ANY WAY OUT

by

Evelyn M. Radford

Pradbin Publishers

Danville, California
2001

Printed in the United States of America.

Library of Congress Catalog Card Number: 2001086965

ISBN: 0- 9708316- 0- 9

Cover Design: Connie Davis Designs
               www.conniedavis.com

Published by: Pradbin Publishers
               Danville, California
               Pradbin@aol.com

Printed by: Amazing Experiences Press
               1908 Keswick Lane
               Concord, California 94518

ii

TABLE OF CONTENTS

AUTHOR'S NOTE

The eleven stories of heroic escape from the Nazis and of starting over in America which make up this book were told to me in interviews that extended over a period of two years. Each of these remarkable people went over with me, again and again, their recollections of life before and after their arrival in the U.S. Their accents sometimes led me to misconstrue exactly what had been said. To make sure that I had heard all the nuances correctly and had faithfully written everything they were willing to share with the world, I redid their accounts until they were satisfied. What follows can be said to be a full and accurate account of what happened to each of them.

(Evelyn) Peggy Radford

PROLOGUE

Hounded by the Gestapo, Walter and each of "The Girls" ran for their lives. Sometimes with the help of some Aryan(s), once by the long arm of Ford Motor Company, usually by their own daring, they fought their way to freedom. They abandoned wealth, left family behind, tore up their roots, and galvanized by fear, fled. After escaping the looming terror of Auschwitz, Bergen Belsen, or Thereisenstadt, after 1944, places where their lives would have ended if they hadn't had the necessary wit, courage, and unmitigated guts to brazenly slip through the fingers of Hitler's minions of madness, one by one, the eleven European Jews whose stories make up the bulk of this book eventually found their way to a safe haven, an Elysian retirement community called Rossmoor Leisure World in Walnut Creek, California.

My exposure to Rossmoor and to them began when the college where I taught responded to Rossmoorians request that courses be offered on their campus rather than ours. Diablo Valley College was too big and too confusing. 18,000 students crowded the walks, too many cars crowded the parking lots, too many buildings covered too many acres, there were too many stairs to climb and too much hustle and bustle as students piled out of and poured into classrooms. Everything was too much. On their campus they had classrooms, and among their over 7,000 residents they had plenty of students. All they needed were teachers. In 1979 I went out on the first wave of instructors to see how it would work. It not only worked, it was an impressive success.

Class limitation was set by the fire marshal. Enrollment was limited to the number of people allowed to occupy a given room. I always added a few to my American history rosters for Rossmoorians travel, they have visiting relatives, they get sick. They are never all present. Unlike the on-campus Diablo Valley College students who enroll in a class, then drop when they get a job, or when they feel like they're failing and leave to avoid a blemish on their GPA (Grade Point Average), or find a different instructor they think will be easier - the reasons are myriad and no class roll is secure for three weeks - in Rossmoor no one dropped out.

It was exciting to teach well-educated, well-traveled, mature students who were eager to learn. I met wonderful people from all walks of life -- all professions, all levels of affluence, naturalized and native born Americans, residents who had come from all over the United States. From the first semester on, after the word got around, course after course the front row of my class was filled with bright, inquisitive people, all of whom had foreign accents. They seemed to know each other well. They knew little about American History, however. They wanted to learn all they could about their adopted country. They made me feel like I had a fan club. When, at last, the computer said no more -- I'd taught all I was scheduled to teach at the college and neither they nor I could repeat the courses -- they set up a howl.

"We'll pay you ourselves!" they cried. "Teach us anything."

I was flattered, but they asked too much. After weeks of cajoling, I agreed to create six to eight weeks courses on the history of -- we went all over the world and delved into all kinds of social problems. In return, they would pay me what the college charged them per course, AND they agreed to allow me to come to the homes of those I chose, tape recorder in hand, to interview them. It was the clique of foreigners I wanted to know more about.

The whole class agreed, but when I singled out the front row every one of them demurred. "Darling, you don't want my story." "Darling, I've never done anything." "Darling, you'd be bored." I had to remind them that they'd promised. The first story I heard astounded me, and the next left me weak. These people had miraculously escaped the Holocaust! I was mesmerized, and fiercely indignant. I resolved to drop the idea of adding a chapter to an oral history project at the college. I would write their stories and share them with the world. Such stories of human courage in the face of man's inhumanity to man, and their Phoenix-like rise from the ashes of destroyed lives, need to be heard again and again in our pampered American isolation.

Fay Obsfelt, who didn't want to be part of the project because her son would do her story one day, was the only one bearing a tattoo from her years in the camps, but she was not the only one herded into three and a half years of slave labor on a starvation diet. Stephie Necheles, who did want to be in the story, left Germany in the 1920's and thereby did not qualify. She was bitterly disappointed to be left out. There were others whom I did not include because they escaped too easily, coming out before the Nuremberg laws were passed. Ilse Schiff, one of the early departees, is included because of her special role in the lives of the others. After the husband with whom she fled, an eminent surgeon, died, she married Walter. His story reads like a tortured suspense thriller. Also, Ilse was "mother hen," as Miriam called her, to the rest of them.

Once safely in America, all but Magda had to begin at the beginning. They lived out the American dream as other immigrants before them had done. They met each other in Rossmoor, a veritable "Valhalla" for the retired, which was as far away from Europe as they could get short of going on to Asia. Because they needed to connect with people who understood the pain of their past, and because they became genuinely fond of each other, eight of them bonded in a group called "The Girls," and shared their lives like a sisterhood. They played bridge, golfed, traveled, took classes, worked in the ceramics studio, did all the things Rossmoor retirees do, and always together. They clung to each other as though still afraid of the gentile world around them, still afraid that the obscenity of the thirties and forties might be repeated.

Each of them lost relatives to Hitler's ovens, some numbering as high as one hundred. All felt guilty for surviving. Recurring nightmares needed no interpretation among them; they knew from their own personal nocturnal encounters with the fearsome past what other's dreams were about. When memories reduced them to mourning and grief they could cry out to each other's receptive ears, and find an echo in the heart of the listener. Many have given up on a God who turned his face away on 6,000,000 of his *Chosen People*. But all of them wear their Jewishness like Joseph's coat with dignity and some defiance. When Ilse meets a stranger, within the first five minutes she says, "I'm Jewish." Then she pulls her hair off her forehead and says, "See? No horns."

Most of the people I wrote about are dead now, the rest are eighty-five or older. Those who died did not die like the millions they left behind in Europe; they died the natural death all human beings are doomed to face. At the end, they were and are surrounded by friends closer than members of an American family.

BRIGITTA

"In my presence, no one speaks badly about the Ford Motor Company!" *That* was her opening statement. I had come to interview Brigitta in preparation for what was to become this book. To be greeted by a declaration of loyalty to the Ford Motor Company was startling. I was not prepared for such a fervent, disconcerting, beginning. Hoping my mouth was not agape, I mentally scrambled to figure out why she thought I would speak badly of Ford Motor Company, or what difference it made if I did. What did Ford Motor Company have to do with anything? I thought I ought to go out and come back in again.

Amused by my stunned expression, Brigitta smiled. "The Ford Motor Company saved my life, not once, not twice, not three times, not even four times. Five times the Ford Motor Company was my savior."

I felt disoriented. Henry Ford had blamed the Jews for their own extermination; even thought Hitler was a benefactor of the human race by getting rid of them. Ford Motor Company had saved her life? "*The* Ford Motor Company?" I reiterated inanely.

"Yes," she repeated emphatically. "In 1937, in 1938, in 1944, in 1945, and in 1957. I'm alive and in America because the Ford Motor Company made it possible for me to live, and to escape." She nodded toward the couch, "Come in, come in. Can I get you anything?"

I could think of nothing. As she settled into a chair so did I. Brigitta is a tiny, pretty woman under five feet tall. She has big blue eyes, an infectious smile, and a deep-timbred, Tallulah Bankhead voice that surprises the listener when one first hears it Uncertain of my bearings, thown off stride by her beginning of this interview, I said hurriedly, "First, I need to learn about your life before Ford Motor Company entered it. I want to know you before we talk about what happened to you after Hitler came to power. We can talk about Ford Motor Company when that becomes part of the story."

She laughed that musical, throaty laugh of hers. "Start wherever you like," she said, "but you'll see when we're through that I owe an eternal debt to Ford which I will never be able to repay."

Brigitta's life was segmented, like a worm hacked into pieces by an angry child. She began life in Budapest, Hungary.

Budapest had been created by the joining of the ancient village of Buda on one side of the Danube River with the equally old village of Pest on the other. Budapest was a city without Ghettos. Jews lived in neighborhoods of their own choosing. Brigitta had little sense of herself as a Jew. As a sheltered, only child, she was overwhelmed by a successful father and a melodramatic mother. Her first escape at the age of twenty-one was to language school in Stuttgart, Germany. That was followed by an incredibly romantic and exciting sojourn in San Francisco where she lived and worked for more than a year. Then she returned to Stuttgart to marry a goy who did not know she was Jewish. They were divorced just as the Nuremberg laws were passed, and he never knew. Then came the twenty-one years of playing hide and seek with two totalitarian governments, both of which wished her dead. She began playing hardball with the Gestapo in 1936 in Cologne, Germany, when she first went to work for the Ford Motor Co.

While other members of "the Rossmoor Girls" had either husbands or parents with whom to plot and plan and carry out escapes, Brigitta was forced to rely on her own canniness and grit to stay alive, and to keep herself and her mother out of concentration camps. In the end, it was Ford that finally pried open the doors in Budapest and let her run to the West in 1957.

Born in 1905, when the twentieth century was newborn and on the threshold of incredible change, Brigitta arrived just in time to be a product of that transition. "Papa" would have liked a son, but since his only child was a daughter he treated her like a boy. He allowed her to sit at his elbow long after the women left the table and listen as he and his brothers and friends talked shop and politics. Paul Konigstein was in the transportation business. He owned a company that imported goods from around the world and shipped Hungarian products to exotic places that neither he nor his child had ever seen. Ports whose names rolled off the tongue like liquid amber were casually discussed in dinner table conversation, along with stock quotations and shipping difficulties. Brigitta listened, and in her imagination saw marvels and wonders beyond anything Budapest had to offer. For her the world became a storybook where all kinds of wonderful adventures awaited an intrepid traveler.

"Someday," she told her father solemnly, "I'm going to get on a ship and go everywhere."

Paul shook his head and smiled. "Princess," he said, " you'll have to marry a sailor to do that. I never get any closer to any of the places where my goods go than our dining table or my desk at the office. Very few people get to see the world. Be content. The place where you are, wherever that is, is so big a world you'll never understand all of it. Don't look someplace else for excitement. It's right under your nose."

Brigitta listened, but she was not convinced. She kept on checking books out of the library about the places she wanted to visit - some day. Brigitta's father had five brothers and sisters and her Mother had eight. They and their spouses were spread out all over the globe. Stories of their lives abroad, coupled with the exposure the family business gave her to the world, made her hunger for new experiences.

Brigitta's romantic nature and her looks were inherited from her mother. Gizella Konigstein was a gay little woman who loved attention. Witty and theatrical, Brigitta's mother longed to go on the stage when she was a girl, a vocation socially unacceptable in her day. Thwarted in her thirst for glamour and recognition, she transferred her ambitions to her daughter. By the time Brigitta came along, the theater was no longer regarded as a pit of depravity for nice girls. With impunity, Brigitta could have the spotlight which Gizella had been denied. Vicariously, Gizella could emote before audiences, could bask in her daughter's reflected glory. The transference of ambition from one generation to the next didn't happen. When Gizella dramatically met the trivia of daily existence with the passion of a Greek Tragedy, Brigitta and her father, helpless to quell the tempest, could only ride out the storm in silence. Forced too often to be an audience to her mother's performances at home, Brigitta had no desire to be consumed by Gizella's fantasies about her own life. A constant tug-of-war kept mother and daughter engaged throughout Gizella's long life.

Undaunted, Mrs. Konigstein programmed her daughter's life with hours upon hours of cultivating the social graces and absorbing culture with a capital C. Brigitta took piano lessons, was dragged to lectures, visited museums in her mother's wake, attended matinees where they sat, front row center, on the wrong side of the footlights. Beaten on the issue of the theater, Gizella shifted her focus to planning her daughter's marriage into one of the great families of Europe. Polished young European ladies spoke several languages: Brigitta studied German, French, and English. When the opportunity presented itself, Gizella said, she would be at home in the parlors of the mighty in any major capitol of the world.

Both her parents believed in education for women so Brigitta was sent to the best schools money could buy. Their house was filled with the books her scholarly father collected, and Brigitta became a voracious reader. She read more than travel books, she read anything that fell into her hands. Precocious and studious, she sailed through school and was enrolled in two gymnasiums for her final year of matriculation: a Hungarian school and a German one. The German gymnasium had been established in Budapest by the German government for the education of the children of German Civil Servants living in Hungary. All of the teachers were imported from Germany and only the German language was spoken in the classes. Her attendance at the German gymnasium was not only for cultural purposes, it was in anticipation of her entering a German University upon graduation.

At the end of World War I, the communists under the leadership of Bela Kun, a Jew, seized power in the newly truncated Hungary, power they held long enough to create social upheaval. Universities were opened to women, public marches for political or social causes were allowed, universal suffrage was the law. When they began land reform they reached too far. The communists were overthrown by the conservatives, and the new government under the presidency of Admiral Horthy (who had never been to sea) undid all the social innovations and imposed a quota system on the University of Budapest. Only five per cent of the students body could be Jewish and none could be female. That system would exclude Edward Teller and Brigitta from attending University in their homeland. All her life Brigitta had expected to attend college somewhere when she finished gymnasium, but, she would now have to go abroad to do so, and a university in Germany was her anticipated place of matriculation. At the last minute, her parents wouldn't let her go. They couldn't give her up. Instead she went on with language training.

4

Finally, in 1926, when she was twenty-one years old, they allowed her to go to summer school in Stuttgart, Germany where her father had friends with whom she could stay. In summer school she could further her proficiency in the German language. She had learned to speak German primarily from her Austrian governess. She had a slight Austrian accent as a consequence. It was hoped that living in Germany for awhile would erase it. Very soon after she arrived, she discovered there were even better reasons for being there than speaking like a native. It turned out to be a magical summer. She studied a little and played a lot. Brigitta had lots of beaux before she went to Stuttgart, but something new came her way in the form of a young German male who was gorgeous, glamorous, suave, intensely sure of himself, and a fine athlete. In college he had been on the ski-jumping team. His name was Erwin Gräber, and he was Aryan to the core. Ambitious, focused, a perfectionist, he was employed as an economist in the sales department of a candy factory.

That summer Brigitta saw no flaws in him. None of Brigitta's previous swains had been Jewish and for her Jewish or non-Jewish was not a problem. Most of her family's friends were Catholic. Religion was rarely discussed in her home; except by her Jewish relatives when they were around. Brigitta had grown up entirely in a gentile world. Because she never thought of herself in religious or racial terms, she didn't bother to tell Erwin about her own Jewishness. Her thoughts were centered on how gorgeous he was, and how gorgeous he made her feel.

Brigitta might not be able to find fault with Erwin, but her parents would have if they'd known about him. Somehow they always found a reason to object to anyone who seemed serious about her. Her mother kept urging her to stay uncommitted so that when she was old enough she'd attract a truly worthy man. Worthy meant rich. Brigitta kept Erwin's existence her own private affair. She never mentioned him in her letters home. The weeks flew by and then it was midnight and her coach turned into a pumpkin. She had to go home to Budapest. There was the usual pledge of eternal love, the usual tears at the railway station, the fervent promises to be true, to write, and so forth. Then, drying her tears, she left for home and headed toward the next chapter of her life. Erwin wrote faithfully, Brigitta answered fitfully. It wasn't that she was fickle, it was just that a new love came along and Stuttgart, after all, was too far away for dancing and flirting and spinning air castles. Letters didn't carry the same zing as the physical presence. Where the new love might have carried her is purely speculative for two things happened simultaneously that ended the current romance, and decidedly put Erwin on the back burner. First, Uncle Charlie came to town.

An intriguing aura clung to Uncle Charlie. Long before she was born Uncle Charlie had fled Hungary under a cloud of disgrace and settled in that most romantic of all places in the western world, San Francisco, California. Humiliated because he failed his examinations for graduation from the gymnasium, in his mind he'd brought shame on his family. The only honorable thing to do was to run away. He went to sea with his best friend who had also failed. They left on a steamer bound for America as cook's helpers. It was not like being apprenticed to the head chef at the Ritz in Paris but Uncle Charlie learned how to make Hungarian goulash with the best of them. The two young "Bohunks," a slang term for Hungarian immigrants in America, wound up in New York just in time for the outbreak of the Spanish-American war. With no pressing business to hold them back they enlisted in the U.S. Navy and sailed off for the Philippines. Uncle Charlie had had no more than a tourist's glimpse of New York City before he left for Manila, but that was enough. After the Great White Fleet had annihilated the pathetic Spanish Navy in Manila Bay, it was sent back to San Francisco to begin its triumphal tour of the coasts of America. Uncle Charlie found his final destination. The moment he sailed through the Golden Gate he knew this was where he'd pitch his tent and make his stand. After two years with American sailors he spoke the language well enough to strike out on his own.

San Francisco neighborhoods were ethnically mixed, there was no Hungarian ghetto like the one he'd seen in New York where any Hungarian restaurant with enough paprika could succeed. A Hungarian restaurant in San Francisco would have to serve excellent food and have a gypsy ambiance if it was to be popular and survive very long. Uncle Charlie put together the right formula. He opened his restaurant, he served wonderful Hungarian food, and he did well. In 1928, he was ready to go back to Budapest to sport his affluence and erase the blot he'd left on his reputation. Brigitta was twenty-two when he arrived, her head was full of daydreams and she was hungry for adventure. She set out to court him. She listened breathlessly to his stories, she begged him to describe over and over the glamorous California city where he'd found his fortune, she lighted his cigars, and in the end she won from him the invitation to go to America she'd been angling for. To her surprise her parents endorsed the idea. At that moment, as though star-crossed, Erwin decided to come to Budapest to take Brigitta back to Stuttgart as his bride. Brigitta fled with Uncle Charlie. Weddings, followed by the consequent house-keeping and babies, could wait. A chance like this might not come again.

Of all the possible ships Uncle Charlie might have chosen for their trip across the Atlantic, he booked passage on the German S.S. Stuttgart. Like rubbing salt in a wound, Brigitta dropped a line to Erwin to tell him of the incredible irony of being on the Stuttgart rather than in the city bearing that name. Erwin's response was an avalanche of letters to Brigitta's parents in Budapest begging for Brigitta's American address. They refused to comply. Their daughter was in no hurry to reinstate anything with Erwin, and certainly they were not interested in her moving to Germany. She was in San Francisco, the darling of Uncle Charlie's Hungarian circle, and busy. She'd gone to work. Paul was proud that his daughter felt she must get a job as soon as she arrived so that she wouldn't be a burden. Uncle Charlie had connections and those connections turned up a job. Brigitta went to work at the Bank of Italy which today is the world-wide Bank of America. It wasn't a great job, what she did was write out money orders in French and German to handle the flow of money sent back home to Europe by new San Franciscans from those countries. But it paid enough that she could feel independent and self-supporting.

Like every other true romantic who sees the "city by the bay" she fell in love with San Francisco. She loved riding the cable cars to and from work, especially down the steep hills where one could look into the first floor windows of a home as the car approached it, then stare into the basement windows of the same house as it passed. She loved the ocean and the bay and the screaming sea gulls and the wet damp air in the morning and the moaning of the fog horns at night; everything delighted her. What's more, as always, there was a man. His name was Jack Grant, a name he'd adopted as he went through Ellis Island coming in from Russia. He was a Certified Public Accountant with the very serious view of life stereotypical of accountants. He had money to spend and he spent it, taking her to dine in all the best restaurants in the city. But every time he wanted to kiss her he parked under a street light to do it. As usual in Brigitta's romantic life, in spite of his unromantic predilection of seeing things at their most practical level, they became engaged.

"If I marry Jack," she told herself, "I'd automatically become an American. He's a citizen so I wouldn't have to go back to Budapest. I could stay right here for the rest of my life."

Her mirrored image frowned. "But you don't love him." She told herself.

"I know." she said, "but I'd become a citizen myself and then I could always get a divorce if it didn't work out." She bent over the washbasin and finished brushing her teeth.

As she ran a comb through her hair she asked herself. "Does it mean that much to stay in San Francisco?"

She looked toward the fog shrouded window and laughed out loud. "Maybe not today," she said inwardly, "but it's better than Budapest."

When Brigitta wrote to her parents about her forthcoming marriage, an event that would keep on the far side of America, they promptly sent Erwin her address. Better she marry a German who lived an overnight train ride away than an American living on the other side of the world. Letters began to flow like a tide into San Francisco from Germany, wildly romantic letters, articulate and pleading. Erwin, Brigitta remembered, didn't need the lights on to kiss her. As the weeks went by the contrast between the man on paper and the man in the flesh was too disturbing to be denied. Cable cars were romantic and so were fogs, but romance in human form was better. She packed her bags and headed back to Europe toward a fate she should have avoided by marrying Jack. In case she never came this way again, she decided, she took the long way home booking passage on a ship going to Calais through the Panama Canal. Best to see that engineering marvel while she was in the neighborhood. In Calais, she caught the boat train to Paris to do the town with Hungarian friends now residing there. She'd play awhile before going on to settle down in prosaic Stuttgart.

Escorted by her Hungarian friends living in the city by the Seine, she reveled in Montmarte and the Left Bank, and soaked up the gay, independent single life knowing this might be her last fling. Finally she boarded a train for Hungary. She really couldn't linger longer if she was going to be on time for her own wedding. She had allowed herself so few hours in Budapest there'd be no time for debates with her parents, especially her mother. She could hear it now. How could she think of marrying someone she'd known only for a summer, someone she hadn't seen since, someone her parents didn't know at all? How could she throw herself away on a mere accountant?

"Brigitta, where is your head?" Gizella demanded as Brigitta emptied out her bureau drawers. "This Erwin has a good job but so do lots of young men. What does his family have?" How will you move around in the best society?"

"I don't know his family," Brigitta retorted, "I'm not marrying them. As for the best society, I don't give a fig for it. "

"You're wrong." her father interceded. "No one ever marries just the person they love, they marry that person's history which includes all the family, living and dead."

"Nonsense," snorted Brigitta. "That may have been the way it was when you were young, but this is the 1920's. Erwin and I are marrying each other and nobody else."

There were tears and more argument for which Brigitta had no time. She packed her trunks and left her parents behind in Budapest. She was off to be a bride and she didn't need rebuke and lamentations to spoil her great moment. They were married at the City Hall in Stuttgart with no parents present, and went off to the mountains for a glorious honeymoon. Erwin was as romantic as his letters for two whole weeks, then it was time to go back to work. From the day she unpacked her bags in the villa apartment Erwin had taken for them in the suburbs of Stuttgart she knew she was in trouble.

When the honeymoon was over, it was over. To her surprise, Erwin was as methodical as she had feared Jack would be. She couldn't keep things neat enough to suit him, she couldn't cope with his insistence that meals be on the table at precise hours, she couldn't abide his lecturing on the right way to do things. The rigid schedule he laid out for her covered when the clothes went out to the cleaners, which days were to be set aside for housecleaning, the tasks to be done and in what order, plus when and with whom they would socialize. He kept her on a strict budget, something her father could never have gotten away with Gizella. She felt stifled. The rigidity of her days was painful enough, but added to that was the shocking discovery that within months of "cleaving only to her forever," Erwin had someone on the side. His ego was so monumental one woman couldn't feed it. He'd married properly, now he was free to be as promiscuous as he chose. When she found out and confronted him with the "I really think you ought to know" information given to her by "a friend" he lied about it. He lied about everything.

"His very breath was a lie," Brigitta says.

Her sense of outrage at his betrayal made her utterly miserable. She had been raised in a home where fidelity was taken for granted and where truth was the cardinal virtue valued most. She couldn't live like this. She hadn't given up San Francisco to be confined to a garden villa by a husband who would not hear of her taking a job, but who was taking himself off to another woman's bed whenever he could without causing another row. They were divorced. His parents invited her to come to live with them. They had long before been forced to face their son's perfidy. None of his family believed a word he said nor were they surprised at anything he did. Family pride kept them from warning the pretty little Hungarian before she got into the family, but they'd come to love her and didn't want to lose her.

"Come to live with us," his mother begged. "You know we love you and we hate to think of you being alone."

"I can't do that," Brigitta protested. "I can't live with you and really be free of Erwin. Every time he came to visit I'd have to leave."

"But he never comes," his mother argued. "We lost him long ago, we don't want to lose you too."

"If I lived with you my mother would be crushed. If I live with any family it would have to be my own and I can't face that." Erwin's mother remained silent. There was really nothing she could say to overrule the fact that Brigitta's own parents had first call on their daughter's life.

10

Brigitta began searching the want ads for a job. What was she qualified to do? One position caught her eye that would take her away from Stuttgart and promised excitement in the bargain. Ford Motor Company of Cologne wanted a translator in English who could type. Undaunted by her lack of secretarial skills she bought a typing manual and with three fingers learned to put a letter on a page in fair order. She got the job. From 1935 to 1937 she worked her way up the ladder of the company moving from translator to Junior Secretary in the Office of the General Manager. However, she had secured the position through a tiny bit of deception. When she filled out the application for the job she did not reveal her Jewishness, she had cleverly skirted the issue through the veil of being a Hungarian. Once she was in Cologne and on the Ford payroll she refused to join the German Labor Pool for fear of opening up the can of worms she'd circumvented at the time she was hired. September 15, 1935, the Nuremburg laws were passed placing all Jews beyond citizenship and forbidding intermarriage between them and German citizens. Erwin had joined the Nazi Party in the meanwhile, and was rising rapidly in that organization. What she didn't need was to have him find out that he had been tainted by marriage to a despised Jew. His retribution would be merciless. There were other people to be feared as well. She car pooled to work with four fellow employees, two of whom she thought suspected the truth.

One day one of them turned to her in the car and asked, "Are you really Aryan?"

"Aryan?" she retorted. "I'm more than Aryan, I'm Hung-Aryan."

They laughed, but she wasn't sure they were convinced. She began to worry. In 1937 Ford opened an office in Vienna and immediately Brigitta asked for a transfer. She told her boss she wanted to be nearer her family in Budapest. The people with whom she worked had known for some time that her father was ill so her request to be nearer home was accepted at face value. No one thought of the possibility that there might be a more urgent reason for wanting out of Germany. They granted her application for reassignment and reluctantly sent her off. In Vienna she breathed freely and settled in to life in the Austrian capital for a year. Then it was March, 1938, and the Germans marched in. Overnight Austria was gobbled up. Hitler annexed the country and it became the province of Ostmark, a part of the Third Reich. Ford now had two offices in Germany, and Ford's European master plan called for only one operation per language group. They closed the Vienna operation and in its stead opened a new office in Budapest. What could be more logical than to send Brigitta to her own hometown where her native tongue would be most useful? Ford put her on the list of employees to be brought into Hungary as part of the company personnel.

She returned to Budapest as a German citizen in possession of a six month's visitor's visa. When she married Erwin she'd been forced to give up her Hungarian passport. As an executive employee of a prestigious, and most welcome, foreign company, a person who had been born and raised in the city, it never occurred to her that she might have trouble with immigration. It was a blow to learn that Ford Motor company, an American firm, was welcome in pro-Nazi Hungary, but Brigitta was not. In Hungary she had become just a foreign citizen, even worse a foreign Jew as well. No matter that she'd been born, raised and educated in Budapest! According to the new political order of things she was an unwanted person to whom immigration did not intend to issue a working permit, much less grant permanent residency. She would not be allowed to repatriate, she had to go. The moment of truth had arrived for Brigitta at last, she had to reveal her Jewishness to her unsuspecting boss.

By that time, however, she had so capably proven her worth to the company that Ford took on the role of guardian angel for the bright little woman they wanted to keep, a role they would fill off and on for nineteen years. They tried to use the influence of their corporate might on the immigration authorities, but that effort was thwarted by the pro-Nazi wing of the government. Implacably, the Hungarian government refused to compromise. Under no circumstances would any foreign Jew be allowed to remain in Hungary on any permanent basis. There was no solution anyone could see. Brigitta would have to leave the country. It didn't matter to the Hungarians where she went, but it mattered to her. She faced a future in which she had no homeland. In both Austria and Germany she was now revealed to be a Jew and therefore a marked woman. She could not go back to either place. For once in her life she was stumped, she couldn't find a way around the impasse.

Then came one of the most bizarre twists of fate in her whole fateful life. In Budapest, Brigitta's family had friends whom she had known all her life. These friends had a nephew who, although a Hungarian citizen, resided in Vienna where he owned a paper factory. The friends went to Gizella and Paul and proposed that a marriage be arranged between Brigitta and their nephew. Such a marriage would automatically make her a Hungarian citizen. Once that was done, and Brigitta had been back in Budapest long enough to have citizenship in her own right, the young people could get a divorce. The nephew, Alex, had no love interest in his life, and was in fact a confirmed bachelor. If Brigitta and her parents were agreeable they would approach their nephew about the matter. Brigitta was desperate. Gizella loved the drama of such an intrigue. When his aunt and uncle approached Alex he too was intrigued with the idea. It was like the plot of a spy novel. He came to Budapest to meet Brigitta and when he saw her he fell in with the plan enthusiastically. He was as romantic as she.

Reveling in the conspiracy, Alex and Brigitta excitedly went off to apply for a marriage license only to have their excitement dashed immediately. They faced further red tape. Since Brigitta was a German citizen she would have to have a permit from Germany to marry a foreigner. That regulation was not part of the oppression of the Jews, it applied to Aryans and Jews alike. Furthermore, the permit had to be issued in Stuttgart where her German citizenship had been established. Brigitta promptly wrote to the proper authorities for the required permission and within days received notice that her request was denied. No reason was given, just a flat out "No." Further correspondence was useless. She'd have to go in person to unravel this; but that was too hazardous. She didn't dare show up in Stuttgart. Alerted already to the fact that there was a vulnerable little Jewess trying to get out of their reach, the authorities would be waiting for her. She wouldn't stand a chance of going into Germany incognito. What was to be done?

The dilemma gave Gizella her great acting opportunity at last. She took stage center, bought a round-trip ticket to Stuttgart, and headed west. It was forbidden for Jews to ride the trains of Germany without government permission. Gizella, caught up in the drama of it all, blithely ignored that little fact. She was traveling on a Hungarian passport, wasn't she? She checked into a hotel in Stuttgart, also a thing verboten for Jews to do without permission. With supreme self assurance, she presented her Hungarian passport at the registration clerk and got by with it. They gave her a room, and, unquestioningly, sent her up with a bellboy. She didn't bother to unpack her almost empty little bag, she deposited it on the bed and went right back down to the street to hail a cab. Arriving at Gestapo Headquarters, she imperiously took the elevator to the upper floor where the immigration office was located. She opened the door and swept regally into the presence of bureaucrats and clerks bent over their desks.

Putting her purse on the counter that separated the waiting area from the work area, she made a production of taking off her gloves. "I've come to get a marriage license for my daughter," she stated.

Gizella did not look Aryan like Brigitta did. Jewish was written all over her face.

"Nonsense!" the official shouted. "She must come herself."

"She cannot!" Gizella's voice rose to match his own as she stood as tall as her five feet height would allow, "I have come for her, you must give the papers to me."

"It can't be done!" his face had turned red and veins stood out above his shirt collar.

"It can be done!" she cried matching his tone of voice. "If you don't give me the license I will kill myself, and all the world will know how heartless you are!"

With that she rushed to the window, pushed up the sash and started to climb onto the sill. Unnerved by a crazy little Jewess with an overpowering presence who seemed quite capable of carrying out her ridiculous threat, the man quickly sorted through the forms before him, took out the right ones, signed them and held them out to her. After all she was only asking for a marriage application, not a business license or something serious.

"Here," he stormed, "Take them and get out of here."

Gizella climbed down from the window, and with an air of disdain haughtily straightened the seams in her stockings, took the proffered papers from him, scooped up her purse and gloves, and, head held high, walked out the door. No stage exit was ever made with more flourish. The moment the door clicked shut behind her she ran on trembling legs to the elevator, ran out through the lobby and all the way back to the

14

hotel. There she retrieved her things as fast as her palsied hands could scoop them up, and, shaking like a leaf, raced for the train. No one stopped her, no one seemed to even be aware that anything was amiss. The clerks in the hotel were not even aware that she was gone without paying her bill.

The train for Budapest was chuffing quietly at the platform as she hurried to a first class car and clambered up the steps. She slipped into a compartment just as the engineer began building up steam for departure. The train pulled out of the station and rumbled across Germany. Scarcely breathing, still expecting the arm of the law to fall on her shoulder, she scrunched down into the seat hoping to be invisible. When they crossed the border into Czechoslovakia at last she let out a whoop and hugged herself with glee. Dancing in the small space between the seats, she broke out in raucous laughter over what she'd done. She'd played her daring role without a misstep and pulled it off triumphantly.

Never entertaining the slightest doubt about her mother's success, Brigitta took the last Danube steamer headed north before the river closed to passenger traffic for the winter. She and her mother and Alex had agreed to rendezvous in the city of Bratislava. Before World War I, when the city had been in Hungary, it was known as Pozsony. There she had an aunt who was married to a gentile who was a famous artist. The Aunt's home would be their meeting place. Gizella, still elated and strutting over her performance in Stuttgart, triumphantly brought the license to Bratislava just hours before Alex arrived from Vienna. Her last appearance in the romantic escapade was to serve as Witness at her daughter's wedding in the Town Hall. After that, there was nothing left for her to do but head for Budapest leaving the entire stage to Brigitta. Brigitta and Alex could not leave with her, they had to wait until Alex could enter his "bride" into his passport, stating that she was accompanying him on a business trip.

To keep the charade from being uncovered until all was clear for a divorce, Brigitta moved into a building where another of her aunts had been living for many years. She took occupancy under her married name. Every building had a concierge and every concierge was required to report regularly to the police any unusual circumstances or events in the lives of their tenants that might indicate that surveillance should be in order. A woman under the age of fifty, living

15

alone, was suspicious. A married woman has a husband. Brigitta was living alone and she had no visible husband. The concierge had to be lulled into unsuspicious acceptance of that state of things. Brigitta and Alex conspired and came up with a plan to convince the concierge that Brigitta did indeed have a husband, and was a self-respecting married woman whose job kept her in Budapest while her husband's business kept him in Vienna. Every now and then, Alex would come for a weekend and take Brigitta away with him. They would make sure the concierge saw them chatting happily as they walked off arm-in-arm down the street, Alex carrying Brigitta's little weekend bag. They would walk several blocks to the apartment of a friend of Brigitta's who was in on the plot. Alex would deposit Brigitta at her friend's house to spend the next two days while he went on his way to visit his family. Sunday night Brigitta would slowly walk forlornly back into the building as though she had just seen her husband off on the train for his return to Vienna, and was facing another lonely period of separation.

During the week, Brigitta was at her desk at Ford, now Ford Motor Co. of Hungary. Her position was that of "Administrative Secretary," a job that located her next to the manager's office. With no private office of her own, she was very visible to the public. There were plenty of German officials who came and went from Ford, men who were in Hungary as technical advisers and trade ministers. They took note that a Jewess held a prominent position in the American Company. Within a very short time, there were complaints from the German embassy to the General Manager of Ford. How, the embassy inquired, could Ford give full employment to a Jewess when there were so many non-Jews available, competent gentiles who should be given such a position at such a salary? The general manager ignored the protests until one day representatives from the German Legation appeared and demanded that she be fired. The general manager assured them the situation would be attended to immediately. The "situation" was "attended to" by creating a Department of Statistics made up of one employee, Brigitta. The new department was located in a back office out of sight. Not only did she continue to work, but she continued to pull down her big salary. If the Germans were aware of the deception, they didn't press the issue any further. Brigitta never missed a day of work until the German army marched into Budapest in March of 1944.

When she had been in Hungary long enough to establish her own residency, she and Alex were "divorced." She continued to live in the apartment she had occupied since her "marriage" until her father died in 1941. At that point she felt obligated to move in with her mother to look after her. The two of them took a lovely apartment in a modern building located in a pretty park on the Pest banks of the Danube. Just as they took occupancy and moved in, shortages of fuel caused by the wartime consumption of oil by the German army caused the Hungarian government to put restrictions on the number of hours every day that any building could have heat, and at what temperature. The big Ford salary made it possible for Brigitta to instantly respond to this exigency. She had a large tile, wood-burning stove installed in the apartment. The stove was built into the wall with heat ducts running to every room. A self-indulgent extravagance, perhaps, but Brigitta's mother had heat all day long while the other tenants in the building bundled up during the midday hours when the furnaces were turned off. Later, that stove, coupled with Brigitta's will to keep them alive, saved them from starvation.

When the Germans marched into Budapest in March of 1944, they took control of the government. They applied the Nuremburg laws to the Hungarian capitol, the last city in Nazi-occupied Europe where Jews had escaped Nazi extermination. First, Jews were ordered to turn over their bank accounts to the new government. Brigitta had no bank account. She'd learned her lesson in Cologne. Always, when she was paid, she immediately converted her salary into large bills which she could carry on her person if necessary. Second, Jews were ordered to turn in radios, ski outfits and jewelry, except for plain wedding bands. A lot of Viennese Jews had gone skiing down the Swiss side of the mountains in 1938 and 1939. Hungary, too, bordered on Switzerland. No Hungarian Jews were going skiing this time. Brigitta and her mother turned their jewelry over to gentile friends who promised to keep it for them until Hungary was a sane and safe place in which to live again.

Twenty-four hours after the Germans marched in, all Jewish telephones were disconnected. There was nothing even Ford could do about that, or about the yellow stars painted on certain buildings that made that apartment house a Jewish enclave. All gentiles had to move out. Conversely, any building not marked with a yellow star could no longer be home to Jews. A mammoth shifting of the population took place. Prior to this time, there had been no restrictions on housing, no special districts much less buildings denoted by the government as Jewish. People lived where they chose to live as long as they could pay the rent. Jews and gentiles began moving in with relatives and friends, even perfect strangers if necessary, in order to take up residence in the politically correct apartment buildings. The building where Brigitta had first lived when she came to Budapest as Alex's bride was not a starred house, therefore her aunt had to evacuate. She came to live with Brigitta and her mother for theirs was a starred building.

At first, the new restrictions were irritating, inconvenient, and restrictive, but on the whole fairly tolerable. True, they were not allowed to be out of their buildings except between the hours of 11 a.m. and 4 p.m., long enough to queue up for groceries and work a few hours at whatever jobs they still held, limiting and humiliating, but they could survive. All Jews were ordered to sew yellow stars on their clothing, and forbidden to go out on the street without having that yellow star clearly in view. Brigitta could no longer go to work at Ford. She was a "marked woman." It would not be safe for her to be found walking in the neighborhood of the company offices. Ford continued to pay her salary anyway. The money was brought to her surreptitiously by Olga Negro, wife of the Assistant Manager of the Ford operation. Olga even gave Brigitta her own identification papers to carry around with her as protection. With her salary coming in as regularly as it had when she could go out to earn it, Brigitta, her mother and her aunt could continue to eat and pay their bills.

Their building had a roof garden on it, and it was there the tenants spent the days of the summer of 1944. Prohibited from entering the city parks or "loitering" on the streets, they sunbathed out of the sight of the police on the streets below, and out of the range of vision of possible spies. Theirs was the highest building in the neighborhood so they gathered above the forbidden streets to play cards, watch the children romp around them, gossip and make jokes, trying to keep life as normal as possible. They were very careful never to talk or, heaven forbid, to laugh too loudly for fear they'd be heard by passersby below. With the rooftop available to them, they could spread out and escape breathing into each other's faces. Otherwise, the crowded conditions of too many people per apartment would have made life untenable. That sun-drenched lofty recreational area was also their escape from the psychological overcrowding which the Nazis designed to help break them down.

As the days grew shorter that fall, and the Nazi throttle-hold tightened on the city, there was a coup d'état in October which tossed out the pro-Nazi moderate Horthy government still clinging to a vestige of power, and swept the rabid Nazi Party of Hungary, the Arrow Cross, into office. The Horthy government had been too soft on Jews to suit the real Nazis. Rumor had it that Horthy's own grandmother was Jewish. At last, 'The Final Solution' was instituted in Budapest. Out of the international public eye, the countryside of Hungary had been scoured by the Nazis from 1939 on. 400,000 Jews had already been carted off to Labor Camps or extermination centers, most of them going to Auschwitz. Many Jewish men had been sent into "labor brigades" which took them to the war zone in Russia as vanguards for the German army. Now the edict came down that all Jewish women in Budapest under the age of forty-five were to report to a certain sports stadium bringing with them three days' supply of food and whatever clothing and other necessities they had the strength to carry. Brigitta, under forty-five, decided it was time to take a walk.

Tearing the yellow star off her coat, Brigitta headed for the suburbs where she knew she could find refuge. Lotte Madrasz, another gentile friend, had always told her that the doors of her home were open if she ever needed sanctuary. Lotte's husband was an army officer at the front lines of the war, and was threatening to desert. In late September, he sent two soldiers and a truck for all their personal possessions and family pieces and moved Lotte and the children to a little town on the German border. They left their house and furniture with Lotte's Jewish cousin, Eva, who was also under forty-five, and also evading the Nazi order. Eva, walking around with the papers of another gentile friend, was now known as "Martha." In Eva's hands, the house became a shelter for refugee Jews. People spent their nights there, then slipped out before dawn. The attic was filled with the papers of these transient residents and the few possessions they had been able to carry with them when they "disappeared."

Brigitta took up residence in Lotte's house with Eva. With Olga's papers in her possession Brigitta could come and go at will. Olga's husband's position with Ford made it unnecessary for Olga to show papers every time she made a transaction. She had Olga's original birth certificate, her original marriage certificate, and her ration cards. The two refugee Jews passed themselves off as two gentile friends whose husbands were away at war. The number of overnight "guests" dwindled drastically, day by day, as the Jews were systematically hunted down and forced into fewer and fewer shelters. The decreased number of Jews on the street made it easier for the police to keep watch over the entire populace so that hiding became more dangerous.

Every day Brigitta would take the local train into Budapest on errands of mercy to Jews hiding out in the city: a little bread, a word of comfort, delivery of a letter, whatever she could do to relieve their isolation and suffering. And each day she would get word to her mother that she was still alive and well. It wasn't safe to go back to the old apartment to see her. A regular courier who came and went from the apartment would attract attention so she always had to find someone new by whom to send her messages. Occasionally, she and her mother even managed to meet briefly. "Martha", made her own daily rounds of mercy which she referred to as her "work." To convince the neighbors that she was an employed woman Eva caught the same train every morning and returned on the same train every night. People got used to seeing her pass along the street as part of the suburban work force going and coming from Budapest.

It was the end of the October when Brigitta moved in with "Martha" and at the end of the month she would have to have a new ration card. Brazenly she took her "Olga Papers" to the nearest ration office and wordlessly handed them over to the clerk.

"So you're Olga !" he exclaimed beaming at her out of blue eyes almost buried under heavy brows. "I am the cousin of Karlos!"

Brigitta's skin crawled. She caught her breath. To be confronted so abruptly by unanticipated danger made her slightly sick. She did her best to cover her agitation. With all the composure she could muster she rewarded him with a delighted smile.

"Are you?" she asked innocently, "Which cousin?"

"I'm the son of Klari." he answered, smiling down into her blue eyes.

"Oh, I AM glad to meet you. How is Aunt Klari?" she gushed.

From long hours of friendly exchanges Brigitta knew all about all of Olga's and Karl's immediate families. She'd also heard about all their extended kinships. Frantically, she tried to run through everything remembered in search of this Karlos. Being as winningly open as she knew how to be, she kept up a barrage of comments and questions about various family events and relatives. Outwardly relaxed, inwardly she was dying. She wanted to scream at him to hurry up, but she dared not cut him off.

"If you see Aunt Klari before I do, give her my love, won't you?"

It was Brigitta's turn upon the stage of life and she rose to the occasion as well as Gizella herself could have played it. Clenching her fists in her pockets to keep from twitching with nervousness, she smiled and chatted as though the whole day stretched seamlessly before her. The poor man never suspected he was not dealing with the real Olga. Finally, after what seemed a lifetime, he handed over the precious ration cards.

"See you next month," he said lightly as she turned to go.

"Unless I lose them." she laughed over her shoulder.

With thumping heart and shaking knees she hurried home to Lotte's house where she went straight to the stove and poured herself a strong cup of coffee to quiet her nerves. One day, after Eva had already left for work, and Brigitta was about to go out on her round of errands, there came a loud, officious knock at the door. Responding as quickly as she could, Brigitta opened the door on an Arrow Cross official who stared at her questioningly.

"Are you Martha?" he demanded. Brigitta's heart lurched, then began to race until she could feel her pulse pounding in her temples.

"I'm sorry, she isn't here," she said, opening her eyes as ingenue-wide as possible. "Did she know you were coming?"

He ignored the question. "When is she coming back?" he demanded.

"Late in the evening after she is through work," Brigitta answered breathlessly. "What do you want with her?"

"She'll find out." he said laconically.

"Well, she won't be back until very late." Brigitta stepped back to close the door.

"Okay, then" he said, holding out his hand to stop her from shutting him out. "I wait."

"But I was just leaving," Brigitta protested. "I have many things to do in the city."

"You can do them tomorrow," he said flatly.

There was nothing she could do but step aside to let him in. He was of medium height and medium intelligence, in fact it was apparent that everything about him was average. Brigitta sat down opposite him with the stove between them. He offered nothing in the way of conversation. The silence became so oppressive Brigitta couldn't stand it. The ticking of the clock, usually unnoticed as a background noise, was so loud it beat on her ears. Brigitta began talking, talking about any bit of nonsense that came into her head. She began to ask questions. She learned all about his family, she heard the story of his life, she chatted and chatted until her mouth was dry and her mind was numb. Unable to do anything but stay in and entertain him, she feverishly searched for a way to get word to Eva that it was not safe to come back. There was no telephone service to the city even if she could have figured out how to make a call without being overheard. She wracked her brain, but she came up with nothing. Trying to beguile him, to win him over, she plied him with coffee, cup after cup. At one point she gestured toward the dirty, crumpled arm band around his sleeve which identified him as the enemy.

"Aren't you ashamed to wear that important symbol when it's in such poor condition?" she scolded. "Here, give it to me and let me wash it for you."

She washed it and ironed it, and put it neatly back around his arm. He seemed pleased with her gesture but only grunted an acknowledgment. She gave him lunch, they played cards and they drank more coffee as the clock ticked and ticked, "Eva, Eva, Eva." Brigitta became literally sick with anxiety. In the middle of the afternoon her heart almost stopped when she Eva's aunt coming across the front yard. Eva's aunt was

22

also hiding out in the neighborhood and somehow Brigitta had to alert her to the danger. When the doorbell rang, Brigitta threw it open and greeted the aunt over-warmly, giving her no time to say anything.

"Oh," she cried. "Are you too looking for Martha? She's not here. Everyone seems to want to see her today, but she's at work. This gentleman has been waiting all day." Brigitta waved a hand in the direction of the unwanted guest behind her.

Eva's aunt was not stupid. She took one look at the Arrow Cross arm band, and bowed slightly in his direction.

"Oh, no, thanks," she said quickly. "I just took a chance that the weather might have kept her home. I have many things yet to do today so just tell her I came by about that fabric she wanted. I located a piece which I'll bring around tomorrow."

With that she hurried away to the train station to waylay Eva so that she would not come home at all. When the last train of the day roared through at 9:00 p.m. and no "Martha" returned the Arrow Cross man finally left.

"I'll be back tomorrow," he groused. "Her staying away tonight won't do it."

"Oh," Brigitta lied smoothly, "she often stays over with a friend in the city when it's too awfully cold like it is now. She may not be back for several days."

"It doesn't matter. Orders are orders. I'll be around in the morning." Curtly he clapped his hat on his head, pulled his collar up around his ears and hurried away, his boots crunching on the icy sidewalk.

As soon as he was out of sight, Brigitta frantically rushed to the attic and carted down arm load after arm load of incriminating papers. With the lights turned out so no one could see what she was doing, she began fueling the fire in the stove with them. Around eleven o'clock there was again a loud knock at the door. Brigitta broke out in a cold sweat. The house was dark except for the firelight streaming out of the open stove. Quickly Brigitta closed the stove door and on cat feet fled to the bedroom, rumpled up the bed, threw on her nightgown as the knocking became louder and more insistent. Still without putting on a light she went to press against the closed door calling out in a sleepy voice, "Who's there?"

"Open!" came the growled order.

"Just a second," she called as she rumpled her hair with trembling hands, "while I put on some clothes."

Returning to the bedroom she hastily changed back again to street clothes, then returned and opened the door. Two men wearing Arrow Cross arm bands stood there silhouetted against the light from the street lamp. Their breath rose like faint smoke around their heads. "Come with us to headquarters," the taller one ordered.

"What for?" Brigitta asked, shivering and peering out into the cold night.

"Never mind," he waved his thumb toward the street behind him. "You'll find out when you get there. Bring your papers."

There was nothing to do but go. Terrified that her true identity had been uncovered or that Eva had been taken into custody and forced to confess her own pretense of being a gentile, Brigitta's legs could hardly support her as they went. In her purse she carried her "Olga" identification which could save her, or incriminate her, depending on how things fell out. At headquarters, she was ushered into an almost deserted hallway lighted by a single unshaded globe hanging from the ceiling. The shorter guard motioned her to a chair where the light from the bare bulb shone in her eyes. She was sure her days were numbered. To her surprise they began questioning her, not about herself, but about a man sitting back in the shadows along the wall.

"Do you know this man?" they demanded, showing her a picture of him.

"Oh, yes," she said, "he is Martha's Uncle Julius." The poor creature in the corner made no motion, seemed not to hear.

"He is a dirty Jew!" Her interrogator interrupted. "What do you know about him?"

"Oh, that cannot be!" she cried. "It is not possible! He is Martha's uncle, a gentile."

"It is not possible!" one of them mimicked. "You will see for yourself."

Looking at the poor man Brigitta felt faint. He had been beaten, badly beaten. Blood covered his face and head, his eyes were swollen to mere slits, his clothes were torn and muddy, he looked exhausted.

"Do you know this woman?" they demanded of him. Fortunately, he only knew Brigitta as "Olga."

24

He peered at her across the dim hallway. "She is Olga," he said hoarsely.

"Do you still insist you do not know who this man really is?" they demanded.

"I have met him, he is Martha's uncle" Brigitta's voice had risen as though in exasperation, "and I cannot believe he is a Jew."

"You will see," snorted the official "Just sit there and wait."

Brigitta was in great danger and knew it. One slip of the tongue and her own cover might be blown. She had met the poor battered man only once. However, she knew a lot about him. He'd been the manager of a large electronics company, and was in fact Eva's uncle, not Martha's. When the Arrow Cross took over the factory which he managed, and hustled all his Jewish employees off to the trains, Eva, with the assistance of her gentile friends, helped him go into hiding. They gave him strict instructions to stay indoors and away from windows, to never go out for fear some former employee might recognize him and report him. Evidently, he'd gone out, alone, for no one else was with him and surely there'd be other victims here if they'd found him in hiding holed up with other refugees in some attic or furnace room. How had they made a connection between him and the real Martha, not Eva? That must have been why the Arrow Cross had been looking for "Martha" this morning. The real Martha was in trouble, not for helping Eva, but somehow over this battered being slumped in the chair across the drab passageway.

Eva had confided to Brigitta that the real Martha was the very non-conformist daughter of a top Arrow Cross Commander, a revolutionary at heart. She was adamantly opposed to the "Jewish Solution" the Germans were imposing on Hungary, and, in defiance of what she considered a horrible policy, she had passed her papers on to Eva to protect her. Had the "real" Martha also been a part of the plot to save this man? If the Arrow Cross knew about the Eva-Martha arrangement, what did they know about the Olga-Brigitta combination? Her palms were sweating and her mouth was dry. What were they waiting for?

The pitiless bare bulb cast long shadows down their faces as Brigitta and the former business man sat in silence after the Arrow Cross men went into a warm office off the cold hallway. Brigitta's attention remained fixed on the half-dead soul across from her. Obviously, his fate had already been decided, he was alive now only to serve as evidence against the commandant's daughter. Almost an hour ticked by on the big clock over the door at the far end of the hall before the outer door opened and the real Martha was shooed in by two young Arrow Cross officers who obviously didn't know whether to act tough or conciliatory.

Instantly, the interrogating officers returned to the hallway. "Do you know these people?" they demanded when she was led into the light where she could see Brigitta sitting stiffly in her chair on one side of the hallway, and the half-dead figure slumped a chair against the other wall.

"I have never seen either of them before in my life." she said disdainfully.

"How can that be?" asked the interrogator, his voice heavy with sugar-coated venom. "This man claims to have been placed in a house near here by someone who said she was you."

"It is not true." She tossed her head and pulled her fur coat tighter around her.

"What is not true?" they demanded. "That you don't know him or that you didn't help him? Do you have your papers?"

"I do not need papers!" she retorted drawing herself up indignantly. "You forget yourself. You know who I am."

"It is you who forget yourself." snapped the officer in charge. "Shall we send for your father?"

"My father has more important things to attend to than one small Jew. I would not advise waking him at this hour over such a poor creature as that one." she retorted.

"Your father might not like being wakened for such a one as that dirty little Jew, but he might be very interested in how that dirty little Jew comes to be placed in a house for hiding, by a woman carrying your papers."

Martha was visibly shaken by their knowledge. She swayed perceptibly as her cheeks paled but she stood her ground. They were relentless in their hammering at her until finally she broke out, "All right!" she shouted. "I helped one decent Jewish woman live. Do you think my father will let you throw me in prison for that?"

"It is a crime against the state, first, to have helped an enemy escape, and second, to allow another person to use your papers to avoid the housing proscriptions," the taller one stormed

"It is not a crime to be human," she insisted.

The officer's mouth curled into a sneer. "When did Jews become human?" he demanded.

They lectured her for what seemed like hours to Brigitta, but, because Martha's father was who he was, they did not arrest her, nor did they wake him out of a sound sleep. They cowed her, finally brought her to tears, then sent her off again with an escort. Unable to make a case against "Olga" at all, as Brigitta kept on proclaiming her amazement that such a deception could have been carried out right before her eyes without her knowing it, they let her go too. She was so convincing that in the end, they became apologetic about having dragged her out on such a miserable night over such an unpleasant issue. They even commiserated with her about having been duped by an impostor, a filthy little Jew of no consequence, assuring her that it sometimes happened to the best of people. One of the officers even gallantly insisted on escorting her home through the cold, dark streets.

Once inside the house, and sure that she was not being watched, Brigitta wasted no time. Burning the rest of the papers as quickly as she could, she threw her few things into a bag and at dawn caught the first train to Budapest. She could never feel safe at Lotte's house again. Life became a nightmare of walking the streets, sleeping where she could find a place for a night, washing in public baths, spending her days in libraries and museums, hiding in dark theaters during matinees, living like a hunted animal. There were apartments where she could go late at night and be admitted inside for warmth and shelter until just before dawn, but the apartments had to be vacated for safety's sake before other people were awake and aware of who was out and about. Days dragged endlessly into equally boring days as Brigitta spent mornings searching out her haven for the night. There were some places to which Brigitta had delivered food while she was still in the suburbs which were not safe to approach now, they might be watched if the authorities were looking for her. Nor could she go home to her mother, her mother wasn't there any longer.

In December, when the Russian armies were racing toward Budapest, Brigitta learned that Ford Motor Co. was pulling out. They contacted her through the real Olga and offered to take her with them in a great caravan of movable equipment, records, employees and their families, which would be headed west to Cologne. They urged Brigitta to go, but they would not risk taking her mother with them. Gizella looked too Jewish for it to be safe. Brigitta was in agony. She desperately wanted out, to be back under the protection of the Company, but she could not leave her mother behind in the new ghetto Eichmann had created, and into which he was forcing all the Jews to take up residence. Choked with tears, from a safe distance she watched them leave. The payments from Ford stopped, and Brigitta was left truly on her own, with only her wits to save them now. Fortunately, Brigitta's wits and her obstinate insistence on the right to life were enough.

Knowing that her aunt and her mother had been among those marched into the new ghetto, Brigitta went calling. Refusing, as always, to accept the unacceptable, she went to the gates of the densely-packed ghetto, sized up the situation, then, outwardly calm, inwardly quivering with fear, she walked into the lion's den. There was still great confusion around the gates as trucks came and went. The gentiles, who had lived in the area from which they were being evicted to make room for the Jews, were still moving out. Jews, dislodged from the nooks and crannies of Budapest where they had been discovered hiding, were still being brought in. In and out, among all these people, tradesmen were plying their wares, trying to sell the Jews anything and everything they could lay their hands on, in an effort to separate the "enemies of the state" from their last shilling. The streets were a cacophony of sound and a jumble of movement. In such a hubbub, Brigitta passed unnoticed into the crowded streets of the cordoned-off area.

House by house she searched, inquiring anxiously at every door for her "Aunt Gizy" whom she said had been her governess when she was a child, and to whom she wanted to say one last good-bye. It took hours of wandering through the chaos that enveloped the area before she found them. Her aunt was speechless when she walked in. The suddenness of Brigitta's appearance didn't surprise her mother at all. Gizella fell in with the charade immediately. She acted the role of the old family retainer as calmly as though they had rehearsed this play many times before. The other detainees in the house were completely unaware of what was happening right in front of them. When Brigitta suggested that her mother and aunt walk with her to the gate, Gizella seized one of Brigitta's arms and urged her sister to take the other.

Slowly, the three women strolled away to the gates, through the gates, down the street, and all the way to the suburbs. It was not sensible to ride the cars with two women who looked so Jewish, the only prudent thing to do was to keep right on walking, which they did. The whole episode was carried out with superb composure, the sickening fear under their aplomb not apparent to anybody watching. Brigitta led them to the home of another gentile friend of hers who had offered shelter some time earlier, and was now called upon to provide it. She welcomed them, though she was obviously terrified by their presence in her home. She was so frightened they knew they could not stay longer than it would take Brigitta to figure out what they should do next. Her fear would betray them all.

It was the dead of winter, every Jew known to the Nazis had been rounded up. The Hungarian population of Buda was living on the knife edge of want and fear. The 'Final Solution' mattered to none but the most deranged ultra Nazis. Ordinary Hungarians, frantic over their own fate in the face of the Russian advance, ignored the Germans' psychopathic witlessness, and let the Jews alone. Brigitta decided they would go home. Playing her Olga trump card one more time, she requisitioned her own apartment, the apartment wherein stood the precious tile stove. "Olga" was granted occupancy, and the three tiny women went walking again, walking calmly across the bridge to Pest, attracting no attention from a population with more imperative things on its collective mind. The concierge of the apartment house had never had a stomach for the removal of her Jewish tenants, and when she saw them coming she looked the other way. They climbed the three flights of stairs to their old apartment, and let themselves in.

The place had been stripped of everything small enough to carry, but the precious stove was there and so were the larger pieces of furniture. Brigitta stood in the middle of the living room and sized up the situation. The apartment was so cold her breath hung like frost in the air. First, they'd have to have some heat, and after that they'd see what was to be done. Whatever had to be done, they were home and that was that. That very day she went out and bought a Christian cross to affix to the outside of their apartment door like so many of their Catholics neighbors had done in the old days when the Cross had been a declaration of faith, not political purity. Then she began her raid on empty apartments in the building looking for firewood.

When the Arrow Cross had packed Jews in yellow-starred buildings into apartments to sardine capacity, Gizella and her sister had been forced to share their apartment with thirty-three other people. By then, Brigitta had gone to the suburbs. The crowding had been so impossible their "guests" had slept on the floors, on all the furniture, slept in shifts wherever they could find room to lie down. thirty-five people had shared the one toilet. thirty-five people never bathed because the water pressure had diminished to a trickle. thirty-three people had been fed what little they could scrape together, yet somehow they had kept the peace among themselves. What was left of Brigitta's well-stocked pantry after their thirty-three guests had been fed was looted by the police when the Jews were taken to the Ghetto. Where was she to get food? Three lives depended on her ability to provide. What could she do? In the affluent Ford days she had had food delivered to the apartment, but there was no phone now with which to place an order, and no delivery trucks moved anywhere in the city. The only food they had, the only food they would have until the city was liberated, were the dried peas they found scattered all over the apartment when they walked in.

One of the thirty-three people forced in upon them in November had been a commodity broker. Aware of what would be the most pressing need in the days ahead, he'd brought with him three large sacks of dried peas. The fateful day the Jews had been ordered to leave the building within the hour, taking only that which they could carry, the peas had been left behind. Once the building was empty, the Nazis had gone through all the apartments looking for loot. Some Nazi had slit every one of the sacks to make sure no treasure was hidden inside. When Brigitta, her mother and her aunt returned, they found those peas everywhere, and they carefully picked up every single one of them as though they were pearls beyond price. For the next four months, those peas were more precious than any gold or jewels would have been. To fight off the cold and to cook the peas, all Brigitta had to do was find the wood with which to fuel the wonderful big tile stove. She began tearing up the parquet floors in bombed out buildings nearby, carrying bundles of dry wood up the three flights of stairs to their apartment. They had heat, something few gentiles in Hungary enjoyed, and they had water procured by melting snow they scooped from the window ledges, in a small pot stuck through a small opening in the blessed stove. Once the snow was melted, they cooked the peas. The peas became breakfast, lunch and dinner, eaten in small amounts to make them last. When Brigitta could find no more flooring within a manageable distance from their building, she began to slip out in the early dawn, or at dusk, and wrestle wooden seats from benches in the park to bring home as firewood.

Since the evacuation of the Jews, the lower floors of their building had been occupied by Swabian refugees pouring into the city from the outskirts of Budapest, frightened people fleeing ahead of the Russians. Swabians were descendants of settlers invited into Hungary in those troubled centuries from nearby Germany to replace the population killed by the marauding Tartars, followers of Ghenghis Khan who rampaged through eastern Europe in the thirteenth century. They had retained their German ethnocentricity and their love for all things German throughout the successive future shifts of political boundaries. Swabians hated Jews as much as the Germans did, but they feared the Soviets more. Usually hate and fear go hand in hand. By the end of 1944, fear had mounted to the point of near hysteria for those who had opposed Russia and allied themselves with the Germans. There was little energy left for Jew hunting. In such a climate, Brigitta reasoned, three little women at the top of the stairs would receive little attention from anyone.

Christmas Eve, 1944, Budapest began to go up in flames as the Russian ring around the city tightened. The Soviet siege began almost simultaneously with the British and American aerial bombardments. As part of a last ditch effort at defense the Hungarian army placed a cannon in the entrance of their apartment building and fired away at a gun emplacement on the opposite bank of the river. Maniacally, however, the Arrow Cross men still left in Budapest obsessively hunted down Jews as Allied bombs set the city ablaze. Any Jew found outside the Ghetto was shot on the site of discovery, and his/her body was thrown into the Danube. Bodies, bloated and frozen, could be seen floating among the blocks of ice forming in the river, or washed up onto the ice-covered quiet waters at the river's edge.

As if to support the Russians in their efforts to free Budapest from Nazi control, the winter of 1944-1945 was the worst winter in memory. Temperatures dipped below freezing and kept on sliding down the thermometer. Horses froze to death in the streets and were hacked up by the starving citizens. Soon the Danube was frozen so solid that had there been anything to ship it couldn't possibly have come to the city by water. Snow, piled wall high along the streets, made foot traffic almost impossible and there was no other kind of traffic available as public transportation dried up when the gasoline supplies ran out. There were no deliveries of fuel oil for the furnaces of Budapest. Most utilities were cut off so there was no gas for heating or cooking, and the bombers early on targeted the power plants that supplied electricity to the city. The water mains froze and repair crews were helpless to cope with the emergency. Civilized life came to a halt.

The bombing of Budapest shattered every windowpane in the city. The pathetically thin little trio on the fourth floor struggled to stuff mattresses into the empty window frames. Those mattresses kept out the cold but they also made the apartment a blackened tomb regardless of the hour, day and night. To relieve the darkness, to be able to live in a dim gloom rather than like bats in a cave, they made wicks out of stuffing pulled from the mattresses, soaked the wicks in oil, then poured more oil in a thin film over a dish of water. They floated the wicks in this suspended oil. The water below kept the wicks from smoking too badly. In silence they huddled together wrapped in whatever they could scavenge from the empty apartments of the building, and listened to the city being destroyed around them. The bombing was terrifying. Every time a wave of bombers came over the city the three little women became as still as mice, as though their silence would send the bombers on to buildings more heavily occupied than theirs. Miraculously, only a corner of the apartment above them was blown away. In the streets below they could hear incessant gunfire, sometimes near, and sometimes blocks away. Since they never went out, the death that stalked the streets was not as frightening to them as the death being rained down on the city by the bombers overhead. By mid-January, the Germans had been driven from Buda, and in February Pest also fell to the Russians.

The end of the fighting relieved them of the fear of being blown to bits by the Russian, American and the British planes, but it did nothing to relieve them of the fear of starvation. That only increased. Brigitta could, at last, get out by daylight to forage for food and wood. The Russians had no interest in hounding Jews, but her foraging was for naught. The food shelves of Buda and Pest were bare. Getting wood was not easy but it was possible. Not too distant from the apartment building was a lumber yard, silent, buried under snow and abandoned. The only lumber left were the heavy cuts stacked outside the building. Brigitta and other foragers had to saw each twelve foot piece into two pieces in order to be able to move it. It took all her waning strength to pull a twelve foot board off a stack, saw it in half, strap a piece to her back and drag it back to the courtyard of their building. She would stagger along bent over so far she was almost crawling through the snow. When she had wrestled the wood to the bottom of the stairs her mother and aunt would come to help wrestle it up the rest of the way to their apartment. If they were frugal with it, Brigitta could bring home enough wood in one trip to last several days. Every morning they would hack away at their woodpile until they had what they needed for that day, then quit, exhausted. Down to 100 pounds fully clothed, Brigitta did manual labor fitting for a man half again her weight to keep them alive. Her stomach growled relentlessly, begging for something more substantial than peas to support her heavy work. There were days when she was so tired that putting one foot in front of the other seemed impossible.

Weeks into their interminable nightmare, the day after Pest was liberated by the Russians, an apparition appeared at the door. Incredibly, her cousin, the son of her aunt, stood before them. His mother cried out in surprise and would have fallen if he had not rushed to catch her. The Russian army was moving forward so rapidly that companies lost track of their officers and battalions and there was no order anywhere. In the confusion, he simply walked away from the labor battalion in which he had been forced to serve, and came back. To his amazement, he found that gentile neighbors had saved his house and his business for him while he was away, convinced that if anyone could survive this terrible time it would be he. He had come to take his mother home with him where he could see to it that she was fed.

It was a blessing, not only for her aunt but for Brigitta. It meant one less mouth to feed even though one less mouth meant very little when there was no food. The peas were running out. Not even two would live long unless something else turned up. Just when hopelessness and apathy were about to overcome her, her guardian angel returned and entered her life again. Ford Motor Co. was to be reopened by the Russians. The new government, which was nationalizing all private enterprise, sought out all the old employees who might still remain in Budapest and called them back into service. Those who reported to work would be paid in food since there was no currency to be had.

As the Germans pulled out of Budapest ahead of the Russians they crated up everything of value: art objects, machinery, livestock, streetcars, private possessions, everything. They loaded their booty into boxcars and sent it out by rail to Germany marked "Gifts to the German People from the people of Hungary." Naturally, they also carried off the contents of all the bank vaults which meant that there was no currency left to circulate. The job to which Brigitta was assigned, as were all the old employees - office help and factory workers alike - was removing rubble to put the factory back in operation. All day she carted off fragments of concrete and twisted pieces of metal until her arms ached and her legs were leaden from fatigue. For simple manual labor the pay was two bowls of thin watery soup and two slices of dank, heavy black bread each day. She ate one bowl of soup and one piece of bread on the job, then took the other bowl of thin soup and the other slice of gooey sour bread to her mother. People, who had not wrestled with wood for weeks as she had, collapsed on the job, but somehow she found the strength to haul herself out every morning and wend her way through the snow clogged streets to the worksite.

When spring came, the farmers cautiously returned to their stalls in the city market with food for those city dwellers who had gold with which to buy. The farmers would not barter and they would not take the new paper money which devaluated as quickly as it was printed. Runaway inflation had sent the Communist currency skyrocketing into the quintillions. Eighteen zeroes followed every figure. People could scarcely pronounce the prices they were charged, much less produce the money. The currency, printed only on one side of the paper, came in blue, or white, or green, or whatever color of ink the Russians found that day. If a puff of wind carried off your money and it fell into the gutter, no one bothered to pick it up. The idea that there was currency in circulation was a cruel joke. Brigitta and her mother once more were lucky, they had gold, they could eat. They had recovered their jewelry from their friends, and among their pieces was a long gold chain inherited from Brigitta's grandmother. They took it apart, link by link, exchanging one link each day for food. First, peas had saved them, and now little pieces of gold were their salvation. The world had become an insane place in which to live.

Along with the return of the peasants to their traditional role in the economic life of the city, along with the blossoming that spring of the stunted limbs of trees which had been shattered by the bombings, came wonderful news from the West. On April 30th, Adolph Hitler and Eva Braun died in their bunker in a mutual suicide pact. Their bodies were soaked with gasoline and burned up. The madman had done the sanest thing of his life, he had left this world. Immediately, the Americans set up a legation in Budapest whether the Russians liked it or not. Brigitta fairly ran to the employment office they opened. She applied for a job as a translator-interpreter-typist. There was plenty of competition for the jobs they offered, everyone wanted to work for the rich Americans, but Brigitta had the edge because of her command of English and because of her past employment with Ford. She got the job she wanted. It was like manna from heaven. The job carried a salary of seventy dollars per month which was paid in American currency.

In the Hungary of 1945, American currency was worth ten times its value in the United States. Besides the pay, she had Post Exchange privileges which were worth even more. The Americans had everything, everything that could not be had for love or money in Budapest shops. She could buy real coffee for nine cents a pound. The citizens of Budapest hadn't even smelled coffee for over a year. She could have milk delivered to her mother again, every day, and neither of them carried firewood up those three flights of stairs anymore. For

Brigitta, there was indeed a Santa Claus, and his name was Uncle Sam.

Brigitta loved the Americans! And they loved her. Before long she was making ninety five dollars a month, and every day she took a little of her money to the street to exchange for local currency. It was foolish to exchange more than that day demanded, tomorrow the exchange rate would be different. She was working for the U.S. Information Service, and they paid in one dollar and two dollar bills because of the ridiculous currency situation. Two people could live on one dollar a day, and a family of four could get by on two dollars. Brigitta stashed away every penny they did not absolutely need. Everyone knew the monetary situation had to be stabilized. Runaway inflation couldn't keep on making smoke out of money. When the currency was depreciated, Brigitta's salary, which had been a king's ransom, became a subsistence income. The American dollar might still be king but ninety five of them no longer bought $950 worth of goods. Furthermore, the Americans refused to give additional pay raises in order not to bring resentment down on their heads from the impoverished populace not lucky enough to find employment in a U.S. enterprise.

One of the first businesses to get back into world-wide distribution after World War II was the American film industry. A newly-formed export bureau was opened in Budapest, and Hollywood lost no time in sending all the backlog of "B-rated" movies they'd made in the past four years into the Eastern European market. Most of them were propaganda films. The United States had a message to deliver as well as a buck to make. Brigitta was offered a job by the export bureau at a salary three times that paid by the Information Service. Her star was again in the ascendancy. Not only did she make much more money than she had been making, but going to work was literally going to the movies every day. She translated dialogue into subtitles to be imprinted on the American soundtracks. She translated anything and everything - advertisements, promotion articles about the films, film credits - anything. Warner Brothers, Paramount, Metro Golden Meyer, she worked for all the big studios and loved it.

Meanwhile, the rest of the population was not faring well. No real recovery from the devastation of war was occurring on any front. As agreed at Potsdam in 1945, 1948

36

brought Hungary's first free election following the war. The Communists lost the election and lost control of the government. Within twenty four hours the infamous coup d'état followed. The Communists seized control of all business life and closed down the film bureau. Censorship of every form of propaganda for the good life in the West went into effect immediately. All Western businesses were ordered out of the country. The new government gave the employees of the export bureau six months severance pay and sent them back into the job market. Brigitta began pounding the pavement. Discouragement followed discouragement. There was no work.

While she was still with MOPEX (the film distribution company), a school for tour guides was opened by the mayor's office in hopes of encouraging tourism in Budapest. When she did not find work immediately, Brigitta enrolled in the school full time to learn everything there was to know about the city and its history. She even acquired a red umbrella in anticipation of leading walking tours around Budapest. But when it came time to take the certifying exam she had to provide a political clearance, a so-called morality certificate. These could only be obtained from the police department. She mailed in her request to the Police only to be notified that she was not certifiable, she was not morally responsible. Gasping with indignation, she marched off to police headquarters to confront them over this outrage. Not morally responsible? A very nice young officer greeted her at the counter. She laid the offensive letter down in front of him.

"What does this mean?" she demanded. "Not morally responsible! What does it mean?!"

"Morally responsible?" He raised one eyebrow quizzically as he steadily faced her anger. "Morally responsible means many things. It depends on the category."

"What category am I in?" The color in her flushed cheeks deepened.

"I can't tell you that," he said kindly, trying to take the sting out of the words. "That's confidential material."

"Confidential? Confidential from whom?"

"From everyone," he said.

"Confidential from the party?"

"Oh no, the party makes the categories and then enters the names."

His tone was the voice of rationality. He was addressing her like a child.

"Can't you at least tell me what kind of list I'm on?" she pleaded.

He sighed. "I'll check." He walked into an adjoining room leaving her drumming her fingers on the counter. In a minute he was back. His face was sad.

"I'm afraid," he said sympathetically, "that you're on a list of persons who can't be certified for any kind of work."

Brigitta gasped. No work at all?! Her face went white and her voice shook. "Please, may I have a copy of the document that says I'm not a morally responsible person?" Her throat constricted over the words.

He should never have given it to her, that list, but he did. The names of all the individuals in the city who were regarded as persona non grata were on that list. In her shaking hand she held proof that she could not work at any state job anywhere in Hungary, ever. With everything nationalized, what other kind of work was there to be had? She poured over the document trying to find some reason why her name was included. There was nothing

"Can you tell me where I can go to get my name off this list?" Her big blue eyes reflected her panic.

"I'm sorry. I can't tell you. I can't tell you because I don't know and I don't dare ask."

She left the police station dazed. Why? What had she done? What was she to do now? If she could not work, how were they to live? For days she walked around numb, dazed, unable to grasp the immensity of the calamity that had fallen on her. Over and over she asked herself Why? Why? but she couldn't come up with an answer. Lying in bed staring at the ceiling one night she decided it was because she had worked for the Americans. She quit listing her post-war employment on application blanks and fell back on her education and pre-war positions as qualifications for employment. Those qualifications should have been enough to get her hired at any job she chose, and did, but within days of being hired she would be notified by phone that her employment had been terminated.

Night after night she lay sweating in the dark, terrified that she would never work again. Her daylight hours were no better. Whipsawed by fear and anxiety, she felt blocked from being able to think her way out of her dilemma. She had her mother to feed, the rent to pay, and somehow keep them alive. One day, as she walked down a busy street in the heart of Budapest, her thoughts as dreary as the day itself, she ran into an old school friend, someone who had also survived the Nazis, someone who could understand what desperation meant. With a sympathetic ear at her command Brigitta poured out her tale of woe. Her friend listened sympathetically letting Brigitta spill out her dilemma before she spoke. Finally she interrupted and turned Brigitta's cloud inside out.

"Brigitta," she said calmly, "you will have a job tomorrow. My husband is the manager of a corporation that makes furnace linings. Never mind," she held up her hand to cut Brigitta off, "you can learn all about it after you've gone to work. The point is that it's not a Hungarian company. The owners are all Czechs and that puts all the hiring in his hands, not the government's."

Brigitta began to cry. "I..."

Again her friend held up her hand. "Tomorrow, you go down to his office," she paused to write out the address for Brigitta, "and tell him who you are. I'll talk to him tonight. I'd have him telephone you but I don't think it's safe. We think we're bugged."

Brigitta tried a brave little rejoinder. "We're not bugged. They've taken our telephone out so I can't influence the operators."

Her friend did not laugh. "They're little better than the Nazis." she said grimly. "The only difference is they don't play favorites. They treat the whole population like they were Jews. There are camps you know. They call them prisons."

Brigitta was at her friend's husband's office before it was open the next morning. Wanting to present a composed sophistication when she walked in she hung around the door pretending to be lost in the early edition of the insipid propaganda sheet that passed for a newspaper. When she thought the staff had had time to settle into the day she walked in and went straight to the receptionist to have herself announced. Compared to the offices at Mopex, the manager's suite in this corporation looked like the anteroom of the shipping department at the film distributing company. The whole interview was over in a matter of minutes and she was hired. The new job was another piece of translating. This time she was to reproduce English language manuals containing installation and operating instructions into Hungarian. She was also to translate technical magazine articles into simple Hungarian layman's language. Young people with less than gymnasium-level education had to be able to understand the specifications given in American measurements which were to be converted into the metric system. Additionally, there were many routine translations requiring precise writing about precise tasks. Even if they had blindfolded her she could not have failed. More importantly, she loved the work. Especially intriguing was the technical library she was expected to manage on the side. Within six months she had moved up to the Research Department of the company, taking her library duties with her.

When Hungary was separated from Austria and her geographic area reduced at the end of World War I, all the bauxite-bearing lands had gone to Czechoslovakia. The factory, for which Brigitta now worked, manufactured refractory bricks made from bauxite. These refractory bricks were used to line furnaces for making steel. Brigitta knew nothing about science, but, since she always wanted to know everything about anything with which she was involved, she got curiouser and curiouser. Why not go to night school and take courses in library science? It wouldn't teach her much about bauxite, or the making of steel, but it would make her a bona fide technical librarian. In the process, she'd learn a lot of things about which she presently knew nothing. At age forty she matriculated, majoring in technical and scientific library studies. Attending school at night, putting in long weekends bent over her books, it took her several years to get the coveted degree, but at last she was a certified librarian, and her area of expertise was technical libraries. Wherever in the world she might seek employment, she'd be qualified.

Brigitta was not a tunnel-visioned workaholic in those years, though it may seem so. The old fun-loving Brigitta had not died. Nor had she gone into self-imposed seclusion. She still attended the theater, operas, and concerts. She went to the movies regularly, seeing only Russian films since Western films were banned. Limited as it was to Communist-dictated themes, movie fare was generally very dull, but the movies were the cheapest form of entertainment in town. Photographic techniques were improving which made many of the films visually exciting even if the plots were too thin to be called more than a series of patriotic vignettes. The price of theater tickets and all forms of entertainment were fixed by the government at a level that was affordable to everybody. She and her mother attended Saturday matinees again, but the old magic was gone. Besides the cultural events there was Sunday in the park with her mother and friends.

Her sex appeal had not shriveled up or blown away either. There was always someone around to escort her wherever she wanted to go. Dutifully, Brigitta brought all her men friends around to meet her mother and Gizella charmed them all, but when they left she picked them to pieces. If Gizy had approved of any of Brigitta's suitors her daughter might have remarried and never seen America again, but Gizy never did. For almost three decades she kept her funny, witty daughter tied to her, in constant attendance.

Brigitta met an attractive man who intrigued her and who worked in the offices of a factory near her own employment. Past experience warned her not to take him home, not to let him come under her mother's eagle eye. They met for dinners out, they attended the theater, for two months they saw a good deal of each other. Then one night, when they had a date to meet on a certain corner to go to a movie, Brigitta arrived on time and waited. Then waited, and waited, and waited some more. He never showed up. She waited long enough not to have to explain to her mother why she had come home early after having told her she would be late. The next day he was not at work, nor the next, nor ever again. He just disappeared. Seven years later, in November of 1956, he called.

"Hello." The voice was as recognizable as if he'd called yesterday.

"Hello," Brigitta stuttered in astonishment. "Where have you been?"

"In prison. Isn't that where everyone goes when they want to get away?" There was a bitter quality to his voice that had not been there before.

"But why?"

Why indeed. Among the educated classes of Budapest, before the tragedy of October, 1956, they jested that society was divided into three groups: those who were in jail, those who had been in jail and those who would be in jail. In this man's case his offense had been one of resistance to the further enslavement of the working class. He was a lawyer, and the personnel manager of a state-owned shipyard, the largest in the country. In 1949, the Communists introduced a new system of wages based on piecework. It meant that only the strongest and most able-bodied would be able to earn a living wage. He protested that this would drive most workers into degrading poverty, but his protests fell on deaf ears. He was ordered to follow the new method of establishing each man's earnings, immediately. He defied the order and continued to pay on an hourly basis. He'd gotten by with it for only a month before he was stopped. The day he was to meet Brigitta for the movies he was called into the head office and never came out. Since Brigitta had been so chary about taking him home to meet her mother he had not mentioned her to his parents. Not knowing anything about Brigitta they did not know to call her to let her know of his imprisonment.

Brigitta hated the Communists, hated them almost as much as she had hated the Nazis. Jews were not set apart by the Russians, they shared the common demoralization that bowed down the rest of the population. They suffered the same impoverishment, they found their lives circumscribed by the same censorship, they were equally crushed in spirit as were their Christian neighbors. They were as ready for an uprising in October of 1956 as anyone else. For three days hope surged through the city as the intellectuals revolted and pleaded with the world to send them aid. Then the Russian tanks rolled in from the countryside where they had been kept since 1945, and in three days the uprising was history. When the Revolution failed, Brigitta was as devastated as the nation itself. She felt as trapped as she had in 1944-45. She couldn't walk across the borders with her friends, her mother was now seventy-nine years old and her walking days were over. There was only one hope of getting out so far as she could see. She contacted Ford-Cologne hoping someone there might remember her.

At Ford Motor Co., people in high places remembered Brigitta. In only a matter of weeks, Ford-Cologne made her escape from Communist Hungary a company project. Several departments were involved in the process, and somehow Ford secured German immigration visas for her and for her mother, visas from Germany which were required by the

42

communist government in Budapest before an exit visa from Hungary could be issued. They mailed papers back and forth from the company to the Hungarian authorities, never involving Brigitta in the paper shuffling. Her participation could have put the project in jeopardy; it had to look like Ford had initiated the whole thing. It became a game in which the company persisted until the Hungarian government gave her the coveted exit visas and the doors finally opened for her escape. Brigitta's relief and gratitude knew no bounds. She and her mother wasted no time in making preparations to leave. Communist restrictions prevented them from taking any furniture or other items on the government's proscribed list with them. They could take only personal things.

"What do they mean, personal?" Gizella demanded.

"Personal means personal." Brigitta braced for a fight. "You know. Your clothes, your jewelry, your makeup."

"That's not what I call personal." snapped Gizella. "That's just necessary. I think it means things like your family's crystal, things you inherited."

"Mother! You're going to get us into trouble. Don't start rewriting the law. Just pack your stuff, things that go in suitcases, and forget the rest. In Germany we'll have enough money to buy more."

Gizella pursed her mouth. "I'm taking my mother's crystal and silver and that's all there is to it. I won't try to take the furniture. It's so shabby I'll be glad to have new, but I don't leave my mother's table service behind!"

Brigitta rolled her eyes and spread her arms helplessly. There were times when the words that came out of her mouth fell directly onto the floor as soon as she spoke them. They never reached her mother's ears. The trick was to know when one of those times was upon her so she didn't get upset uselessly. Besides, with Gizella's chutzpah she might get by with it. She did, but when the packers got through wrapping the lovely pieces Brigitta's mother had sorted out for shipment and throwing them into crates, many were chipped, dented, or broken. Everything else, even clothing beyond the value limit set by the government, had to be sold. Brigitta took the money from their estate sale, converted it at exorbitant black market rates into American $100 bills, then sealed the bills in a plain envelop addressed to her cousin in San Francisco. She waited to mail the envelop until it was time to board the train for

Germany. Crossing her fingers and praying, she dropped it in the Post at the very last minute. If it got there she'd have it and if it didn't, she couldn't take it out with her anyway. In her anxiety to get safely out of the country she forgot to enclose a note to her cousin to tell her what to do with the money. The money arrived and, bewildered by no instructions, cousin Grace deposited it in an account in San Francisco in Brigitta's name to await further developments.

Ford Cologne welcomed her with open arms. It was like the return of the prodigal son. Many of the people she had known were no longer there, but there were some, and it was good to work with them again. She found an apartment for herself and her mother and once they were settled in, she tried to contact Erwin's family. Many times during the war she had wondered about them, wondered if they had lived through the Allied bombings on Stuttgart. They were generous people who had loved her and cared for her. She went to the street where the family had lived, but a new house sat where their home had been. House and family were gone. Only Erwin had survived. Far too busy to join his family for his father's birthday, Erwin was not there when an Allied bomb made a direct hit on the building. He was in his second marriage when Brigitta and her mother arrived in Germany in 1957, and that marriage would be followed by a third and a fourth before his death in the early 1980's.

After the euphoria of being out of Hungary wore off, and after the excitement of being back in the arms of Ford had subsided, Brigitta took stock of the new Germany and found that both she and Germany had changed. Prosperity returned to that country by 1956 thanks to the Marshall Plan. The rubble had largely been removed and the cities rebuilt. People again haunted the beer halls and the bands played in the parks on Sunday. On the surface it looked the same and sounded the same, but it didn't feel the same. Everywhere she turned, she met defensive people who stoutly declared they had not known what the government was doing to the Jews. Nazis or not, there didn't seem to be a man, woman or child who was aware that 600,000 people had disappeared from among them and the largest portion of the missing were Jews. Or, if they were ignorant of the fact that she was a Jew, they would sullenly insist that the only mistake Hitler made was in losing the war.

She was no longer the romantic young woman who'd told her Cologne friends that she was more Aryan than they, she was Hung-Aryan. She'd lived with the consequences of Germanic egocentricity too long. She'd been mauled, brutalized, and terrorized by arrogant, frenzied German narcissism. She rebelled against living under the tyranny of silence her work at Ford imposed on her, a silence that seemed a betrayal of those whose lives had been snuffed out because of the hypocrisy of not knowing: aunts, uncles, cousins, sleeping the peace of the dead; friends with whom she had shared her youth shipped off to camps from which they never returned. Silence would deny her own vividly remembered experiences of paralyzing fear and near starvation, of foraging like an animal for wood, of hiding out like a criminal, of walking the streets without a place to lay her head, of being humiliated, terrorized and vandalized, all because a madman in Germany hated Jews, and the super patriotic German people had closed their eyes to what was going on around them. To come to this place where it had all started and have the monstrous innocence of the populace thrust down her throat day after day was too much. When they told her that the tales of the death camps were Allied fantasy and propaganda she knew she had to get out. The Germans were cavalierly rewriting history in a way that could easily lead to another Holocaust. The next time Nazism reared its head she wasn't going to be there.

Come hell or high water, she was going to San Francisco and she was going to take her mother with her. She began hearing foghorns in her sleep, and daydreaming about little cable cars while she worked. She wrote to her cousin. She needed two affidavits that would guarantee the U.S. government that she and her mother would not be dependents on the public dole. In her letter, she assured her cousin that there was enough money in that bank account to take care of them until she found work. Her cousin was not worried about the money, she had money of her own to burn which she would gladly put up as security for Gizella and Brigitta. Grace contacted the immigration office so that Brigitta need not risk being ordered back to Budapest to do the paper work. It took months of correspondence between Frankfurt and San Francisco before the U.S. authorities were assured that between her own savings and the wealth of her cousin, which would be available as the backup security required, she was a safe risk. For the last time Brigitta bid Ford Motor Co. good-bye. It was the only tie in Europe she hated to break.

The two little newcomers arrived in San Francisco in 1959 on Gizella's 80th birthday. Relatives, and friends of their relatives, people whom they knew and some they had never met, threw a birthday party to end all birthday parties. It was a glorious beginning.

Things came together very quickly. Through a chance encounter, Brigitta learned that Children's Hospital in San Francisco was feverishly looking for a medical librarian. She didn't know much about medicine, but she knew scientific libraries. She got the job and within a few years was elected president of the Northern California Association of Medical Librarians. One day in 1965 she received a call from the head of the Pink Ladies organization at the hospital.

"There's a woman down here I can hardly understand. She's a Hungarian, she says, and she wants to volunteer. Do you suppose you could help me out and talk to her?"

"Of course," Brigitta answered. "Send her up."

The woman was Magda, Magda Zahler Markowits Oudegeest. Brigitta had seen her perform in the dear dead days of their youth in Budapest. Magda was elated to be recognized and remembered. She had just come to America and was at loose ends. Her husband was looking at property in Rossmoor, a new community that would, in time, fill a whole valley and where Brigitta herself would one day reside. The friendship that has bound them together for thirty-four years began that day. Today, Magda's needs fill much of Brigitta's life, for Magda never learned to speak English well enough to mind her own business when she became a widow again.

In 1970, after eleven full, happy years in America, Gizella died. Brigitta was sixty-three. Life seemed both empty and free. She was alone, and she missed Gizella. Still, she had no one but herself to watch over, no schedule but her own to keep. After more than three decades of having to put someone else's comfort and safety and needs before her own, she was free to come and go without accounting to anyone about anything. She had her mother's little dog for company, and a lovely apartment near the hospital where she worked. She ate out or in, depending on her mood, she chose the movies she saw and the books she read without a debate about her choice. She was liberated. But oddly, it was not enough. An emptiness persisted long after she quit missing her mother. One Sunday, to keep her weekend from ending on a lonely note, she called friends who lived high up on Mount Davidson, a peak in the ridge of hills that runs at an angle across the southern section of San Francisco.

"I need company," she said bluntly. "Could I come and share your morsel tonight?"

"Of course you can, my dear. You know you're always welcome," was the answer. "But, it will be more than a morsel. We're having a few guests over."

"Why didn't you say so ?" Brigitta scolded. "You would have let me break in on your dinner party like some poor lost soul you couldn't turn away. I wouldn't think of it."

"No! Now listen up. You'll like these people and they'll love you. One of them is even a single man so you'll make the table come out even. Please come. I should have thought of it when I was planning this little supper."

Too lonely to do more than politely demur, Brigitta allowed herself to be persuaded. Not wanting to make an entrance, she arrived earlier than the other guests. Her hosts were still in the last throes of getting things together. "I thought I could see your new terrace before the others came. I want to go up by myself while you finish whatever you're doing."

Brigitta climbed the slope to the new terrace her friends had created out of some brushy land that was part of their lot. Above the house by almost a full story, the view from the terrace of the Pacific was grand. Below her lay a spectacular sweep of the ocean, at that hour aglow with the light of the last rays of the setting sun. A half disk of orange-red sun hovered on the horizon. Brigitta was so mesmerized by the beauty before her, so lost in the dramatic pinks and reds of the sky above the water, she did not hear the approaching steps of someone coming into the new garden behind her. The goddess of love could not have created a more perfect setting in which to kindle romance. Brigitta, who had decided long ago that it was too late for Cupid to do any more damage to her life, learned that love knows no season. The footsteps belonged to Fred Schneider. Startled, Brigitta turned to face the nice little man with the friendly face who returned her gaze so steadily, so openly, she was caught off guard.

"Oh, she gasped, "I didn't hear you coming."

He smiled his disarming smile. "I didn't mean to frighten you. Our friends sent me up to fetch you down for dinner. I'm Fred and you must be Brigitta."

"I am," she said turning back toward the stone steps leading down, "I invited myself for dinner. I hope you don't mind."

"How could an old widower like me mind a pretty dinner companion like you?" he said, his wonderfully crinkled face alight with pleasure.

"Oh, come now," Brigitta laughed. "I'm a little beyond being a pretty woman."

"You know better than that." his tone brooked no pretense.

Brigitta's heart skipped a beat. The sky overhead was now pale pink in the fading sunlight. She hoped the flush she felt in her cheeks would be seen as reflection of the color overhead. Could something wonderful be dawning as the day faded? Nov. 7, 1970, only months after Gizella's death, they were married. After 37 years of battling the worst life could throw at her, Brigitta had someone to watch over her.

They found an apartment high in the western hills of San Francisco near the University of California Hospital. It was a splendid location. From their balcony they had a hundred and eighty degree view of the Bay and the Golden Gate, and all the way to the Farallon Islands. What was more, the dog was welcome. It may sound perfect, but it was constantly windy high up on that hill, and when the city was cloaked in fog the gray emptiness around them was hauntingly lonely. The summer fog made every day a dreary replica of the day before. To break the monotony, they went out to Contra Costa County to visit Magda. In the hills around the Oudegeests' place there were lovely places to walk among the deer which grazed the swards of Rossmoor. Fred was enchanted. They decided to leave the city and move out to where the sun shone most of the time.

Fred lived another twelve years. When I met Brigitta in 1986 she had been a widow for four years. She and Magda, now also widowed, were bound together by their Hungarian origins, Magda's need for an interpreter, and their mutual membership in the circle of "The Girls." Rossmoor was and still is their sanctuary.

MAGDA

The hushed sounds of dawn did not waken the compound as usual. No one had slept. Bright tropical sunlight edged the rim of the gray horizon with gold. Palm fronds creaked softly in a breath of a breeze. This hour of the day had always been magical for Karoly before he'd been betrayed. Though the human beings in it were not abed, the world he was leaving stirred sleepily awake as he stood on the terrace, hands thrust deep into pockets. Cocks heralded the approaching sunrise, then came the soft cooing of doves nesting in the shrubs around the house. Peacocks on their perches along the roof line, stood, rustled their feathers, and sent forth their first raucous shrieks of the day to announce they were about to start patrolling the grounds. Sounds of softly padding bare feet on the hard-packed earth under the breadfruit trees whispered the arrival of the few servants left to serve the big house. A few short weeks before, twice their number lived beyond the row of hibiscus planted as a privacy screen, privacy for the masters of the compound, and privacy for the servants who made their masters' lives so princely. More than half of the servants' quarters were empty now.

Behind Karoly stood the magnificent house he and his partner, Bandi Von Kiss, and their families occupied. Half of the living quarters belonged to the Von Kisses, and half to Magda, Marika, and him. The gynecological clinic occupied the rest of the mansion. Inside the living room of the Markowits' quarters, Magda sat rigidly perched on the edge of a deep lounge chair. Karoly came in from the terrace wrapped in angry silence. Magda stared dully at him as he paced up and down the length of the room. At the other end of the big double house, Bandi's family, drenched with tears, gathered in their own living room waiting for the Japanese to come to cart Karoly, Magda and Marika away. Karoly wanted it that way, had insisted on it. "Distance yourself as much as you can from us," he'd argued. "Make them think you're glad to see us go. It won't make it any easier for either of us if you rile them."

Filled with emotion beyond expressing, they stood looking haggardly at each other the night before. There was nothing left to say. Bandi had berated himself mercilessly over Karoly's entrapment. It was his fault Karoly was here. He'd lured the young surgical assistant to Surabaya in order to double the staff of his one man clinic. In the hospital in Budapest, sixteen years ago, his much younger face had been alight with excitement as he'd played pied piper to Karoly's burning ambition and thirst for adventure. As for Karoly, he could hear as clearly as ever his partner's eager voice as Bandi said, "Come on, Markowits, give yourself the chance of a lifetime. Come on out to Java and go into practice with me. We'll be rich as kings!"

Karoly did not blame Bandi for what was happening now. He, Karoly, had been eager for it, eager for the palmy world of high living Bandi extolled as they stood side by side in that little scrub room off the operating theater. During the night a spring storm had dumped wet snow on Budapest leaving the streets a slushy mess. The thought of sun-drenched days where money grew on trees was irresistible. Kiss was a fine doctor. It would be good to practice with him. Karoly, avid for a piece of the action, left Magda behind to wait while he tried it out. The money had poured in as promised. The two young doctors had become as rich as kings. In such a setting who could have foreseen the events of today. Karoly Markowits was to be carted off like a penniless convict to face God only knew what fate, and all because he was a Jew.

Last night, the two men had wrapped their arms tightly around each other for a long, long last moment while Magda and Marika stood by silently weeping. On their side of the house this morning the Von Kisses, all four of them, braced themselves against the sound of lorry tires on the crushed shells of the long driveway. The Japanese were always punctual. When they posted notices of events to come, those things happened right on schedule.

Marika, her woebegone little face red and swollen from crying, went to where Karoly strode up and down the long, high-ceilinged room and threw her arms around his waist to stop him, to seek comfort from him. The slender little body trembled with fear as she pressed hard against him, fear for which he had no words of reassurance. The round-eyed little ten-year-old and the powerfully built middle-aged man fused to form a single silhouette against the early morning light coming through the window behind them. Magda shivered as she watched.

Mournfully, she fingered the patterned fabric of the upholstery under her. Her beautiful home! All the lovely, tasteful things they'd collected to furnish this magnificent house. As she looked around at all she was leaving the lump in her throat swelled until she couldn't breathe around it. In the muted light of this dawn an unnatural silence muffled the world outside their windows. For thirteen years she had woken every morning to the comforting sounds of chattering servants, dogs snuffing about, the wind sighing through the palms. Now the stillness was like a vigil for the dead awaiting the keening cries of grief still to be raised. She shuddered again and wiped her eyes.

"The Goddamned old fool!" Karoly exploded. Neither Magda nor Marika responded to his outburst. He'd erupted like that for over a month, ever since they learned that the Japanese had a special fate in store for the Jews of Java. That fate had been designed in Berlin, but they'd been betrayed into it by a religious zealot, a stupid old self-anointed, modern-day Jeremiah.

"Jew!?" Karoly shouted when Number One boy brought in the bulletin the Japanese had issued. "Hell, I don't even own a prayer shawl!"

"Yes you do, Daddy. It's in the chest in the hallway," Marika's eyes danced with pleasure at knowing something he didn't.

"Not anymore, little melon," he snorted. "That prayer shawl became incense three weeks ago. I had a Buddha priest bless it and burn it for me."

He turned hotly to Bandi, "If I had known where to find a Shinto Shrine I'd have personally burned it there myself. Some of those little bastards are Buddhists, aren't they?"

"Their Buddhism is about as deep as your Jewishness," Bandi retorted angrily. "Your prayer shawl wasn't the problem, and burning it wasn't the solution."

The problem, and "The Final Solution," didn't have anything to do with anything in Indonesia. The madness of Europe seeped into Asia through that damned Tripartite Treaty that said the Japanese would turn over the Jews they captured in Asia to Hitler. The old Jew had set them up to be incarcerated by Hitler's allies. Bandi didn't turn Karoly's name over to the Japanese, the old fart did. The Dutch never kept records identifying people by religious affiliation. There was no way the Japanese could have sorted the Jews out of the Europeans without a spy in their midst. The stubby, holierthan-God old fool striding the streets of Surabaya wrapped in his woolen prayer shawl, even on the hottest days, his yarmulke askew on his head, looking for prey was the betrayer. Walking into any gathering, without a by-your-leave he sonorously launched into his sanctimonious braying about the sinful assimilation of the Jews into the ways of the goyim. Theatrically, he would thunder about a Jew's duty to God until everyone present was embarrassed for him. For the past five years he'd carped constantly about tradition and obligation, insisting that all the Jews of Surabaya must contribute to the building of a synagogue and a Hebrew school. No one, not one other Jew in the whole city, had wanted those buildings but him.

The crazy old fool had made up lists of every Jewish family in Surabaya, lists on which he made notations about who had sons or daughters who were not receiving religious instruction, and how much he thought each household could afford to contribute toward a religious center. One little fanatic for Judaism had delivered him, Karoly Markowits, and his family, along with every other Jew in town, into the hands of the allies of another little fanatic who was bent on obliterating all adherents to Judaism from the face of the earth. The universe was reeling under a monstrous joke perpetrated on the human race by half-crazed, ideologically mad little men. And where was this God who had chosen the Jews to be His people while all this was happening? This God the demented old fool prattled about? Bitterly Karoly stared at the wall and moaned, a long shuddering sound came from the depths of his being.

Instantly alert and anxious, Magda looked up. "Are you all right, Karoly?"

Karoly didn't answer. A fresh wave of fear swept over her. Without Karoly she would be lost. She depended on Karoly like she'd depended on her father before him, trembling when either man lost his calm. Never had anyone expected more than for her to delight and to entertain. Never had she been expected to deal with the world on its terms. She had been born into a magical circle where strong people surrounded her, directed her, indulged her. Not once in her whole life had she been forced to face a hurdle alone. Without Karoly standing between her and whatever lay ahead she was lost. How could it all have come to this? How could it be that she, Magda Zahler, the darling of theater audiences all over Europe, daughter of Emil Zahler one of Budapest's foremost physicians, wife of a very rich and very charming man, how could it be that she was going away in a truck to some unknown fate taking nothing more with her than what she could cram into one little bag small enough for her to carry?

Why had her father and Karoly let it come to this? If only she could turn the clock back three years to 1939 she'd be safe in Budapest. In the beginning, the outbreak of war in Europe seemed remote and far away. It had nothing to do with life out here, or the family back home. Hitler would never invade Hungary. Hungary would remain free of Hitler's control because of the Arrow Cross, a strong pro-Nazi Party which had put pressure on the Horthy government to maintain an alliance of sorts with Germany. The alliance would keep Hitler at bay. Hungarians at home and abroad wanted desperately to believe that Hungary could remain neutral as the war flowed around her.

If they had gone home in '39 this would not be happening to them. When Holland was overrun in 1940, consternation bordering on hysteria broke out all over the Dutch East Indies. It was too late then for any Hungarian to get back to Budapest. Many of their Dutch friends packed up and went home to be with relatives no matter what the future held. Some of the Brits had gone home later when the Blitz of London began. It was a curious thing, this need to be in the Mother Country to share the fate of their countrymen in the line of fire. Karoly and Magda talked it over and she allowed him to persuade her that the best thing they could do was to remain where they were. The Dutch East Indies would be protected by the British and Dutch navies.

"You know the Brits and the French will beef up their forces out here. They've got India, and Burma and Indochina and Singapore to lose if they don't!" the pundits at the club said. The skeptics said, "Hell, they'll never get started in time to send anything out here." Karoly's optimism made him side with a third group who trusted the might of America. America, they said, would protect the sea lanes to the Philippines. Magda had overheard a heated exchange in the club bar one day and came home full of fear. Bandi snorted, "The Brits can't get the Eighth Army out of Europe, much less send anything out here."

Karoly tried to hush him because if Magda became hysterical they'd be in for it for hours.

"Forget about the British," he admonished them both. "It's the Americans who will save our ass."

The Americans! The thought gave them all comfort, lulled them into thinking they were in a safe backwater of the world's currents where events would swirl past but never overflow them. America would never let Japan move farther south than Indochina. Then came December 7, and the invincible Americans were caught with their pants down. All sense of security vanished with Pearl Harbor. After that, no one wasted any more time trying to figure out which way the war would go. However it went in the long run, in the immediate future they had to deal with the tidal wave about to hit them. Within days of their surprise attack on Hawaii the Japanese were bombing Batavia. Frantically, people began digging air raid shelters in their yards and in the parks. Karoly and Bandi had a huge one excavated on the compound grounds, one large enough to shelter their families and all the servants with storage for ample supplies as well. Karoly even had a mammoth four-inch thick table built for the house so that, should there be no time to run across the compound to the shelter, when the bombs started falling they could dive under the table for protection.

Whatever their plans for Batavia the Japanese were obviously bent on pulverizing Dutch port facilities. All Dutch naval bases along the sea lanes to Singapore were hit and hit hard. Surabaya was one of the first targets. Day after day, bombs fell on the harbor facilities and even onto the city. Traffic was disrupted, businesses shut down, life came to a halt. One day a rumor spread like wild fire through the neighborhood that Marika's school had been hit. For Magda, until that moment, the war had seemed like a surrealistic drama, "over-directed and under-rehearsed." Instantly it became very real and very personal. She tore out of the house running wildly through the debris raining down in the streets from falling buildings and walls. When she reached the schoolyard and found that the building had not been touched, that the rumor had been only a rumor, she was too shaken to be rational about anything. Ignoring the pleas of the headmaster she took her child home where she could hold her close and hopefully safe. If any of them were going to die they would all die together. Marika had not been back to school since.

A few days of incessant bombing and all the shop windows in town were boarded up. Europeans awakened to the fact there were no Japanese left in the city. Fore-warned, they had taken to the hills. The British sent transports in to remove British women and children from the Indies and carry them back as far as India or Australia, a lucky few going all the way home to England. Stubbornly, foolishly, the Markowitses and the Von Kisses persisted in their belief in the might of the Americans. The Yanks would catch their breath and before the Japanese could actually invade they would move enough of their remaining Pacific fleet into the waters between Java and Indochina to block the Japanese southward thrust. They argued that point of view to all who would listen but inwardly doubt began to creep in and take over. To hedge their bets on the Americans Karoly and Bandi began converting every form of wealth they owned that they could bear to part with into platinum bars, jewels, gold, whatever was small enough to be hidden or carried away with them should they be forced to run.

The Americans didn't catch their breath in time. After the fall of Singapore even the most determined optimists faced the reality that Java would be invaded. Within weeks, soldiers from the celestial kingdom controlled the streets of Surabaya. They took the airfield, they seized the radio stations, they blocked all communications with the West, quickly closing every avenue of escape. All European nationals who had clung to their holdings in the Dutch East Indies rather than flee took cover as best they could. Some retreated to distant plantations they owned, or country places owned by friends living away from the city. Their belief that they could escape the wrath of war in the countryside was blasted when they found that the Japanese were very interested in plantations and what they produced. The people of the countryside were no safer than the people in the cities. The Javanese and the Chinese were ignored by the Japanese so long as they didn't raise their heads above the kow-tow submission expected from them. But the Europeans! They all looked alike. To the conquering Japanese, Jews were just more westerners to hate like they hated the Dutch, the Americans and the English. They had no special interest of their own in them, but they had an agreement with Hitler which they meant to keep.

Among the first people the invaders scooped up was the old man and his lists. Once the list was in their hands they began systematically scouring the city for the people whose names were now known to them. Of course Dr. Markowits, with all his wealth and prominence, was one of the persons underlined in the old man's address book of prospective donors. The Japanese intended to put the Jews into labor camps. It would probably be a long day before they could actually turn them over to Hitler; if they had to feed them they were determined to get as much out of them as they could. These Jews would earn their keep and a whole lot more. The Dutch rulers of the islands, along with other European nationals, were put into special sections of the cities thereby creating new White Ghettos. Later, the occupants of these White Ghettos would be organized into labor battalions. Residents in the white ghettos were humiliated, starved and robbed of everything that could be sent back to Japan, but not otherwise abused. Except the Jews.

For a time Magda and Karoly were left free. Karoly's skill as a gynecological surgeon and the clinic he operated with Dr. Kiss were vital to the well-being of the conquerors until Japanese medical personnel could be imported. The conquerors didn't want epidemics of communicable diseases to thin the ranks of their captive labor force. Magda, Marika and the Kiss family remained closeted in their shared home attended by the servants still in residence. The rest slipped away in the night as soon as the bombing began. Karoly and Dr. Kiss made house calls, kept office hours and ran their clinic. They cared for bombing victims regardless of who they were. Neither doctor had any illusions that the situation would long remain as it was. Once the Japanese had ended all Dutch resistance and brought in enough professionals of their own, they would no longer be exempt from the fate of all the other Caucasians from the West. They could do nothing but wait and play out the hand the way it was dealt. Even so, they were determined to find a way to keep as much of their wealth out of the hands of the rapacious Japanese as they could. Bandi believed there was a slim chance that, though Karoly would unquestionably be taken because he was a Jew, the Japanese might let him, Bandi, continue to live in his half of the house and carry on the practice alone.

"It makes sense," he argued. "This clinic is needed in this city. We've got a lot of important patients the Japanese will want to placate. They may not even take you."

"Don't kid yourself." Karoly's tone was bitter. "There hasn't been a Jew yet who was big enough to be exempt." He raised his wine glass to the light to look at the color of the contents and avoid the eyes of his partner.

"But Karoly," Magda's voice rose hopefully.

"But nothing, Magda." Karoly interrupted her. He put down the glass and impaled her with his eyes. "Don't hope! Don't believe. You start hoping and believing and you'll get us into trouble sooner than we're going to get it anyway. Just keep still and stay out of sight!"

Magda's lip quivered but Karoly did nothing to soften his words. What he and Bandi had to do was be realistic, not wish for a different outcome than the one they were facing. The immediate thing was to find a way to protect their wealth. Bandi thought that what they needed was a huge iron safe, one so heavy the Japanese couldn't cart it off like a piece of furniture. They should get their own bank vault and put it right in the house where it would be under Bandi's watchful eye after Karoly was gone. The Japanese would undoubtedly strip the commercial banks of all their currency, rip open all the safe deposit boxes, take over all international loans, loot the homes of the Europeans, and in countless ways root out all the sources of wealth as soon as they had the populace under control. Therefore, a huge iron safe, one so heavy it would take a squadron to move it, might be the safest way to try to hold onto the collections of precious stones, ivory carvings, and small art objects, that Bandi had been greedily collecting for almost two decades. He would tell the Japanese the safe held drugs and medical supplies and precious instruments.

Karoly had no faith in such a scheme. However, he was willing to give anything a try that might keep some of the priceless pieces safe. It took some searching to find what the two partners wanted but they found it, a behemoth, iron monster large enough to hold art objects too large to hide elsewhere. A Herculean task, it took more than a dozen dray men to get the safe into the house. A door frame was taken off and the monster rolled in on log rollers. The job was so difficult Karoly let himself believe it might work. To blow it open would destroy whatever it contained. The larger

57

sculptures Bandi had been collecting, and most of their own paintings, they turned over to Chinese friends who promised to return them when the war was over and Java was liberated. Once the safe was full they had to find a place to hide the small stuff: platinum, jewels and gold. Karoly had converted as much of his Art as he could into portable wealth urging Bandi to cover his behind by doing a little of the same.

"Buddy, if they clean us out, you're gonna lose more than I am. There's a lot more Art out there to buy once this is all over, if you've got the money. If I can, I'm gonna reduce mine to the smallest size possible, then stash it away someplace where they won't find it"

For once Bandi listened. The two of them began searching for a sure-fire hiding place for their treasure. One Sunday morning they packed the touring car with picnic baskets and all the requisite paraphernalia for a day in the country. The two families drove out of Surabaya, seemingly headed for an outing. Some miles out of Surabaya they drove into a forested area where they had picnicked many times in the past.

"Put out the food ladies," Bandi called cheerfully as the two men casually strolled away through the trees carrying a number of bundles.

"You'd think we had an audience," teased Karoly. "This play acting is overdoing it, don't you think?"

"You never know old chap, you never know. The grapevine around here is faster than the telephone service."

Bandi whistled a merry little tune which belied the effort he was making to walk lightly along. The bags were heavy. Behind them the women fell in with the script and began chattering away about nothing at all as the children played around them. With time-consuming care, Magda began constructing sandwiches while Bandi's wife played with the children in a sunlit little clearing near the road. If anyone was watching, it all looked very innocent.

In the middle of a clump of trees they could easily identify later, the men halted and dropped the heavy bags to the ground. Karoly stood guard over the treasure, casually lighting a cigarette and blowing smoke rings into the air, as Bandi went back to the car for the spade. For almost an hour the two doctors dug furiously spelling each other every few minutes. They dug until they had a hole deep enough and wide enough to

58

hold all their treasure with a foot to spare on top. They wanted it so deep that any casual disturbance of the forest floor would not reach their bundles double wrapped in oil cloth. Rain, and the perpetually damp forest loam, would do to their treasure what Nature did to anything left to rot in the ground. With everything carefully packed into the hole they set about piling in stones and dirt until the hole was full and mounded high. They tapped the loose dirt down with the back of the spade packing it hard. Finally, they covered the raw earth with sod so that anyone walking over the spot could not see or feel any difference in the ground underfoot.

"Done," gasped Bandi. "I don't think anyone will ever see it." He walked back and forth over the new sod several times as his breathing returned to normal.

Karoly stood back and eyed their handiwork from every angle. "You'd have to have a map to find that," he gloated with satisfaction. "It looks like all the rest of the ground around here." He grinned at his partner. "That was work, man, I need a cigarette."

"I thought I was in pretty good shape," Bandi panted reaching into his shirt pocket, "but I stretched a few muscles. I'm gonna pay for this tomorrow."

The two sank down on the grass, as Bandi lit up. "Here," he said to Karoly. "Have one on me. You've earned it."

Karoly grinned. "Thanks," he said laconically, "You're a real sport."

The two of them lay back on the grass staring up into the tree branches overhead. As Karoly exhaled slowly, savoring the knowledge that they had planned and planted well, his gaze drifted to a tree nearby. Horrified, his heart skipped a beat and he choked on the smoke. Perched in the tree like little monkeys were three small boys who had watched the whole process.

In a flash he was on his feet waving his arms frantically. "Get the hell out of there!" he shouted up at the children.

Bandi scrambled up in fright. "My God, Karoly!" he exclaimed. "They'll go back to the village and before we're out of sight the whole neighborhood will be out here digging."

"Well, we can't leave it here, that's for sure," moaned Karoly. "What a mess!" Almost in tears the two tired men dug out the hole and carried the bundles, which seemed far heavier on the return trip, back to the car.

It took days to hatch another plot but the one they came up with was a masterpiece. They would bury some of it in a new place and hide the rest in a wall of the house. They tore the plaster off a section of the wall in a room on the Markowits side of the house. Then they slipped much of their repackaged treasure down between the studs, re plastered the damaged area, and repainted the entire room so there'd be no difference in color over that one spot. During the operation, the women stood guard against the unexpected entrance of one of the servants. Karoly and Bandi worked at night after the skeletal household staff had gone for the day. When this war was over, when they were all back together again, when the postwar future they were preparing for arrived, they'd be sitting like kings right where they'd been before the Japanese made such a mess of things. Unless, of course, the house itself was destroyed. They'd found a different place in the forest and buried the rest. They'd done all they could and now they waited for the Japanese to further the drama and take them into custody.

Magda rose and walked to the door leading out onto the terrace, brooding over the turn of events that had put them in jeopardy. If the old Jew had not made his lists, had not kept his records, had not authored a "Doomsday" book of all the Jews of Java, they wouldn't be sitting here in the middle of the little pile of things they could take with them wherever they were going. Instead of the eerily silent house behind her, they should be having coffee and crullers and the newspapers out on the terrace as usual while servants moved through every room of the house behind them. Ordinarily, the only place you go without servants being under foot was the bathroom, and in all likelihood there'd be one waiting at the door for you when you came out. Today there were no sounds, no visible servants, no crullers. Choking back sobs that involuntarily rose in spite of her resolve to be brave, Magda mentally echoed Karoly's curse. "Damn him! Damn him indeed!"

Karoly held Marika close letting her draw what strength she could from him as he stared stone-faced at the wall. Since the day the Japanese began bombing Java and the Americans hadn't been there to stop them, fear had dogged his every waking hour. Dread had lain like a thick blanket on his chest since the notice was posted that the Jews were to be subjected to special treatment because of a treaty provision the Japanese made with the Germans honoring that cold, merciless Axis schemata for the world's Jewry. His natural optimism had deserted him. He struggled continually to keep up a facade of calm to quiet the others. Bandi, unabashedly, dissolved into tears daily.

Late spring, 1942, the order came at last. Those Jews of Surabaya not yet in custody were instructed to be ready to leave their homes at 6:00 a.m. on specified days carrying only what they could manage by themselves. Karoly emptied all the money left in the house into the safe and bid his patients good-bye. Weeks before, Magda had turned all her personal jewelry over to another Chinese friend to keep for her until this was all over. The sound of a truck motor and the crunch of heavy wheels on the clam shell driveway brought her instantly to Karoly. Marika let out a sharp squeal of terror and buried her face in Karoly's shirt front. Her father loosened her arms from around his waist and tilted her chin upward so he could look directly into her eyes.

"Liebchen," he said softly, "remember. Heads up!" He took her hand and led her trembling to the door with Magda trailing behind. An open, slat-sided cattle truck, already partially filled with standing people, drew up before the entrance. Before the vehicle was fully stopped, two Japanese soldiers hopped down from the cab, rifles in hand. The tailgate was let down and the three Markowitses were hustled unceremoniously up onto the truck bed. They made no eye contact with the other passengers. It seemed rude to look upon the shame of another. No one spoke as they roared down the driveway and out into the road. Block after block, the truck canvassed the neighborhoods to pick up more and more people until the human mass became so dense no one could move or slump down.

It was terrifying. Someone else's breath was in your nostrils and yours was in theirs. Within two hours the sun was high enough overhead to beat mercilessly down on them compounding the sense of being suffocated. When the truck stopped or started it did so with a jerk that threw everyone forward. Before they could get their footing the erratic motion of the truck threw them backward again. The driver had no regard for his passengers, they were cartage, not people.

61

Magda gave way to tears becoming almost hysterical while Marika clung to her father in frozen silence. It took all morning to fill the truck to its absolute maximum capacity. About noon they pulled up before the Surabaya Prison on the outskirts of the city.

Waiting Japanese let down the tailgate and ordered them to jump. Most fell to their hands and knees on the gravel drive and when they were on their feet again the soldiers began shouting and gesturing for the men and older boys to form one line, the women and smaller children another. In panic, Magda realized that she and Marika were about to be separated from Karoly. She began to wail. A hard punch in the back delivered by a menacing guard silenced her immediately. As for Karoly, despair filled him. How would they get along without him? Why were they being separated? He started to make a stand but just ahead of him a man who protested was beaten to the ground, his head split by a rifle butt. It was terrifying and humiliating. Karoly Markowits was used to pandering servants and praise from his patients, he was not accustomed to being herded and prodded along like an animal. Seething with anger, he stood silently rigid in the lengthening line.

It was days before he learned the full extent of the nightmare that had descended on them. Within hours of the Markowitses being taken prisoner the Japanese had come again to the big double house and carted off the Kiss family too. Wasn't Dr. Bandi Von Kiss the partner of a Jew? It was a ruse for clearing them all out of the big house so that the Japanese could come in and strip the place of everything, including the iron safe. To this day Magda doesn't know how much wealth they lost in that methodical looting but it had to be a lot.

In the salad days just before the war the two doctors had had a visitor, a Dr. Barbara Lloyd Still. Dr. Still was on a world tour so poorly timed she was caught in the Dutch East Indies and interred for the duration with all the other Europeans. After the war she wrote a book about her experiences entitled, "Dr. Barbara." It contains a chapter on her visit to the home of the Doctors Markowits and Kiss. In that chapter she describes their practice, their lifestyle and their environment. Her book is the best inventory that exists of the haul the Japanese made when they cleared the place out:

"Drs. K.(iss) and M.(arkowits) - the former a gentile the latter a Jew - had the wealthiest clientele in Java, composed mainly of Chinese merchants and Arab bullion dealers. Their joint house was air-conditioned throughout and was full of precious furniture, carpets and ornaments. In addition Dr. K. owned a collection of jewelry and precious stones. A great deal of priceless Chinese porcelain and much else that any museum might be proud to show.... Dr. M. did not hoard. He owned a villa up in the hills, as luxuriously appointed as the joint house, and lived there for part of the year.... They had three cars, ten servants and entertained lavishly, without any thought of investing in precious stones."

Once separated by sex, the Jews were herded into separate but adjacent barracks. Visually the two groups had no contact with each other but their exercise yards were adjacent, separated only by high walls over which they could call back and forth to each other. The Japanese tried to keep the prisoners from communicating, but with l25 women and children and only a handful of guards to enforce the regulations the odds were in favor of the more courageous inmates. By the time the Markowits were herded into captivity the Japanese had incarcerated almost 50,000 Jews in various locations in the Indies. Controlling that many people required a sizable investment of manpower. To substitute technique for personnel, they resorted to brutality severe enough to cow their captives into submission. Using such methods, fewer guards were needed to control so many people.

The women's barracks had been built around a large empty square where the prisoners could be lined up for inspection, instruction or discipline. All around the square, were single cells enclosed on three sides. The fourth side, the side opening onto the square, was nothing more than an iron gate equipped with a heavy lock. The cell block looked like an animal shelter with cages around the entire parade ground. Each cage was approximately four feet wide and six feet deep. They had been designed to hold one prisoner, but the Japanese crowded five into each. Magda and Marika were squashed in with another woman and her two children. The only bedding provided was one thin mat per person. The five of them had to sleep spoon fashion in order for them all to lie down at the same time. When one turned over they all had to shift. In the mornings, they were almost as tired as they had been when they lay down the night before. Within a few days they were so exhausted they could have slept anywhere under any conditions. At that point, Magda and Marika, like many others, began to sleep on the walkway outside their cell under the overhang that ran all the way around the building. There they could stretch out and talk privately to each other in whispers. When a guard came by they quickly feigned sleep until he moved on.

Hunger was another weapon the Japanese used with exquisite skill. The Jews were given rations far too meager to sustain health, the portions so small everyone was constantly hungry. In the beginning, Karoly fared a little better. Since the Japanese had extended their forces over too great a portion of the world to be able to supply enough medical personnel of their own, they fed the European doctors enough for them to function well.

Whenever a woman or a child became very ill, Karoly was brought into the women's building to care for the prisoner who was down. Sentries hovered over the scene so that he and Magda could do no more than look guardedly at each other. The first time he'd come, Magda cried out his name and started toward him only to be stopped dead in her tracks. A guard snarled something she could not understand, but there was no mistaking the cane in his raised hand. After that she and Marika looked hungrily at Karoly but made no effort to cover the ground between them. As for Karoly, he was enraged to see how thin his wife and child had become. The Japanese would do nothing to purify the water even when he pointed out that the prevalence of illness was not only due to a lack of food but also to the foul water that stood in barrels in the sun. The Japanese allowed him so few drugs for the prisoners there was nothing he could do about Marika's dysentery which began almost the first day of her imprisonment, and continued unabated for three long years.

Once they began to sort themselves out, Magda saw many women she knew among the prisoners. Many had been guests in her home for Karoly loved to entertain and the Markowitses were famous for their parties. Their soirees were always lavish and anyone who was anyone at all was invited. The double house was so spacious it could handle large

64

crowds and Karoly filled it at least once a month. One of the first people Magda spied was Lilly Krause! Only a few nights before she and Karoly had sat entranced at the concert Lilly had given in the concert hall in Surabaya. One of the foremost pianists in the world, she was on tour in Java when, like Barbara Still, she was hauled off to prison by the Japanese who saw her as nothing more than another Jew!

"Lilly!" Magda cried. "How did they find you?"

"I wasn't hard to find," said Lilly bitterly. "The account of the recital carried the information that I was a Jew and in what hotel I was stopping. They came this morning. The desk called me to tell me to get dressed and to pack a small bag. When I protested the clerk broke into tears. 'Miss Krause,' he said, 'I can do nothing. They are here and they want you.' I packed a bag and I came down ready to give their officer a piece of my mind. Instead, he slapped me across the face and shoved me out the door." Lilly stared over Magda's shoulder at a guard striding across the courtyard. "Beasts!" she hissed. "Nothing but beasts."

Magda's hands flutter at the neck of her dress. "Don't talk so loud Lilly, if they hear you...." Her voice trailed off as she glanced fearfully about.

Lilly looked at Magda in wonder. This was the famous Magda Zahler she had heard so much about, the Mrs. Karoly Markowits who had been so radiant at the party held after her concert? This trembling creature? She reached out and linked her arm through Magda's. "Come, let's find a place to sit and talk."

There hadn't been much time for talk that first day. They were no more than seated with their backs to the wall than they were ordered out to the open square to be lined up and counted. It was late in the second afternoon before the two women found a shady spot under the overhang and sat down again to lean against the prison wall. "Magda," Lillie began, "I've heard that you were as good a pianist as you were a dancer, good enough for the concert stage if you had bent your talents in that direction. Didn't you study at the Academy?"

"Did I study at the Academy!" exclaimed Magda! "If he had to have a daughter on the stage my father wanted a pianist, not a dancer." She laughed remembering. "Even Madame Pallay could not convince him that the stage was a proper place for his child."

"Then why did you dance? Why didn't you play?"

"Ah!" Magda's face was radiant. "When I am up there dancing I am the creator. When I was up there playing the piano I was an instrument for somebody else's creation. My father was so disappointed." She stared dreamily at the palm fronds waving over the low roof of the building on the other side of the open space.

At her debut, her first public performance, Dr. Zahler came that first night to the Concert Hall in Budapest. He had been astonished at how mature she seemed up there before this crowd. He admired her dancing, though he didn't fully understand the modern craze for interpretive soloists. But he still resented her exposing herself so blatantly before the crowds that filled the hall. The stage was for the daughters of the lower classes, not the daughter of Emil Zahler. Ilonka Zahler, on the other hand, was swept up in the magic of the evening. Her child was taking Budapest by storm and she loved it. The applause thrilled her as much as it would have had it been for her. Remembering, Magda could hear again the murmurs of delight from the audience and feel again the heat of the footlights on her face.

Thunderous applause filled the hall. An ovation that would have satisfied a seasoned prima ballerina poured over the sprite of a child trembling in the spotlight. At that moment, fourteen-year-old Magda Zahler was the darling of Budapest, the magic child who danced on fairy feet. Poised, exuberant, captivating, she moved with the grace and fire of a mature danseuse. "Little" Magda hugged the applause to her pounding heart, eager for more such evenings. In the ensuing decade there would be many more such evenings. From capitol to capitol she danced her way across Europe. The press called her "Hungary's Isadora Duncan." Like Isadora, Magda created all her own material. She was six when her mother first took her to Madame Pallay, the prima ballerina of the Royal Opera House in Budapest. Madame Pallay had been impressed with the little six-year-old's natural talent and her wonderful imagination. She had enthusiastically taken Magda as a pupil. From then until Magda was fully launched on her career, she spent three afternoons a week at the Royal Ballet School.

When she was sixteen, on a trip with her father who was soliciting funds from American Jews in Chicago and New York, for two months Magda danced on stages across the United

States. After she returned from her American triumph, Madame Pallay made her her assistant, then tried to seduce her away from the stage to become her partner in the management of the Royal Ballet School. Her arguments fell on deaf ears, Magda's need to dance outstripped any interest she might have in teaching. Teaching could come later when she was too old to dance, just as it had for Madame Pallay. As for the piano, though she'd studied at the world famous "Music Academy", Hungary's Juilliard School of music, the piano was physically too confining.

Magda turned to Lilly with a smile. "If I had stayed with the piano I would have had to walk in your shadow all the way. I didn't have to stand in any body's shadow as a dancer."

"I wish we'd known each other in Europe rather than getting acquainted in this hell" Lily said.

Magda shrank back fearfully against the wall. If Lilly didn't hold her tongue they'd really learn what hell was like. "Lilly, darling," she whispered urgently. "You'll get us both killed! You can't talk like that in here."

"I can talk however I want to talk whenever I want to talk." Lilly argued vehemently. "I will not kow-tow to the little bastards no matter what they do.

Magda started to rise. "You're talking crazy and you know it," she hissed angrily. "I don't want to sit near you if you're going to go on like that. I don't want to get killed."

Magda never found out who got Lilli out or why, but within days Lilly was courteously invited to pick up her things and go. Courteously! It was a shock to see how quickly the Japanese could change countenance when it suited them. Somebody somewhere must have pulled some powerful strings. After Lilly's departure the days dragged by in utter boredom. The Japanese kept them busy by organizing work details. They cooked, they cleaned, they did laundry, they had latrine duty, they stood for hours in silence in long rows while the guards taunted them, trying to irritate someone beyond endurance. Any movement or murmur and the victim would be punished before the whole group to terrorize them all. Life was mean and brutish and dehumanizing. The only recreation they had was guarded talk when the guards were too distant to hear.

Marika busied herself about the prison taking care of the younger children while their mothers worked. From time to time, she would come to lean silently against her mother for

67

reassurance. Only at night, after they stretched out under the overhang, would the child turn to Magda to talk. Magda tried to entertain her there in the warm darkness with stories of her own childhood, stories which comforted them both.

"You should have seen those big black horses clattering down the streets!" she would tell Marika. "Their hooves made sparks fly from the cobblestones. Oh, it was fun to ride up top with the coachman. I loved those horses! How I did love those horses. So did Grandpa."

"Tell me about Grandpa." Marika would beg and Magda would tell her story after story.

The joy in her mother's voice always made Marika feel good. She thought she could remember Budapest but she couldn't be sure. Maybe her mother had told her so often about the storybook city that she had created a picture in her mind made up out of hearsay rather than from real remembrance. Through her mother's stories, Grandpa was becoming almost as real to her as her father. A tear rolled down her cheek in the dark sometimes during the stories about how Grandpa adored Grandma. Grandpa had had to make his way in the world, but Grandma had been born to privilege. He delighted in showering her with things. Grandma rode out on her social rounds in an elegant enclosed carriage behind a team of black horses as spirited and handsome as the Zahler family who owned them. One of Magda's favorite memories, which she recounted over and over, was of riding to school each morning up top the black carriage, sitting in the coachman's lap, holding the reins as though she was driving. Erzsi, her older sister, sat sedately inside the carriage pretending to be their mother. The coach wheeled up to the school with a flourish which always caused a stir on the playground much to Magda's delight. She would scramble down from her high perch while Erzsi dismounted from the carriage like a great lady. Both of them loved their daily "entrance."

"Erzsi was not a bit like me," Magda would say. "She went on the stage to please Mama but she hated it."

"Why did Aunt Erzsi get a divorce?" Marika asked one night.

"Oh," Magda would answer drowsily, "I think she only got married to get off the stage. After she had a baby Grandma didn't push her any more."

68

Marika buried her face deeper into her mother's side. She didn't want to go on the stage either. She didn't like being in dance recitals. If they ever got out of here she was going to speak to Papa. Maybe he could get Mama to let her alone and not make her dance. But if she didn't learn to dance how could she go to America?

Some nights Marika wanted stories about the trip to America. "My father was a very important man," Magda would always begin. "The Jews of Budapest turned to him for leadership always. It was for them we went to America. They needed help."

World War I brushed the Zahler family lightly. It was the aftermath of the war that engulfed them as it did all of Hungary. At the peace tables in Versailles in 1919 Hungary was disconnected from Austria as the Austro-Hungarian empire ceased to exist. The King was forced to abdicate and the government was taken over by the Communists. The Communists held Hungary in thrall for seven long months. Kun tried to strip the magnates of their lands and nationalize all the new young industries that had sprung up during the war. A counter-revolution erupted led by the conservatives whom Kun had tried to dislodge from power, power they had exercised for centuries.

Because Kun was a Jew, a wave of dormant anti-Semitism broke out. Midway through the nineteenth century anti-Semitism had been buried by the Minorities Act, but now a series of anti-Jewish laws were put into effect by the new regime headed by the Protestant, "Admiral" Horthy. Businesses owned by Jews were confiscated or ruined. No Jew could hold public office, or even vote unless he could produce census records to prove that his family had been in Hungary for five generations. No ethnic group could send students to the Universities in greater numbers than their proportion of the population. The Jews made up approximately 6% of the population so 6% of the students could be Jewish and only 6%. Many a young Jew had to leave Hungary in order to secure a University education. Edward Teller, the world-famous nuclear physicist, was one of those. Clubs that had long been open to Jews now eliminated their names from their membership rolls. The Jews of Hungary were in trouble and they needed help. The leading Jews of Budapest met at Dr. Zahler's home to decide on a course of action.

"Help will have to come from America." one said.

"From the United States government?" asked another.

"No. From American Jews. We'll send a delegation to all the cities where there are Hungarian Congregations and plead for money with which to fight Horthy."

"It could work," mused another. "But we need someone who is known in America. Someone who has connections. You have relatives there, Emil, you lead the delegation."

Emil had a large family of half brothers and sisters in America, some in New York City and some in Chicago. Emil's father had had three wives, each bore him children. Emil was the older of two sons who were the children of the second wife. The first wife's five children had emigrated chain fashion to the United States, one reaching back to help the next make the leap across the Atlantic. Those five had all done well in the new country. Some were enough older than Emil that they were now grandparents. That made a lot of American Zahlers to visit as he toured on behalf of the beleaguered Jews of Hungary. Magda begged to go with him.

"Magduska, this is a serious business! I am not going on a holiday, I'm going to raise money. I'll have to speak night after night. What will you do?"

"I'll go to the theater," she beamed. "You can put me in a cab and have it come for me when the performance is over. Please!!"

"Out of the question." he declared stoutly.

"Emil," Ilonka interceded, "she can spend time with your family. You always say you wish we could know them. They never come here so why not let Magda go with you? At least one of us will know them."

Emil knew he was licked when Ilonka sided with either of the girls, but especially Magda. He relented on one condition: she was to patiently and obediently follow him around and stay out of his way. Magda made a solemn oath to abide by the limits he set on her going, then danced off to eagerly pack her bags. They took ship for New York in November, 1921.

Having danced professionally for two years by that time, Magda's fame preceded her to America. Even aboard ship the social director prevailed on her to give a dance recital in the grand ballroom of the ocean liner. The first-class passengers loved the show. Though he swelled with pride at her performance, Dr. Zahler was annoyed. The attention she was receiving would go to her head. After her performance there wasn't a spot on the ship where he could get away from people eager to tell him how precocious his daughter was.

"I feel like I ought to be a trained seal," he snorted one night. "Then we could do a real act for them."

Magda immediately went into an imitation of a waddling seal. He had to laugh. When they reached New York, theatrical agents surrounded them trying to sign her to a contract for a tour of the United States. Dr. Zahler reached the end of his patience.

"I did not come to America to follow my daughter around from one theater to another," he exploded.

But the pressure was too great: the family wanted it, Magda wanted it, and certainly the agents wanted it. So, added to the responsibility he carried for the fate of the Jews at home, he now had the additional burden of watching over his daughter while she pranced before the American public. Forced to choose among the various agents, he finally settled on the "Harmonia R.T." Artists' Agency because they agreed to schedule her performances to coincide with his itinerary.

The tour began at the Lexington Theater in New York City, December 11, 1921. SZINHAZI UJSAG, the Hungarian Theatrical Journal of New York said of that first performance:

"A recent arrival in the United States is Hungary's youngest classical dancer. sixteen-year-old Magda Zahler who is the personification of grace and youth. (She) has danced in most of the European capitals. Her style of dancing resembles that of Isadora Duncan while her interpretations are clever and original."

The leading newspapers of every city they visited were just as full of praise. Her American family ate it up, and even the busy Dr. Zahler finally was secretly glad he'd given in and let her come. By the end of the third week in December they were in Chicago. Fund raising in Chicago went smoothly because of his sister's connections. Money and pledges poured in. What made it even better, Magda had no engagements in the windy city.

From Chicago they went to Cleveland where both of them had engagements and where they celebrated Magda's seventeenth birthday on Christmas Day. It was mid-January before Emil's work was completed and by that time Magda had fallen in love with the United States She didn't want to go home. Her father was not amused.

"Stay in America alone?" he shouted, "Are you out of your mind? You promised you'd not be a bother. How can you even think of such a thing?" Magda didn't mention it again, she went home to Hungary but she never forgot America.

"Mama," Marika asked, "What do you think would have happened if you had stayed in America? Would you have had me?"

Magda laughed and cuddled her close. "I'd have had you, liebschen, no matter where I'd stayed."

"But you wouldn't have met Papa!" protested Marika.

"Well, you would have had a different Papa, that's all, but I would have had you just the same." Magda stroked her child's hair and held her closer.

Marika was silent for a long while and then she said, "I'm glad you didn't stay in America."

Above her head she could hear her mother's breathing become even and slow. Marika snuggled in against her and closed her eyes. That night they enjoyed several hours of sleep before the air raid sirens went off. Every night when the whine of airplane engines were dimly heard followed by the first faint explosions, Marika was instantly on her feet heading for their cell, her mother right behind her.

In the following weeks, as the bombing came closer to the prison, there came that peculiar shrieking sound of air being split by hurtling objects. After a breathless moment came the shock wave of sound that followed the contact of bombs hitting their targets. At the first sound announcing another air attack, guards came pounding into the courtyard shouting and swearing, driving them back into their cells. Guards slammed iron doors, locking them as they ran. Pity the poor prisoner who didn't move fast enough to get inside in time. Next morning she'd be lying where she had fallen, dead from the blow on the head she had received for not getting into shelter fast enough.

The first time they'd been locked up during an air raid a great uproar had ensued. "If the building is bombed we can't get out!" women shrieked. "Don't lock us up this way!" At the morning lineup next day they learned never to protest again.

Summer came and went, and through the dull heat of July and August they sat around the edge of the square in a stupor by day and slept the drugged sleep of hot humid nights after the sun went down. The only light in the prison came from the guard towers. Magda lost all track of time. She wasn't sure what month it was, much less what day of the week. As the air became a little lighter with the advent of Fall, their miserable, now familiar, world was violently shattered. The men were all moved out. Without warning, without the rumor mill giving any hint of impending change, one morning the men and boys were loaded into lorries, packed in as tight as sardines, and driven away. All the women whose husbands and/or sons were in those trucks were wild with grief. Magda couldn't take it in. Separated though they'd been, hers had been the comfort of knowing that Karoly was near enough to know if anything happened to her or Marika. From time to time she had heard his voice, had spoken to him over the wall, had been able to see him from a distance. Now there would be no Karoly. What was she to do without him? Where were they taking him? When would she see him again? The enormity of it felled her.

She became ill, ran a fever, was sick for days before the new prison doctor, a gentile captive, one of those moved in to take the place of the Jews in the men's prison, was allowed to see her. Through it all, Mrs. Teitler, another of the prisoners whose only crime was to be born Jewish, looked after Marika. Mrs. Teitler had a son who had been on the other side of the wall with Karoly, and who was now transported to a new fate along with Marika's father. Mrs. Teitler knew Karoly would take care of her son as gladly as she now cared for his daughter. For days Magda talked and moaned in her delirium. She was back in Budapest, back at the beginning of Karoly.

The magic year Karoly Markovits came along was 1925. Over the years Magda's father had many young surgical assistants, all of whom he brought home to meet his wife and daughters. Magda was used to bright young doctors. She was also used to stage-door Johnnies, she'd run the gauntlet of all kinds of them. Her career so filled her life she never had time for the young assistants or the stage-door Johnnies until the night she walked into a party and there was magnetic, urbane, sophisticated, handsome Karoly Markowits. Karoly Markowits knew what he could do with women, and Magda was no exception. A gynecological surgeon eight years older than she, at twenty-nine Karoly was ready to fall in love and settle down. Twenty-one, a desirable young woman untutored in the art of coquetry offstage, Magda was ripe for the plucking. The fact that she was the daughter of one of the most prestigious doctors in Hungary added to her allure. Their courtship was not a lengthy one, Karoly was not a man to wait for anything he wanted. Within weeks of their meeting he proposed and she accepted.

Before a date could be set, however, enter Dr. Bandi Von Kiss. Dr. Kiss was an internist of exceptional ability and personal charm. He'd gone out to Java in 1921 to make his fortune. European doctors were in high demand and could charge astronomical fees in the Far East. He had come back to Budapest on a sabbatical to bring himself up to date on the latest developments in medicine. Choosing to study at the hospital and medical school where Karoly was first assistant to that institution's famous professor of gynecology, the two young doctors met and became fast friends.

"Bandi says this and Bandi says that," Magda complained one night as they trudged through the snow along the promenade on the banks of the Danube. "All the time, what Bandi says seems to be like the words of God."

"You're just jealous," Karoly teased. "You think he's going to take me away from here."

Magda was worried. She'd listened to Karoly's fantasies about the magical East, the world Von Kiss described so romantically. She knew in her bones that Karoly wouldn't be able to resist the siren call of the good life when Bandi urged him to go back with him and try it out for himself. Nothing could hold him back, not even her.

"Magda, darling, don't be like that," he pleaded when she wept. "If it's all make-believe I'll have had a good adventure and be right back. But if it should be real - just think Magda what life could be like. We'd have it all!"

When Von Kiss returned to Java in 1926 Karoly went with him. Before he left he laid out a time table for Magda. If Java truly was the land of Arabian Nights for doctors he would apply for a Dutch license to practice medicine in that part of the world. He'd set them up in a lovely home and then come for her or send for her. They could be married out there. He never offered her a choice for it never occurred to him that she wouldn't wait.

74

Left behind, she went on dancing, she went on flirting, she went on going through the motions of being a world-famous dancer appearing in every major capitol of Europe, but it was all a filler, a matter of marking time until her life could really begin again. In Paris. she danced "Peer Gynt," possibly one of the most difficult of all pieces of music to interpret. Her star was at its zenith. Andre Kertesz, famous Hungarian photographer, Hungary's Ansel Adams, photographed her draped dramatically on a couch. In that photograph her legs and arms curve away from her body in a wondrous configuration it would take a contortionist to replicate. That photograph became as famous as either its subject or its creator. It is still included in every major article that appears on Kertesz. It hangs in every show of his works and has been the inspiration for other photographs by other photographers. Connoisseur Magazine carried a print of one imitative work which sold in 1990 for $150,000. There is no doubt about the blatant interpretation of the Kertesz photograph.

In 1965 HARPER'S BAZAAR did a feature story on the six women who gave Paris "an uncommon radiance and bravura" in the 1920's, accompanied by full page photographs of each of the women. There was Magda laid out on that couch again. The caption under the picture read: "Magda Zahler -- what capacity for caprice -- her exuberant caricatures took us by storm." The NEW YORK MAGAZINE in November of 1987 carried a feature story about the work of Andre Kertesz. Again Magda looks out languorously at something beyond the camera's eye. In 1988, GLAMOUR MAGAZINE ran the photograph in an article on beautiful women. One half expects to find Magda curled up in that impossible pose yet today.

Karoly was an instantaneous success. Even Bandi had not prepared him for how much money, how VERY much money, came pouring in. He wrote glowing reports of the easy life Europeans led: the servants, the parties, the luxurious surroundings. He wrote that he had applied for a license and had entered into a partnership with Von Kiss in Surabaya, a seaport city of some importance. As usual, everything happened as Karoly planned. Her parents lost interest in Karoly Markowits. Ilonka urged Emil to find Magda another young doctor, one who was rooted in Budapest if what Magda wanted was to find someone like her father. Both her parents talked and talked about how dreadful life in the tropics could be.

"Magda, be reasonable," her father implored. "We don't know anything really about all the diseases you'll run into out there."

"But I'll be married to a doctor!" she argued. "We aren't going to live in a hut somewhere with flies all over the place. Karoly says people employ servants to do nothing but keep the bugs away."

Ilonka looked up from her petit point in exasperation. "Magduska, how are you going to survive in such a backwater. There's no culture out there!"

"Culture!" Magda protested. "What do you know? Karoly says European artists come there all the time."

"Second-rate European artists!" shot back Ilonka. "What first class Artist would go all the way out there to appear before all those barefooted people. Karoly is trying to pull the wool over your eyes."

"Surabaya is a big city, Mama!" Magda's voice betrayed her rising anger. "Karoly says it's the Paris of the Far East. You'd think Karoly had lost his mind to hear the two of you talk."

"I think you've lost yours," snapped her father. "You wanted this great career. Well, you got it, but you're going to throw it away to go off to a place filled with monuments to monkeys."

"I'm going off to the Dutch East Indies to marry Karoly Markowits. Monkeys haven't anything to do with it." Magda retorted.

"I wonder." said her father as he stalked away.

To think of her married and living in a far-off place they couldn't easily reach was a dismal prospect for Magda's parents. If only she would meet someone else. But it didn't happen, Magda wouldn't let it happen. She'd made her commitment and that was that. The letter finally arrived telling her to come. Just like that! Pick up and come. Magda was floored. She'd never believed he wouldn't come back for a proper wedding in Budapest before the two of them honeymooned their way back together. How could he ask her to make that long trip alone? Someone always traveled with her. In the secrecy of her room, out of sight of her mother, she cried her eyes out.

Ilonka was furious. Her daughter was to be married in a heathen place with no family to attend the ceremony? It was unreasonable. That became the most tragic aspect of the whole affair to the mother of the bride, the wedding without family. When Magda went right on with her packing, Ilonka, at last, planked her feet down firmly.

"I'll not have it," she announced after dinner one night as they were leaving the table. "I'll not have you going halfway around the world unchaperoned and unmarried. It isn't decent."

"Decent!" Mother! This is 1928! Women don't get "chaperoned" any more. I haven't been "chaperoned" for over two years, and I've traveled everywhere."

"You've never been on a train overnight more than half a dozen times since I quit going with you." Ilonka's voice rose. "And I don't care if it is 1928, no daughter of mine is going half way around the world to rendezvous with any man, not even Karoly Markowits."

She took a deep breath as if to brace herself against Magda's reaction, then announced, "There will be a 'glove marriage' before you go!"

" A glove marriage!?" Magda was aghast. "How archaic! I won't do it!"

"There's no other way!" her mother declared. "Either there will be a glove marriage or I'm going to Surabaya with you."

Magda burst out laughing, but one look at her mother's face sobered her up. Ilonka was not laughing. Her foot was down and the whole family knew that meant no further discussion would be entertained.

Magda wailed and begged, but Gibraltar would have been easier to move. Emil tried to reason with his wife with no better success. The household bowed to the inevitable and set about making preparations for that ancient Jewish ceremony of marriage by proxy. They held the stilted affair in the Zahler living room with only the family present. No jubilant reception followed, only a little supper for the family with a Jewish wedding cake. It had pacified her mother, but it was no wedding at all as far as Magda was concerned. Instead of snuggling into Karoly's shoulder on her wedding night she cried herself to sleep alone in the bed where she had slept since she was a child. Depressed, feeling unloved, unrespected, and very unmarried, she set off the next day on her long journey toward a future shrouded in mystery. Her mother went with her on the long train ride to Marseilles, weeping all the way. Ilonka's misery was so intense that by the time they reached the seaport Magda was almost ready to turn back.

After a long, lonely voyage, plagued the whole journey with seasickness, at last the ship nosed its way into the wharf where Magda spied Karoly holding a huge bouquet of flowers waiting to welcome her. He was scanning the faces above him as the crew secured the ship and let down the gangplank. Magda melted. Throwing kisses across the space between them, she wiggled her way to the head of the gangway and literally ran down to throw herself into his arms. Tanned, happy and excited, he greeted her with astonishing news. Anticipating her apprehensions, aware of her disappointment over the drabness of her archaic wedding, he'd planned a big surprise for her.

"You're going to have your wedding, darling," he whispered into her hair, "as grand a wedding as you could possibly have hoped for. Bandi's wife is busy right now putting the finishing touches on an affair fit for a princess! Just you wait and see."

It was indeed a wedding for a princess. The "arrangements" at the country club, where the ceremony and the reception were held, were like an imperial ball. The two doctors' circle of friends, plus all the other elite of Surabaya society, were dressed elegantly in silks and modish styles straight out of the pattern books from Europe. The ravages of the post World War I depression still held much of Europe in its grip but they were not evident in Java. All was pomp and ceremony and champagne and laughter and music and dancing until almost dawn. It was a prophetic beginning for the pampered life she was to live out there on the rim of the world, a preview of indulgence that could never have been forgiven in the austerity that still hung over economically depressed eastern Europe. Now, thirteen years later, all the glamour of the past seemed lost forever, and she was able to conjure it up only out of her fever-induced hallucinations.

Once the fever subsided, Magda recovered her physical health quickly. It was her lack of interest in anything around her that frightened Marika and kept Mrs. Teitler busy allaying the child's fears. Magda could not avoid her work assignments, those had to be done, but every motion she made was mechanical. There was none of the old spontaneity, no alert watchfulness, none of the signs of a will to survive that had been evident before. Mrs. Teitler tried to pull Magda out of her gloom by remembering better times.

"You know, Magda, I was never in your home. We didn't move in the same circles. Tell me about your life out here."

"What is there to tell? You know what it's like to live out here?"

"I know what the life of a Dutch Civil Servant is like, but I don't know what the life of a rich doctor's wife is like. Tell me."

Magda shivered slightly. How privileged she'd been! The opulence of their life was an embarrassment here in this prison where existence centered on the next morsel of food. Talk about the cornucopia of privilege and pleasure that had been her fare before the Japanese came seemed frivolous in the present situation.

"Well," she began hesitantly, "it was a big change from Budapest. You know, I can't make Europe real in my mind now. It's like I was born out here, full grown."

"In a household that big with that many servants," Mrs. Teitler persisted, "a lot of funny things must have happened."

Magda smiled wanly. Something always happened. More than a dozen servants and their families lived on the property, all of whom were at her beck and call. They were underfoot constantly. She wasn't allowed to even go to the kitchen for a glass of water. Protocol demanded that she ring a little silver bell for every service she wanted. When she rang, a houseboy, dressed in an immaculate white tunic and trousers cut off halfway up the calves of his legs, approached on his knees. He awaited her command, then went to the kitchen for a glass of water, or ordered her car around, or filled the house with flowers, or executed whatever her wish had been. It took twice as long to do anything than it would have if she'd been allowed to do things for herself. Nevertheless, the mysterious chain of command that governed life out here had to be respected. A chauffeur was always at ready to drive her wherever she wanted to go. Custom did not allow her to drive herself.

"I wanted to go somewhere one day." she laughed. "I don't remember where for sure, to the club I think, and since I couldn't drive myself, the chauffeur came around in the little roadster to take me. I scrambled in while he held the door open wide, and off we went. Then the car broke down. There I sat in the hot sun while the chauffeur went trudging off down the road to find a telephone. After awhile he came back to tell me that we'd have to wait until Number One boy brought another car. I was wringing wet with sweat by then. Pretty soon, here came Number One boy, and, just like they were serving a queen with all that bowing and scraping, they ushered me from one car to another and the chauffeur and I went on our way while Number One boy waited for the tow truck.

"What about your school? When did you start that."

"Not until Marika was well past two. At first, I helped Karoly in surgery. I did it for over a year. Karoly told me everything to do and if I didn't do it fast enough he yelled. My God how he yelled! I was glad when they got somebody out from Holland who was trained." She stopped talking as though she'd lost interest in what she was saying.

"Then you had Marika," Mrs. Teitler prompted.

"Then I had Marika." Magda's voice lifted. "But," she said sadly, "you know how it is out here. Always the servants do everything. The babu took care of Marika. I could hold her sometimes, but the Babu did everything. Then we went to Budapest."

They had gone to Budapest for a sabbatical and taken Marika and the babu with them. They would stay a year in order for Karoly to get in touch with all the new developments in medicine. After four long years in a land of fantasy Magda was glad to be back on familiar ground. In Surabaya life was so frivolous, so gaudily rich, she couldn't adequately describe it to her mother. The enormous sums of money she'd bet on card games at the club seemed obscene in the telling. Karoly loved to gamble and he wanted his wife to play for high stakes too. There'd been an unreality, like play-acting, to the life she lived in the Far East. Going home was renewal. She reveled in being back in her town surrounded by old friends. She delighted in showing off her child and watching Marika's grandparents devour her.

It wasn't all homecoming and play. Karoly did advanced study in surgery while Magda learned to be an x-ray technician. To be near the hospital where Karoly was working, they took a hotel suite in the heart of the city. After long days at the hospital, the "babu" kept Marika while they poured themselves into the night life. They ate in their old favorite restaurants, went to the theater, partied with friends, and generally "lived it up." Magda even made a stage appearance for old times sake. In the holiday breaks from the hospital, they took trips to St. Moritz to ski. The year passed so swiftly it was time to go back to the ironclad rules of the rich in the Indies before they were satiated with the people they loved and the places where they could be themselves.

Crated and snug in the hold of the ship, was an x-ray machine, the latest model they could find. When the new equipment was properly installed in the clinic Magda went back to work. That x-ray machine gave Karoly and Bandi an advantage over other doctors in the city so quickly that within weeks it was decided to replace Magda with imported technicians. Once again she took up the life Karoly thought ought to give her pleasure. Again she went to teas, played tennis, gossiped and visited as long as she could stand it.

"I had to have something to do." Magda said firmly. "Karoly had his work and there were servants for everything around my life. At night there were always people. We had fun but I had to have something for me to do that was mine, that no servant could do for me, something that Karoly would approve of. So, I opened the school.

Every time they went home to Budapest after that first trip, rather than being reluctant to leave, she had been eager to get back to her school in Surabaya when their sabbatical was over. They'd gone back to Budapest in l936 and stayed six months. They returned in l938 glibly promising to see everyone again in another two years. That was four years ago and only God knew if she'd ever see any of them again. Tears trickled down her face and she slumped back against the wall.

Mrs. Teitler interrupted another retreat into depression. "I wish I could have seen you dance at the charity ball three years ago. I wish you could dance for us here."

Startled by the mere thought of it Magda looked at Mrs. Teitler in horror. Was the woman actually suggesting that she call attention to herself in this place? The guards would beat her to death if she tried to do anything so diverting, so frivolous.

"Oh, don't worry." Mrs. Teitler hastily reassured her, "I know you wouldn't dare do one pirouette, much less really dance. I'm not going to let them know what you can do. But' she sighed "it would be nice."

In the fall of 1939 she had performed with a touring orchestra from Hungary at a glittering charity ball that had been major news for the local paper. That same fall she'd had an experience that could have made the pages of the NATIONAL GEOGRAPHIC. She was presented at the court of the Sultan of Batavia, and after the ceremony she was photographed standing behind the turbaned sultan seated Turk fashion on satiny pillows, his barefoot wife beside him. Both were heavily bejeweled. Like the western traveler in one of Richard Hurlburt's vagabond books popular at that time, Magda stands behind their majesties dressed like a correspondent for Life Magazine.

"I got the giggles," Magda said, telling Mrs. Teitler about it one morning after she had fully recovered. "There they were, the sultan and his wife and all the officials, all barefoot. You think you'll get used to that, but you don't. I felt like the elephant who's stuck his head and trunk through the back of the tent and no one but the photographer knows he's there."

The women had little to cling to for sanity's sake. Night after night there was little sleep as the tortured and the hurt wailed and cried. One of the Japanese pastimes was to hang the men by their arms, then burn them with cigarettes. Stretches of bamboo matting for walls where doorways in the wall had once been left slits the women could peak through in fascinated horror to watch the macabre scene. Shrieks of pain while the torture went on pierced the very souls of the listeners as it was intended to do. After the Japanese tired of the game and went away, the groans of men left hanging like so many sides of beef until morning kept everyone awake. It got to the point where Magda no longer responded to any of the agony around her. Her mind became numb and her feelings blunted.

Burdened by monotony, one day followed the next without change in their listless routine. The New Year rolled around without notice. One could only guess what month it was by the stages of vegetational maturation, the only measurement of time they had. Early one morning in January of 1943, without warning, the women and children were ordered out of the prison. Bewildered, confused, and sorely afraid, they followed their guards to the railroad siding. The guards told them nothing, merely herded them along like animals. They were loaded into open railway freight cars, packed in as usual until there was no room left in which to move. It took all afternoon to fill two cattle cars. No water was provided and there was no way a woman could relieve her bladder without wetting herself. Children peed on themselves and whimpered in embarrassment. The relentless sun overhead made everyone sweat profusely which brought on itching to add to their misery. Magda thought she'd faint but Marika's terror didn't allow her to give way to her own hysteria this time. There was no Karoly now. She had to be calm and alert and strong if they were to survive.

Finally, in late afternoon they were ready to depart for wherever they were going. As the train built up steam to pull out of the station they heard the roar of British bombers making their first sortie of the evening. Shells fell like rain on the rail yards all around them. Commercial buildings along the railroad right-of-way collapsed in heaps of rubble, fires broke out, any truck that moved was strafed. Women and children screamed uncontrollably while some fainted and hung limp in the press of humanity adding their dead weight to the nightmare of the others. Panic in the face of impending death was a contagion. Probably it was over in a matter of minutes but it seemed like an eternity before the roar of departing planes died away and there were no more whistling sounds of falling shells. In the eerie silence that followed, the crackle of fires and the thick pall of smoke that hung over everything made a surrealistic back drop for whatever was to follow. Creosote ladened smoke made the air almost unbreathable, while the stench of vomit compounded the indignities of the setting. Fire consumed buildings only a stone's throw away but no fire companies came to save them. Embers and falling ash covered the rail yard and the prisoners as well. People cried out as hot sparks hit them but no one came to their rescue. There was no one to come, the Japanese trainmen had taken flight when the first bomb left the belly of the plane carrying it.

Hours dragged by and still no one came near. Perhaps the Japanese had given them up for dead. Torpor settled over the exhausted women. A heavy human silence settled over the scene, broken only now and then by a child's wail or the quiet sobbing of a woman who had reached the limits of her endurance. As dusk grew deeper, the fires along the railroad tracks burned everything to the ground, leaving only smoldering spots of flame here and there. The heavy black smoke drifted away and an abnormal stillness, deeper than silence, settled over the land. Magda surrendered to the probability that she and Marika would die right there on a railroad siding at the edge of Surabaya. Night fell and now every woman and child stunk with her own excrement. The blessed darkness was strangely comforting. At least the blinding sun no longer revealed the desolation around them.

Magda's legs began to prickle and go numb. Marika alternately whimpered, then was still. The night winds turned cool and they were all grateful for the heat of the bodies around them. When dawn came at last there was scarcely a woman in the crowd who held out any hope of their being rescued. Magda was only vaguely aware when the train started moving just as the sun came up. The bombing had not altered the plans of the Japanese at all, it had only delayed their execution. These women and children had been selected for shipment to a destination plotted out by the Japanese army and that's where they were going even if the tides of the sea were reversed.

Way out in a barren, remote part of Java the Dutch had built a military base sometime in the past which was now to be converted by these women and children into a farm. The Japanese army was having difficulty securing supplies from the home country. At the battle of the Coral Sea and the battle of Midway, both of which occurred six months after the attack on Pearl Harbor, the Americans had taken command of the sea lanes to Southeast Asia leaving the Japanese south of that line stranded and on their own. Food was in short supply.

It took thirty-six more hours of hunger, and thirst, and bladders that overflowed, monstrous assaults on the limits of endurance, before the train finally stopped and the boilers of the engine shut down. They were there, wherever "there" was. A few of them had not arrived, they had given up life along the way, unable to bear more. Others had succumbed into a blessed catatonic state from which they could not be roused. Magda looked out through the slats of the cattle car and prayed to God that this was not their destination. It was the most desolate place she had ever seen. A treeless plain, once used for gunnery practice, stretched out as far as she could see. Off to one side was an array of buildings that had fallen into such decay that surely they couldn't be used to house human beings. For the Japanese these people were not human beings, they

84

were work animals to be stabled. They were expected to turn those hard-packed gunnery fields into productive garden plots. Scrawny skeletons of Jewish women and their half-starved children, equipped only with the most primitive farm tools, were to produce food for the Japanese army! It was insane.

The abandoned buildings were once large barracks built to house men temporarily stationed here. The whole Barracks area was surrounded by high barbed wire fences. Evidently, the Dutch soldiers had had to be guarded and fenced in too to keep them from deserting such a dreary post. Each of the barracks was actually one humongous dusty room with bunks built into all four walls. The bunks were two feet wide, unmattressed, nothing more than wooden platforms made of planks roughly eight inches wide, some of which were missing. Two people were assigned to each bunk built to hold one grown man. Once there had probably been tables and benches in the center of the room where the men could play cards or write letters but now the open space was bare. There was no place at all to sit except on the bunks or the concrete floor. When they were not in the fields, everyone was confined to these large rooms whose only light came from windows just below the roof line. The center of each barracks was the only playground the children could use. The children moved listlessly from one gaunt adult to the next seeking reassurance; but the women could scarcely be roused to respond, they were too worn out. Not one moment of privacy was available for anybody.

Every morning, those who passed for able-bodied were rousted out before dawn and sent into the "fields" to spend another day under the hot summer sun swinging a hoe to cut the granite hard ground into clods. When rain fell they kept on working even if the soil gummed up on their hoe blades and bent the vegetation heavy with water making it almost impossible to chop away at the weeds. Vegetation came up faster than the prisoners could clean it out. Only the smallest children and those too sick to do hard labor were exempt from the back-breaking work. Sick enough to be excused from work usually meant a matter of a few days before the victim left the barracks permanently, carried away with the garbage taken out by the trucks that brought in their meager supplies.

Because of the foul water Marika's dysentery never ended so that she was too weak to work. She played quietly with the little children, sitting in the shade of an overhang outside.

The children were so traumatized by the brutality surrounding them few showed any energy, creativity, or imagination. They whispered when they spoke, glancing furtively about, wary of bringing attention down on their heads. Marika's only hope for survival was for Magda to somehow lay her hands on enough food to keep them both alive. Marika needed food at frequent intervals for everything she ate went through her too quickly to do her any good. Faced with the knowledge that Marika's life lay in her hands, something happened to Magda. She became unflinchingly determined to live, and to have her daughter live as well. Whatever she had to do to get enough food for her child she'd do, and do it to the best of her ability.

All those years of dancing now paid off. Magda entered captivity in excellent condition, strong and supple, and she knew how to use her body so that she put the least strain on it no matter what she was forced to do. If work could save them she'd work, she'd work two assignments. She'd put in her day in the field, then she'd help in the kitchen at night. The cook often slipped her an extra sweet potato for Marika. Magda carried heavy sacks, hoed in the rock-hard earth, cleaned latrines, and twice a week she kept the fires going in the kitchen using a hand bellows. Sometimes she was so tired she worked in a daze. Sometimes she was so weary that, without Marika, she would gladly have laid down and never gotten up again. She knew that the least sign of weakness on her part would be the end for them both. The Japanese had no pity for the weak, they wore the women out and threw them away.

Week by week, a miracle was happening. The old parade ground, and every other inch of the enclosure, was yielding to their ceaseless effort and coming under cultivation. Watered by their bucket brigades, the sun-baked soil proved to be immensely productive. The vegetables these spectral women and children were growing, but which they were absolutely forbidden to taste, were plump and juicy and tantalizing. Anyone caught with food in her mouth or hidden in her clothes was brutally beaten. A string bean or a pea pod found tucked inside a bandanna or a bodice brought the wrath of the guards down on the heads of the entire prison population as well as giving the guards reason to beat one creature into insensibility. The next morning after the theft was discovered, everyone would be lined up in the hot sun and forced to stand until they collapsed. There was no feigning fainting for when a woman or child went down a guard rushed forward and jabbed the crumpled figure with a stick to make sure there was no play-acting. If the person was truly unconscious she was carried inside and thrown into a bunk and left to revive on her own. If the person was not unconscious, merely succumbing to fatigue or emotional exhaustion, she would be beaten to a point just short of death. Now and then the guard doing the beating underestimated the strength of the poor wretch he was flailing and killed her. Such a death was invariably followed by a snort of disdain and the corpse left where it lay until the next morning when it was slung into the back of the garbage truck and carried away.

The prisoners were forced to witness such bestial behavior every week even when no legitimate excuse for punishment existed. One sadistic Japanese officer who visited the camp every seven days, would stand, feet apart, hands behind his back, watching the morning lineup until every woman and child was accounted for. Then he would arbitrarily choose some woman from their ranks to haul to the front of the group and beat into unconsciousness while the rest watched. When Japanese officers came into the camp for any reason everyone was supposed to kowtow deeply from the waist, palms together in front of their faces, and no one was to look up until the officers had gone. To straighten up too soon brought more punishment. Once Marika came up too soon and an officer hit her across the face with his hand so hard she had the print of his fingers welted on her cheek for hours. Punishments, hunger, overwork, emotional exhaustion - only one out of three of the women and children who came into the camp left it alive.

The key to survival was to have three attributes: grit, wit, and native physical strength. Magda surprised herself by having them all. She could always see a way to make something out of the slimmest opportunity. One circumstance that came to her attention was that the Japanese fed the pregnant women who came into the prison more food than others received. If the baby died in childbirth, and many did, the bereaved mother was kept from field work to be a wet nurse for the children whose mothers had died in the birthing process. Magda saw a way to get more food for Marika, maybe even a little more for herself. She offered to wash diapers at night for part of these lucky women's ration. Weak and tired they welcomed the offer. Too desperate for her own child's life to put a value judgment on taking food from one abused human being for another, Magda wrung out diapers until her arms ached. Sometimes she was so exhausted that when she got the precious food back to Marika she fell into a stupor leaving the child to eat alone.

The cooks in the kitchen watching her day after day working fiercely to keep her child alive, always even tempered and willing, began slipping her a bun now and then for Marika. Magda would go shuffling off as fast as she could with hands cupped around the treasure to keep it warm until she could pass it to the starving little wisp lying listlessly in the bunk. Food was also beginning to enter the camp surreptitiously from outside the barbed wire. Native Javanese working the land outside the camp came to know some of the prisoners working along the other side of the fence and took pity on them. When the progress of work carried someone close to the fence row a small handful of prepared food, perhaps nothing more than a ball of rice, would be passed surreptitiously through the wire.

Aware of the growing support for the prisoners from the community outside, the Japanese guards tried to keep the two groups from any contact at all. They could not prevent all contact, be everywhere at once, for they were too few in number. So a rotation process began. Periodically, the women were moved from one camp to another. Never were they allowed to remain in one place long enough to establish empathetic relations with the Javanese community around them. After leaving Surabaya prison, Magda and Marika were in three different camps during their years of imprisonment.

The Japanese refused any affiliation with the International Red Cross. In other theaters of war the Red Cross put prisoners in touch with their families back home, but the Japanese wouldn't entertain such a foolish practice. There was no outside contact of any kind, no war news, no news of Karoly, only unreliable rumors about the growing native unrest throughout the islands of the Dutch East Indies. Whispers circulated about an underground which was organizing against all foreigners, along with fragments of rumors that the war was going badly for Japan. How could anyone believe anything whispered through fences and passed along from woman to woman? Day followed day in cruel repetition of the day before with no end in sight and no change in the prison routine. Then, unbelievably, incomprehensibly, without warning, one morning in July of 1945, the gates of the camp swung open and Lord Mountbatten himself rode through. He was standing in the back of a touring car, looking down with anguish into their gaunt, stupefied faces.

"It is over," he said gently. "The Japanese have been defeated. Soon you can go home." He paused and waited for them to grasp the significance of what he'd just said but all the faces turned in his direction looked blankly at him as though no one could understand the spoken language. "Even though it is not safe to let you go now, you are free," he continued. "There is a civil disturbance in the streets that makes it unsafe for you to be on your way at this time, but you are no longer prisoners. Your guards will see to your safety from the violence outside for their lives now depend on how well they protect you."

Like everyone else Magda stared up at him open-mouthed. Could it be that the garbled tidbits of information that had come through the rumor mill about a breakdown in Japanese authority in the civilian population were true? No one had believed the reports that the Javanese were the ones rebelling, not the Dutch. The Javanese were docile, peaceful people. It had been said that a leader had risen up among the native people who would eliminate every overlord from the soil of what they, the Javanese, were now calling Indonesia. She and the rest had brushed aside the few rumors they'd heard as mere wishful thinking, but here was this flesh and blood Englishman earnestly telling them that the war against the Japanese was over and a new war had begun. Magda's mind raced. She found it harder and harder to focus on what he was saying. Inured to accepting Japanese oppression as the natural order of things, what this Englishman was saying seemed sheer fantasy.

Finally the meaning of Mountbatten's words began to register in spite of her disbelief. How else to account for the presence of this man? But if they were free why were they still locked up? What kind of freedom was that? The guards who had beaten and tortured them for so long were to become their protectors? She couldn't imagine them without whips and prods and tyranny. If the Japanese were defeated, why was it necessary for the Javanese to make a 'civil disturbance?' She looked around in bewilderment. Over? How could it be over? The guards had given no hint that change was in the air. The tall neat man continued to talk and Magda tried to force her wandering mind to concentrate on what he was saying but it was difficult.

"The Dutch forces have landed and are trying to quell the riots in the streets" he said, "but at present any European or Japanese caught by those mobs is likely to be tortured and killed. It is best that you remain here with these men to protect you," he waved his little baton at the guards.

Magda looked fearfully at the guard nearest her to test the proposition and couldn't believe the transformation. The familiar arrogant posture that demanded submission had slumped into a slight, subservient stoop that made her think of the houseboy at home. A frightened, apologetic smile quivered at the corners of his mouth. From habit she quickly turned away looking straight ahead, shoulders braced expecting the blow that before would have fallen on her shoulders for the audacity of looking full face at her captors. There was no blow.

"I want to be sure you understand," Mountbatten raised his voice, "You are free, you may go as soon as it's safe to leave. We'll provide you with what food we can, and provide whatever necessities we can lay hand to, but these riots have the docks tied up. We cannot bring in supply ships at the moment. Neither do we have transport to offer. When the time comes for you to leave you may jolly well have to go out on your own. Meanwhile, you are safer here."

Magda felt a little pulse begin to beat hard in the hollow of her throat. Free?! It was over?! She shivered. She and Marika could go home?! A few women around her began to weep softly, some laughed hysterically, others embraced each other clinging to a friend as if to find confirmation in that simple act that their ordeal was indeed at an end. Here and there a woman went up to a guard and spit on him. It was incredible to watch. The guard would smile deferentially, wipe off the spit, and bow low. Mountbatten watched the scene in silence for a brief moment, then wearily saluting them he ordered his driver out the gates of the prison. When he was out of sight Magda stirred. Wrapping her arms around herself she rocked back and forth crooning as she let it all sink in. Free! It was the most beautiful word in the world. She broke and ran pell mell for the barracks.

"We can go home, darling!" she cried, sweeping Marika off her feet. "We can go home to Papa!"

"Go home!?" Marika asked incredulously. "We can go right now?"

"Not right now, darling, but in a few days for sure."

"Home!" The wonder in Marika's face broke Magda's heart.

"Yes, home liebschen, we can go home to Papa." She tilted the child's head back and kissed her on first one cheek and then the other.

Going home to Papa didn't happen in a few days. The gates to the prison remained closed for weeks. The situation outside got worse, not better. No supplies came in. Food was more scarce than it had ever been, and now the guards were as hungry as they. The soup became thinner and thinner. Life seemed to be slipping away just as it promised to be opening up again. Then one day American bombers appeared overhead, so low one could see the wonderful star on the underside of the wings. Big black bundles and boxes tumbled out of the bellies of the planes dropping inside the fortress fence. The sky seemed full of parachute umbrellas carrying manna to earth.

It was food! Wonderful, glorious food, food in abundance, the most marvelous sight they had ever seen. It was unbelievable. As the packing crate sized bundles fell around them they laughed, they cried, they raised their arms in thanksgiving to the pilots overhead. Then they fell on the containers frantically ripping them open. The planes came back the next day to repeat the shower of blessings. The former prisoners and their emboldened guards began to gorge. It didn't take much to fill shrunken stomachs, but a few wouldn't quit eating. They kept stuffing themselves until they were sick and threw up. Like clockwork, after that, the Americans flew by on their milk run. During one of the early drops, when they still couldn't believe such a thing could happen, one of the women gazing skyward became so transfixed that a big carton hit her in the head and killed her. Killed by abundance after all those years of deprivation! Only the Gods of the demented could laugh.

At last came word from the Dutch that if any of the prisoners had friends in Batavia to whom they could go for shelter, they were free to leave at anytime. There'd be no danger of starving, the Americans were dropping food everywhere they were told. As Mountbatten had warned, there was no help from any source in securing transport. When the Dutch had said they were free to go they truly meant that they were free to make it on their own. It was intimidating. For three years they had not dared take one step without orders or permission. The idea of striking out on one's own to go halfway across Java the best way they could left one woman in tears. Magda tried to comfort her.

"Look," she said. "If we could make vegetables grow in this hellish place, we can find our way home. Now stop crying. Think about Home. Don't think about how difficult it will be to get there, think about Home. The very word "Home" was a thrill to say out loud. She could hear it being said all over the compound.

"We stood there inside the gate peeking out like little children." Magda remembers. "We were holding each other's hands. Then we tried it out. We put just one little toe out to see what would happen and when nothing happened we ran."

A goodly walk away from their prison ran a railroad that brought supplies for the camp, a railroad that ran on beyond the military camp to the end of Java. They'd heard the train go by every day since they'd been there. Always the train whistle had been the loneliest of sounds. It beckoned to a life from which they were cut off. When the women reached the platform the first train that came through had people clinging to the tops of the cars, hanging from the steps, bulging out the windows. The train stopped, but no one got off and there was no hope that any of the Surabaya-bound women could get on. After three more trains came through, all just as crowded, they realized they'd never get away if they waited for space for them all.

Sooty twilight was giving way to coal black night before Magda managed to push onto the bottom step of the ladder on a passenger car. Shoving Marika ahead of her so that the child was wedged between herself and the man on the step above them, Magda was able to grasp the handrail on either side so she could entrap Marika and keep her pressed against the man above them. Her strength renewed by the American food, the diaper washing and bellows pumping yielded its harvest. Her muscles were stretched taut as the wind tried to pull them off the train. Hour after hour they hung there. Finally, those on the steps managed to force their way into the corridor of the car where Magda and Marika collapsed in a heap. For three nightmare days of physical endurance they fought their way onto trains so crowded there was literally no room for them until Magda made room. They waited on platforms for trains going in their direction shivering with fear they'd not be able to get on. Once they stood on a platform in the middle of the night while somebody's bombs fell all around them. Marika and Magda were both screaming at the top of their lungs by the time it was over. Then, miraculously, they were there! Tears rolled down Magda's cheeks as they dismounted in the Surabaya train depot.

The Red Cross was already at work in Surabaya when they arrived. They had lists in abundance: lists of stray people trying to find each other, lists of homes where people would give them shelter, lists of the places where the food drops came in. Magda looked at the long queues in front of these posted lists and impatiently struck out on her own. If Karoly was alive she knew where to find him. He'd be with the first friends he made on the island, a Chinese citizen of substantial worth who probably had bought his family's way out of imprisonment. If Karoly wasn't there, those people would know more about him than the Red Cross could tell her.

The streets were a maze of debris. She and Marika picked their way carefully through the rubble. Landmarks had disappeared. Whole buildings were gone. But with unerring instinct, Magda led them to the house of their friends and found it intact. Marika began to cry. Trembling with hope, Magda led her up the steps and rang the bell.

The door opened and there before them stood -- Karoly! Karoly! Thin, gaunt, but alive. No one moved for a long stunned moment, then shock gave way to joy!

"Mein Godt! Mein Godt! They're here!" Karoly cried as he scooped them into his arms. Their bony little bodies pressed against him as they tried to become one with him.

"Oh, Karoly, Karoly, Karoly!" Magda repeated over and over showering his head with kisses. "I can't believe. I truly can't believe."

"Papa!" Marika sobbed into his neck, "I wanted you. All the time I wanted you."

Karoly held them away from him as best he could with four arms wrapped tightly around his neck. It had been two years since he'd seen them and, in spite of everything, Marika was taller. Her growth had not been stunted. Relieved, he hugged her tight to him again. They wept, the three of them, and hugged and kissed and laughed and clung to each other and talked all at once while their friends looked on with tears streaming down their faces. They couldn't get enough of touching and looking and kissing and breaking out in tear-filled laughter again and again. Then, in the middle of their ecstatic reunion, there was a pounding on the door.

"Good God, what's that?" cried their host. He clapped his hands sharply and a servant came on the run. "Look out to see who's there." he ordered. "But send them away. We don't want anyone coming in."

The servant sprang to the door, opened it just a crack then shut it sharply. "Master must come," he whispered urgently, "Others must hide!" He was visibly shaken.

Their host pushed the Markowits family back under the staircase out of sight and with beads of perspiration popping out on his forehead, went to the door where the pounding threatened to break the door off its hinges. Opening the door, he blanched. The man on the stoop before him carried a machete in one hand and with the other played with the handle of a knife tucked in his belt. He wore ragged seaman's pants and was barefoot. A huge hulk of a man, he stared fiercely down on their host. Their host managed to keep his wits and composure, in spite of the wild gaze directed at him.

"What do you want?" he asked.

"European in this house must come to Market Square tonight at eight o'clock with suitcase. We know he here, he no come we come get him and we get you too! You make him come or you be dead tomorrow.!" The voice rose theatrically.

"Why is he to come?" asked their host. "What has he done!"

"Never mind! He come or else...." Pulling the knife from his belt he brandished it in their host's face. "He come!"

Karoly was shattered. This couldn't be happening now, not now after everything they'd been through. The man leaped down the steps brandishing his machete over his head as he went. Their host quickly closed the door behind him.

"Who was it?" Karoly demanded. "Have you ever seen him before?"

"No," replied their host as he shot the deadbolt to barricade the door. "It has to be one of Sukarno's thugs,

94

though. They came thronging in last night from the countryside and they're in control of the streets now."

The four adults stared stupidly at each other. Had they escaped the Japanese only to face death at the hands of the Javanese? "Don't go." begged their host's wife. "We'll slip you away."

"All three of us?" Karoly asked. "And what would happen to you?"

Husband and wife stared at each other and were silent. "I have to go," said Karoly hopelessly. "I have to go or we all die. Maybe they're only trying to extort money from us Europeans. Maybe they think we've had some hidden on us all these years."

Magda threw her arms around him and buried her head in his chest. "I won't let you go without me, Karoly. I won't."

"Don't be foolish," said Karoly sharply, then pulled her to him in remorse. Less than two hours ago he didn't know whether she was alive or dead and now he was yelling at her again.

Magda didn't answer. The threat from outside the door had thrown her back into the silence of the past three years, the silence of those who dare not speak. It was foolish of her to suggest going with him. What would happen to Marika if anything happened to her? She and Marika had learned they could do without Karoly, but Marika could not do without her.

Karoly packed a small bag and was gone before night descended. Those left behind could only wait. They strained to sort out street sounds that might tell them what was going on outside their doors. Servants were sent out to scout for news. They didn't return. Interminable hours went by. Finally Marika fell asleep, but there was no sleep for Magda. Late in the middle of the night, when they had almost given up hope, the doorbell rang. Quickly dousing the lights their host leaped to the door and cracked it slightly to peek out. There stood Karoly silhouetted against the inky darkness. His host pulled him into the darkened house and hastily closed the door behind him.

Karoly went directly to Magda and clasped her to him. "Oh God!" he groaned. "I thought I'd never see you again."

"What's going on out there?" demanded their host in a loud whisper.

"You won't believe it." Karoly rasped, his voice filled with horror and revulsion. "They're slaughtering every European they can lay hands on."

Magda tried to pull back but he smothered her against his chest, holding her so tightly she could hardly breathe. He poured out stories of butchered men who had reported as ordered, literally hacked to pieces by Javanese armed with machetes. No longer supine before their colonial masters, filled with pent-up hatred for all the years they'd been forced to labor for their overlords, they were creating a literal blood bath.

"The cobblestones are so covered with blood you can hardly stand up!" Karoly shuddered remembering. "I didn't think I had a prayer. I crouched down as soon as the butchering began, then scuttled like a crab into an alley. When I was sure no one had seen me I lit out for home."

He reached out a shaking hand and grasped his host's shoulder. "I hung to the alleys, honest to God. I went blocks in the other direction before doubling back. No one saw me. I know they didn't, but we've got to get out of here! We've got to hide."

"Hide where?" his host demanded. "You can't go to your house. There's no one there to guard you, to feed you, to watch over you. You have to stay out of sight right here. There's no other way."

"Yes. Yes." nodded his wife. "The servants can be trusted not to tell. I don't know where they are right now but we'll see to it they don't talk."

"What do you mean, you don't know where they are right now?" asked Karoly in alarm.

"We sent them out to find out what they could about you," she replied. "They haven't come back...".

"They won't learn much in that melee." Karoly interrupted her. "There's more chaos in that square than there ever was in prison. These Javanese don't even know how to conduct a revolution! The killing that's going on out there will make their own people puke when it gets out. Sukarno must be a fool."

"Oh no," said his host gravely. "Right now he's letting the people have their revenge, but when he's ready, he'll pull them in like dogs on leashes. The people will heel!" He clapped his hands and Number One Boy appeared magically. "We have to hide these good people for a few days. What can you suggest?

Number One boy bowed low. "In my quarters, master. No one will look for them there."

"You're taking a big risk," Karoly protested. "If they find out you sheltered us from your own people they'll cut you to ribbons."

Number One boy smiled mysteriously. "They will never know." he said flatly and turned away.

For days the Javanese roamed the city looking for prey. Then the British managed a temporary break-through. Gurkha troops from Nepal, part of the British forces that had entered Indonesia to drive out the Japanese and hold the islands until the Dutch could arrive, tried to bring order out of the total chaos that gripped the city. Even they proved helpless to do more than form a driving wedge to clear a path going from street to street to rescue all European nationals holed up anywhere. Leaflets were dropped on the city to alert prospective evacuees to the British plan. Lorries, protected by the Gurkhas, were to range throughout the city to pick them up and transport them to waiting ships which would carry them to safety in Singapore. The Markowits' hosts eagerly brought the leaflet to Karoly. They were not going themselves, they had too many friends in high places among Sukarno's people to need to go. Though he insisted they didn't mind the tension of hiding Karoly's family if he chose to stay, didn't Karoly think it would be wise to leave? The Markowits packed their few things and when the lumbering lorries came down their friend's street, they gladly became evacuees.

At the wharf, pandemonium reigned. People milled about on the dock. Magda and Karoly arrived and began pushing their way close to the ship anchored dockside. When the gangway was let down the Markowitses were still far back in the crowd. By the time they got aboard, all the cabin space had been taken and there was nothing left but a spot of deck here and there where one could throw down a sleeping mat. The little trio could not even get near the rail to watch Surabaya slip away into the green haze as Java faded into the empty horizon. Magda and Karoly, swept one way and then the other in the milling crowd, were hesitating about where to claim a spot when suddenly Karoly let out a whoop easily heard above the din.

"Bandi! My God, Bandi!" Furiously he began pushing his way through the crowd leaving Magda and Marika standing in the midst of their little pile of luggage.

"Karoly!" Bandi's tired, thin face lit up with joy as he saw his partner coming toward him. "Oh Lord, it's Karoly!"

The two men fell on each other. Arms locked in a bear hug they rocked back and forth wordlessly, too overcome to say anything. At last Karoly croaked, "I can't believe it." His voice was husky with tears. "I gave you up for dead two years ago. I thought I'd never see you again."

Bandi smiled tremulously as he pulled away and wiped his eyes. "I gave myself up at least once a month from the day we all got hauled out of the house. But I was sure they'd done you in when they took you out of Surabaya prison. I could keep you in focus until then. A little moll here, a little moll there, and information was available."

"How the hell did you get hold of any moll?" asked Karoly in astonishment.

"Oh," answered Bandi acidly, "Number One boy and I have a little agreement. I'll have to tell you about it some time."

Crossing the Straits the Von Kisses and the Markowitses, along with Dr. Barbara Still who was also on board, slept together out on the deck. The cabins below were fetid and overcrowded; sleeping on the cool wooden flooring was the best arrangement after all. Having had little experience with beds for three and a half years, they could delay getting reacquainted with such civility. Certainly the deck was cleaner than some of the places where they'd been forced to bed down.

Overhead, the velvety black sky, studded with stars that sparkled like diamonds, stars so near Magda felt she could reach out and pluck them to wear in her hair, hung magically above them. Warm tropical breezes scented with the smells of the sea, blew over them. There hadn't been such peace for years. Sleep was out of the question, they talked long into the night. The two men lay apart not far from their wives and children so they could talk privately.

"Have you thought about how we can get back into practice?" Karoly asked. "The Dutch are bound to win this thing in the long run."

"We're going home to my in-laws in Holland on the first transport we can catch," said Bandi flatly. "I don't care who wins out here, I want no more of this place."

Karoly gasped. "I never thought of a future without you if we both survived." he cried. "I don't want to think of it now". Bandi was silent. Karoly lay quiet, struggling to take in this new possibility. A future without Bandi?! The silence between them became pregnant until at last Karoly rolled over on his side so that he could see his old friend and partner's profile.

"When I thought you'd probably already gone back if you'd gotten away, or when I thought you might be dead," he confessed, " I did think about what I'd do if I got out and you weren't here. I can't go back. You can, we can't. We have to stay here or immigrate to a place like Australia or America, someplace that will take us in. We never took out Dutch citizenship so we can't go to Holland and we can't go home to Hungary."

"Why not?" Bandi wanted to know.

"From what we hear the Russians are stripping Hungary clean worse than the Germans did. We don't know much, we haven't been able to get any word through the Red Cross. We don't know whether we have any family left or not."

Bandi's voice was husky. "The Goddamn Germans made a mess out of Holland but at least it's ours again and it can be rebuilt." He reached out and gripped Karoly's wrist. "I'm sorry," he said softly, "the Boche should never have gotten into Hungary. She held out so long. I've been hearing the same things you've been hearing. In the end, Budapest was bombed into rubble. God, Karoly, this war has made chaos out of everything."

Karoly rolled over on his back and lay very still looking up into the vast arc of nothingness that reached to the horizon. He made no effort to free himself from Bandi's grasp, he needed the comfort. He hadn't faced the prospect before that he and Magda would be completely orphaned out here. The chatter of the women made him want to cry. Even their friends were going to be taken from them. Bandi released his grip on Karoly's arm and lit a cigarette. He handed it to Karoly and lit another for himself.

"What about the stuff we buried and the stuff in the walls?" Karoly asked at last.

"You mean if the Japanese didn't find it?"

"They didn't find it, Bandi. I know they didn't find it. I know it in my gut."

"Well, if they didn't find it and you get back there just send me my share. I wouldn't go back for a penny of it." Bandi's snarled.

"Come on, man," Karoly pleaded. "With what we've got in there we can live as well as we ever did."

"Karoly, I'd rather be in partnership with you than practice any other way, but I'm not going back. I never want to see the place. I'd never again trust anyone out here."

"But Number One boy...?"

Bandi snorted. "Number One boy will come to Holland once we get there. That's the deal I made with him and I'll keep my word, but I hate him as much as I hate the Japanese. He made me beg for favors, made me beg for information, and always there was the threat that if I didn't swear to get him out of here when the war was over he'd betray our friends who hid our stuff. I began to hate the stuff too. It stopped being "My art," "My jewels," "My money." and became just stuff. I had to sell my honor to keep him from turning innocent people over to the Japs. You can round up the stuff up and sell it if you want or you can leave it where it is. Probably it's all been carted off to Japan by now, anyway."

Lounging on a coil of rope the next day, Dr. Still told all who would listen about her research project which she intended to pick up in India rather than Java. "Isn't it wonderful?" she babbled. "We all have something to carry on into the future. Some kind of work that needs to be done."

Karoly shrugged. Bandi would work in the Netherlands, Karoly would go back to Surabaya, if possible. Magda would reopen her school. But it would never be the same. The world was not just changed, it was distorted. But, with the balmy wind in their hair, the sea breezes in their faces, the warm sunlight on their backs, he felt comforted and at peace in spite of wounds still healing. If he could just float for a time, let the world become hospitable again, maybe things would turn out all right in the end.

In Singapore, they were taken by lorry to an old fort built long before the war. This fort, however, was a far different experience than the prisons they had occupied for the past three years. The gates on this place were wide open at all times. There were mattresses on the bunks, there were toilets and showers, and best of all there was plenty of food. The Red Cross saw to everything. They were free to roam the city at will, visit the bazaars, hang out in the cocktail lounges of the hotels, drink coffee at sidewalk cafes, live like Europeans again all day and all night if they wished. They only had to return to their barracks to eat and to sleep.

They began running into all sorts of people they had known. It was like homecoming week in a small town. Throngs of people came and went in all directions. Troops, battle-weary and eager to return to their own beds in their own homes, were headed west as returnees who had fled from the Japanese came back to resume life as they had known it, or to rebuild in the new situation. There were Americans and British and Indians and Chinese, a truly international olio of businessmen, politicians, service men and civilians, all moving in and out of the city fueling the wide-open night life. For Magda and Karoly it was like a second honeymoon, but for little Marika it was like rebirth. She had been hurt by her travails far more than her parents knew.

The titanic struggle between Sukarno and the Dutch was won by the Dutch at last, and the Markowits family prepared to "go home." Four years of unimaginable horror had gone by since they'd left their house. Four years in which first the Japanese and then the Javanese had had the run of the place. What would they find? Had it been destroyed in all the fighting that had gone on in Surabaya? Had it become an Aegean Stable? Were all the walls intact? They went shopping for linens and simple dishes and pots and pans, the bare essentials with which to get started, things they wouldn't find in Surabaya now. The Red Cross advanced them the money. When transport was at last available, they boarded ship and headed south. They had seen the Kisses off for Holland, they had bid Dr. Still 'God Speed,' they had watched a lot of friends and acquaintances head for the West. Those headed South and East were few in number, and none of them were more than acquaintances of theirs. Like all the returning exiles, they were headed for a familiar place which had become foreign and strange because of the war's nightmarish interruption of life. Karoly lounged lazily against the rail watching the ship's wake close behind them as he pondered the future.

Marika came to lean against him. "Papa" she said. "Do we have to go back? Why can't we go to Holland too?"

He put his hand around the back of her neck and turned her face to him. "We can't go to Holland, darling. We're not Dutch. And we can't go to Budapest. The Russians are there. Surabaya is all the home we've got. But why are you fretting? We're going to get you a new horse and a couple of dogs and some peacocks again and life is going to be like it used to be. You don't have to worry, it's all going to be all right."

Solemn eyes looked up at him out of an inscrutable face. There were no tears, no frowns, nothing. He was baffled. These days he never knew what was going on inside her head. Somehow, during these past three years, under a facade of calm detachment, she had hidden away. Now she asked for nothing and she offered little of herself. It made him uneasy. But Karoly Markowits was not a man to dwell on complex problems that offered no quick solution. She'd be all right once they were settled in again. Young people got over things quickly if you made light of them. Absentmindedly he stroked her hair as he looked out to sea.

Off to the south he could see the dark thin line that would become green Java when they approached near enough for it to take form. His mind leaped to arrangements that would have to be made once they stepped ashore. They would have to take a bus to get to their house, the Markowits didn't have cab fare. And if they found the place intact the first thing he'd do was knock out that plaster! He practically salivated at the thought of all that loot waiting for them. If the house was there and "it" was there they'd have the money to get all the help they needed to restore the compound to what it had been, and after that, "let the good times roll." After what they'd been through life owed it to them.

On the Surabaya wharf all was bustle and business. The slow leisurely pace of the past, marked by the cheery calling back and forth of porters as they ambled about, had disappeared with the War. This day there were no porters to be seen. They had to locate their cartons of goods themselves and find a drayman to carry them away. There was no "number one boy" obsequiously bowing and scraping as he cleared their path before them. Karoly left Magda and Marika standing out of the way of the foot traffic while he gathered up their few cartons. A more frustrating effort was to find a drayman who promised to deliver them the next day, not chop chop this afternoon as of yore. The luggage taken care of the next hurdle was to learn where to board a bus going to their part of town. The streets were still littered with the refuse of war. Little had been done to clean up or rebuild. Karoly began to sweat. Once familiar streets with their neat rows of houses sitting sedately behind their neatly trimmed hedges were snaggle-toothed with here and there a house still standing amid vacant lots with bare foundations or piles of rubble where a house had been.

The bus stopped at the foot of their long drive. The house had never been visible from the street but the state of the grounds which they could see from the road caused his heart to plummet. Rotting vegetation lay in mounds where it had been blown against standing trees, relics of palm fronds lay scattered over the tall uncut grass. There had been no maintenance whatsoever of the crushed shell driveway. They walked in silence up the drive. At the bend in the drive where his heart had always warmed when he caught sight of the house, Karoly gasped. Shabby, neglected, but otherwise undamaged, intact, there it was. Whooping with joy they dumped their luggage and ran pell mell for the front door. Using the key Bandi had given him, with trembling hands Karoly opened the door and stepped inside.

They tiptoed into the foyer and stood silently listening for sounds. The house was still as an empty church. Not one stick of furniture or one drape was left of their gorgeous furnishings. The place had been stripped bare. Someone had swept the floors not long ago and washed the windows. Magda walked as quietly as she could through all the rooms to check and not a single pane of glass was missing nor were there water stains on the walls or ceilings. Somebody had done the best they could to maintain the interior of their house though neglecting the outside and the grounds.

Karoly had but one concern. He strode quickly to the room they painted that night four long years ago. Four solid walls greeted him. He peeled off his jacket and hurried outside to the terrace to fetch a large stone. Finding one he could scarcely lift he brought it in and smashed a hole in the plaster where he thought the boxes lay. Thrusting his arm through the opening he felt around. It was there! It was there! Their fortune was as snug and secure as when they'd sealed it in! He sat down on the floor, pulled up his knees, buried his head in his arms, and wept. Magda stood stunned for a moment then danced with abandon from room to room crowing with delight. Fearfully, Marika watched them both from the hallway. Daddy had knocked a hole in the wall and Mama thought it was wonderful.

Their hidden treasure amounted to a king's ransom in the economic shambles of post-war Southeast Asia. They were rich again, they were home again, the world had changed but they were ready for whatever lay ahead. It was unbelievable. Karoly immediately bought all the medical equipment he could lay his hands on, some new and a lot more used. Anything new was hard to find in a goods-starved world. The Chinese friends, to whom they had entrusted their portable art collection and Magda's jewels, returned every precious item to them. Not only had they been good custodians of their trust, it was their servants who had kept the interior of the house clean and ready for their return. Bandi's "stuff" was gone beyond recall. Karoly hoped it had been shipped to Japan and been bombed into nothingness by the Americans. Best of all, when he dug up the platinum bars they were all there.

As soon as the clinic could be scoured, painted and refurbished, Karoly went back to work. All his old patients who were still in Surabaya returned and brought new ones. His practice flourished from the day he reopened his doors. He was so busy he longed to have Bandi come back but every letter from Holland bore the same message. "Never Again in Java!"

Magda reopened her school. Students poured in as they had before the war. Tutors were hired to help Marika make up for school time lost in prison. By late 1946, goods from Europe began to reappear in the shops of Surabaya and on the surface pre-war life resumed. But the old colonial aspects of life were dead, torn asunder by war and revolution. Several of their former servants returned: the chauffeur, one houseboy, and the cook who couldn't tell time except by the sun. They were changed too. The houseboy no longer approached on his knees. Magda could jolly well go to the kitchen for her own glass of water. The cook, whom Karoly had taught how to prepare his favorite Hungarian dishes, now had ideas of her own and threatened to quit every time they tangled over the menu. Loyalty was one thing, subservience was another. The servants and their families no longer lived in the little houses on the compound but, with the higher salaries they demanded, rented apartments in the city. The old free and easy society had been sobered up. No one lived as ostentatiously as before the war, and no one was cavalier about tomorrow. A new breed of European was coming in and the old breed of Javanese had been transformed.

Months went by before concrete information about their families in Budapest came from the Red Cross. All the anguish of their own experiences resurfaced with each communication from Hungary, making them vulnerable all over again. More devastating than stories of the depravation of the still living was the listing of those who had died. It was staggering. Aunts, uncles, cousins, friends, acquaintances - the roll call seemed endless - all gone. Dr. Zahler's life had been spared for the same reason Karoly's had been spared; the people with power needed him. After Eichman came to Hungary to clean out the Jews, Dr. Zahler's gentile patients had gone to the Germans on his behalf and succeeded in keeping him alive and in their service. He was even allowed to make house calls. As he walked the streets making his rounds without harm, his relatives were loaded onto trains headed for Auschwitz and Bergen Belsen.

At the end of the war Ilonka's heart began failing and in 1948 she died. Magda was called home to be with her in her last illness. For weeks she sat at her mother's bedside, holding her hand as they went over the good times of the past and the bad. Together they mourned all the relatives who had died in the cause of the satanic dream of history's greatest megalomaniac. When Ilonka was laid to rest, Dr. Zahler wanted to go home with Magda. There was nothing left for him in Hungary. The Communist government would not allow it. He was still needed. For eight more years he lived in his house among his ghosts, and continued to see patients, but the vital spark in him was gone. He died in the 1956 Hungarian uprising, victim of a stray bullet which penetrated his thigh while he tended the wounded in the streets. How long he lay in the cold and snow before the Russians found him and took him away to a hospital no one knows, but it was long enough for him to develop pneumonia. His death came so quickly Magda could not get there in time to say good-bye to the father she adored. Budapest became a mausoleum for her, a grave yard she never visits.

By 1948, Karoly's practice was booming. The house was refurbished as elegantly as it had been before the war. Once again, life centered around the club and their friends. Marika became seventeen and old enough for college. Academically, however, she was far from ready. The lost years in the prison camp had not been made up so quickly. She needed tutoring to bring her up to college entrance level. In Chicago, Magda had a cousin, the daughter of Emil's younger brother. In Chicago also was the renowned Parker Schools for girls where individual attention was given to every student as they advanced at their own pace. Marika could quickly recover lost ground in such an atmosphere, or so Magda and Karoly thought. Magda called Suzanne for help. Could she negotiate with the school and take Marika under her wing?

When summer came Magda and Marika left Java by ship. Air travel was still too difficult for civilian flight; besides airplanes terrified Marika. The bombings of Indonesia, first by the Japanese and then the liberators, had left her traumatized by fear at the mere thought of boarding a plane. She wouldn't even ride the Ferris wheel in the amusement park. They booked passage by ship and sailed for New York, where after a brief visit with the relatives, they took the train to Chicago. Chicago thrilled Magda, but the city overwhelmed Marika. Its elevated trains were so noisy, its streets were so crowded with pedestrians and cars, people in the streets were so dwarfed by the tall buildings. Everything was covered with soot and grime and the crowds were so intent on getting to where they were going no one had time to stop to visit along the way. Everything was constant motion. She tried to see it from her mother's point of view, tried to appreciate the wonderland of elegant shops, the extravagant night life and the first-rate theaters, but she could not. She wanted to go back to the quiet of their compound before she even unpacked her bags.

Magda stayed a month, trying to acclimate Marika to the new world into which she was being thrust, then left on schedule believing that once she was out of sight all would be well. It was not. Marika did not adjust. Life was too competitive -- on the streets, at the school, even among the young people cousin Suzanne threw in her path. She was a child again left in her prison bunk to cry alone. She lost weight, she withdrew, she became so maladjusted that in despair Suzanne wrote to Karoly that she thought it best to send Marika home. At that moment, Magda was with her mother in Budapest saying good-bye. It was December before she was free to come for Marika after one and all gave up on the Chicago project. Suzanne took Marika to New York, put her on a ship for Amsterdam, and Magda headed for Holland to meet her.

Long weeks at her mother's bedside had drained Magda emotionally. She was too strung out to deal with Marika at the deeper level where Marika's needs lay. Instead, she put all of Marika's pain on the shelf until they could get back to Karoly. She booked passage on the first ship leaving for Surabaya, then checked the two of them into a hotel to wait. They celebrated Magda's forty-fourth birthday on Christmas Day, 1948, alone in Amsterdam, just the two of them in a hotel dining room. Christmas behind them, Magda called Mrs. Teitler who had also survived the Japanese internment, and was living with her husband and her son in Amsterdam. Mrs. Teitler came immediately when she learned they were to be there over New Year's Eve. She insisted they come to a party she was having. Magda welcomed the invitation but Marika hung back.

"I won't know anybody," she wailed. "I hate parties! Why do you always do this to me? Why can't you just go by yourself? Why do you always have to drag me around like a pet poodle?"

"Because you're young!" Magda argued. "Because you need to learn how to be with people. It's no good your just being by yourself all the time. It's the same at home! You never want to go to the club parties either. Marika, you've got to learn to mingle!"

Wearily Marika gave in and the two of them arrived at the New Year's Eve party gorgeously gowned. Most of the guests were Magda's age but there were a few younger people. One was Max Teitler. Marika was 18, Max Teitler was 31. They had been through what few of the other young people around them could understand. They were thrown together that night with nothing in common but their experiences under the Japanese but that was enough for a beginning. Magda could hardly believe how animated Marika became in Max's presence. She laughed at everything he said. She flirted with him outrageously. Magda couldn't keep her eyes off the two of them over in a corner excluding themselves from everyone else. It never occurred to her that what she was watching was the fairy princess meeting Prince Charming. From that night Max Teitler and Marika spent every hour they could together. Within days they were announcing to Magda their intention of being married immediately. Magda was frantic. What was she to do? This was not what she and Karoly had in mind at all. After what seemed an interminable wait she managed to get through to him by phone. Hysterically she poured it all out through the static on the line while Karoly cursed.

"Karoly," she shouted, "You say I should bring her home. How can I bring her home if she won't come? How?"

"Put her on the phone," he commanded. "I'll make her come home. I'll put a stop to this nonsense right now."

Marika went to the phone, crying and pleading as she talked to her father, but he would not budge. He would not give his consent and he forbade Magda to give hers. Without their consent Marika could not be married, she was not old enough. Karoly left her no choice but to leave with her mother when the ship sailed. At the dock she clung to Max weeping uncontrollably until Magda was ready to scream. On the ship going home to Surabaya she continued to weep, and for six months after her return she wept copiously, continually. She wept and wrote letters to Max. Finally, in absolute disgust, Karoly threw up his hands and let her go. So, sans husband who would have no part of it, Magda took ship once more for Amsterdam to plan and execute a wedding for which she herself had no heart. It was a marriage that has not only endured but for more than forty-five years has been an uninterrupted love story. In 1953 little Frits Teitler was born and then, at last, Grandpa Markovits capitulated. The little boy became his crown prince.

Two years later, in 1955, after the situation in Indonesia had deteriorated to the point where life for all Europeans became intolerable, Karoly called it quits. Sukarno's newly independent Indonesian government was bent on driving the Europeans out. Karoly and Magda had no desire to be removed by force a second time. They decided to cash in their chips while they still could and go back to Europe. Karoly sold the practice, Magda sold the dancing school, they sold their houses, the one in the hills and the double house in town. Then they packed that portion of their worldly goods they could use elsewhere and left the rest behind them in the land where they had spent all the years of their marriage. But where were they to go? Not to Communist Hungary! The only place to go was Amsterdam.

Karoly's Dutch license to practice medicine was valid in Holland, so without breaking stride, he opened a new office. There was more competition in Amsterdam than there had been in Surabaya, and too much competition to open a clinic. Nevertheless, he soon had a respectable practice established. Magda contented herself with an exercise studio. The demand for exercise studios in Holland, where a bicycling population got plenty of exercise on their own, was not great, but she had enough pupils to satisfy her need to be teaching. They bought a lovely home and tried to sink roots into the marshy soil of Holland, but Amsterdam was not Budapest any more than it was Surabaya. They floated on top of life in the Dutch city. Even though they had many friends, repatriates from the artificial Dutch world of Java where Europeans had floated above the native Indonesians like oil coating the water, or other Hungarians who had fled from their subjugated homeland to this sanctuary, they did not dig deep roots. Then abruptly Karoly died. Though a diabetic, like many another doctor he thought himself immortal. Counting on insulin to take care of the disease, he continued to smoke fat cigars, drink fine wines, indulge in gastronomic feats that would have floundered even a non-diabetic. A gourmet by nature, Karoly consumed enormous meals of the richest foods produced by the finest chefs in all the best restaurants. Sauces, cheeses, red meats, he ate them all with gusto. Wine, women and song. Wasn't that what life was all about? That's the way he had lived and that was the way he died. A massive insulin reaction killed him.

For the first time in her life Magda was alone. For the first time there was no strong man to lead her through her days. Max saw her through the tangle of lawyers and estate inventories she had to deal with, but once the aftermath of Karoly's death passed she was very much alone. Dinners with friends, her studio, her grandson, and little else. The hectic pace that had always filled her days was reduced to a crawl. Two years later, when she met Maarten Oudegeest, she was "ripe for plucking. Originally from Amsterdam, Maarten was a naturalized citizen of the United States. He owned a plastics factory in New York and one in his birth city. He was in Holland on business when he met Magda. He had not come

109

looking for another wife but he found one. He took possession of Magda like he possessed everything else in his world.

They were married in l965 and set out on a world tour. First, they flew into New York where Magda's family awaited them and where Maarten had many friends whom he wanted his bride to meet. While they were in New York, Magda visited Andre Kertesz, now an American citizen. He photographed her again in the old pose on the couch in his apartment. She was obviously older, but was as supple as ever.

After a month on the East Coast, they headed across America. Maarten had narrowed down his preferred location for retirement to the Bay Area in California. Once they arrived, San Francisco felt more like home than any place she'd been since she and Karoly left Surabaya. There was a European flavor to the city not found anywhere else in America. In the Spring of l966, while searching for a place to live, an article in the SAN FRANCISCO CHRONICLE caught Maarten's eye.

Out in Contra Costa County, on the sunny side of the Berkeley Hills, a new community was being created Magda and Maarten went to see it. By late afternoon they had purchased a square on a map where, four months from that day, a unit would be ready for them So Magda came to America and to Rossmoor, a long way from Java where being a name on an old Jew's list had done her in. Maarten died after two decades of golf and parties and good living in a community which was home to people from all over the world. Magda became a widow for the second time. Today, at ninety-six, after hip replacement at age 88, she goes wherever she likes but needs a walker for balance. In her imagination she still dances across stages and thrills to the applause. Once a year she makes the long trek to spend two months in Amsterdam near Max, Fritz and Marika. Her daughter still will not fly.

Recently, the Ansel Adams Gallery in San Francisco had a showing of Kertesz photographs. The famous "Magda" picture hung on the outside of the gallery. When the museum curator learned that the subject of the picture was still alive and living in nearby Rossmoor, they sent a car for her. Magda was photographed beside the life-sized blow up of herself immortalized by Kertesz. This time there was no curling up on a couch. Rather she stood beaming her wide vibrant smile at the camera, obviously delighted not to have been forgotten.

FRIDA

Life along the Graben, Vienna's main pedestrian shopping street which runs from St. Stephensplatz to Kohlmarkt Strasse, was warm and lively. The city's best shops lined the mall while the upper stories of those buildings were divided into apartments, spacious apartments that housed many of the professionals who worked in the old city. The great Cathedral loomed over shoppers and residents alike reminding them of the omnipresence of the watchful eye of the church. During the day the street was filled with busy shoppers and hand carts delivering goods to the business establishments that kept the Graben humming. Children who lived in the apartments above the stores darted in and out among the busy throng adding to the energetic bustle along the street. But when the Vespers Bells announced the ending of the day the shops began closing their doors and, if the weather was good, the residents of the neighborhood came out to stroll with their families along the emptied sidewalks and have a coffee at one of the outdoor cafes. While the parents sat and gossiped the children played up and down the little store-fronted lanes leading from the Graben to parallel streets behind.

The Kwiatkowskis, all five of them, loved the neighborhood. It was home. When the twins were born in l903, two identical little girls when a son had been hoped for, their father bought an apartment house facing on the Graben. The lobby of the apartment house was tucked in between two little shops and the apartments upstairs spread out above them. The building was to be an investment for the children's future. When a brother was born two years later his name was added to the title of ownership along with the names of the twins. When Frida and her sister were children they fantasized that they owned the whole Graben. This was their world, all of it, and they reveled in their fancied role as proprietors of such a marvelous kingdom.

The years of their childhood were the last years of the Austrian Empire's magnificence. Grandiose flights of imagination went with the romance of Light Opera which was Vienna's favorite form of entertainment. The Strauss family's music still held Vienna in thrall as did the gypsy music coming from the "Cellars" below street level. Some of the finest restaurants inside the Ringstrasse were located in these

"Cellars." Frida and her sister grew up in the rich musical culture that was the signature of Vienna. When the twins reached school age they were sent to convent schools over their mother's objection. She did not want a convent education for her daughters.

"I don't want them to grow up ninnies like I did." she protested. "I want them to know how to do something! I want them to be able to make it in this world on their own."

"My daughters will never be shop girls!" Mr. Kwiatkowski shouted.

"They won't be anything," his wife fought back, "they won't know how to do anything."

"They'll be what women are supposed to be, what you are." he stormed.

"And what am I? What do I know? Am I a great pianist? Can I carry on a decent conversation in French? Am I a great painter? I didn't learn enough of anything to be anybody."

"You're my wife, you're the mother of three children, you're the mistress of a good house, and you are a fine hostess. What else is there a woman should want?"

"Something in my head." she cried. "To know something."

Her husband had ceased being incredulous over such nonsense. He'd heard it over and over. She refused to accept the fact that a woman's worth was measured by her husband's success.

"We've covered this ground before." he said in his most patriarchal tone. His wife pursed her lips and was silent. His implacable, stubborn insistence on a way of life that was fading all around them was infuriating. The twins went to convent school and they learned the social graces so they could enter the world like butterflies leaving their chrysalises, but Frida's mother's rebellion had more influence on her daughter than did all the preaching of the nuns. Frida's maternal grandmother shared her daughter's disdain for the schooling her son-in-law prescribed for women. Her own life had been spent in silent rebellion and she intended to see to it that her granddaughters would have no need to rebel. She had the money to send the twins to Teacher's college when they left the convent in 1921. The girls came to count on Granny to provide for their liberation. There'd be a struggle, but with Mama and Grandmama, and Grandmama's money, behind them, they'd not have to quit school as soon as they were of marriageable age. There was a big wide world out there and in this new century they were not going to be politely pouring tea when grand things were going on outside their doors.

The twins entered gymnasium just after World War I broke out and were matriculated two years after the war ended. The war removed most of their options. All of the father's plans for his daughters, as well as the grandmother's counter ambitions, were washed away when two generations of wealth disappeared in the chaos of Austria's defeat. All that was left of the affluence they had enjoyed and had expected to continue to enjoy was the apartment building purchased when the twins were born. Frida and her sister were reduced to going to Business College, a long step down from all their expectations. Once she was immersed in accounting, however, Frida felt she'd found the stairway to what she wanted. To her surprise, she found she loved business and figures. She majored in Economics and minored in Accounting.

Unlike the situation in the United States, accounting was not a closed field for women in Europe. Upon graduation in 1924 the twins went to work. Throughout the 1920's, neither Vienna nor Mr. Kwiatkowski recovered from the economic doldrums created by the late war. Her father was never able to put together again the necessary investment money to start over, nor could the economy of a big city surrounded by a little country seem to find its way either. Times were tough year after year throughout the decade. The whole family was lucky that both of the girls found work right out of school. With an income of her own, Frida could be as independent as she liked. She and her father jousted constantly, but he was weaponless. The ancient right of a father to withhold his daughter's dowry if she did not accept his choice of a husband was gone, a husband was no longer a necessary choice. Unconvinced, Mr. Kwiatkowski, forever the autocrat, ordered the family around as though his authority over them was undiminished in these new circumstances. His pride would not allow him to allow his children to pay room and board, nor move out on their own.

"Save your money!" he exhorted them constantly. "Save your money!"

As a concession, the twins remained at home and Frida saved some of her money. To be twenty-one in 1924 with a little spending money in her pocket was a heady thing. The gayety of Vienna's past days of glory returned without the hidebound formality of pre-war etiquette. Chaperones were out, flaming youth was in. There were dance halls where respectable girls could go to dance, with or without an escort. Like her flapper sisters in America Frida loved to charleston to the jazz which had taken over in the cabarets. Skirts were short and so was hair. Frida wore the new styles and had her hair bobbed nearly giving her father a stroke. Unescorted, she haunted the dance halls. Decent women, in her Father's book, didn't do any of the things Frida was bent on doing. Life became a game of Frida outwitting her self-appointed arbiter of taste and morality.

She gleefully remembered one party in 1929 that didn't end until 3 a.m., not an unusual hour for Vienna's night life to shut down. It was a costume party and audacious Frida had donned sailor's pants and jersey, saucily tipped a sailor's cap down over one eyebrow, and had a riotous old time. At 3:30 she tripped into the foyer of their apartment building, a cigar clamped between her teeth, her bell bottom trousers flapping around her ankles. Humming a jazzy number she'd sung lustily at the party, she danced her way through the front door and came to an abrupt halt. There sat her bathrobed father, arms folded over his chest.

"No decent woman goes out dressed like that!" he roared. "How dare you shame your family this way?!"

Frida felt blood flood her face all the way to her hairline. She resented being robbed so abruptly of the good feeling left over from the party. "How dare you wait up for me like I was a child!?" she shot back, eyes blazing. "I'm twenty six years old and I have a job which pays my way in this world. How dare you shame me by sitting down here in your bathrobe like some police sergeant off duty."

"No respect!" he shouted. "No respect for me or for your mother."

"Leave my mother out of this!" She pushed the sailor cap back on her head and flipped cigar ashes on the floor. "If she was my age she'd do the same thing. As for respect, you don't get respect by demanding it. You don't get anything by demanding the way you do. You don't know how to live so you don't want anyone else to either."

"Live!" he was approaching apoplexy. "You call what you're doing living? You play like a grasshopper. You and your sister. Twenty-six years old and no husbands, no babies. You are a disgrace to womanhood!"

"Womanhood?!" suddenly Frida was convulsed with laughter. "Oh me, oh my. Womanhood! Depend on a man to know what womanhood is." She whipped off the cap and spun it around her finger holding the cigar in her other hand out of the way.

"La Dee Dah! Dear, dear father. The l9th century died and was buried and you didn't even read the obituary." Still laughing she mockingly danced a few little steps across the floor toward the stairs then headed up them two at a time. "See you in the morning!" she called over her shoulder.

"It already is morning!" her father shouted after her. From around the turn in the stairs her laughter floated down to where he had begun his slower ascent. He didn't know what to do about her. She had no respect at all.

At work Frida knew terrific success. She rose rapidly in the firm until she became head of the accounting department. Then in l930, the firm was liquidated and removed to England. After that she went to work for a textile manufacturing company and, again, just as swiftly, climbed the ladder until she was assistant to the chief accountant. Her office was located near the private office of the plant manager. The manager had a son who was a research chemist for a carpet manufacturing company nearby. Chemistry was a field forced on him by his father. Fathers, especially Jewish fathers, had that kind of control over their sons in those days. George Loeff, handsome, sensitive and talented, had enrolled himself in the University of Vienna as an Art History Major. His father had promptly marched down to the University and re-enrolled his son in the chemistry department. George knuckled under and became a brilliant chemist, one of the first among dye experts in Austria. Several times a week he stopped by the textile factory on his way home from work to walk with his father to the car line. In his father's office he met Frida.

George met Frida right under his father's nose and kept on meeting her that way. She would remain at her desk until he arrived so they'd have a chance to chat and flirt and laugh before the senior Mr. Loeff emerged from his office, then the three of them would walk out together. Soon he was calling for her at the apartment on the Graben, taking her to the theater, to the cafes, to parties in the homes of his wealthy circle of friends. They had picnics along the Danube, and on Sundays took day-long excursions into the Vienna Woods on the slopes of the hill west of the city. In the 1930's, Catholics and Jews freely intermingled in Austria. Position in society was based on wealth and family; the older the family and/or the greater the wealth the higher was one's position in the best circles. George's family, an old and respected family that moved in the best circles, held a prestigious position in society. George was a most desirable catch for any girl, Catholic or Jew.

Within months, George and Frida were ready to announce to their respective families that they were going to be married. They didn't ask permission. As far as they were concerned the old forms were out. There was rejoicing in both households. George's father already appreciated Frida's good mind and equable disposition, while Mrs. Loeff delighted in her vitality and initiative. Her fun-loving nature amused them both. George needed a little livelier approach to life, his mother thought, more spontaneity and less introversion. Frida's father was especially ecstatic. Frida was marrying at the level he'd wanted for his daughters. Frida's mother boasted to all the neighbors about George's charm, his good looks and, of course, his family's wealth.

"Your sister is going to be a Mrs. Somebody." Mr. Kwiatkowski crowed proudly one day to Frida's twin. "George should have lots of friends for you to choose from. You'll both wind up in the social register."

Frida's sister looked at her father in mocking innocence. "You think Frida's going to settle down and be a little housewife?"

Mr. Kwiatkowski frowned. "Why do you say it that way. Of course she'll settle down. She won't need to be a housewife though, she'll have servants like her mother-in-law."

"And I suppose you think she'll have babies and be a 'True Woman'?" Her voice remained pure saccharin.

"And just what is this 'True Woman'?" asked her father belligerently.

"You know," she shrugged. "It's what you always wanted her to be. A porcelain doll lady who has no desires except to be a helpmate, a doting mother, and a gracious hostess."

Mr. Kwiatkowski exploded. "If it's a 'True Woman' to do the things women are meant to do, then yes! It's what I want for you too! What's gotten into you?"

"Nothing Father," she said laconically as she rose and brushed past him out of the room. "But you might hope she'll be happy."

There was nothing but happiness in the Loeff household. "We're so pleased." George's mother's voice fairly glowed. "With Frida's personality and George's mind the next generation of Loeffs should be dynamic."

"Yes, " her husband said. "Dynamic and successful. I can see him now, George Loeff III. Tall, blue eyed, with George's brow and mouth. You know about the naming of Jewish children, don't you Mrs. Kwiatkowski?"

Frida's father who had been listening to this exchange, relishing the thought of a grandson, experienced a little twinge of resentment. The Loeffs were brushing aside Frida's Catholicism rather cavalierly. The Jewish naming of children for dead relatives? He knew. What about the Catholic naming of children for Saints? But, he had to admit, if he was the father of the groom rather than the father of the bride he'd make the same assumption. George and Frida were not present when the exchange about babies took place. If they had been the meeting would probably have become volcanic on the spot. The lifestyle they anticipated had nothing to do with family, or church traditions and expectations. Being ever so modern, Frida had no intention of giving up her job, and George insisted from the start that they have no children. He had no desire to become a link in a long Jewish dynasty. George and Frida were having a wonderful time the way life was, why change anything except their marital status? The betrothed and their parents were seated in the Loeff library when the two central figures in the coming event innocently set off fireworks that put an end to any plans for a big wedding.

"I guess I'll have to be looking for a replacement for Frida soon," Mr. Loeff said.

"Why?" George sipped his brandy and raised an eyebrow at his father. "She'll be just as good an accountant married as she is single."

"Oh, no question about that" Mr. Loeff smiled benevolently "but at your ages you won't want to put off having a family. It'll be too dangerous for Frida soon." He turned and smiled affectionately at his daughter-in-law to be, "You should have been a mother a decade ago." he said.

117

"Frida isn't ever going to be a mother," George said quietly, cutting Frida off before she could say something stingingly funny.

Mrs. Loeff gasped. "My dear!" she exclaimed, her voice heavy with sympathy. "Why didn't you tell us? Why can't you have a child, or is that too delicate to talk about here." her glance swept the men present.

"Yes, why can't you?" demanded her father. He turned to her mother. "Why didn't you tell me?"

"How could I tell you what I don't know." said a very surprised Mrs. Kwiatkowski. "How do you know you can't?" she asked Frida.

"No one said she couldn't." George was exasperated by their reactions and fearful of some outrageous outburst from Frida. "I said she wouldn't."

Mr. Loeff turned on Frida. "You won't? Why not, or don't you think we have a right to know?" He rose and walked to the fireplace to poke angrily at the embers. He was obviously struggling hard to hold his temper in check.

Frida giggled. "I promised George I wouldn't." she said.

"She promised you!" Mr. Loeff's turned indignantly to his son. "What on earth would prompt you to extract such a promise? Don't you want a son?!?"

"Nor a daughter." replied George calmly.

"No children at all?!" Mr. Kwiatkowski strode over to loom above his daughter.

"Nary a one!" she looked up at him with dancing eyes. "Nary a chick nor child."

"Why not?" demanded her mother.

"It would get in our way." Frida sipped her drink relishing the bombshell.

"Get in your way!!?" roared Mr. Kwiatkowski.

"Yes." George rose and stood facing the two older men. "I don't want to be a father. I don't want to be the family stud. Frida and I are getting married because we want to be married to each other, not because we want to be parents. If somebody needs to carry on the family name," he said coolly, "let my brother do it. Saddle him with the honor."

"But you are the eldest!" The chords stood out on Mr. Loeff's neck.

"I didn't choose to be," George said levelly. "And I don't choose to fill the role Jews have always assigned to the eldest son."

"You'll reconsider this or there'll be no wedding." threatened his father. "You must be out of your mind. This is adolescent nonsense. I was willing to help you provide a home for Frida, a home worthy of the wife of my son, but I won't subsidize any such idiocy as this. A home has a family in it, not a couple of empty-headed pleasure-seekers."

Frida rose and went to stand before Mr. Loeff. "Father Loeff," she said laying her hands on his arms. "I don't want the kind of home you want for me. I want to keep my job, I want life to go on like it is. I've never been the kind of woman my father wanted me to be and I'm not the kind of woman you evidently want me to be either. I'm just the kind of woman George wants. Can't that be all right with you?"

"No." he said flatly.

"Will you fire me?" Her blue eyes danced with wicked glee.

"I never fire a good employee." he said. "I had hoped you would be my good daughter."

"I will be," she kissed him on the cheek. "I can be a good daughter without being a mother, you wait and see. And I'll probably be a better daughter without children than I would be with them hanging on my skirts and taking up all my time."

"It won't do." His tone was final.

George and Frida slipped away a few days later and were married in a civil ceremony at City Hall without a single member of either family present. They went back to their respective jobs without breaking stride and continued their pursuit of fun and fortune. They moved into an apartment in the building on the Graben and Frida not only kept her job, she took over management of the building. Papa paid his rent along with everyone else. She had inherited a little autocratic streak of her own.

In spite of a seething undercurrent of unrest in the country from 1933 to 1938, life was a bowl of cherries for Frida and George Loeff. They floated on top of the everyday life in Vienna, they ignored the tension building around them, they were unaware of the fissure that had developed in Viennese society, separating the laboring class from the rest of the populace. Then Austria was gored by a major revolution in 1934 as the workers of the urban centers tried to wrest control of the government from the old hands which had continued in office since the Great War. After 1919, the politicians running the country steadily shifted toward the right as the economic situation of Austria did not improve. One segment of the right wing was the Austrian Nazi Party, which ferociously put down the rebellion when it broke out in the smaller outlying factory towns. Escalation of the resistance brought riots into the streets around the factories of Vienna. For weeks, life was hazardous throughout working class neighborhoods and around the university where student sympathizers battled the police in support of the unionists. For two years the country was in turmoil, but the Loeffs kept on with the good life as though politics had nothing to do with them. Every sunny Sunday, well away from the districts in turmoil, they attended concerts and strolled in the park dedicated to Mozart beside the canal. Saturday nights, they haunted the cabarets or attended the theater. They spent many midweek evenings sitting around with friends discussing philosophy and Art and the latest movies from the United States. They, and their wide circle of friends, were dedicated to the new life being fashioned by cinema offerings from Hollywood, and European film makers. Avoidance of traditions of the past and politics of the present was a cardinal virtue among the "literati." For them, Austrian Nazis were funny paper people who simply could not be taken seriously. The volcano building under their feet, a volcano which would bury the past forever and make politics the most important aspect of life for many a long weary day into the future, was ignored.

March, 1938, when Der Fuehrer's troops marched into Austria, George and Frida Loeff were stunned awake. A frightening new era was born, and overnight George, the Jew, became a hunted man. Those Jews who held high positions were the first to feel the wrath of Hitler's hatred for the despised "race." Too well-educated, too highly placed, too important in his company to escape immediate notice, George was among the first victims. He was dismissed from the rug factory. His father escaped prompt dismissal from the textile factory because the firm was owned by Czechoslovakian interests, and for a time the Germans made no move toward foreign-based corporations. For months, the Nazis walked softly around any of the industrial enterprises home-based in Prague. There was no point in arousing the Czechs to the possibilities the Nazis might have in mind for them.

The next blow for George and Frida landed when the Germans took a census of the Austrian population revealing all of the Jewish-Gentile marriages. Such marriages were denounced from the pulpits of Nazi orthodoxy, the newspapers now firmly under German control. They were labeled "abhorrent and unnatural." Frida became a target for those Viennese who pandered to the occupying Germans, people who had either been closet Nazis, or who overnight were reborn as proud Aryans. Rabidly anxious to please the conqueror, formerly tolerant Austrians launched into a campaign to dissolve all these detestable marital liaisons through the force of public opinion. Frida was visited by members of the neighborhood committees of the Nazi Party. They ordered her to divorce her Jewish husband as an act of Austrian patriotism. At first she laughed them to scorn, but when day after day as she rounded a corner on the streets and ran into a member of the neighborhood committee, and night after night, when she came home from work to find more "Aryans" lying in wait for her in the lobby, she stopped laughing.

"Don't argue with them, Frida." George begged. "It will only make it worse."

"But you can't ignore them!" she stormed "they won't let you. Every time I even go to the toilet at work someone follows me and shouts over the partition at me."

"You think I don't know?" George retorted. "Only today, when I went out to market, there was a bunch of harpies outside the grocers whom I never saw before, but they knew me. 'Jew bastard.' they yelled. 'Why didn't you marry a kike like yourself?' One of them spit on me and another knocked my hat off and kicked it into the gutter."

"It's none of their business!" Frida snapped. "I'd like to pull hair, I get so mad."

'You pull hair and we'll both be in jail." George warned. "They'd love an excuse."

"What are we to do?' she demanded.

"What can we do?" he answered helplessly.

Her family began to be harassed too. People knocked on her father's door at all hours and left leaflets denouncing mixed marriages. Her parents, like Frida and George, received phone calls in the middle of the night. Both the Loeffs and the Kwiatkowskis became terrified by the attention focused on them because of this "profane" marriage. Then the cajoling and persuading slowed, and the threats began. Anonymous voices on the other end of the line promised to castrate George, to rape Frida, to kill the "damned Jew." Their families began to fear for George's life. For several years, prior to the Anschluss, George's brother traveled back and forth to Riga in Latvia on business. March 12th, 1938, he was winding up some business in Riga just as news of the Anschluss hit the worldwide press. He simply did not come home. He stayed in Riga out of harm's way. Both families agreed that George should go as quickly as possible to join his brother.

The Jewish community in Riga was receiving and aiding Jews pouring in from all the eastern European countries about to be overrun by Hitler. They sent word via George's brother that they would find a place for George if he wanted to come. George needed no urging, he was ready to fly at a moment's notice, but Frida wanted a different solution. She wanted them to go out together. The moment the Jewish repression began, she and George went to the Australian embassy to file for immigrant status in that tolerant country. They also filed with the American Embassy, but there was little hope that anything would come of that application. The United States had accepted the Anschluss without protest. They noncommitally added Austria to the German Quota without increasing the number of Germans to be admitted into the United States. It would be years before the Loeffs names could reach the top of the German list. In order to leave together, Frida and George were willing to accept entrance into any neutral country. Weeks went by, and it became obvious there was no possible way to spring the two of them at the same time. George would have to go out alone, and Frida would have to join him when she could. She bowed to the inescapable. But how to get him out?

The Jewish enclave in Riga quickly obtained the necessary permits from Latvia for George to come into the country as a political refugee. They found a room to let near his brother, and rented it in his name. They secured a teaching job for him with which he could support himself. However, the required exit permit would have to be issued by the Austrian government, now under German control. George made application for the exit permit. He was stonewalled by a mountain of paperwork the Nazis put in his way. Requests for private records were interminable, then disappeared once the Loeffs had complied. Public records seemed to get shredded before George could retrieve the documents the Nazis demanded: birth certificate, tax records, deeds and titles to any properties he stood to inherit, every scrap of identification he could produce. Frida began making the rounds carrying the requests herself hoping that her gentile status would carry the day. Instead of securing the necessary documents, she found herself facing a constant barrage of denunciation about her marriage wherever she went. If she brought in tax records, she had to meet with another interrogator or small committee to talk about her unholy marriage before being allowed to talk to the official with whom she needed to conduct business. No matter how many requirements were met, the government produced more. There seemed to be no resolution to George's situation and no peace to be had as long as they remained married.

Finally, at still another family conference held to discuss ways and means, someone came up with an idea that might work. It was proposed that a shrewd move might be to let the Nazis think Frida was capitulating, was succumbing to the incessant pressure she was under. If she went to the immigration authorities alone and applied for a single visa in George's name they might think that the younger Loeffs were separating, that with George safely out of the way she would get the divorce. The ruse worked. Deluded by the urgency with which she pleaded for an exit visa for George alone, the papers came through quickly. In January, 1939, George dusted the soil of Austria from his feet and headed North. To keep up the illusion that the couple was separating, Frida did not accompany him to the train, only his mother and father went to see him off.

Austria began to suffer from the brain drain the Nazi Jewish policy had inflicted on the annexed country. 80% of the Viennese doctors were Jewish and most of the country's scientists. Most of the Jews leaving Austria that year were among the intellectual elite, assisted by influential gentiles not yet cowed by the invaders. Only after that talent was put to work by the Allied countries that accepted them, did it become obvious just how stupidly blind the collaborators and the Nazis had been. The chemists, almost without exception, went to work in weapons development and war materials production for the enemies of the Third Reich. January, 1939, George was launched on his long journey to become one of them.

In Riga, refugees were not allowed to hold any of the jobs the government listed as "work," but teaching was not so categorized. Teaching was so poorly paid that a man could barely earn enough in the classroom to keep body and soul together. It was not regarded as a profession that needed to be protected against the tide of incoming professionals. George went into the "non-work" of teaching High School Chemistry. The job would keep him alive until Frida could get out to join him. The situation in Riga was unique in European politics. When, in the summer of 1940, Hitler signed the Non-Aggression Pact with Stalin they agreed that Latvia would go to Russia in the event there was any change in political boundaries, changes which in fact were already on the drawing boards in both Berlin and Moscow. Those drawing boards were hidden from the eyes of the rest of the world. Both signatories to the agreement wanted time to prepare their separate blueprints. So long as the two nations respected the treaty, Jews were safe in Latvia for the Russians had no plan for Jews remotely similar to those of Hitler. Too many of the Party Leaders in Russia were Jews themselves. The Loeff brothers were safe for the time being. Now the focus turned to how Frida was to go out without arousing suspicion.

She didn't dare apply for a travel permit to Latvia, the Nazis would have known immediately that they'd been duped and would not let her go. The Riga Jewish committee again took a hand in the Loeffs' affairs, and made contact with a family in Estonia. Through their intercession, the family invited her to come to them for a visit. In order for any Austrian of whatever "purity" to travel outside the state, proof had to be presented to the authorities that the applicant had been invited to visit someone, somewhere. Secondly, the would-be traveler had to give the authorities the address of the family with whom they would be staying, the location where they could be found if Austria wanted to find them. A temporary travel permit for a good Catholic gentile, who was in the process of divorcing her Jewish husband, to visit friends in Estonia was easy enough to obtain.

Frida kept the letter of invitation constantly with her so it couldn't get "lost," as so many other papers had during their efforts to get George out. She had a whole new wardrobe made to see her through whatever lay ahead. Among the clothes she ordered were a sturdy wool suit, a sturdy wool coat, two or three good light-weight dresses, two or three heavy wool skirts, and a couple of heavy knitted sweaters. A stout leather purse, underwear and blouses completed her "traveling wardrobe." She was not leaving as a fashion plate, she did not wish to attract attention to herself, she was leaving prepared to survive. In the midst of her preparations she had a discrete phone call from her mother-in-law. Mrs. Loeff suggested they meet to discuss "your separation." With all Jews' phones tapped, people spoke in code. Let the authorities think Mrs. Loeff wanted to talk about the imminent "divorce."

They met at an open air cafe in the park where they could talk in plain view of watchful eyes and not be overheard. Mrs. Loeff came right to the point. "Frida, I have something for you. George's father and I would love to give you and George the money to see you through, but you know how it is with us now. Every transaction we make is known at Gestapo Headquarters immediately.

Frida stirred her coffee and sighed. "We know, Mother Loeff. We know." She wanted to reach out and touch her mother-in-law's cheek but she didn't dare. "If only we could take you with us."

Mrs. Loeff looked away, her eyes wide to check the tears. She breathed deeply until she had herself in hand, then she turned again to Frida. Her voice was husky with emotion. "None of that my darling." she said.

She stretched one hand, balled into a fist, across the table. "Put your hand over mine, Frida, and I'll withdraw mine as though I didn't want you to touch me. What I'll leave under your hand is the best we could do for you. They came to me from my mother. We thought you could get a pair of shoes made with hollow heels and put one of them in each shoe. When you get to wherever you're going, they will get you started."

For a long moment Frida stared at the closed hand lying on the table then looked pleadingly into Mrs. Loeff's still face. There was no response. Forcing herself to match her mother-in-law's tenuous self-control Frida leaned forward as though to plead a case. She followed her instructions and wrapped her hand around her mother-in-law's fist. Mrs. Loeff extracted her hand as though burned by Frida's touch. Frida's palm rested on two solid objects. She wrapped her fingers around the gift and made a fist of her own. Pretending to feel rejected, she leaned back in her chair and returned her hand to her lap. She stuck both hands in her pockets and stared across at George's mother.

"Whatever this is, Mother Loeff, we'll always be grateful."

Mrs. Loeff rose abruptly dabbing at her eyes. "Thank God you didn't have that baby." was all she said before hurrying off.

Only when she was safely home did Frida take her hand from her coat pocket to see what she had been given by the doomed mother of her husband. Her heart almost stopped. There in her hand lay a pair of earrings fit for a coronation! They were perfectly matched, and exquisitely cut. Their brilliance dazzled the eye. Each earring was a solitary diamond which weighed at least 2 1/2 carats. She stared in wonder at the jewels. She'd never seen them before. They must have been locked away in a vault for a very long time. Suddenly she was racked with sobbing as tears coursed down her cheeks. Her mother's, Mrs. Loeff had said. These diamonds must have graced George's grandmother's appearances at the opera and at great balls held in the days of the Empire. They were too grand for lesser occasions. Frida knew she'd never wear them. Their loveliness was too decadent for this brutal age. Their only value lay in what they'd bring when sold. Every ugly thing about the present rose up in contradiction to the beauty in her palm. These priceless diamonds must again be hidden away, this time in such an inglorious hiding place as a pair of shoe heels.

In March, she used the letter of invitation to secure the government's permission to take a vacation, and boarded a train for Riga where, according to her ticket, she would transfer to another train to get to Estonia. To avoid suspicion that anything more significant than a holiday was underway, only her twin sister went laughing with her to the station. All the way across Czechoslovakia and Poland Frida held her breath. Every time there was a passport check her heart pounded in spite of the fact that there was no red J stamped on her documents. The trip passed uneventfully and she arrived safely in Riga without mishap. When the train pulled in George was on the platform waiting for her. Frida came down the steps and George wrapped her in his arms like a drowning man hugs a life preserver. They were almost delirious with relief. For days they honeymooned, they clung to each other, they repeated their vows of love over and over, but when the euphoria passed they faced the grim reality that they were transients in a place where they could not stay, yet they had no other place to go.

George earned so little in his position as a teacher they barely had enough income to pay the rent on the tiny apartment the committee had secured for them. They used up what funds Frida had brought with her and, as a refugee, she could not get work. They couldn't pay for passage to Australia or America should either country offer them sanctuary without using one of the earrings, and it was too dangerous in their situation to be trying to sell diamonds of that value. Their families in Vienna had to come through again and again. Between the time Frida left in late March, before the outbreak of war September I, 1939, Frida's twin sister made several trips to Riga to bring them money to tide them over, and to help them with the cost of immigration should they be able to find a place to go. Each time she returned to Vienna, she made the rounds to hound the Australian and American embassies on her sister's behalf, but nothing ever came of her efforts.

They were not the only ones living on tenterhooks; life for George's and Frida's families was constantly worsening as the Nazis methodically strangled Austria. First, George's mother and father had to turn over their lovely home to provide housing for high-ranking Nazi officials. They even had to leave the furniture for them. Soon after March, 1939, when the Nazis overran Czechoslovakia, George's father was dismissed from the textile factory. The Loeffs were forced to turn over all their stocks and bonds and jewelry and Art collection and bank accounts to the warlords and were reduced to destitution. Frida's family, while distancing themselves from the Loeffs publicly, had to meet them surreptitiously to share as much of what they had, or that they could get their hands on in the way of food and fuel, to keep their daughter's in-laws alive. Life became a nightmare on both ends of the umbilical cord that stretched across so many miles of hostile territory.

The outbreak of total War in September, 1939, changed everything for George and Frida. Russia marched into Latvia soon after Germany marched into Poland, and the ties with

Vienna were irrevocably broken. There were no more visits from Frida's twin sister, no more support from home, no more contact of any kind with those they'd left behind. Even more ominous for the three Loeffs stranded in Latvia, once that country was pronounced a province of Russia, Australia immediately closed her embassy there and returned all the papers they had on hand to the applicants still waiting for visas. To relieve the population pressure in her new province, Russia offered Russian "citizenship" to all intellectuals hiding out in Latvia, Jew or non-Jew. Each of the three Loeffs faced a horrendous decision. There probably would be safety in accepting the offer of Russian citizenship, but Russian citizenship would put an end to their dream of immigrating to Australia or the United States. They debated and debated.

George's brother's was in the most dangerous spot of the three. If Jews refused the offer of Russian citizenship, anyone holding a passport marked with the infamous red J would be shipped to Russia to work in the coal mines. George was protected by Frida's unmarked passport, but his brother was naked before this monstrous choice. In the end he refused "citizenship" and George and Frida had to watch helplessly as he was herded onto a train carrying a load of workers toward Russia to be impressed as slave labor. The slight young man with the spectacles didn't stand a chance of survival. It was only a matter of months before they learned that he died within weeks of arriving at the mines.

Shocked by the news, their own plight loomed larger than before. Their situation grew more and more desperate as weeks went by, and their number at the U.S. Embassy remained a long way down the list. If they couldn't go to America where were they to find refuge? What was to become of them? One day, after another fruitless trip to the embassy, Frida was disconsolately climbing the stairs to their apartment when she smelled gas. In a flash of intuition, she knew exactly what was happening. Heart pounding she ran frantically up the remaining flight and burst into their tiny apartment. There was George with his head in the oven, the gas turned on, and a farewell note to her lying on the table. She went to pieces.

"Why?" she screamed, racing to turn off the jet, "Why? What are you doing?!"

"Without me you could go home," he moaned. "With me you'll die here like I will."

Hysterically she raged at him. " Are you mad? I gave up everything to be here with you. I left my family! I could be safe in Vienna with my sister! I could still have my job! I'm not a Jew! This is your fate we're living out, not mine! I've been through hell for you and now you think I could go home? I can never go home! It's too late! How could you do this? You would really take the coward's way out and leave me? You're all the home I've got!"

She put the palms of her hands over her eyes as though she could not bear to look at him. "Why!" she demanded, her voice muffled by her wrists. "Why?!"

George stared up at her wordlessly, his eyes pools of weariness. He lifted his hands in a futile gesture then let them fall helplessly into his lap.

Frida turned away and made a circle of the room rubbing her temples and shouting at the walls. "Because fiends hound us? Because we can't find our way out? Because your brother is dead? Thousands have died and millions more will. People who have the courage to live will live. But you! We're still alive! We still have opportunity. Something will turn up! But you, you want to throw everything away." Her lip curled contemptuously as tears poured down her face.

"What did you think I'd feel for the rest of my life?" she sobbed. "Ashamed! That's what I'd feel. Ashamed that I married a man who couldn't see it through. How can you say you love me, and think of doing this to me." Her voice rose to a wail.

She stopped walking and bent over almost double. Bunched up she rocked back and forth on her toes. It was an amazing posture. "Weak!" she moaned, "Weak."

George sat queasy in his chair, his head between his hands, his elbows on his knees while tears dripped down onto his shoes. At last, when exhaustion began to take over, Frida collapsed into the chair across the table from him.

"Why?" she asked once more, pleading for an answer that would make it all right.

"I told you," he sobbed miserably. "I told you."

"It isn't enough," she said in a drained voice. "It isn't enough."

George looked up into her bewildered tired eyes and reached out a hand across the table to cover hers. She did not withdraw from his touch but she did not return the pressure. They sat locked in silence until the day ended and the world outside their window was engulfed in darkness. Then, without a word, Frida rose, undressed, and went to bed. There was little conversation between them in the ensuing days, but every time she left for the embassy, George went out to walk the streets, never remaining in the apartment alone. Neither of them ever mentioned the incident again, but it was always there between them.

Since Latvia was no longer a free nation, the U.S. Embassy at last was forced to close up shop, like it or not, and obey the Russians' orders to get out. During the final days between the announcement that the Americans were leaving and the locking up of the premises, Frida frantically haunted the place trying to wring a visa from the staff. Everyone knew the ambassador still had twenty four valid passports to be awarded before he boarded a train to Sweden and headed for Washington, D.C. The decision as to which of the thousands of applicants should receive the few precious documents kept him awake nights. Finally, he threw quotas out the window. He wasn't going to be limited in his choice by nationality. He made the decision to choose whom he would choose from among those persons he felt would make the greatest contributions to the United States as new citizens. It was a cliffhanger for people whose very lives were at stake. The day before he was to leave, the Ambassador finally announced the names of the lucky ones among the thousands who not could follow him to America.

Because of his scientific background, George and Frida were chosen! Only twenty four priceless pieces of paper, and two of them were theirs! It was a miracle. An outrageous, incomprehensible miracle! They couldn't grasp it. Worthy people with far higher quota numbers than theirs had been passed over while they were handed the greatest gift they would ever receive. It was an indecent fairy tale, and numbingly unbelievable. They were shaken by the sudden reprieve. It was embarrassing to face those left behind whose fate was as dangerous as their own, especially those with small children whose lives might now be forfeited. But guilt was not enough to offset their inexpressible relief. THEY were out of the jaws of the Nazis, THEY were on their way to America!

The Russians stipulated that all those who received the twenty four visas would have to have them processed for exit in the Moscow office of the American embassy since Riga was no longer a national capital. It meant two long expensive days to get to Moscow, and another two expensive days in the Russian capitol while the paper process necessary for departure was completed, but there was no way around it. The Soviet loved the trappings of bureaucracy even more than Americans or Germans. From Moscow, the only open path to the West was due East across the vastness of the U.S.S.R. All routes across Europe had been closed off by the furious fighting between the armies of Hitler and Stalin. Frida and George did not complain. Properly stamped visas in hand they hustled their bags to the train and climbed aboard as quickly as possible. It took more money than time to get the paper work done. Prices were astronomical in Moscow. It also took more of their slender funds for hotel bills and food than it had for the tickets on the Trans-Siberian Railroad to Harbin. Unchecked wartime inflation was sending the Russian economy into orbit. By the time they found their seats in their assigned compartment on The Trans-Siberian Express, they were financially on the ragged edge of insufficiency. There was so little left of their slender immigration funds they would have panicked if it had not been for the fortune in the heels of the shoes on Frida's feet.

When they left Moscow it was mid-August, 1940. The countryside was green and lovely. Frida sat beside the train window staring unseeingly as Russia and its variegated landscape rolled past. George watched Frida. Since that awful day when she'd found him in the act of taking his own life, she had spoken few words and eaten almost nothing. A little cereal, a swallow or two of soup, a soft-boiled egg half-eaten, an apple. She was wasting away in front of him. Her clothes hung loosely on her athletic frame. It was frightening. Her sorrow was so deep he didn't know how to disturb it. He was miserable. It took five long days for them to cross Siberia and reach the Manchurian border, five days of silence between them, five days of suspended animation while crossing a landscape so tranquil it was hard to imagine that a war was raging behind them.

The moment the train slid across that invisible line drawn on maps that delineated one area as Russia, the next as

Manchuria, Japan controlled their fate. The train was immediately shunted onto a siding where Japanese soldiers boarded the cars. With no exceptions, they made all the passengers on board their prisoners. Armed with machine guns, they systematically robbed everyone of their cameras, confiscated some passports and visas without explanation, and forced their owners off the train. Luckily, neither the Loeffs, nor the rest of the escapees from Latvia were detained. They were allowed to continue on in chilled silence to Harbin where they changed trains for Diaram. At Diaram, they were herded like cattle onto a ship bound for Kobe, Japan.

The island of Honshu rose like a mystical landscape from the Pacific as they approached. Mount Fujiyama, clad in an ermine head covering, provided an ethereal background for the lush terraces in the near distance. Deceptively serene, Japan beckoned like a peaceful oasis afloat on a watery desert. But reality closed in the moment the ship was tied up at the dock. Immediately, the twenty four emigres faced the serious problem of how and where to get transportation to America. War between the United States and Japan lay a year away, but relations between the two countries were already stretched taut by suspicion and rival ambitions for Southeast Asia. Few passenger ships sailed from Japan for America, and those that did were overbooked. A lot of Asian-Americans wanted to go home, fast.

The emigres decided to break up into two groups, one half of them would search out all the travel agencies in the city. The other group would canvass the ship captains whose vessels were anchored in the Harbor. The men would go to the wharves, the women to the agencies. Anti-British as well as Anti-American feeling ran high in Japan in 1940. England was at war with Japan's ally, and the British Navy was controlling the sea lanes of Southeast Asia inhibiting Japan's movements in that direction. It was wise for all blond people to stay off the streets so as not to attract attention to themselves. Frida was decidedly blond. The rest of the twenty four looked Mediterranean and were far less conspicuous, but Frida stuck out like a beacon. Her blue eyes, blond hair and fair complexion coupled with her tweed suit made her look terribly English. They left the hotel in groups of three. Arm-in-arm, Frida placed in the middle between two companions to protect her, her little team set off in one direction while George and two other men headed for the docks.

Before World War II, most Japanese men still wore kimonos. Japanese men in western dress were primarily young radicals and students. The hatred of these young people for the English and their American cousins was even more intense than the hatred directed toward those two nationalities by the less idealistic general population. The streets of Japanese cities were almost all cobbled, and in high heeled shoes a woman had to pick her way along very carefully. The three women were making slow progress down a hilly street that led to the harbor when suddenly Frida was hit solidly in the back sending her sprawling to her knees on the hard stones. The wind was knocked out of her, her stockings were torn, and her knees were bleeding. The indignity of it all, the suddenness of the attack, and the helplessness she felt left her in tears when she recovered her breath enough to cry. She turned over and looked up into the faces of two young men in western clothes looming over her, separating her menacingly from her friends, shouting incomprehensible obscenities at her. As the tears poured down her face they laughed raucously, mockingly, all the while continuing the barrage of insults she could not understand. Obviously they were trying to attract attention to themselves and their patriotism. Then abruptly their tirade was interrupted by a man, obviously an Englishman, who strode angrily down the hill waving a walking stick in the air. He shouted something to them in their own tongue which caused them to break off their abusive philippics almost in mid sentence. Scornfully, they turned and stalked slowly away in haughty silence. While the Englishman stood guard, Frida's friends helped her to her feet. Unable to stop sniffling, she stood brushing herself off, trying to regain her composure. When she could speak she turned to her rescuer.

'Why?" she asked, "What did I do?"

"Nothing," he said. "You didn't do anything. Where were you going? I'll walk with you and explain as we go. It's best not to stand around in this neighborhood."

The man walked with them to the nearest travel agency, and as they walked he laid out for them the explosive situation they'd walked into.

"Japan's a powder keg," he said. "It's only a matter of time until it explodes. All we Westerners are trying to get out ahead of the maelstrom. I've been trying for months to sell my business so I can go home, but they want to steal it from me, not buy it. The prices I've been offered are insulting."

He opened the door to the agency and stepped aside to let them enter. Without missing a syllable, he continued: "No Westerner is welcome here, but the Americans and we Brits are hated more than anyone else. Germans have a fairly easy time of it because after all, Japan has a treaty with Germany. Japan is not at war with the United States yet, but everyone but the isolationist Americans knows that it's only a matter of time. Neither country can afford to back down out here. The Japs are already, technically at war with England. Both Englishmen and Americans walk lightly and sleep lightly on this side of the globe. Anyone unlucky enough to wind up here finds it too uncomfortable to remain. It's best you get out of town as fast as you can."

There was no need for him to urge them on. They had no desire to see any more of the anger around them. As they assured him fervently that the only thing they wanted was a way to get out he gallantly offered his services as an interpreter. He made inquiries for them in Japanese and learned that there was an eighteen-ton freighter bound for Seattle out of Kobe on which they could book passage.

"You won't think much of the accommodations," he said. "These old freighters are smelly and damp and crude. It'll be more like buying steerage on an immigrant ship than modern ocean travel. But I'd take it if I were you.'

"When will there be another passenger ship? A real passenger ship?" one of the women asked.

"Maybe not at all. It depends on the course of events. This kind of ship is the best you can count on running until war actually breaks. I don't think you dare take the chance on a better ship coming in."

They looked at each other, silently agreeing, then turned back to their benefactor. "Tell him we'll take them."

All twenty four were crowded aboard a vessel that regularly carried few passengers. Life on the ship, they found, was all the Englishman had warned them it would be. The food was plentiful but plain, which didn't matter to Frida who continued to starve because she could not swallow. There was plenty of clean water. Otherwise they were as cold and as miserable as immigrants to the United States in the l9th century had been. Winter storms bumptuously churning the seas kept most of the little group of homeless wanderers seasick and listless in their narrow bunks. The storms sent the vessel far north of its usual route which added considerably to the length of the voyage. For six debilitating weeks they lived in the dim light of the ship's hold. All of them were exhausted by the time they reached landfall, but none so completely worn out as Frida. Her normal weight of l30 lbs had dropped off since Riga to ninety-one. When the ship disgorged its cargo, human and otherwise, onto the docks in Seattle she was physically a wreck. She had to have food and she had to have rest or she wouldn't survive.

As soon as they disembarked, George went to Jewish Services for help. He knew of no other source. The placement committee at Jewish Services found a family who had offered earlier to take a couple temporarily until the Committee could place them. They were given an address, placed in a cab and sent off to their first encounter with Americans. It was as inhospitable a sanctuary as could be found. The host family took one look at Frida and put them in an attic room which was damp, unheated and freezing cold. The family was sure she was diseased. And when they learned the Loeffs had come steerage from Japan they were sure that both of them had picked up vermin along the way. There was a toilet up there in the attic, and a wash basin, but no tub or shower, nor would the family allow them to use one of theirs. The roof leaked and in the perpetual rains of Seattle they had to sleep under opened umbrellas night after night. The bed was never completely dry.

"I think I'll die here." Frida whispered to herself one day. She sighed. "What a long journey to such a grave."

George went job-hunting, but for a refugee there was no job to be had in Seattle in l940. They had come a year too soon. Government contracts for Boeing Aircraft had not yet been issued. Wartime employment had not opened up. The depression was letting up enough for Americans who had been out of work for a decade to begin to go back to private employment, but there were not enough jobs to have spares for newcomers. The best George could find was a job plucking chickens at the local poultry plant. All day he worked bent over the great tubs of steaming water into which the chickens were plunged to loosen their quills from their skin. While George sweated Frida lay alone in the damp cold bed listening to the rain spattering off the umbrella over her. She developed a cough which kept them both awake at night as they lay huddled together to keep warm. At the end of ten days their hosts appealed to the relief committee to give them relief by getting these sick strangers out of their house. Assessing the local employment situation, the committee decided the Loeffs would have to be moved to another city. Seattle offered no work for a research chemist. The only job the committee turned up anywhere on the West Coast was in San Bernardino, CA., a job in a grain elevator where George would be expected to hoist fifty pound bags of wheat to his shoulder and carry them up ramps into railroad cars. Obviously, this puny little man, who had never done a day's manual labor in his life, could not do that.

George was in despair. He still dreamed of returning to research, to a laboratory where his training, talent and experience could be put to use. Research laboratories are located, as a rule, in very large urban centers or in Universities. Frida wanted the committee to find a place for them in New York. In New York she had relatives and they knew a few people there who luckily had escaped from the old country before them. The Seattle committee contacted New York Jewish Services which unhesitatingly refused their request. New York was awash with refugees coming out of Europe via Britain, Holland and France. They informed the Seattle committee that the West Coast would have to take care of its own problems. On the West Coast the only major city where such laboratories might be located was Los Angeles.

To move anywhere in the United States, a refugee had to produce a letter of guarantee from a guarantor, a sponsor, who promised to provide for the refugee(s) should he/she/they not be able to provide for themselves. The only other place besides New York City where they had any contacts was Chicago. In Chicago lived Frida's twin sister's, sister-in-law, who was married to a cellist with the Metropolitan Symphony Orchestra. Chicago offered no hope as a haven for the windy city was up to its eyeballs in its own refugee problem, but the cellist had lots of contacts in Los Angeles. He got in touch with a musician friend of his working in the movie industry, a member of one of the big movie company orchestras. This man was Jewish and his parents had been immigrants themselves. Satisfied by the Chicago cellist that the couple stranded in Seattle were people of drive and ability, the cellist, someone who only knew of them third hand, sent the precious letter guaranteeing sponsorship required for their removal to Southern California. The Seattle committee was so relieved to have them off their hands they gave them tickets for the train ride along the west coast through scenery so beautiful it was balm for the soul. Frida roused from her lethargy at last. To be heading for the sunshine of California after sodden Seattle was like being given a ticket to Paradise. Better still, for the first time in over a year she was traveling toward the future rather than running in paroxysms of fear from the past.

With the last, this time the very last, of their immigration money, they rented a little apartment in Culver City and furnished it from the Salvation Army Store. George kept being amazed at how the empty purse continued to produce the absolute minimum needed for the immediate crisis. He went job-hunting. Frida was still too weak to do more than walk a few blocks to the market and back with a small bag of groceries. The irony of dragging herself along with almost no money in her pocket while balanced on diamonds worth a mighty ransom delighted her. Until now, she'd stretched out their slender funds and stretched them out again without disturbing those earrings, and she had no intention of breaking open her shoe heels at this point. She had walked on a small fortune from Austria through Poland to Latvia, from Latvia to Moscow, from Moscow to Japan, from Japan to Seattle, and from Seattle to California. In all that walking those earrings had come to seem like the thread of life that kept her from losing her way. They were her assurance there was a future. To spend them now was unthinkable. Some day, maybe, they would buy a home for her and George if there was no other way to acquire one, but until that day she would continue to walk on them. They might be the means by which the family, George's parents and her own, could be brought to safety, the means of reunion with her beloved twin.

George found work so quickly they had no time to worry. Research chemists were as scarce on the West Coast in 1940 as ostrich eggs. He found a job in the laboratory of a dye factory, a far cry from esoteric research, but light years away from chicken plucking. His salary was large enough that they could eat and pay the rent easily. When George came bursting in with the news, Frida wept for the first time since she'd turned off the gas in Riga. As the days went by and they both relaxed into the knowledge that their nightmare was truly over, Frida began to put on weight. Color came back to her face, her hair, that had become as dull as a twine wig, had luster again, and her confident stride returned. It was only a matter of weeks before she was ready to go back to work herself. Like George's pure-science, her accounting went up in blue smoke. Women in the United States were not accountants. Bookkeepers, yes, accountants, no. She had to settle for a bookkeeping job at Woolworth's in Los Angeles. It was boring, it was not a challenge, and in her eyes it was demeaning. Since American firms were not impressed with her European experience nor with her European education, she decided to enroll in University Extension Classes at night after work. They had little to teach her, but they had the precious diploma she hoped would open doors for her into a career worthy of her background. She went through the exercise. She got a degree in Accounting, but what she wanted, to become a Certified Public Accountant, eluded her. Women couldn't even be licensed as Certified Public Accountants in 1941 in the United States of America. The "old boys" network had things sewn up tight. Men had locked the door on most professions, locked it from the inside, and no female outside was allowed entrance. Professions in business were especially male preserves. How long George would have mixed colors or Frida kept books if World War II had not broken out, is, of course, pure conjecture. War did break out, and, like a lot of underprivileged Americans, George and Frida got their chances at last.

With the mobilization of the United States' male population, jobs opened up everywhere. Military contracts were let that demanded highly-trained personnel, most of which had already gone off to fight. George went to work for Hawthorne, a California company that camouflaged ships, and other weapons of war. Here was Research and Development (R&D) work to do at last. Quickly he became head of Hawthorne's chemistry department and stayed in that job for the duration. In fact he stayed in that job for the rest of his working life. When the war ended, Hawthorne went into the detergent business. George found himself creating soap, not shadows, until he was forced by a series of heart attacks to retreat to his Art books.

In the twinkling of an eye, World War II scrubbed American scruples about women doing men's work. Frida went to work as the accountant for a firm employing 3,000 people. Her skill and competence became glaringly apparent as men left for military service and women who had never balanced a check book before were hired to replace them. Frida had to take over the training of these neophytes. 4F (physically unfit for military service) young men found themselves being trained by a woman rather than a drill sergeant. The world had turned upside down it seemed. But once they became literate in accounting, the men moved on into positions of management leaving Frida behind. The discrimination against females had not disappeared after all, it had only been loosened to meet the emergency. Frida complained bitterly to the top brass, but her protests fell on deaf ears; women could not become part of the power-pack world of male control. Women did not sit in private offices or make policy. She quit.

For the rest of the war she did accounting and bookkeeping for companies too small to set up a whole department. Never having worked for small businesses before she found the one-woman office had its rewards. She did not have supervisors who knew less than she did. She was not going to train some male child who would then be advanced over her because of what she'd taught him. Alone in her work, she was her own boss. But such jobs had no advancement. Then the war was over, the boys came back, the accounting world became solidly male again, and the doors closed permanently on any hope Frida had for recognition and acceptance. That is, the doors were closed until the Marshall Plan rescued Europe from its economic prostration.

The Marshall Plan created Volkswagen, and before long Volkswagen came to Culver City. Volkswagen had a European view of women in the work place. Also, Volkswagen needed someone who understood European business practices as well as being familiar with the intricacies of the American market. Being fluent and literate in the German language was also an asset few people in the United States had acquired by the start of the post-war era. Not withstanding the rest of her background which Volkswagen appreciated, her language facility was the most important feather of all in her cap. They snapped her up and presented her with a ladder a woman with her qualifications could climb after all. A woman with her qualifications could climb the ladder until she reached the level of company officer, that is. No woman could become controller of the company or have a key to the executive's washroom. Frida had to settle for the job of assistant controller with an office of her own, her name in black letters on the frosted pane of glass in the door, and most of the perks of the upper echelon hers for the taking. The Controller attended the all male Board meetings and went to the executives' lunchroom, but the assistant controller ran the financial arm of the business. Frida accepted the limitations of the job and stayed with Volkswagen until she retired.

Their financial worries behind them, George resumed his pursuit of Art History. He haunted the Huntington Library, he attended lectures at museums, he filled their house with Art books until he had acquired the largest private collection of published works on Art in California. Frida developed a circle of friends with more prosaic interests with whom she spent evenings while George was attending lectures. She and George shared pleasure in the theater, concerts, dinners with friends, and spirited discussions of the events of the day. Altogether, they were content with the life they had built around good food, good company, and their home -- except for the ever-present haunting guilt about the good life that had come their way. Frida could not slough off the past. The more affluent she became the more she agonized about the family left behind in Austria. From the day they arrived in the United States a constant refrain ran over and over in the back of her mind. 'How is it with them now?'

In the earliest days after their arrival in Los Angeles, she had written daily to her family, but the letters were all returned marked "Undeliverable" because the U.S. government could not get mail into areas under Hitler's control. Allowing mail to come through from the United States would have helped undermine the Nazis when those letters refuted much of Geobbels' propaganda. The Germans were keenly aware of how critical it was to keep Europeans from knowing the truth. One of the lies the propaganda mill of Germany was grinding out furiously was that all refugees who fell into the hands of the Americans were held in concentration camps where they were starved and overworked. Frida's twin's sister believed the blatant untruth, and grieved herself sick over Frida's fate. George and Frida contacted the Red Cross hoping that through them they could let the family know they were safe and well, and working only for themselves. The Red Cross was swamped with inquiries about relatives trapped in Nazi-held lands, far too busy to reverse the flow of their concern. Not until 1943 did they get word through to Frida's family, and thereby, hopefully to George's, about George's and Frida's snug harbor.

When the Japanese bombed Pearl Harbor and America went to war, Frida's and George's hopes soared. Now Austria would be liberated. Now the Jews would be avenged. Such illusions kept them from despair for a time, but illusion withered as the months dragged on and America did not make a landing in Europe. What they were spared knowing for the time being, was that George's parents had been among the first Jews from Austria to be part of The Final Solution. They were rounded up soon after Frida left and were taken out of Vienna to die in a concentration camp. Frida's family had been unable to lift a finger to save them, their own lives would have been lost too if they had tried. The first letters to come through from Vienna after the war brought George and Frida the tragic news. By the time those precious letters arrived, however, they were prepared to hear it. News reports coming out of Europe in May and June of 1945, accompanied by news photos to make the blood run cold, had been filled with horror stories of the concentration camps the Allied forces had overrun and "liberated." The extent of the Holocaust, as the story unfolded, left no room for hope. Only a most miraculous miracle could have saved George's parents as prominent as they were.

As for Frida's family, there was only her father and her brother left when Austria was opened up by the American forces. Her father had remained stubbornly monarchist in his political leanings throughout the war while the rest of the family had joined the Social Democratic Party after the occupation began, and it became expedient to do so. While the Nazis held Vienna in thrall, her brother had been put to work in a locomotive factory, a position he loathed but was helpless to leave. Once the locomotive factory closed down at the end of hostilities, the postwar shambles of the European economy left him nowhere to go. Her twin had married a kind man of very limited sensibilities. A dull marriage and constant grieving over the deprivation she thought Frida was enduring, gave her bleeding ulcers, a condition that needed expert attention.

When the Nazis, by driving the Jewish doctors out of the country or killing them off, reduced medical care available in Vienna to the skill of medical students, they set medicine back a century in quality and expertise. Frida's sister had to have surgery or die. Either a student performed the operation or there would be none. The student who performed the surgery on Frida's twin let the scissors slip sending them through the stomach wall into the pancreas. She came out of that surgery with diabetes which led to alcoholism. Without knowing that Frida was prospering in California, she died a few precious weeks before the liberation of Vienna. It was such a waste. Long lives were the rule in their family, not the brevity of forty-three years.

For weeks after the revelation of the mini Holocaust which had struck her family, Frida's hysterical grief frightened George. He could see the same over-reaction setting in that had almost cost her her life in 1940. He never suggested that either of them go back to see for themselves, but in 1951 a letter from Frida's brother made it impossible for Frida to remain safely distant from the scene of so much sorrow. The Kwiatowskis' apartment building was to be seized for back taxes. Her brother was helpless to stop it. Since the apartment building was now half hers she had to act or their father would be out on the street and their inheritance lost. Her brother could scarcely afford the postage stamp to send the letter to Frida telling her about the impending disaster.

"They've already sent Father an eviction notice," he wrote, "and he's about to lose his mind. You know father. His pride has been sustained by owning that building. No matter how bad things got he was still a landlord. Now he's nothing. Ever since Mother died, he's shut himself off from the world so that his only contact is with the neighbors he meets as he sweeps the lobby."

The letter was a long rambling plea for help and a thinly veiled manipulation of her guilt over being so well-fed and so solvent while they were living on the edge of want. Frida read the letter over and over and knew it was time to spend one of the diamonds. In 1951 a two-and-a-half carat diamond could work wonders in the shattered economy of Europe; one such diamond could save the building. The prospect of flying left

Frida almost convulsed with fear. But there was no other way. She could never take off enough time to cross the United States by train, take ship for Europe, then board another train to travel halfway across Europe. In this crisis she had no choice but to look her fear of heights in the face and conquer it.

George and Frida had taken out American Citizenship as soon as their five years were up. She had no problem touring the world if she wanted to. Her American passport would take her anywhere. She bought her airline tickets, she raided the drugstores in their neighborhood for Dramamine, and she took one of the diamonds out of the old shoes hidden in the back of her closet. She would wait to sell it in Amsterdam to avoid paying the exchange fees on the money. She would open an account in Amsterdam and write checks on it in Vienna.

That trip was as terrifying as she had expected it to be. All the way across the Atlantic she kept the hostess-nurse busy with airsick bags and cold cloths, and when the plane landed in The Netherlands she got down on her knees to kiss the tarmac. Once in Vienna, she paid off the indebtedness on the dear old apartment building. That done, she spent a little money to make her father more comfortable. She spent hours reminiscing with her brother, visited her mother's and her twin's graves, and walked through her favorite old haunts of the city so filled with memories. Everywhere she turned she ran into ghosts from the past. She could not find a single member of George's family, nor could she find any record of their passing. They simply disappeared from the city records leaving no trace of where they'd been sent. Not only had the people who had made up her life disappeared, but the physical world she had known was not the same. There wasn't a single street in the old neighborhood untouched by the war. Nothing she did or saw gave her any sense of being "home." She felt lonelier than she had ever felt in her life. Vienna, without her mother and her sister, was an empty landscape. Her father was only a shell of the old autocrat. Try as they might they could find nothing to talk to each other about. Nothing remained of the textile factory which George's father had managed or the carpet factory where George had worked. Her past had been totally demolished. When her visit came to an end she literally fled from the scene of such harrowing sorrow.

She had promised George that while she was in Europe she would search all the records of every country where he had had relatives to see if she could locate any living member of his extended family. The search took her through records and graveyards in three countries, including West Germany. Just to set foot on German soil was a physical effort. It sickened her to breathe the air of the country that had produced Hitler and then supported his madness. Resolutely, she fulfilled her promise to George but she found no tracks left behind by anyone. They had all disappeared as completely as if they'd been vaporized. The trip was one long psychological endurance contest, and a constant flood of overwhelming grief.

Along the way she visited a village being created for orphans of the Holocaust. All the children she and George had chosen not to have were there: gaunt, undernourished, frightened, psychologically as well as physically emaciated. They sat on playground benches without moving. They stared with quiet eyes at something Frida could not see. They didn't smile or laugh. When they played they played very quietly staying in one spot. The war was six years behind them but they seemed not to be aware of the changes those six years had wrought. Frida, walking among them, tried to elicit some vitality from them, talking to children who listened politely and smiled faintly but held themselves aloof. She resolved that when she got back to Los Angeles she would retrieve that other shoe from the closet and unleash the power that was hidden in its heel. It wouldn't bring anyone back who had been annihilated, but it might give life to a few of the wraiths still living.

The last particle of the old life, the remaining diamond, she gave to the children of that village in her name, in George's name, in her twin sister's name, in the name of George's brother and George's parents. Wrapped up in that gift was all the grief, the despair, the buried anger she had carried with her since March 12, 1938. Years later, when her father died and she returned to Europe to bury him, she re-visited that village. Her heart swelled with pride over what her mother-in-law's gift to the future had accomplished. The young people, the sad children of her first visit, to all outward appearances had become as normal as teenagers in America. They crowded around her to ask her questions, they wanted to know all about the United States, and when they learned she was from Los Angeles, the home of movie stars, they bubbled over with excitement. She watched them play soccer, and she was their guest at a musical recital. She heard from their foster parents about their plans for the future.

Those children who had been so disinterested when she first met them that she'd feared they'd just sit out the rest of their lives, were now filled with dreams as multi-colored as hers had been at that age. She met the teachers in the village who confirmed for her what their foster parents had told her, that the future was not lost with the past for these kids, but open to all kinds of possibilities. A great healing settled over her. For the first time since she'd boarded the train for Riga the agony of her own past slipped away in that village and she was completely at peace.

George and Frida bought their house the American way, with a mortgage, not diamonds. They toured the United States on vacations since touring did not require flying, and they enjoyed life. When George was sixty-four he had to throw in the towel on his career. His misbehaving heart set him free from the workaday world. He could spend whole mornings or afternoons with his Art books while Frida was away at her desk at Volkswagen. Frida was amazed at his serenity, his uncomplaining acceptance of his illness. During the next twenty-two years he underwent surgery six times, but he was never took on the mantle of an invalid. All he needed to be at peace, besides his beloved books, was the company of his beloved friend, his wife. He died in 1986 and the following year Frida moved to Rossmoor. George had a niece, his only relative who escaped the Holocaust, living in the Bay Area. Over the years she had become the only family Frida had. With George gone Frida wanted to be near someone she could call her own. Already suffering from heart trouble herself when she came to Rossmoor, Frida died two years after moving in. Following her last heart attack, which did not carry her away immediately, Miriam was a constant visitor, taking her food and in essence holding her hand. Lu took her "chicken soup," in the form of little delicacies she thought a heart patient could eat. With their usual solidarity "The Girls" made her last days as pleasant as they could. They took her in as a fellow refugee, and briefly made her one of their own.

TRUDY

"I never see a brilliant sunset but what my blood runs cold." Trudy said. "I literally shiver, and have forebodings of great upheavals."

There was a brilliant sunset March I2. The German army marched across Austria all day and by late afternoon was entering the capitol. Sunset found those arrogant Aryans still coming over the hill west of the city. The sky overhead was filled with bloodshot clouds of crimson spattered with gold. It was as though the heavens were heralding the coming of the Boche. The colors of the sunset intensified and expanded, shimmering off every gilded cross atop every church spire in the city. Windows threw back the radiance, treetops were aflame with color they would not flaunt again until autumn. Silhouetted against the glorious cloud banners behind them, those tall "barbarians" terrified Trudy. She became almost ill with the premonition that the way West had been closed forever. Closed to her personal dreams, and maybe, an awful maybe, to life itself.

Sunday, with the Germans in complete control of Vienna, Trudy tried to escape her father's repeated optimistic arguments which she knew were nothing more than whistling in the dark. She couldn't stand to hear him say again and again. "They won't do it to us, not here in Austria. The world wouldn't let 'em. Austrians wouldn't let them. We're too civilized for that here."

She went to the home of a friend who had left for America only a month earlier. Toni wanted to become a master chef. She left school at the end of the sixth form to become a trainee in a large Vienna hotel and when an opportunity came to be a trainee at the world-famous Savoy Hotel in London, she'd plunged into the study of English in order to master the language. Busy cooks didn't have time to translate for foreign help underfoot. For a year she remained at the Savoy in England, acquiring by association a standing in the world of culinary arts which would be invaluable in the United States where she intended to go. Americans were still awed by any association with the Crillon in Paris or the Savoy in London. In the great restaurants of New York she would have no trouble finding work. Feeling herself ready to move on to bigger fields, Toni had come home to obtain the necessary visa for the United

States, and was on her way barely a month before the Germans arrived. Toni's mother's brother, a resident of New York City, and a U.S. citizen, had sent the affidavit she needed and would watch over her when she arrived.

Trying to escape the nightmare of what was happening around her Trudy went to her friend's house to talk about Toni's big adventure, to see if there'd been word from her. There had been no word from Toni, but Toni's mother had words for Trudy. Unlike Trudy's father, Toni's mother was convinced that all Jews within the reach of Hitler were in trouble. A no-nonsense woman with no illusions to defend, she lectured Trudy.

"You have to get out." she insisted. "All the young people must go. The future of the Jews demands it. Go to London!"

"But I have no skills," protested Trudy. "How can I get an exit permit?"

"You don't need skills. You're young and strong. You can work."

"Work at what!"

"Work at anything. Be a maid. Your family had a maid who went to London, didn't she? Domestic permits can be had."

"But mother says I don't even know which end of a broom sweeps." Trudy cried, wringing her hands.

"Then take care of children. Be a governess. Just get out while you can."

"But I can't speak English!" wailed Trudy.

"Then learn!" snapped the woman, losing patience.

The two spent the rest of the afternoon examining one avenue for employment after another, but the discussion always came back to children. Upper class people all over Europe had governesses for their children, especially the English.

"Go to London," the woman kept exhorting her. 'You already have friends there!" She began listing all the girls Toni and Trudy knew who were living in London working as domestics or au pairs.

All the way home on the street car Toni's mother's words rang in her ears. By the time she reached her house she had worked up the courage to present the idea of leaving to her parents. She was sure they'd raise the roof and the decision would be made for her, but all day the radio had carried one

148

pronouncement from the conquerors after another. Her parents had been glued to the unfolding drama. Trudy repeated the entire conversation she'd had with Toni's mother.

"She says I should begin English lessons right now before I even have the papers. She says I should go down tomorrow to apply for a visa and then tomorrow afternoon get enrolled at a language school."

To her surprise, her parents didn't consider the idea preposterous, nor did they laugh when she told them that Toni's mother had suggested she might even marry an Englishman and send for her whole family. Instead, tears came to her mother's eyes and her father couldn't find his voice for a spell. The three of them talked through most of the night about how it could be accomplished. At times her mother waffled.

"I can't bear to think of it," she'd sob, "If you go I don't think you'll ever come back. You'll stay in England and I won't be able to see you or my grandchildren."

Trudy's father shook his head irritably. "She isn't even out yet and you have grandchildren on the brain! Would you rather she stayed here in the path of the Nazis?

"Of course not!" Trudy's mother dried her eyes but kept her handkerchief ready. "But why does it have to be this way?"

Her husband spread out his hands helplessly, "Maybe God knows but I don't!"

He turned back to Trudy. "To get a visa you have to have a diploma or a certificate. A diploma from a professional school of some sort, or a certificate that vouches for your skill at something. A man I know, he's gentile but he's a good man, has a daughter who runs a kindergartner over near the Ringstrasse behind the Opera. I'll call him in the morning and see if she'll take you on as a helper. I could pay her a little something to be "training" you. It's a licensed school and a letter from them saying you're an employee should do the trick. Unless you can think of something better?"

Trudy couldn't think of anything at all. The next morning she found a private teacher for the English lessons, and made her first trip to the Immigration office to get the papers to apply for a visa. Her father's gentile friend's daughter did better than take Trudy on as a trainee, she gave her the title of "Assistant to the Head Teacher." When Trudy returned to the Immigration Office a month later with her request for a work permit as a "domestic" the permit was handed over with no difficulty at all. She rushed home with the precious paper tucked safely in her purse.

"I got it!" she cried waving the paper above her head as she rushed in. "I got it. I'm going to London! Can you believe it? There wasn't any trouble at all. I just walked in with the letter from the teacher and they gave it to me without a word! I'm on my way!!"

But it wasn't that easy. Before the family could celebrate her good fortune they learned that in order for her to be granted an exit visa under the new Nazi regulations which had new rules for departure, her father would have to present his tax records to the authorities to prove that he didn't owe the State any back taxes or fines of any kind. From what they'd heard, the Nazis went over every Jew's records with a fine tooth comb and usually they found something to hang them up, at least for a time. Many Jews didn't bother to leave by the front door, visa in hand. They took off on skiing trips from which they didn't return, or went over the mountains on foot leaving everything behind.

In the past only the person leaving had to prove they were not ducking out on any debts or obligations which remained true for Gentiles. But Jews were a different category.

Her father took his tax records to the appropriate office, proved he owed nothing, and unavoidably brought immediate attention to himself and his income in the process. He was the manager of a large import business, a highly paid executive. The company imported carpets from the Middle East and cleaned them before selling them to the public. Rugs from the Middle East were full of sand and camel dung and getting them clean enough for the colors to stand out was a rather sophisticated process requiring a sound knowledge of chemicals and dyes. After the tax matter came the check of police files to prove that no member of the family had a record of misdemeanors or arrests. Only when these checks had been completed satisfactorily was Trudy free to apply for the coveted exit permit.

In the fearsome days after the Nazis arrived in Vienna, while she waited for permission to leave, Trudy had to go to one of the government offices on business. Just a blue-eyed, brown-haired, pretty young girl with little experience of officialdom to guide her, as she approached the counter where she was to transact her business, she saw two lines. One was very short, the other very long. Seeing no reason to wait longer than necessary, Trudy slipped into the end of the short line. Within a few minutes she was face to face with the Nazi clerk with whom she had to confer. He took her papers, looked at her quizzically and said,

"You are Aryan, aren't you?"

"Oh no," she said breathlessly, her eyes wide with fright.

"You're sure?' he insisted.

"Of course I'm sure," she responded.

"I can't believe it," he said sadly, shaking his head. "You'll have to go to the end of the other line." She was a long time getting to the counter again.

Everything checked, all the procedures complete, Trudy expected the visa to arrive in the mail as promised, but another month went by before at last she obtained final clearance for departure. That month of waiting had exposed her to one experience after another that removed any lingering doubts she or her family had about whether her going to London was wise or not. One of the experiences that wounded her deeply came from such an unexpected source she was crushed by it. As she waited for clearance to leave she began to list all the people whom she would lose out of her life, people she would miss seeing again. Among them were members of the faculty at her secondary school. Trudy set about to say good-bye. There was the language teacher who had once drawn a little sword for her one day when she was a Freshman and was stuck on the word for saber in a French exam. She remembered how the woman had taken a pencil out of Trudy's pencil box and idly drawn that little sword on a slip of paper then put the pencil back in the box without ever looking up.

They arranged to meet for coffee in the Cafe Mozart behind the Opera House. Sitting across a little table from the woman, with half-eaten cakes and coffee growing cold before them, without preliminaries unsophisticated Trudy blurted out that she was leaving. A triumphant smile crossed the woman's face.

"Good. Good." she said with great satisfaction. "It will not be safe for you here now that we National Socialists are in control. My brothers have had their Nazi uniforms in the closet for months waiting for this day and when they put them on last month we were all thrilled. Austria will come into her own now. We'll be rid of the Jews who have held us back and sucked us dry. Be glad you are going. What is coming will not be pleasant."

Shocked, Trudy's anger was at last aroused. From that day on she couldn't wait to shake the dust of Austria from her feet. As the Nazi noose tightened around the Jews of Vienna, those who had buried their heads in the sand in the earliest days of the invasion had to give up being ostriches. All of her extended family began thinking of escape. Conversation centered on nothing else. If they couldn't extricate themselves, the older generation argued, they had to figure out how they were to get the younger generation out. The day Trudy left, one of her aunts and her parents accompanied her to the train. It was May 25, 1938, ten weeks after the Anschluss, and no one any longer looked upon her departure as an adventure. It had become flight, pure and simple. At the station her aunt handed her a sack of cherries.

"Here," she said. "You can spit all the way across the rest of German soil."

Trudy tried to choke back tears as she looked down from the train window at the forlorn little group standing on the platform. How long would it be before she saw them again? What was going to happen to them now? As the train began to move she wanted to leap off and stay there to protect them but too much had gone into getting her out of harm's way for her to turn back now. She had to face the future, whatever it brought. From Vienna the train was routed through Frankfurt where another aunt lived, one of her mother's sisters who was a Czech citizen. The Aunt came to the station to share the few minutes Trudy would be there. Trudy left the car to join her aunt over a cup of tea and was terrified by the swarms of Brown Shirts on the platforms and in the waiting room.

"Come with me," pleaded Trudy. "Come to England. You have your Czech passport. You can travel on that."

"What would I do in London?" the aunt asked anxiously.

"I don't know but we'd find something. If you stay here you'll be killed."

"Oh child," admonished her aunt, "don't say such dreadful things. I'm not going to be killed. Why would anyone want to kill me?"

"Why do the Nazis kill anybody?" Trudy demanded.

There was too little time to argue it out. Trudy had to get back on the train. As the engine's big wheels began to turn she leaned out the window and shouted to her aunt, "Think about it. And don't wait very long, it'll be too late. Do it now!"

Almost a year to the day after the Anschluss, the Nazis marched in to Czechoslovakia. Terrified by this turn of events Trudy's aunt left Frankfurt on the spur of the moment. Having made no disposition of her worldly goods and no provisions for living abroad, she came to London. Arriving almost penniless, she was turned over by Jewish Relief to a shelter in a rundown section of the East End where the standard of living was so much lower than what she was accustomed to in Germany that she was horrified. Never had she seen such want, such deplorable housing, such filthy streets. If Germany had people this poor she at least didn't have any this slovenly. To compound her feeling that she had fled comfort to come to absolute deprivation she learned what many another refugee from the Continent learned to their dismay. She found that her command of the English language, pure textbook English, was incomprehensible in the streets of London. She couldn't understand anyone, including the tradesmen, and they couldn't understand her. She might as well have never studied the language at all.

For a long agonizing month she fretted about what to do, the one short month in which the doors to Germany were still open. Trudy urged her not to give in to despair, not to go back, to leave everything there and take her lumps as a refugee. She assured her aunt that things would get better when the British got organized, that she wouldn't have to spend her whole life in a London slum, that she'd only have to be there until the two of them figured out what her aunt could do to work her way out her current situation. She might as well have been spitting in the wind. Continuously, her aunt thought of all she'd left behind, of the small savings she could retrieve from the banks, and of the valuable household possessions she could sell. If she went back and took care of the business she should have taken care of before she flew the coop so precipitously, she could exit Germany with something in her pocket. She went home to close out her life there. From Frankfurt she wrote one letter to Trudy, the last anyone ever heard from her. In the vain hope that she would be allowed to immigrate with the government's permission, to go like a law-abiding citizen not like a hunted animal, to leave with dignity, she said, she feared she had forfeited her life. She had. When Trudy tried to locate her at war's end there was no record of her.

Trudy left Vienna in the morning, and the next day the Nazis appeared at her father's factory. They arrested him, his brother and his brother's son. Then they went through the carpet-cleaning factory and carried away one of the Jewish employees. Fear swept through the entire Hebrew community. Her father and his brother were interrogated for hours then released the next day, but Trudy's cousin was not so lucky. He was taken away and interred, exactly where no one knew. Every inquiry was rebuffed and the fate of the nephew seemed more and more hopeless as day after day passed without word from him. Months later a letter came to the carpet-cleaning company from a dry goods concern in Switzerland. The Swiss were looking for someone experienced in the art of refining and cleaning carpets. They intended to expand their business and they planned to buy the machinery they would need from the company her father still managed. If they purchased the equipment they needed someone who knew how to use it.

Her father screwed up his courage and took the letter to the same authorities who had warned him away when he had come before about his nephew. Surely the request from a Swiss firm made it a different matter than just a Jewish Austrian firm seeking one of its own skilled employees. The clerk took the letter and curtly informed her father that the matter would be taken under advisement. Months more passed, then, without forewarning the nephew returned one day from the concentration camp where he'd been held. There was joy unspeakable at his return, heightened into ecstasy when it was learned that he was to be permitted to take the job in Switzerland. Days of breathless waiting followed for the necessary exit visas to come in the mail. When they came, not only did they cover the nephew's departure, but his wife was to be allowed to go with him. What was more, they could take their household possessions with them. It was unbelievable. Who had performed such magic? The family wasted no time on such frivolous questions, they bent to the task of getting another of their young out of harm's way.

It was fairly simple to pack him up for the company had been in the hauling and transfer business as part of their whole operation. His furniture, which included an ordinary spice rack that could be found in any European kitchen and which had many little drawers in it each labeled for a different spice, was crated and delivered to the cartage company along with everything else. Not waiting for his furniture to be packed and shipped since all of them feared there might be a new directive issued against the Jews which would close the door, he left Austria ahead of his goods. On the day of his departure, late in December of 1938, some of the family again went to the station to see one of theirs on the way to freedom. There were tears and embraces and much murmurings of shalom and mozeltof as the family clung to another member being torn from their midst, possibly never to be seen again. Then the conductor cried "All Aboard" and the nephew and his wife tore themselves away to climb the steps of their car. As the train pulled out of the station, Trudy's father ran along the platform shouting up to his nephew who was leaning out the window to wave,

"Be sure to have caraway soup as soon as your furniture arrives. It's very good for moving day."

Passersby turned to watch the well-dressed man dashing along the platform shouting such homey advice up to the equally well-dressed young man leaning out the window. A few even stopped to laugh. But when her cousin uncrated his goods in Switzerland, in the little drawer in the spice cabinet marked caraway among the seeds lay Trudy's mother's diamond ring.

When Trudy arrived in London she was met at Victoria Station by three friends already living in London who had been alerted by her father that she was coming. Also at the station was her new employer and her young daughter, a child who was taking German at school. After the exuberance of the four girls' meeting had spent itself Trudy's employer and her daughter carried her off to their home outside London where she was expected to be an assistant maid to the housekeeper. Nineteen years old, totally unskilled at domestic chores, Trudy was in over her head. The job lasted a week. Another position was found for her, this time in the home of a family in

Greenwich where there were three children, none of whom spoke German. Their complete care fell on Trudy for almost the entire day, every day. Their mother was a tennis buff who spent her time on the courts.

Trudy's feeble English left her helpless with the children who could defy her by pretending not to understand her. Without the mother at home to interpret, life became a nightmare. On her first Sunday off Trudy went to visit one of the three friends who had met her when she first arrived. She had been given directions about how to take a bus to London, then a train to Croydon, then transfer to another bus which she would find at the entrance to the underground station. There was one difficulty with the directions, they failed to tell Trudy that the bus made a circular tour of its route so she boarded going in the wrong direction. Trudy finally arrived, having made almost the full circle of the bus route. The family was seated and waiting for her. Her friend Magda had a tight schedule. She was to usher at a benefit concert in London and couldn't be late. What she'd planned to do was that after tea she would ride back as far as Charing Cross with Trudy where she would go on her way to her concert and Trudy would take a bus back to Greenwich.

At Charing Cross, Trudy, anxious not to delay her friend further, pulled at the heavy door and had opened it just a few inches. The train gave a jerk as it came to a halt and her finger got caught as the door slammed shut again. Her finger was almost severed. It bled all over the place. Forgetting that there was a hospital just across the street, Magda took Trudy to another Viennese friend who lived not too far from the concert hall and turned Trudy over to her. The friend's husband rushed her to the office of a doctor nearby who looked at her hand and said that he couldn't do much then because the hand was badly swollen by that time. He would bandage it, he said, and wait until the swelling went down before stitching it up. Meantime, she'd have to carry that arm in a sling.

"How can I take care of kids like this?" she cried. "What am I to do?"

Her friend's husband drove to Greenwich, told Trudy's now ex-employers what had happened, and picked up Trudy's things. She would stay with them in the interim. Once her hand healed, Trudy found a job in Kensington with a family who had one little boy. They welcomed Trudy into the family and having decided to retain her, set about improving her English by correcting her, reading to her, urging her to read to herself, and letting her learn from their son. The result was that Trudy had a charming composite of distinctly upper class English accent overlaying her Viennese German.

London was a city charged with excitement and pleasure. She took the little boy to Kensington Gardens where he could romp under the big trees, feed the ducks on the pond, chase squirrels he never caught, and scuffle through the leaves. On her days off, with her own earned money in her pocket, she haunted Woolworth's, a place she thought was Paradise. As the weeks and months went by, more and more of her friends and cousins showed up in London. They made up quite a little community. In the park she met new friends who were also au pairs like herself. They chatted away while their little charges played, they noshed on the sweets the street vendors brought their way, and all of them gained weight. It was a balmy period of safety and comfort that was not to last.

The Underground stop nearest Christopher's home was Earl's Court. The underground station at Earl's Court is a huge affair on several levels. At the far end of the level where Trudy got off the lift there was a great hall that was used for city receptions, political rallies, gatherings of Service Clubs, and any other purpose for which the citizenry wished to pay a fee. Or so it was until the air raids began in May of 1940. Immediately, the hall was converted to a shelter. One day when Trudy turned into the passageway leading to the street near where she worked, the hall was filled with Brown Shirts shouting the same slogans she had heard so often in Vienna. Though she couldn't see them she could hear them, and it terrified her. She scurried past, her heart in her mouth, and hurried back to the shelter of her employer. She rushed through the front door and slammed it behind her, her face the color of her gray muffler.

"Whatever is the matter?" Christopher's mother asked.

Trudy poured out what she'd heard. "They're not fit Englishmen, those hoodlums" the woman said angrily, tossing her head disdainfully. "Pay no attention to them. Nobody pays any attention to them, strutting around and play acting the way they do. Most of them never get beyond sixth form. They don't work, they just roam around puffed up with their own

157

importance. Well, they'll be in real uniforms soon enough if their hero attacks England."

Trudy said nothing more, but she was not reassured. She remembered her father's brave words when the Germans marched into Austria. Her confidence in her present security evaporated. Christopher's parents must have felt some of the same unease for late in the summer of 1938 they began to talk openly about how Hitler would not be stopped by any pacific promises made at the forthcoming Munich Conferences being held to hoodwink Chamberlain. They arranged to send Trudy and Christopher to the Cottswolds where they would live with a lovely farm family who were friends of Christopher's parents. The woman in the Cottswolds opened her heart and her home to the pretty little foreigner, and to the delightful little Christopher. To keep her mind off the impending war, her hostess taught Trudy how to cook. Those few days in the country before the conference began in Germany were sunny, filled with innocent sweetness, but then there was Munich and when war did not come Trudy and Christopher were returned to London for the year of "the lull before the storm" - the winter, spring and summer of 1938-1939.

Back in Vienna, after Trudy's departure in May, the family began plotting to get their younger daughter, Susan, out to safety in England also. She was too young for a domestic's work permit. She was in her third year of a four-year trade school program where she was learning textile and carpet weaving. Not a bookworm like Trudy, it was Susan's hope that she would obtain a certificate from that school that would qualify her for a work permit as a weaver. Each of the students had to make a little carpet to prove their competence before they could receive their certificate. However, early in their occupation of Vienna the Nazis ruled that no Jew would be allowed to remain in technical training. Susan was allowed to remain only long enough to finish her carpet and then she had to give up her education. She has that little carpet to this day.

After Crystal Night in November of 1938, British Jews at last woke up to the plight of the Jewish community in Germany as well as in Austria. Wealthy English Jews organized to offer refuge for Jewish children from the beleaguered areas. "Children's Transports" were chartered which brought children out by train to Hook Van Holland, then by ship across the channel to London. Susan was too old to be shipped among the children but if she could come as a children's helper she would be able to escape. It took some months for her to get into one of the "shipments" as a "helper", someone who would care for the younger ones during the long journey, but she finally succeeded. The little refugees were identified like packages. Labels were hung around their necks bearing the name of the person to whom they were being sent, and identifying the "contents of the package" by stating the child's name, place of origin, age, and the names of its parents. Trudy met the "shipment" with which Susan was traveling, March 15, 1939, the day Hitler marched into Czechoslovakia. Having no place of her own to take her sister, the best Trudy could do was let Susan be apprenticed out as an au pair in a small boarding "cache" for babies. There she was badly overworked, paid nothing but a little pocket money from time to time, and was utterly miserable, Susan was stuck until July when she turned eighteen. Having reached the magical age for a work permit she applied and got a job as a mother's helper.

When Hitler and Stalin signed a non-aggression pact, Christopher's parents wanted him out of London again, as quickly as possible, safe in Torquay where the mother superiors of a convent in that town agreed to receive the child and his nanny. So anxious were his parents about Christopher's safety that Trudy and the boy were packed off to Devon the very next morning. Never having been religious herself, Trudy was amazed to see such a huge place used to house only a few women who seemed to have no purpose in life but to pray. She was constantly surprised and pleased by the many kindnesses shown her by the sisters. They never pressed her to attend worship, they respected her Jewishness, they saw to her every need, and on the morning of Sunday September 3, 1939, two days after Hitler marched into Poland, she was invited by the Mother Superior to come and listen to the wireless with the rest of the household. Trudy was decimated by Chamberlain's announcement of war. It was a cruel blow. She burst out weeping uncontrollably. Her parents and all the rest of the family still in Vienna were trapped, they would never get out now, even if she met and married an Englishman. Many members of the family, besides herself and Susan, were out of harm's way, almost all of their cousins. Some had gone to Australia, a few to Palestine, others to

France, a few to Holland and to the United States, and there was her cousin in Switzerland. But the older generation - her parents and their siblings, her aunts and uncles - concentrating on getting the younger generation away to freedom had sacrificed themselves for the future of the family.

Christopher was five years old when school opened that fall so his vacation from school was extended since he was in Torquay out of harm's way. He did not begin his education until after Christmas. Trudy had four months in which to look the job situation over before her employment would be terminated. War had financially hit Christopher's family hard. They couldn't afford to keep her just because they had grown fond of her. She found a job in Cornwall. Susan was in Devon, an inch away on the map, but days away due to the limitations of wartime travel. Susan had found work with a young family of two small Children. When war was declared the young father had been called up for military service so they had decided that the children and the wife should leave London and take refuge in the south of England. Another young woman and her two children moved in with Susan's employer to share expenses, thus Susan had all four of their children in her care. In the midst of this upheaval in the fall of 1939 came Yom Kippur.

Trudy and Susan planned it all out. They would ask for leave to go to High Holy Day services in Exeter where they heard there was a big synagogue. It was not easy, travel was difficult all over England. Permission was granted, and the two girls went to Exeter for the Day of Atonement surrounded by the ghosts of their family trapped in Europe. It was almost like a purging for them both. They were free and together, and their accompanying guilt had to be expiated. The bitter sorrow and the bitter sweetness got all mixed up together. Then it was over and they went back to waiting out the war along with their employer families.

Life was better than it had yet been in England in spite of the declaration of war. Cornwall was a beautiful place, like a painting. The landscape was made up of grassy dunes near the ocean, flowering meadows back behind the dunes, rugged coast, outcroppings of boulders and granite in the meadows giving light and shadow strong contrasts, and further inland were the shrubby windswept trees so characteristic of coastal England. Trudy's soul expanded on sunlit days, but her imagination was fired when the fog shrouded everything. She particularly enjoyed pushing little three-year-old Pixie in her pram as little Billie walked along beside her chattering away along the country roads tucked between hedge rows which served as windbreaks. If she could have stopped time so that neither she nor the children ever grew any older she would have.

Over the whole landscape, however, lay a breathless waiting. War had been declared, but there was no war. The Germans were totally occupied with the Polish Adventure in the East, while the Brits were frantically trying to prepare for a war the dimensions of which were as yet scarcely understood. The hiatus came to an end early in 1940 when German forces finally faced west from Poland and turned their fury on the Scandinavian countries. With Norway completely subjugated by the end of March the German might was turned on the Low Countries and France By the end of June the entire Atlantic Coastline of Europe was a springboard for the German army. Before France was secured, in May of 1940, the fury of the German air raids on England began. For the next three months those air raids pulverized English cities and terrorized the populace. Completely helpless to do anything to ward them off, refugees and citizens alike huddled in shelters and prayed that the city above them would still be there when they emerged. Trudy was not the only future Rossmoorian trapped in underground bunks in London is those days. Lu Hahn was there with her husband and children. Years later, in Rossmoor, she and Trudy would relive the nightmare of their terrible months.

When the Blitz first began in May, all "enemy aliens" were ordered to leave the coastal areas of Britain and return to London. Now the full impact of being a refugee hit Trudy. There were curfew laws that applied to aliens which had been rather more or less ignored until the bombings of London began. When she arrived in England she'd been issued an Alien Registration Book which she was instructed to carry with her at all times. Every change of address, every change of employment, had to be recorded in that book. Now the curfew laws were sternly enforced. Very quickly, two emigration officers came to interview Christopher's parents as to their observations and impressions of their son's nanny, and to interview Trudy in great detail about her family and her entrance into England. They took her registration book away with them and kept it for two whole days. When it was returned it was stamped, "Passed by the Tribunal." Though uninformed about the procedure the sisters had received a security clearance. Neither Trudy nor her employers understood what that meant, but Susan, whose registration book bore the same imprimatur, understood; it gave her permission to work in Wales.

The Americans had shifted Austrians to the German lists for immigration purposes after Hitler invaded their country and the British, aware of the potential danger of collaborators among the refugees, people's whose families' lives were at stake if they did cooperate with the Germans, quickly followed suit. All German aliens were now enemy aliens and all were to be confined to the city of London where they could be kept under close surveillance. Trudy and Susan were forbidden to own a radio. The government feared short-wave radios over which messages might go out to enemy fleets hovering off the Coast. Forlornly Trudy packed her things to move back to the city which was nightly being pulverized by the Blitzkrieg.

Through the efforts in her behalf of her Cornwall employer, she went directly to rooms in a decent boarding house when she arrived in London and there she was directed to a job as chambermaid in another boarding house nearby. No children to care for this time, instead she would clean twelve rooms each morning after the guests left for work. Every day the landlady of the house urged Trudy to be quick about it and hurried through her own work so the two of them could go to the "flicks" in the afternoon. It lightened the tension of life in wartime London, and it kept Trudy from brooding. What she brooded about was that this was no job for the future. in the interim of war it was a congenial harbor, but for the future it was a backwater with no outlet into the mainstream of life. Life had become a see-saw. Every time things went right something had to go wrong.

In the middle of one of the interminable air raids that sent everyone scurrying to the cellar to wait for it to pass, Trudy was taken to the hospital. She was dangerously sick with German measles. She developed a cough that left her exhausted. She was so sick she was only vaguely aware that, as the ambulance dodged its way through the streets, the city was taking a terrific pounding. At the hospital the ambulance had to park in the courtyard to wait for the waves of bombers to pass over their area before the doors to the hospital could be opened and personnel emerge from the nearby air raid shelters to admit patients. When the ambulance attendants turned her over to admitting she was shunted off to the children's ward where all contagious diseases were quarantined. For over three weeks she lay ravished by high fevers, in severe pain from pleurisy. When she was finally released she had to stay with friends while she regained her strength. Meanwhile, her job had gone to someone else. The twelve guest rooms needed cleaning whether Trudy was there to clean them or not.

To complicate life as fully as possible, in the midst of the blitz of bombings that kept sirens wailing all night accompanied by thunderous crashes of bombs and crackling sounds of breaking glass, with London living on its nerve ends, the furniture their parents had sent out in anticipation of leaving themselves arrived in England, great crates of it. The wharves were under constant aerial bombardment. Trudy received word that she had a shipment which needed to be removed immediately, or stored. Because the waterfront was pounded night after night, storage became shorter and shorter in supply. It was months before Trudy could make arrangements for the crates to be carted off, months of paying for storage that provided space to sit out in the open on the docks in all kinds of weather. Finally, she arranged for it to be taken, still crated, to the hotel Christopher's parents had purchased in Torquay. They had bought a resort hotel as a possible retreat from the severity of life in the capitol, an investment which was failing to support itself, much less help them out.

Back in May when the authorities cleared the seacoast area of people who might be a hazard to Britain's safety, Susan, falling back on her weaving skills, went to live with relatives in Whitchurch and easily found employment in a textile factory in the Treforest Trading Estate halfway between Cardiff and Pontypridd. Once she had a place to live and a place to work she had to get the permits: (l) to live there, and (2) to work there. After all, Cardiff was a seaport city not open for residence to enemy aliens. Driven by the dearth of experienced weavers, all of whom were in uniform somewhere in the empire, permission was granted

Because of her skill and her bubbly personality, Susan forged ahead in the company. Then, just a little over a year after coming to Whitchurch, she too became ill. She had such a severe case of strep throat that the doctors said her tonsils had to be taken out. Under age, she could not put herself into the hospital let alone authorize surgery, Trudy would have to go to Cardiff, sign her into the hospital, and give her permission for the surgery to be done. Getting the necessary paper work completed for her to make the trip to Susan in Cardiff, required an insufferably tedious bureaucratic piece of persistence. She badgered officialdom almost daily to let her leave London, but it took months of dialogue through the mails for her to "spring" herself. It took so long that it was the summer of 1941 before the operation could be scheduled.

Trudy sat outside the operating room, as her mother would have done had she been there, and did a lot of thinking about the two of them and the future. Susan came through the operation with flying colors, she was young and in good health, her hospital stay was not long. During the few days she had to remain under the doctor's care the sisters talked it over. They came to the conclusion that it was time for them to set up housekeeping as a family so they could be there for each other in such exigencies as this without all the trials of permits to overcome every time they needed each other's help. Since Susan's job was far more satisfactory than the kinds of work available to Trudy in London, Trudy was the one who needed to move. For Trudy to come to Cardiff she had to have a job in hand and an apartment to go to. It took weeks, but Susan used her wits and everything came together: job, apartment, and permission. They were free at last to have some semblance of family life on their own. They arranged for the eight or nine crates in storage in Torquay to be brought to Wales.

When the crates arrived, it was like Christmas and Chanukah all rolled into one. The shipment had left Vienna before September 1 of the year before, otherwise it would never have gotten out. The crates contained a plethora of lovely things their parents had hoped to live with when they got out. Only one magnificent old desk from the Vienna apartment was among the pieces of furniture made to specification for the smaller apartments of London and America. There were couches and a couple of chairs of new modern design, and chests which contrasted dramatically with the old mahogany desk which looked like a grand old Czar reigning over the soft, lighter woods that were used in the new furniture. Trudy always suspected that somewhere in that desk was a secret drawer. Otherwise, why else send it? But they never found it. Years later, when Trudy and Susan finally sold the piece they wondered what great treasure they were giving up.

Besides the furniture, packed among pillows and bedding and smaller chests, there was a plethora of wonderful silver cutlery. Silver pieces they remembered from their childhood. The girls were overwhelmed by the bounty. When the Nazis had forced their mother to turn over her silver, like all the other Jews in Vienna, she had yielded up the twelve place settings of big heavy sterling which the Nazis expected her to have. She burned the lovely old silver chest in which all her treasures had been stored. She broke it apart, piece by piece, and stuffed it into the stove so it could not give her away. The rest of the silver she secreted out to her daughters in these crates. The girls divided it between them when Susan left England to go to Australia after the war, but years later Susan sent her portion of the treasure to Trudy.

"These don't fit my lifestyle," she wrote. "You take them."

In addition to the silver, there was crystal and china, and linens enough for a lifetime. What furniture Susan did not take with her to Australia when she left in 1946, Trudy used until she left England. Then she sold it along with the bulky china to raise money with which to begin again in the United States. She brought only the silver, the linens and a little of the crystal to America.

There was a plastics factory located in the industrial estate where Susan worked that made jewelry for export. Jewelry was a far cry from weaving looms. Tired of the heavy looms, Susan became a jewelry designer and maker. Deft and quick, she so impressed the managers that within weeks of being hired she was made a forewoman. Empowered by her position she was able to secure a job for Trudy in the same factory, but Trudy didn't like the repetitious work. She was a people person, not a machine tender. Within a few months she was scouring the want ads. She found just the thing. The City of Cardiff needed an assistant in a day nursery the city operated for the benefit of working mothers. She loved the work from the first day. The children came from families representing all the nationalities a seaport city attracts. She cheerfully remained at the day care center until the war ended.

At the plastics factory Susan met an engineer, a Jewish refugee like herself, whose wife was very ill with tuberculosis. His son, a child born in 1936 in Vienna, was living with friends to prevent him from contracting the disease. Willie, the engineer was bending if not breaking under the burden of his wife's care. Tender-hearted Susan tried to help and in the process fell in love. When the wife died late during the war, romance blossomed and in 1946 they were married. When immigration to Australia opened up they decided to give the young nation a try. They were British citizens by then so they had no difficulty with immigration.

"Come go with us," Susan begged. "You'll have no one here once we're gone."

"No." Trudy answered. "I'm going to America. That's where Papa and Mama wanted to go, and that's where I've always wanted to live. I'll wait here until my number comes up and then I'll leave England. I have enough friends in New York to make myself a family."

"You sound like you're going to make a sandwich. You take one Trudy and slap her between two friends and you have a whole meal. Friends aren't the same as family," Susan pleaded, "come with us."

Susan's pleas fell on deaf ears. Trudy waved them off to Australia and went on with her waiting. The Austrian Quota of the U. S. Immigration System had been reestablished at the end of the European war without Trudy being aware of the change. The old Austrian list had been wiped out in 1938 and no list existed in 1945. Austrians were in luck that year. Because of her ignorance about the matter she was still on the German list which stretched ever longer and longer. Germans with family already in America who applied long after she did were given priority over her.

But before either of the sisters left England, when the war in Europe ended in May, 1945, Trudy and Susan tried to get in touch with their parents in Vienna. They wrote letters, letters which were returned marked "Address Unknown." They tried telephoning, and after weeks of waiting to get through on the jammed international lines, they learned that their old phone number now belonged to someone else. They began contacting every soul, every agency, anybody who might be able to give them any kind of information about their father and mother. They wrote to their cousins in Switzerland, they went to the Jewish Information Center at Woburn House, they contacted the Red Cross, and the United Nations Refugee Agency. With the Allies overrunning the concentration camps news coming out of the continent was sickening and terrifying. The two orphaned sisters could not accept such a fate for all the older generation left in Vienna when the Final Solution hit that city. The best information Trudy and Susan could obtain was that their mother and two of their father's female cousins had been taken to Poland in 1942 and put to work in a labor camp there. Their father, who had been in the hospital at the time of his wife's abduction, was not removed from Vienna until early 1944. Beyond that, only one uncle had managed to save himself.

In the Fall of 1945, Trudy moved back to London. Nannies with her wealth of experiences were in high demand now that the children were returning for their wartime exile, some having been shipped all the way to Çanada. The newspapers were full of ads. Relocated in London from Wales, Trudy had to find a dentist. Immigrants look for other immigrants to serve them when they can be found, they cling to each other for safety. In London there were several Viennese dentists, refugees like herself. Trudy found one. Not only was he Viennese but so was his assistant. Three years into Trudy's employment as a nanny, her dentist's assistant got married and gave notice. The search began for her replacement. Trudy came in to have her teeth cleaned and checked during that period and when she came through the office door the assistant had a bright idea.

"When are you going to quit living with children and come into the grown-up world." she demanded.

"What do you mean?" Trudy was startled by such a direct assault.

"You know what I mean. How many years have you been telling children the same old stories, and teaching them to wipe their noses? It's time to do something else!"

Trudy bristled. "Like what!" she demanded.

"Like taking my job here when I quit. You'd be working with adults more than children. You'd be assisting the doctor and filling out all his purchase orders and billing his patients and doing whatever he dreams up for you to do. And when five o'clock came you could put on your hat and coat and go home to your own place. You wouldn't have to put anybody to bed but yourself and you could go to the flicks when you wanted to."

"But I have no experience," Trudy protested.

"Experience? What's experience? I'll teach you what you need to know about this job and so will the dentist. Come on, what do you say?"

Without waiting for an answer, the assistant presented her boss with the idea as an accomplished fact. "I've hired you an assistant to take my place, "she announced

The dentist was delighted with the choice and after a week on the job so was Trudy. For two and a half years she was a competent, satisfied, Girl Friday. Then, at last, in 1950, her visa number for America came through! In a whirl, she closed out her life in Britain, said good-bye to London, and headed West to the friends in New York. She spent three years working as a dental assistant in New Rochelle and then in the spring of 1953 she received a letter from a friend who had earlier moved to Berkeley, CA. Her friend urged her to come out to the lovely University town by the Bay for a visit. Trudy leaped at the offer. She flew as far as Chicago where she visited a cousin before going on to California. She took the Zephyr from Chicago on to the West Coast so she could see the countryside along the way. The Zephyr tore across the landscape of The Great Plains, a topography devoid of any relieving features. The sky was so vast, the land so flat, the horizon so featureless except for the little towns with their grain elevators that lined the right-of-way, that when she saw the Rocky Mountains looming up before her, their magnificence contrasted sharply with the empty world in front of them. She was enthralled.

When the Zephyr pulled into the train shed in Oakland, CA. where all train passengers disembarked to take the ferry on into San Francisco, she was met by the friend, a Hungarian girl named Liesl. Liesl had not escaped the Nazi snare. She wore long sleeves to hide her tattooed number. She had been liberated by the Americans when they overran Auschwitz. Liesl whisked Trudy away immediately to her lodgings in a charming hillside cottage.

Berkeley was a wonderful place in those days with its woodsy winding streets that snaked up into the Berkeley Hills where custom built cottages hid behind shrubbery that also sheltered deer and raccoons. On the lower slopes of the hills was the great University surrounded by a grand array of architectural masterpieces, homes built for the rich and famous who lived there. The returning GIs attending America's universities on the G. I. Bill exacerbated the massive housing shortage of Post World War II America. Any room anywhere was a prize to be won, sometimes amid stiff competition. Rent controls existed in Berkeley which kept housing affordable in spite of the population pressure. Her friend had a room which she'd occupied for some time but recently she'd been lucky enough to find a nice apartment. Almost with her first breath she told Trudy that she was transferring her residence that very day and that Trudy was to inherit her present quarters. In fact, she announced triumphantly, she had already notified the landlady that a friend was coming who would be taking over her place. Trudy was dumbfounded. She had come for a summer, not for a lifetime. Such small things determine our fate. A single room in a charming cottage in a strange city where housing was tight and Trudy would never go east to live again.

Once she grasped what a plum was hers for the taking, Trudy plunged into the scenario someone else had prepared for her. She took the room and immediately began looking for a Job in THE CITY. She had no problem. She enrolled with a placement agency which quickly located a position for her with an ophthalmologist at 655 Sutter St. A job with a doctor felt exactly right. Every morning she took the E train across the Bay Bridge to the terminal, then walked up the hill to the office. In the long run it might have proved too tiring to make such a long trip both ways every day but in Trudy's life nothing was ever long-run. Before the calendar flipped through the months of the year, fate again put a fork in Trudy's path that would change her direction and make over her life. As always, her network of refugee friends was instrumental in creating this superlative change.

Her friend Liesl had a cousin living in Richmond who was married to a doctor, and she and her husband took both girls under their wing. When Trudy's first Christmas in California rolled around this lovely couple brought a basket to each of them piled high with fruit and all the other goodies they knew neither of the girls could afford. Pinned to the wrapping on each basket was an envelop containing a check and a note saying that the money was to be spent on something each wanted and couldn't give herself. Liesl bought a coveted pair of alligator shoes with her money but Trudy gave herself a vacation. Something Trudy had wanted for months was to visit Los Angeles. In Los Angeles lived a friend of her mother with whom she had faithfully corresponded throughout all the years since she'd left Vienna. Her boss added to the gift of the check by granting her a few days off. Trudy took an overnight trip on a Greyhound Bus and went south.

After checking into a hotel in Los Angeles, Trudy made a few telephone calls which led to a joyous reunion with her mother's old friend. Her mother's friend insisted that when Trudy returned to the Bay Area she was to call the bachelor son of one of her oldest friends. Always open to any new contact, Trudy made the call when she got home. The son answered the phone.

"Do have dinner with Mother and me tomorrow night." he urged after she had explained who she was and why she was calling, "We never eat at home and we're usually in restaurants among strangers. Let us pick you up and carry you off with us for an evening. No dullard would ever be put upon us by mother's friend. I'm sure we'll enjoy meeting you. Give us a chance."

Encouraged by his warmth and good-natured voice Trudy accepted the invitation and enjoyed a rather dull but pleasant evening. When mother and son dropped her at her door he insisted that they have dinner the next night without his mother.

"Mother has a friend over the same night every week and on that night I slip away. Please don't make me eat alone."

Unable to refuse, though not eager for another evening like the one just spent, Trudy reluctantly accepted the invitation. The next night they went to eat at the world famous Claremont Hotel. In those days the gardens around the sparkling white wedding cake Victorian building were extensive and quite beautiful. After dinner they strolled along the garden paths which were well lit by light from lanterns hanging all along the edge of the porch that encircled the hotel.

"My role in life, " he said expansively, "is unabashedly to play cupid. I'd make a good yentel if I do say so myself. Marriage is not my cup of tea. I've known that since I was a boy, but I love to bring people together who ought to know each other."

"And do you propose to match me up with someone?" she asked.

"Of course," he replied smugly. "It won't be hard at all."

"Oh, I don't know," she said flatly. "At thirty-three I'm a little long in the tooth. I've managed to keep my life intact until now, I think I can hold out a little longer."

"Ah, but wait until you see what I come up with," he gloated.

When he dropped her off at her door that night she went in glad to be rid of him. He was insufferably sure of himself. As for his matchmaking, she was sure it was just hot air, conversational stuffing. But to her surprise he called her a few days later, triumph ringing in his voice.

"Trudy" he said, "I have a very interesting man for you."

"You have?" Trudy's voice carried her startled disbelief.

"Didn't I say I would?"

"Yes, but..." she sputtered.

"No buts," he admonished her. "You just have to trust this old fool."

"Neither old nor a fool," she retorted, "but you're right, I have my doubts."

She agreed to meet him and his "catch" for lunch the following Thursday. It might be fun and certainly she could get rid of him, she was a free agent. That morning she dressed very carefully, just in case, and when she left the office for lunch she warned her boss that she might be a little longer than usual. She took a cab to the restaurant and walked in a little nervous about the prospect of having this egotistical "yentel" really pull one out of the hat. He did. The interesting man was Sam.

Sam had heard the same "a very interesting woman for you," and had also been reluctant to come. His secretary had to push him.

"What's the big deal?" she said. "You have lunch and maybe the coffee will be good and maybe not. The girl the same. What have you got to lose? So you already know a woman in Los Angeles. She's in Los Angeles, this woman is here. You don't like her you've still got L.A."

April lst, l954, April Fool's Day, fate gave Trudy a winning hand. The matchmaker brought another woman along to make it a foursome and Trudy took an even longer lunch hour than she had prepared the doctor for. Conversation never lagged and when Sam asked as they left the restaurant if he could drop her at her office she jumped at the offer. Ever practical, always living in the present not the future, she asked him to stop at her bank so she could cash her paycheck which she'd received that morning. It would give her one less errand to run on her way home that night. For some reason that tickled Sam. As he let her out at the office he said, "I might call you. Would you go out with me?"

"Maybe." she said, thinking she'd never hear from him. But the very next day he called.

When Trudy married Sam she left her job with the ophthalmologist and moved into Sam's apartment. When the notice of their marriage appeared in the Chronicle an old friend of Sam's called to congratulate him.

"I've got to meet this new wife of yours," he said. "Wim and Ilse want to meet her too."

"You're in for it," Sam laughed as he hung up the phone. "I guess we'll have to make the rounds so everybody can see the prize I've won."

Wim and Ilse Schiff soon called to invite Trudy and Sam to a big dinner party where many of Sam's friends would be gathered to meet the new bride. Before the evening was over Trudy and Ilse were fast friends. Ilse took Trudy under her wing introducing her to all her friends, meeting her for lunch when she could get away from Wim's office where she worked as his receptionist, sharing guests from the East Coast with the Flamms.

"There's a really nice flat right next door. They've just redecorated it and it's ready to rent." Ilse's father said to them over dinner one night in 1960. "Sam, you want I should go find out about it for you?"

Sam wanted. Sam and Trudy moved in around the corner from the Schiffs and for 8 years as neighbors, Trudy and Ilse were almost inseparable. Friends of one became friends of the other so that whoever Ilse brought into her circle automatically found Trudy part of their experience as well. Ilse always found time for one more dinner party and always the dinner guests were a wonderful collection of congenial people. The hostess with the mostest, they called her. Altogether, life was full and rich for Trudy and Sam.

Then in 1965, at the age of sixty-four, Sam had his first heart attack. He'd worked too hard too long. The heart attack scared him. From his hospital bed he told Trudy to try to sell the business, he wanted out. He dictated an ad for her to put in the paper, an ad that brought him a buyer while he was still flat on his back. The deal was perfect, the man had the necessary financing and he wanted immediate possession. So before he was freed from the hospital Sam was freed from the workaday world and could go home to recuperate without a thing to worry about. They spent their days quietly, enjoying walks around the Marina Green and the Palace of Fine Arts, pausing to feed the ducks and geese on the little lake in front of the marvelous rotunda,. They loved to sit on the grass on sunny days and watch the children launch their little sailboats across the reflections of Bernard Maybeck's masterpiece shimmering in the water of the lake.

May, 1967, Sam and Trudy made their fourth trip to Israel to visit Sam's son, Gabi. They went in order to meet the new baby boy born in Aug. 1966. In the midst of their lovely visit the Suez Canal Crisis broke out and Nasser of Egypt crossed the Sinai desert. The night before they were booked to leave, Gabi had a party for them and invited all his friends. The house was full of young couples when the first knock on the door came. One of the young men was called out and whisked away. Immediately, the atmosphere became somber. Everyone knew what it meant. Before the evening was over most of the young men present had been summoned out and carted off for military duty. The next morning when Trudy and Sam took a cab to the Tel Aviv airport there were women and children and old men out and about, busily at work, but in the entire kibbutz not a single young man was left.

In 1973, Sam and Trudy made their last trip to see Gabi and the family. Sam's heart had supported him well for eight years but shortly after they arrived in Jerusalem he had a massive heart attack and died. It was as though Sam had waited for one more trip, then another, but always with the intention of planting his bones in Israel.

They buried him in Jerusalem, the Holy City he loved so much. Even though Trudy had known for years they were living on borrowed time she wasn't ready to be a widow when death made her one. Sam, handsome Sam, good-natured Sam, Sam the caretaker, had so filled her days she didn't want to face the future without him. She returned alone to the empty house with the too many stairs and echoing footsteps. For nineteen years Sam had taken care of her and when his will was read she learned that he had taken care of her future as well. She wouldn't ever have to go back to work again. At fifty-six, in 1978, she moved to Rossmoor where many of the people she'd met through Ilse now lived. It was Trudy's entrance into Rossmoor that formally brought "The Girls" into existence. In 1990, the first of a series of little strokes overtook her, and in September of 1992 Trudy's death created a major void in their circle. She was the youngest and the first of them to go.

LU (Louise)

Rain streamed down the panes of the window overlooking Kingsbury St. Kingsbury ran its paper-strewn way through one of the most dilapidated neighborhoods of St. Louis. Louise sat alone, dully stirring her coffee, staring out the window of an indifferent little apartment in an unlovely building that flanked the sidewalk of the shabby street. Her mood was in tune with the dismal day outside. Richard was in England in the army, Elizabeth was in school, Rudi was out selling lighting fixtures, and she had nothing to do but keep house, work she had always loathed. The dreariness of trying to make a hospitable home for her family out of the mean little three rooms the four of them occupied constantly overwhelmed her. The slender sandwich on her plate lay half-eaten while the coffee in the chipped cup grew cold. Too dispirited to maintain her customary ramrod erect posture she rested one elbow on the faded oil-cloth covered table and let that hand support her head. She looked indifferently at the boring food on her plate and was struck by a sudden thought. Her life was like that sandwich! The part she had already lived through, had already eaten, had plenty of filling, but the second half, her life today, as well as the yet to be eaten portion of sandwich which lay before her, promised to continue to be tasteless and unappetizing.

In spite of her valiant and defiant resistance to the malevolent forces that had mangled her life these last few years, where was she? The only thing to commend her efforts, the only thing she had to show for the battle she'd fought, was that they were here, and alive. She should be grateful for that. She'd saved them from Auschwitz, or another camp like it. She'd out-fought the Nazis, and accomplished their escape to England. When the British tried to confine them on the Isle of Mann she'd forced the door open again, and gotten them to London where they survived the Blitz. When Rudi's distant relatives who had sent the certificates of sponsorship tried to take Elizabeth from them she'd battled their wealth and power and kept their child with them. But, after all that, was this the future she had struggled so hard to achieve? Was this miserable apartment, and this low class neighborhood to be the environment in which her children would grow up? Was she to end her days grubbing out an existence on the meager living

Rudi, frustrated by the difficulty of doing business in a strange language, brought in? Where was the promise of the good life that the word "America " evoked in the rest of the world.

A tear dripped off the end of her nose. She lifted her head, fished in the pocket of her apron for a handkerchief, and blew hard. Self-pity was the lowest form of human expression; it embarrassed her that on dull days like this she frequently gave in to it. The thing to do was make herself too tired to feel. Crying over what was lost was not going to bring it back, or make things better. It certainly wouldn't bring Babbet to America to look after her. She reached for the scrub bucket and filled it with water at the sink. Seizing a stiff brush she got down on her knees and attacked the worn linoleum. Her half-eaten lunch remained on the table where she'd left it. Elizabeth would finish it when she got home. Vigorously pushing the brush around in soapy circles, Louise let her memory carry her back to happier times where she could feel proud again. The youngest of four children, adored by the governess who came to Louise's family as a young woman and poured her life into theirs, the beginning of her life had been wonderful.

On a generous corner lot in a quiet neighborhood in Aachen, Germany stood their large stone square house. Set back from the streets that ran along two sides of the property, the house was surrounded by manicured lawns and lovely gardens. It was the home of Jonas Hayman, a distinguished looking man in the best German autocratic manner, owner of a textile factory at the outskirts of Aachen, a man noted throughout the city for his philanthropy. The Hayman home was located on the west side of Aachen near the Belgium border. Not a stone's throw away from their home another language was spoken, another government prevailed, another way of life was lived. The nearness of the border played a major role in their lives, in the best of times and in the worst. Jonas had made a good life for himself, his wife and his two sons before the girls ever came along, one close behind the other. The baby, Louise, (forever after called Lu) was his favorite of all the children. Maybe his preference for her stemmed from the fact that she was pretty, like her mother, or maybe because she possessed a certain unquenchable spirit like his own. Whatever it was, as she was growing up Louise always knew that the constant clash of wills between her and her father was their way of belonging to each other.

Jonas' wealth made it possible for him to indulge his beautiful, spoiled wife with everything she desired. She had plenty of servants to do her bidding, to mind her household, and to raise her children. Whatever wrinkles chance put into the fabric of her life were smoothed over, ironed out through the constant vigilance of her husband. Mrs. Hayman entertained often with ladies' luncheons and teas, presiding over the festivities with all the graciousness and protocol prescribed for cultivated women in the nineteenth century. Nothing was ever ostentatious, everything was done quietly, elegantly and graciously. At one of Mrs. Hayman's socials the guests could count on plenty of food, wonderful food, trays full of delicious tidbits served unobtrusively by discretely attired maids. Never did Mrs. Hayman's servants wear those fancy little French uniforms which were all the vogue. The children were never invited in to meet the guests, but they were allowed to peek from the hallways and the staircase where they could keep an anxious eye on how much food was likely to be left for tea in the nursery later on.

Behind the big house, in a little stone cottage facing the side street, lived the chauffeur and his wife. The chauffeur's wife worked in the big house as a maid. On the north side of the rear garden was a greenhouse tended by the gardener who came every day and kept the big house filled with flowers. When Louise was seven, a governess was added to the household staff to teach the children French. It was she who heard their lessons, oversaw their meals, and tucked them in at night. For Louise, the last in line, she became a surrogate for her mother who received her children each afternoon at day's end, then sent them off to their evening meal with the governess. She and her husband dined alone. The governess became such a fixture in the family that she remained long after Louise was grown and gone. In 1933, she nursed Mr. Hayman through his long lingering illness, and after he died, the governess continued on as Mrs. Hayman's companion. She was still in residence five years later when Louise and her family fled Frankfurt and took refuge in the big stone house, protected by the gentile German staff. For weeks as they hid away, any of the servants could have betrayed them, and prevented their escape to England, but their loyalty never wavered.

For the first fifteen years of her life, Louise knew little of the world that lay beyond Aachen. Then came World War I. Aachen lay directly in the path of German armies headed for the Western Front. The city was a major railway center, and troop trains poured through on their way south to France. War began August 7, 1914, and within two months both of Louise's brothers had been drafted into the army. The younger, her favorite, was sent to the Tyrol where he was stationed in the Dolomites. One day in 1915, the telephone lines that led into his army camp were cut by guerrilla fighters from a nearby village. Louise's brother volunteered to go out alone to repair the damage. He was cut down by snipers and became the first German casualty in the mountains of northern Italy. Her older brother was sent to Serbia where he contracted malaria. So the brothers came home before the war was a year old, one to be buried, the other to suffer periodic bouts of malaria for the rest of his life. Eighteen years later, upon the death of their father, the responsibility for carrying on the family name and business fell to this surviving son.

For Louise and her sister, the war was rather a jolly affair - in the beginning. They volunteered for Red Cross work in the summer of 1916, and were assigned to cooking meals for soldiers coming and going across the border into Belgium. Some days they pushed coffee trolleys along the railway platforms as the trains pulled in, which was more fun than cooking. But when the trains started coming back from the Front lines in France pulling ambulance cars filled with boys little older than themselves, the fun drained out of it. It stopped being a lark altogether when the war turned sour for Germany and the lines of cars headed for hospitals deep in the heartland of the nation began outnumbering the cars carrying replacements into the breaches of Germany's trenches. By 1918, when the tide reversed completely, the mood of the girls was sober and scared. November 11, the outgoing flow ceased altogether. No more troops went into France. The incoming tide of returnees threatened to drown Germany in a sea of exhausted, hungry, disheartened young men who left their youth in the mud of the battlefields. They shuffled along the roads leading home, silent, weary, beaten, too many to be fed by the limited staff available to serve them, even if the food had not run out.

They were still coming when the Kaiser was forced to abdicate and go into exile in Holland. The people of Aachen lined his departure route, weeping silently as they watched the long entourage of black automobiles escorted by officers on horseback cross the border. Louise remembered the lonely silhouette of a great horse and rider etched against the dark, bare branches of the trees, the silhouette of a general who rode beside the car carrying the Kaiser away from Germany. At the border the general saluted the sorrowing people watching the symbol of German might leave them leaderless behind.

"It is over," he said as tears rolled down his face, "You are all free to go to your homes and try to resume your lives. May God bless you."

They went home, but there was no resumption of life as it had been. Within a few days the main roads out of Belgium into Germany were filled with Belgian soldiers coming as occupation troops into the first German city in their path. They did not come to keep the peace, they came for revenge. Every indignity heaped upon the Belgian people while they were occupied was to be replicated in Aachen, and as far East as Belgian occupation extended. Killing the population outright was forbidden by the Declaration of Peace signed by the conquering Allies at Versailles, but the Belgians passed ordinance after ordinance designed to grind down and humiliate every German, regardless of sex or age. Civil Rights disappeared completely. Each night hostages were taken from the wealthiest families and locked up in the City Hall. If Aachen remained quiet through the night the hostages were released the next morning. If, on the other hand, there was any disturbance of any kind in the city, the Belgians killed their captives and left their bodies for days on the City Walls to putrefy as a warning to the rest of the populace. Mr. Hayman became obsessed with fear for his daughters. The Germans had raped Belgian women, would his daughters be raped in retaliation? He put Yale locks on their bedroom doors and locked them in at night as though Yale locks would protect anyone against rifle butts slammed through wooden panels. Fortunately, no harm ever fell on his family and his house was never vandalized.

Belgian occupation didn't last long. Before spring, they were replaced by the French, and the French occupiers made the Belgians look like school boys led by a timid tutor. One of the first French measures was to put a nine o'clock curfew into effect. Anyone foolhardy enough to venture out after that hour could almost be assured of being a victim of rape, mayhem, or murder - at the very least a beating. Parties began before nine and lasted until after 6:00 a.m. when the curfew was lifted. There were no latecomers to any social event. Hysteria took over. Disillusioned, ill-nourished, irritable under the constraints of occupation, humiliated, the young people of Germany mocked all tradition. Nothing was sacred. Manners and morals went out the window. It was not only a time of radical political change, it was a time of social disorder. An old way of life had died and there was no discernible form to the future. The occupation of Aachen lasted an interminable two years.

Before the war, Louise had the usual upper-class, German education. She'd gone to private elementary school, then to the same finishing school her sister attended before her. It was a serious mistake where Louis was concerned. Finishing school was not for her. Her sister learned needlepoint at their mother's knee, Louise devoured novels, hiding away in some corner of the house, out of sight, where no one would know what she was reading. She read as hungrily as she ate. At sixteen, with the world at war, Louise knew she was too old for a simpering housemother to come into her room at night to tuck her in. She protested to her father that she didn't belong in that smothering atmosphere, and when he wouldn't listen she left school and went home.

When her father enrolled her he'd guaranteed a full year's tuition. Though his daughter was no longer in residence, he had to pay anyway. Mr. Hayman was furious. For punishment, he sent Louise to his aunt in Berlin for the winter and sent her sister along to keep an eye on her. What punishment! The Hayman girls had a rollicking good time in the big city. They attended the theater every night, they promenaded the boulevards by day, they were on their own, as carefree as birds. Their aunt refused to be a jailer. The sophistication of Berlin was heady, it made poor old Aachen look dowdy indeed. But the winter ended, and with the coming of summer they were ordered back home. When they returned, they began their Red Cross duties which occupied them for the duration of the war. To Louise's lifelong sorrow, when she walked away from finishing school she walked into an impasse with her father which denied her the University education she longed for. Mr. Hayman would not pay twice.

The Hayman mill was not the only textile mill in town. There was another, and a Mr. Hahn managed it for its absentee owners. Mr. Hahn had two sons. Rudi, the younger son, was tall for his age and very handsome. He and Louise were thrown together constantly when they were children and from early adolescence they took it for granted that some day they would marry. The Hahns watched their puppy love blossom into a binding relationship with delight. Mr. Hayman, however, was adamantly opposed to such a union. He thought young Rudi was a light-weight, "a boy" too immature for marriage. He ordered Louise to look for someone else. Ordering Louise never worked. Orders made her back hump like a hissing cat and, once ordered, nothing could move her.

Rudi's mother died when he was a small boy. His father quickly remarried taking as his bride a young widow just returned with her little daughter from St. Louis, Missouri, the heartland of the United States. Americanized, Rudi's step sister knew no class consciousness. She was a little democrat in her attitudes towards adults and children. Her spontaneity and frank friendliness disarmed children raised to mind their manners and remember that "children should be seen and not heard." She innocently did what none of them dared to do. Herr Professors did not speak to children outside the classroom and children never approached Herr Professors, inside or outside the classroom, except with great formality. One day the little girl danced up to the headmaster on the playground, twirled around in front of him and demanded that he admire her new hat. Stunned by such rudeness, the other children waited for the sky to fall, but after a startled pause the Herr Professor mumbled something inaudible and not unkindly turned away. Louise took in that little vignette and held it in her heart. "Someday," she told herself, "someday I'm going to get out of here and go to America."

Rudi's stepmother indulged and petted him, and allowed him to grow up a dilettante, learning a smattering of this and a bit of that, generally having his way with the world. It was no wonder that Jonas Hayman warned his daughter against the handsome young will-o-the-wisp.

"That poppin-jay is good for nothing but dancing and playing." Jonas said with great distaste.

"That 'poppin-jay' is going to be your son-in-law" Louise retorted. "You should try to cultivate him, not castigate him."

"Cultivate him?!" her father snorted, "I don't have to cultivate him. He's like a weed, he's underfoot all the time."

"He's not underfoot! He's here only when I invite him, but after we're married he'll be here as often as I am." She smiled smugly to annoy him.

"You will have to do everything a husband should do." he thundered. "He will never amount to anything."

"I will pick my own husband," Louise shot back. "And you don't need to worry, we won't need anything from you." They were brave words Louise later had to eat.

At twenty-three, fed up with the aimless life she was forced to live because her father would not hear of her working, Louise married Rudi. It was a small wedding for Rudi's father died six weeks earlier and the rituals of mourning would not allow a lovely, big affair like her sister had enjoyed. Technical director of the factory, Mr. Hahn took control of the business upon the death of his boss, and immediately after Rudi's wedding announced:

"I will not have that young wastrel on the staff!" Unceremoniously Rudi was booted out by his own father.

A financial settlement was made, a modest sum which Rudi promptly squandered. Louise never knew where the money went. The bridegroom thought he'd married a rich girl whose family would care for them so he could see no reason for being prudent, to save or invest. But Mr. Hayman was not cut off the same bolt of cloth as Rudi's father. He gave Louise a dowry, a much smaller dowry than her sister received, with the stern warning that he wouldn't give the young couple a cent of allowance. Part of her sister's dowry had been a lovely new house with the first private swimming pool in Aachen. Her sister had married an Aachen boy who met Mr. Hayman's standards. He would dutifully bring his wife to dinner at the Haymans every week.

"My sister was a TRUE WOMAN," said Louise tossing her head in disdain. "She loved to dust and polish furniture. I wasn't like that. I wanted to be a modern woman. I wanted to know more than just how to keep a house."

Rather than have Rudi unemployed and penniless, the technical director found a position for him in a branch plant in

Frankfurt-on-Maine. Rudi and Louise would not be coming for dinner at the big house in Aachen after all. In marrying defiantly, just as in leaving finishing school defiantly, Louise had put herself in straits from which there seemed no escape. In Frankfurt, Rudi received the title of "Representative." In other words they gave him nothing to do, and at a very small salary for doing it. Frankfurt, in 1922, was as short of affordable housing as was every other German city after World War I. If you were not born in the city of your residence your chances of finding a decent place to live were slim at best. The young couple found two rooms in a boarding house where the landlady was even more destitute than they. Her conditions for letting them have the two rooms were that they would feed her and her staff.

The young Hahns began drawing on Louise's dowry for the necessities of life almost as soon as they were married. For three years they drained her funds while life remained static, mean and narrow. Then Louise was pregnant. Their situation did not merit having a family, their income was too small and their quarters far too cramped. Nevertheless, ready or not, they were going to be parents. She had no enthusiasm for this intrusion of a child into her stunted life. When, Richard, a son was born, he was long and well formed and beautiful. As soon as she held him against her she cast him as her compensation for lost dreams and the narrow straits of the last three years. The old governess came for the confinement of her darling, and when she saw the stringent life Louise was forced to live she was horrified. The full impact of just how tight things really were became apparent the day she asked Louise to advance the money for a dressmaker and Louise had to admit that she couldn't. The governess was disappointed in not getting something fashionable from Frankfurt, but not getting a new dress was inconsequential in the face of the fact that Louise's dowry was gone. Tight-lipped, the governess went back to Aachen and confronted Mr. Hayman.

"How can you let her live like this?" she demanded. "She's your daughter and she's living worse than any of your servants!"

"She chose her path!" he protested. "It's her own doing."

"And I suppose you never made a mistake, or needed to be forgiven for anything when you were young?" Few people dared to talk to the master of the Hayman house as the governess freely did whenever she chose.

Mr. Hayman blustered but was abashed nonetheless. He contacted Louise and asked her to come home for a visit. It was humbling for the proud man to have to ask one of his own children to spend some time with him, she had not been back since she married. He'd missed her and had needed an excuse to contact her. It was equally humbling for Louise to be forced by poverty to go home when she felt so unloved and abused, but she went. Mr. Hayman offered her a monthly allowance with only one string attached, that she come home every month for a few days. Louise had to accept the terms because she had to accept the money. So, once a month she took the baby home to his grandparents where Mr. Hayman doted over him, and Louise's mother vicariously fondled him as she watched the governess hold him and feed him and bathe him.

Louise hated those visits. The big dining table groaned with sumptuous food in stark contrast to her own simple fare. The conversation always turned on how well her brother and her brother-in-law were succeeding, or what her sister was doing to her house. Every topic seemed to Louise to be a rebuke aimed at her for having made such a poor choice in her selection of a mate. Always, she returned to Frankfurt in angry tears only to have Rudi scold her for being so emotional. However, life was easier with the allowance. The Hahns could afford the theater now and then, and new clothes when they needed them. Little Richard grew fat and happy, a lovely baby, and Louise made a friend or two. Life was looking up.

Then Richard was four, and Louise was pregnant again. She was staggered by the enormity of it. Another child would eat up the allowance from her father. She felt helplessly trapped. Just when her son was almost old enough to go out the door to school so that perhaps she could go out the door to work, she was going to start over on another child! During her next trip to Aachen all her bitterness boiled over during a shouting match between her and her father that made the air crackle. It started over something trivial but quickly mushroomed into a major fracas.

"You should have been a lawyer!" her father raged at one point.

"If you hadn't denied me the university education I wanted I just might be one!" she shouted back.

"Get a divorce!" he commanded. "I'll take care of you."

"You can't tell me what to do!" She threw her head back in that imperious Hayman posture, her eyes spitting fire. Then abruptly she put her hands over her face and began to cry. "I can't get a divorce." she sobbed, I'm pregnant."

Silence, broken only by her crying, settled over the room like a heavy blanket. Mr. Hayman cleared his throat but found no words. After a startled gasp, Mrs. Hayman turned to stare out the window. No one received her news with joy, no one offered any sympathy, not even the governess could frame a congratulatory little speech. Mr. Hayman raised her allowance a little and Louise crept back to Frankfurt humiliated once again, and filled with despair. With another mouth to feed, the depression that had gripped the country since 1919 not letting up, how were they ever going to get ahead? The next seven months passed glacialy slowly. Again the governess came to see Louise through the birth, and again Louise's mother remained at home. This good Catholic woman took a second generation of Jewish children to her heart and became the grandmother to them that their natural grandmother could not, would not be. They named the pretty little girl Elizabeth, a name beloved by Catholics and Jews alike. With big round eyes in an oval face Elizabeth was as pretty as her name. Louise was delighted with her. She would hold the baby close and wonder how she could have wished not to have this little miracle. Committing Louise's father to a further increase in allowance before she left for Aachen, the governess secured the full time services of Babbet for her darling.

Babbet was a simple village woman old enough to be Louise's mother. When the Hahns came to live in the rooming house, Babbet was the old landlady's cook. She became the Hahns' maid as well, tidying up their quarters was part of her job. She never charged Louise anything for her services knowing that they were already paying for the food she ate. Babbet's niece came to live in the house to be the upstairs maid. After her arrival she took over the care of the Hahns' quarters but she had to be paid. Louise paid her with bits and pieces of her trousseau which her own simple life gave her no opportunity to wear. Not long after Elizabeth was born the Hahns moved into a small apartment and Babbet came to live with them. She worked for room and board only, refusing a salary.

The wrath of the Nazis fell on Frankfurt months before it fell on Aachen. As a border city Aachen was a window on the West. Frankfurt was inland and out of the world's view. Frankfurt Jews were generally wealthy and very visible in the life of the city. They were leaders in the community: in education, in the Arts, and in their benevolence to the poor. They had endowed the city with museums, parks and clinics. Once Hitler came to power, overnight they became pariahs. They were treated to the same kinds of indignities and the same denigrating segregation that marked race relations in the United States in the l930's. First, they were excluded from the public swimming pools. Next, their children were forbidden entrance to playgrounds around the Plaza area in the heart of the city. Following that, the children's ordinance was passed that ordered Jewish children off the streets except while in transit to or from school. Jewish teachers were fired from their teaching posts; some disappeared, others obtained exit visas and left Germany. Schools where Jewish children were numerous began to close as the Jewish children were forced into segregated schools. In those segregated schools, a handful of teachers taught all eight grades in one room. Elizabeth found herself in a room with 63 other children. There were not enough chairs so she sat the first day on the lap of one of the older students. While one grade level was reciting the rest were supposed to be studying. It was a mockery of education

It was no longer safe for any Jew of any age to be seen on the streets alone. Every morning, when Elizabeth and Richard left for school, Louise began a vigil which ended only when they were safe inside her door again that afternoon. She lived in terror of some new decree that would separate her from her children. Louise and Rudi tried to keep life as even for the children as they could, and as sane for themselves as possible. At night they played games with Richard and Elizabeth, helped them with their homework, and on the surface kept up the appearance of things being normal. They rented weekend retreats outside Frankfurt where for two days they could laugh and walk and live as though the fearful world behind them had disappeared. But every Monday morning it all began again. Not many weekends of escape lay before them before the Nazis tightened the noose around Jews even more tightly, and no longer allowed them to leave the city for any reason. Week by week, life became more tenuous and more terrifying. Louise began to plot their escape from Germany.

Rudi's step-mother's relatives had been treated like family whenever they came to Germany for visits. The St. Louis kin were wined and dined and partied to the hilt when they were in Frankfurt. Surely they would send affidavits to clear the path for the Hahns to go to America. Confidently, Louise sent off letters never expecting any hesitancy on the part of "their Americans." Knowing they wouldn't be able to take any money, stocks or bonds out with them, she wracked her brain for ideas of enterprises they might successfully pull off once they were in St. Louis. A good German restaurant might work. She was a good cook and a good organizer, but restaurants were risky, especially in depressed times like the 1930's. She thought of a rooming house like the one they had lived in when they first came to Frankfurt, but a rooming house would only provide them with shelter and food, there was no profit in an enterprise like that. What about a small hotel where they could have a few permanent guests, but operate a large dining room? They could make enough doing that to live well and send the kids to college. Having made the decision, Louise set to work with a will to prepare for the new adventure. In an apartment upstairs in the building next door lived a Maitre de with whom she chatted most mornings as they waited for the postman. She wooed him into teaching all four of the Hahns how to wait tables. Elizabeth, only ten at the time, today laughs and says she still knows how to carry three plates on one arm.

Satisfied that her plan would work, Louise bought ten beds and all the linens for them, and shipped them to Amsterdam. She shipped dishes, cooking pots, table linens, everything she could buy in Germany to be used in America. Safe in Amsterdam, beyond the reach of the Nazis, her future could be stored until she had an address in America to which their belongings could be shipped. That done, she began to telephone the American embassy in Stuttgart, almost daily, waiting anxiously for the affidavits to arrive. Right after the New Year of 1938 she was told that an affidavit had arrived, but it was only for one Rudi Hahn, and his daughter Elizabeth. Louise couldn't believe it. She took the train to Stuttgart to pick up the affidavit, convinced the Embassy was in error. But it was true. She and Richard were not covered. She wrote frantically to the St. Louis clan imploring them to straighten it out. The Hahns could not leave without affidavits for all four of them. They would not leave in pairs. Living in the limbo of possessing only two affidavits, the strain of daily life in Frankfurt began to strangle them. Unable to be inactive any longer, Louise hired a car and a chauffeur whom she felt she could trust and, leaving their apartment intact so as not to arouse suspicion, the four of them took a circuitous route to the north to escape detection, and fled to Aachen, to the safety of her mother's house.

Life for the Jews of Aachen was so little disturbed in the beginning of Hitler's aggression against the Jews that in 1933 Mr. Hayman died his slow diabetic death convinced that the horror stories he heard from other parts of the country were either grossly exaggerated or would never happen in his town. Within weeks of his death, his son-in-law was scooped up and sent to Auschwitz. Any residual feeling of "it can't happen here" was wiped out instantly. The brother-in-law was released almost immediately, but panic gripped the whole family. "It" had reached Aachen, and the wealth of the Haymans had singled them out for the first attack. Louise's brother lost no time in transferring the family's assets to Holland, all the cash, all the stocks, every negotiable thing. When he had stripped their possessions as close to the bone as he dared, with only the house and the mill left, he quietly disappeared with his family across the border. Soon after, Louise's sister and her husband followed him into exile. Mrs. Hayman and Louise's family were all the family left in Germany. While Louise remained in Frankfurt Mrs. Hayman was completely dependent on her servants without whose loyalty she would have been helpless. There was enough continuing income from the mill to maintain a modicum of comfort, but funds were running low when Louise and her little family descended on the household in 1938.

The arrival of four refugees created consternation. If the Nazis learned that Rudi was on premises they believed occupied only by one old woman and her staff, he was doomed and the staff would be charged with helping a Jew, a crime against the state. Rudi, consumed with fear, was reduced to trembling pulp. He became a virtual prisoner in his mother-in-law's home. Everything hinged on the loyalty of the servants, a state of mind that could change at any moment. Mrs. Hayman's household staff presented good reason to be alarmed.

The gardener was a member of the Nazi Party. He must not know of Rudi's presence. From the moment he reported for work in the morning until he left the premises in late afternoon, eyes peered through the lace curtains at him, constantly watching his movements. If he rang the bell to receive instructions, the house became as silent as a tomb. The chauffeur was no Nazi, and his wife was not only not a Nazi she was so outspoken against the ruling party that the family feared she'd inadvertently bring the wrath of the authorities down on their heads. The maid was so devoted to the family that her agitation over the new situation left her a nervous wreck. Louise was afraid that her anxiety would alert the neighborhood that something was wrong at Mrs. Hayman's. The hairdresser who came each day to do her mother's hair had a Gestapo boyfriend who dropped her off and picked her up. When he had to wait, he sat in the kitchen and drank coffee, gossiping with the cook. That worthy was such a gregarious soul Louise wanted someone to sit in the kitchen with them to monitor their conversations. While any Jewish household simmered with fear under the best of circumstances, in 1938 the Hayman home became a pressure cooker. One thing that may have held the Nazis at bay for so long was that in 1929 Mr. Hayman had the long porch of the house which faced onto the side street closed in, and there he'd operated a soup kitchen for Aachen's poor until his death.

During their weeks of residence in Aachen Elizabeth was sent to school. Now almost ten, she was enrolled in the nearest school which admitted Jewish students. Each day she came and went as any little girl would come and go who was living with her grandmother, but she was admonished every morning when she left the house to never mention her father. The child lived in constant fear that she would say something which would betray him. She was never allowed to leave her Grandmother's yard after school, and neighbor children were told that Mrs. Hayman was too old for them to come there to play. Most of the time after school, and after supper before bedtime, Elizabeth went to the chauffeur's lively home for company. The chauffeur's wife inwardly wept over the little child whose life was so precarious and whose days were so lonely. She spent time listening to Elizabeth prattle on and entertained her as best she could.

Richard was tutored at home. A loyal employee at the factory came to the house at night and taught him all he could learn about the technologies of weaving without being able to lay his hands on any of the machinery. Louise wanted him educated for survival once they were out of Germany. Artistic, gifted, sensitive and very bright, the weaving business held no charm for Richard, but Louise was adamant. He must learn what he must learn. In the first days of their stay, Louise went about the neighborhood as casually as though she had brought the children home for a visit while Rudi sat in an upstairs room out of sight reading whatever he could lay his hands on. But once her presence in the neighborhood was taken for granted, Louise began writing daily to Stuttgart. She carried the letters to and from the post office herself so that the postman would not become suspicious. Finally, word came that a second affidavit for Louise and Richard was on hand and could be picked up at the office with proper identification. It meant a dangerous train ride to Stuttgart that she must make alone. There was still the hurdle of Exit Visas ahead. Louise made the trip, dressed poorly and inconspicuously like a simple char woman. Safely back in Aachen, she wrote to the Gestapo in Frankfurt requesting that the forms for exit visas be sent to her by mail. To her dismay she learned that she had to apply in person in the police jurisdiction of Frankfurt where she was registered. That meant going back to their apartment.

"We have to go back to Frankfurt!" She wailed as Rudi sat by his upstairs window reading.

Startled, Rudi looked up at her, going pale. "Why!?" he demanded hoarsely.

"Because we have to apply for exits at the police station in Frankfurt in person!" She collapsed into a chair with the frightening notice crumpled in her hand.

"In person? No!" Rudi's strangled refusal was adamant. Louise's temper flared.

"What do you mean, 'No!' You don't say 'No' to the Nazis! You say things that sound like you're saying 'yes' even when you mean 'No.'" Her voice rose in spite of her effort to keep a lid on her emotions. The servants would overhear her.

"YOU make them think you're saying Yes." Rudi whispered fiercely. "I'm not going." He gripped the arms of the chair as though resisting being pulled to his feet.

"We both have to go. It says so here in this letter." Bending over him, she waved the wad of paper in his face.

"I don't care what it says in that paper. I'm not going. I'd rather try to run across the border in broad daylight than go back to Frankfurt." He was sweating profusely. "You have to do it, Lu, you have to do it. I can't. I can't!""

Lu looked at him in disgust. "You can't do it, but you'll send me!" Her nostrils flared.

They argued for over an hour, but Rudi would not yield. His terror was so great Lu alternated between feeling pity for him and wanting to kill him. In the end she knew it was up to her, all of it. Wearily, she pushed her hair back off her face and walked out. So, the word was spread around the neighborhood that Mrs. Hahn was returning to Frankfurt to be with her husband for a time but that the children were staying on with their grandmother in her absence. Even though they had paid the rent in advance before leaving for Aachen so that the apartment was still theirs, Louise was afraid. A "Jew apartment" was not a safe place to be. She threw herself on the mercy of Babbet to give her shelter.

From Babbett's, she began calling friends. She needed information. Before she entered the lion's den of the Gestapo office, she needed to talk to someone who could tell her how to go about obtaining an exit visa before she tried to do it. One of her old neighbors sent her word that there was a man with a mustache at the Immigration Office who was sympathetic to Jews and she should approach him when she went. He was especially susceptible to women, her informant told her. Louise dressed in her best suit, gathered up her courage, and set off for the City Hall. Outwardly, she gave the impression of being calm and in complete control as she entered the building and quietly asked for directions to the office where one obtained an exit visa. She was directed to an upper floor which meant taking the elevator. Fortunately, it was empty which gave her time to collect her courage. When she reached the door marked Immigration she hesitated only a moment, then took a deep breath and throwing her shoulders back, swept in. Casually gazing around the room, she was horrified to see not one but three men with mustaches seated behind desks, each of which was flanked by a visitor's chair. For one wild instant she didn't know whether to run or to throw up. She stood rooted to the floor until one man raised his head from his work and looked directly at her. That contact was like an electric shock that galvanized her into action. She coolly let her eyes travel over the other faces in the room as though searching for someone in particular. Then feigning recognition, she walked over to the man who seemed to her to have the most gentle countenance of them all.

"Good morning." she said, "I've come to fill out applications for exit visas for myself, my husband and our two children." She made it sound as though it was the most reasonable request in all the world to make.

"Why did your husband not come himself to fill out these papers?" he sneered. "He is the head of the family, not you."

The sneer made her flush with anger but Louise answered steadily enough, "My husband is away on a trip."

Loud laughter broke out all around her. To a Nazi, a Jew being away on a trip meant only one thing, he'd already been picked up.

Tossing her head haughtily, Louise said steadily, "When the papers are ready my husband will be here to pick them up, never fear."

Affected by her pride and her plight, the mustached man looked at her appraisingly then got together the papers that were required for application and went over them with her, step by step, telling her what had to be done and the order in which it must all happen. Louise watched him with narrowed eyes appearing to be intent on his instructions, all the while unfolding a mad plan in her head. When she leaned over to pick up the papers she said sotto voice,

"Why don't you come by my apartment tonight?"

Startled, the man looked up and read what he wanted to read in her eyes. She was one elegant, lovely woman. Such a woman and such an invitation were not to be missed. He nodded almost imperceptibly, and Louise left on trembling knees. For the rest of the day she walked around the apartment caught between terror at what she was doing and a fierce determination to see it through. So much hung in the balance, perhaps their very lives. That night when the doorbell rang she opened the door of the apartment and stepped aside to allow the mustached man to enter the foyer. Expectations were writ large on his face. Louise coyly closed the door behind him, then skirted past him briskly before he could take charge of the situation, beckoning him to follow. She led him straight toward the kitchen. Surprised, he followed saying archly,

"Where are you taking me?"

"Never mind," she answered, "you'll see."

In the kitchen, before he could touch her, Louise swung an arm out and pointed to the refrigerator. "There!" she exclaimed. "It's yours if you'll help us."

Before him stood one of the first American Frigidaires to ever come into Germany. It was one of the last presents Louise had received from her father. The man stared at the Frigidaire and then at Louise as the light dawned in his eyes. She had tricked him. And, luckily, it amused him. Such an appliance was beyond the wildest dreams of a lowly clerk like himself, and she had known that. Never would he be able to afford such luxury. He laughed heartily as all thought of sex flew out the window. Then he bent to inspect the refrigerator. He opened the door and he closed it, not once but several times to be sure the light went on every time. He slid the trays in and out obviously pleased with the ease with which they moved along the track. He ran his fingers sensuously over the smooth surface. He peered inside to check for chips and stains.

"Free?" he demanded, turning his head to look her full in the face his eyes alight with lust - for the refrigerator.

"Free," said Louise firmly, "if you help us."

He stood back and folded his arms over his chest looking at the gleaming white extravagance with the pride of ownership shining in his eyes. Then he looked admiringly at Louise and chuckled. "I'll do what I can." he said.

He did all he could, but in the end the regulations overran him. Rudi must come in himself. The visas could not be issued without the personal signature of the male head of the household affixed to the documents in the presence of an Immigration Officer. Reluctantly, Louise sent for Rudi. Traumatized with fear, Rudi spent some of their precious money on a sleeping car for the four hour trip from Aachen to Frankfurt riding with the blinds drawn all the way. To his surprise the visit to the Immigration Office was uneventful. The papers were signed, an appointment was made with the Gestapo for packing, and they went back to the apartment to dismantle it. With a Gestapo agent present to make sure nothing was packed that was disallowed, they had to crate everything for shipment. The Gestapo plastered every crate with manifests detailing to the last item the contents within. The wages of the Gestapo men for the hours they spent in supervising the packing the possessions of their victims had to be paid for by the victims themselves. That ate away more of their slender funds. Next, all bonds, stocks, jewelry, and portable wealth, had to be turned over to the Nazis. They were given receipts for everything, receipts they thought were worthless.

"Ridiculous" Louise snorted. "Receipts that can be turned in to whom for what!?" But she kept them all the same.

At last it was done, everything that was required. The refrigerator was hauled away, the crates were shipped off to the warehouse in Amsterdam, the apartment was given up, and they sent for the children. When Elizabeth and Richard arrived, the four of them checked into a hotel which they had prepaid, along with their tickets to St. Louis, before turning over their remaining funds. Such advance payments were allowed; after all, the money was being spent in Germany. They expected to stay at that hotel for their last night on German soil - and then it happened. Rudi was arrested! Less than twenty four hours to go, within one day of escape, and the ground was wiped out from under their feet! They took him right from the hotel lobby and pushed him into a staff car which sped away with sirens going full blast. Like a very bad movie Louise stood frozen, too stunned to react, while they carried him off right before her eyes. Her head swam and her knees went weak. Then she shook with fury at the sadistic hypocrisy of the Nazi betrayal and fury released her from the paralysis which had kept her immobile during the crisis.

That night she sent the children back to Aachen with a driver, gave up the hotel suite and moved in with a friend. Until daybreak, she walked the floor too angry to sleep, planning her next move. The following day she telephoned Gestapo headquarters and demanded to know where her husband was. It was obvious they'd expected the call.

"You have everything we had!" she shouted over the phone. "Now give me back my husband."

"You may have your husband," the cold voice on the other end of the line informed her, "when you return the visas you were issued."

"Return the visas!?" she cried. "I will not! Never! Where is my husband?"

"He's in the City Jail and that's where he will be until you turn over the visas. He can rot there for all we care."

Louise slammed down the receiver. Without those visas they would never get out alive, and without Rudi she couldn't use them. The Nazis had her cornered. Government regulations would not allow any woman to go out of the country alone, particularly a woman with children. Another long night of walking the floor and wringing her hands followed while her mind worked furiously. By daybreak she was exhausted but she had a plan which she promptly set in motion. She went to the City Jail to make sure Rudi was there and to make sure they understood she would not turn over the visas. The next day she made a return trip. The third day she gave one of the jailers 60 marks asking him to buy bananas for Rudi.

"My husband loves bananas," she said in what she hoped was a distraught, wifely tone. "If I knew he was getting something he liked to eat this would be easier for me."

She knew Rudi would never see the bananas, that the jailer would pocket the money, but 60 marks a day probably would keep him alive, twenty four hours at a time. Loathing the simple-minded man she had to hoodwink, she made the trip every day, and every day she again simpered like a helpless housewife and gave up another sixty marks. She hired a lawyer with money she obtained from her mother, but the lawyer was forced to leave Germany for defending a Jew. She hired another, and the same drama was played out. By the end of three weeks she had watched three lawyers disappear from Frankfurt without Rudi being released from jail. Then the Nazis made her another offer. They could see that from somewhere she was getting money. They meant to get all of it they could. She was told she could buy Rudi's freedom for 25,000 marks. It was a ludicrous, preposterous offer! The extortionists already had all her wealth. Her mother couldn't raise a sum like that. There were no more resources to draw on. Then she remembered a banker in Aachen, a gentile who had been a friend of her father's and who had done business with the factory. She telephoned him and dumped her tale of

195

woe into his lap. Without a moment's hesitation he promised that the 25,000 marks would be telegraphed within the hour. He was as good as his word.

Money in hand, Louise phoned the Gestapo to tell them that she'd meet their terms. They told her to bring the money in person to the sixth floor of the Gestapo building where she would turn the money over and receive the papers for Rudi's release. Louise was sure it was a trick. It couldn't be that simple, but she had to play it out the best she could. She went to the sixth floor of the Gestapo Building and imperiously faced the smirking faces of the men waiting to spring their trap. When they ordered her to hand over the money she blazed away.

"You will not get my money until I hear with my own ears you give the order over the telephone for my husband's release. Until I hear you say it, and I'm convinced the warden heard it, you don't get one cent!"

They could have taken it away from her forcibly and she knew it, but her ferocity overwhelmed them. There was no more dickering. They put her on an extension and she listened as the Gestapo agent in charge gave the warden the order for Rudi's release and she heard the warden agree to do so. Satisfied, she flung the money onto the counter and without waiting for another worthless receipt raced for the elevator. Out on the street she frantically hailed a cab and headed for the jail. She was a nervous wreck by the time she got there, sure the Nazis were not through with her. When the cab pulled up at the curb and there was no Rudi waiting outside the jail as promised, she nearly collapsed. Stricken, not knowing what to do now, she sat in the cab staring blindly at the building. Then there was Rudi swinging jauntily down the street toward her. Three weeks without a bath, a shave or a haircut, the moment they opened the doors of the prison and let him out he took himself off to the nearest bath house and barbershop. Pleased with his appearance he was hurt by the fury Louise poured out on him.

"How could you do it?" she screamed. "How could you frighten me so? I thought they'd kept you, that they'd tricked me! How could you go off like that as though it was over?"

Rudi climbed sulkily into the cab saying nothing. He sat in the corner and pouted as Louise ordered the cab off to the station where they caught the next train for Aachen. The precious visas were still in her possession. There were still two more obstacles in their path before they could actually leave the country, obstacles they would have to handle from the sanctuary of her mother's home. While she was embroiled with Rudi's arrest and incarceration she discovered she was pregnant. They had exit visas for four people, not five. She also learned that, though the Germans might let them out, in order for England to allow them in they had to have $l000 on deposit in London. $l000! No Jew could leave Germany with more than ten dollars per member of the family in their possession. Where could she get $l000 from outside Germany that could be deposited in London? And what was she to do about the pregnancy? She was living a hideous, endless nightmare from which there was no waking up..

Her brother in Holland could help with the money if he would, he had never forgiven Louise for marrying Rudi. If he would help, if he did come through with the money, and if she could abort the baby before anyone knew about it, then maybe they'd still be all right. She could think of no other way around either problem. She couldn't eat, she couldn't sleep, and every day the situation in her mother's household grew more tense. She wrote to her brother and pleaded with him to make the required deposit. He refused. Fear turned to rage. He had to turn over the measly thousand dollars, measly to him, impossible for her. He had taken all the assets with him into Holland that her mother could have drawn on to help them. What right had he to refuse? What kind of pressure could she apply that would work? At last she thought of a former neighbor of theirs in Aachen who might have enough influence over him to make him come through. She contacted the neighbor who was now living in Switzerland.

When the Jews began to disappear from their home neighborhoods and word leaked out about where they had gone, Louise had the foresight to go to this neighbor, who was a jeweler, and pay him to make a bracelet of pure platinum for her. One of the jewelry fashions of the day was chain-link identification bracelets. One could buy them made of pot metal at Woolworth's, or find them made of sterling silver in department stores, or purchase them in the most expensive jewelry shops worked in silver or gold. Platinum could look like pot metal at best, or like silver even though it was the most expensive of all metals. Behind drawn curtains in his home the jeweler made the bracelet and when he turned it over to Louise he said, "Wear it casually as though it means nothing. Some day it may save your life." Soon after completing the bracelet he had taken his family and gone to Switzerland. Louise called him up.

Appalled by the callousness of her brother, the jeweler took the next train through France and Belgium to Holland and confronted him. When her brother crossed the border into Holland four years before he had gone sans passport, sans work permit, sans exit visa. He had simply walked down the street and across the border after shipping all his household goods to Utrecht. He had no right to be living and working in Holland. The jeweler pointed out to him that though the authorities might overlook his lack of proper papers as long as there was no difficulty, if there should be a lawsuit........? The jeweler didn't have to draw a detailed description of what could happen. Louise's brother deposited the money in London in Louise's name, and when he mailed her the pass book the jeweler went home. One of her problems was solved but she still had the other. The idea of an abortion was abhorrent to her. How could she destroy an unborn life? She was in agony over it. But if she didn't abort this child what about the two she already had? If the authorities suspected she was pregnant they'd never let them out, and none of them would survive. She had heard about physical examinations at the borders as a way of preventing the departure of Jews who had managed to get exit visas through fair means or foul. To whom could she turn? She went to her old Aachen doctor and confided in him.

"What can I do?" she wept.

"I don't know liebschen, I don't know. If I aborted that baby both of us could be killed. You are a healthy woman. There is no medical reason why you can't carry that child full term. You know the law. I can't help you! I wish I could but I can't."

She did know the law, the law that forbid any woman, gentile or Jew, from aborting, and forbid any doctor to perform such an operation. The penalty for patient and doctor alike was death. She turned to a neighbor in despair. "What can I do?"

"What you do," said the neighbor, "is go to the butcher's and buy calf's liver, the younger the better. Then you bring it home and smear bits of the tissue all over your nightgown and on your crotch, between your legs, and down the inside of both thighs half way to the knees, make sure everything is good and bloody and that there are little bits of tissue inside your vagina. Be sure to get it on your nightgown and your robe like fresh blood. Be generous. Then you go back to that doctor in the middle of the night and tell him you have pain and you're sure you are miscarrying. He will do it then, I know."

Louise listened in fascinated revulsion. Did she have the nerve? She thought of Elizabeth and Richard and knew she had no options. She followed her neighbor's directions, she smeared herself with the blood and the tissue so like placenta, and dressed in bloody night clothes rang the doctor's bell in the middle of the night. In a room in an upper wing of his house which he had set up for emergency operations he finished Louise's "miscarriage." If he was suspicious he never let on. Weak from a real loss of blood, Louise crept home to weep. A week later, while she sat waiting in the doctor's office for her follow-up appointment two Gestapo agents walked through the waiting room, opened the door to the inner office, and ordered the doctor out. Louise went cold with fright. What did they know? She caught a glimpse of the doctor's white face and heard him say, "Let me go in the other room and get my coat" and while she waited frozen with fear that they might turn on her she heard the nurse scream. The doctor had swallowed cyanide. Stricken with guilt, horrified that she might have tricked him into death, walking on wooden legs that threatened to collapse under her, Louise let herself out the office door and numbly went home. The way was momentarily clear but at what cost! The doctor's white face rose up before her in the middle of the night and at odd moments when she was tired for months after.

They boarded the train in Aachen for the few minute's ride to the Dutch border where they would have their last encounter with the Nazis. As the train came to a stop all the Jews were ordered out onto the platform and there they were arrogantly searched for any contraband jewelry or money in excess of the forty dollars a family of four was allowed. In the lining of her coat Louise had sewn a diamond and sapphire ring. Her mouth was dry with fear as they ran their hands over her clothes but she had done her work well, it was not discovered. The guards made the process as humiliating as they could. One of them even slit Elizabeth's mama doll open so that all the stuffing hung out in order to make sure nothing was hidden inside the voice box that cried plaintively when the doll was tipped over. Finding nothing they herded them brusquely back onto the train. The little family sat in rigid silence, scarcely breathing. A few minutes after the train was in motion again they saw signposts in the Dutch language go past the window. It was Louise's fortieth birthday and something inside whispered, "It's your birthday. It's a new beginning."

As if to give further evidence that their lives were truly upward bound, her mother's faithful German maid was waiting for them on the platform alongside the train at the first station beyond the border of Holland to deliver Louise's platinum bracelet. This German gentile girl had risked much so that Louise could have a life preserver. With that bracelet she could buy a future. She wore that bracelet triumphantly out of Holland, stubbornly through the nightmare months in England, and defiantly through the pinching poverty that awaited them in St. Louis. Somewhere along the way, in Louise's mind, that bracelet became Richard's college education, too sacred to spend. Louise wore it proudly until her death. There never was a college education.

They paused only briefly in Holland before moving on to Britain where they would have to stay until their number came up on the German quota for admission to the United States. Stepping off the train onto "this green isle, this England" of Shakespeare and confirmed civility, Louise laughed and cried while Elizabeth danced up and down. They were out of harm's way where events in Germany couldn't reach them, or at least they thought they were. Louise tossed her head and said to her little family "One step at a time. The worst is behind us." They picked up the $l000 in the London bank and bought train tickets to Bradford in Yorkshire. Louise hustled her family north as quickly as possible. London was too big, too noisy, too expensive, and too overwhelming. From the North, as soon as they had an address, she would write to the American Embassy in London so they would know where to notify them when their number came up. She chose Bradford as their temporary resting place because the finest textile schools in England were located there. Richard would continue the education begun in Aachen in case college did not materialize. At l4 the boy was almost six feet tall and more fully developed than other boys his age at the school. It gave him a decided edge. Though he disliked the textile business while holed up in his grandmother's house with a tutor, in the school he thrived. He was the only member of the family not eager for the affidavits to arrive.

As an alien without a work permit, Rudi was not allowed employment. England was full to overflowing with refugees, and English workers did not want their jobs underbid by interlopers. So, they had to begin to spend the slender remainder of the $1000. They ate tight in the small apartment they found. Then their meager resources were further strained when Louise's mother arrived. The first thing Louise had done after arriving in Bradford was to write to London. The second was to write letters to Holland and to Aachen. She had to get her mother out of Germany. She could not leave her to her fate. Again she turned to the brother, who again refused, and who again knuckled under when push came to shove. In late summer the family in England became a family of five. No deposit had been made for her mother, but bribes had been paid and Mrs. Hayman's servants had assisted in the conspiracy that "sprung her." From the moment Mrs. Hayman arrived she was a burden, a huge emotional burden. She complained about the lack of servants, she complained about their cramped quarters, she complained about the cribbing paucity of amenities they could afford on their limited funds. And she wouldn't consider securing an affidavit for the United States. She would wait right where she was for that beast in Berlin to die so she could go home. It was August of 1939. The beast would not be trapped in his lair and die until long after Louise was in America and Mrs. Hayman lay under British sod.

When Hitler marched into Poland, and war was declared in England, Rudi volunteered as an air raid warden. He wanted to be useful, be part of the effort, but England was afraid of her refugees. She began to sort them out and put them into categories. Anyone coming out of Germany was listed as an enemy alien, fleeing Jew or not. All Germans were rounded up and packed into restricted areas away from installations or facilities essential to the war effort. Nothing could convince the British that they were not housing Third Reich vipers in their bosom who would like to blow the United Kingdom sky high. The British reasoned, when they reasoned and didn't just react, that whatever the cause for their departure from

Germany the refugee became a threat to England because he/she might have left family behind whose fate depended on that refugee's cooperation with the motherland. Rudi was rounded up with the rest of the German males in the North of England and went to "jail" again. Like common criminals they were brought under guard to Liverpool and from there shipped across to an improvised prison of seaside hotels on the north side of the Isle of Mann. Guard patrols were posted around the periphery of the former resort area, day and night. Elizabeth and Richard were frightened. Louise tried to assure them that this was temporary, that Rudi would be back, that everything would be all right, but ten days after the men were carted off a woman officer came to take Louise and the children into custody as well.

"What about my mother?" demanded Louise.

"She's too old and frail for where you're going. We'll leave her here." the officer said impatiently.

"Alone! Never! Let me make a phone call." Louise drew herself up ready to fight.

"No phone calls! There's no time. Now, move on!" The officer motioned toward the waiting bus.

Louise sat down on the steps of the house defiantly. "You will have to carry me." she declared. "I make a phone call or I don't go."

The officer, red-faced with anger, looked down at the intransigent figure below her. In the silent contest of wills that followed the uniformed woman knew she'd been bested. "All right!" she hissed. "One phone call and make it snappy!"

Louise put in a call to a German friend residing in Britain who agreed to come and get Mrs. Hayman, and to keep her until other arrangements could be made. Other arrangements were never made and the friend had to bury the forlorn lady from Aachen by herself.

The women and children gathered up by the police were warehoused in an empty school on the west coast of England to await transportation to Liverpool where they would be transferred to the south end of the Isle of Mann as soon as the hotels there could be vacated and made ready. Among the women crowded into classrooms converted into dormitories was a woman from Berlin with whom Louise became friendly. This woman was so despondent over being hunted down a second time that Louise feared for her sanity. Among the few possessions

Louise had with her was a small cache of drugs she'd brought from Germany. She raided her precious store and gave the woman valium every day, talked to her hour after hour until she could convince her that life was worth the fight.

"Don't let them beat you." she reiterated angrily again and again. "Don't ever let anybody beat you. You can win if you set your mind to it."

Louise was so compelling in her arguments for living that the woman revived, but for Louise the whole world had become the enemy. No one was to be trusted. Every turn of the road revealed another obstacle to be surmounted. Every time she won a battle there was another to be fought. From then on, whoever or whatever she encountered would be viewed as a challenge to her right to exist until she was convinced that no harm lay in that direction. Furthermore, she was sure she had to do battle alone, she couldn't count on anybody but herself.

Their stay in the school house was short. In a few days they were herded onto a train for the short journey to the seaport and the waiting boats that would take them to their place of incarceration. At the Liverpool station they were lined up in a column like school children on a field trip and marched from the train to the wharf. Along the line of march townspeople had gathered to throw stones at them shouting "Dirty Kraut! Hun!". Richard, being taller than the rest and male as well, was targeted more than the others. That march ended his childhood. A small boat was waiting to transport them to their detention area. The government had converted the whole island, hotels, cottages and boarding houses used in happier times as a vacation spa, into a massive concentration camp. Intended for family vacations at the seashore, each unit was small. Louise refused to be separated from either of her children which meant that Richard had to fold his six-foot frame into the bathtub every night. His height and his physical maturation made him a target for every sex-starved woman and pubertal girl in their building. Richard was set to work sweeping the hallways and staircases. Louise went into orbit over the situation. She stood guard the whole time he worked. Girls planted themselves provocatively in his path. Women made suggestive remarks. Invitations were tossed his way, most of which, in his innocence, he didn't understand. Filled with wrath Louise stormed into the office of the warden who made the work assignments and demanded that she come see for herself what Richard was up against.

"Just you look and see if you'd want your fourteen-year-old son to be in a mess like that!" Louise demanded. "He's just a little boy no matter how big he is."

The woman watched and listened and reassigned Richard to less public tasks. The hotel in which they were housed was operated by an Irishman with avowed anti-Semitic prejudices. Paid by the government, a government newly at war and over-burdened with monumental challenges, he was assured a fixed income per inmate regardless of what they were fed or how inadequately they were sheltered. The manpower shortage of war did not leave civilian personnel to oversee the comfort and well-being of prisoners of war. The diet was sparse and devoid of vitamins. Louise dipped again into their dwindling reserves to go to a nearby village each day to buy food for her children. Medical services were almost nonexistent, one doctor had been provided for 7000 women and children. Those who had come to the camp pregnant received the least care of all. Midwives could deliver babies, he said. What he was concerned about was the possibility of epidemics of communicable diseases. So women delivered other women's babies as village women had done for centuries. Life became an endless battle for the most minimal sanitary conditions and for supplies with which to care for each other. Throughout the community the great cry was, "What have we done? Why do we deserve this?" Wars raise many questions and provide few answers. The only answer to their cry was that the British were scared.

While they were incarcerated on the Isle of Mann Elizabeth had her twelfth birthday. Louise trudged off to the village bakery early that morning to buy up the whole day's output of doughnuts. All of the people in their building were invited to a party. Never had so little been served at any party Louise had attended, but rarely had there such a festive spirit. With so few pleasures to relieve the monotony in the encampment, Elizabeth's party was exciting and memorable. Secretly, Louise wept.

Fortunately, not only did Phoenix rise from the most desolate ashes, the human spirit is resilient and forever upward bounding. One of the women decided the children's education should not be interrupted any more than could be helped. She organized a school, drawing the faculty from among the most talented women in the camp. School became not only something to do, it became the focus of life in the community. Then out of the blue came an unexpected offer from the British government. The women were all called together to hear the proposal. Australia was to be opened up to all who would go. A great hubbub ensued. Many women were instantly for it, many against it. There was such discord over the proposal that the camp was split into angry factions. Finally, calmer voices carried the debate by demanding that they be allowed to consult with their husbands before making such a momentous decision.

Frustrated, the government agreed to a meeting. One day they were all lined up like school children again, and marched north across the island. They had gone a short distance when they saw an approaching column of men. Men and women broke ranks and began milling about searching for each other. A tower of Babel ensued when nearly l0,000 people began debating the question of emigration to Australia in the middle of the island. When Louise and Rudi found each other they answered the question for themselves without even asking it. They were not going to Australia, they were going to St. Louis, Missouri in the United States. They would consider no alternative. Rudi insisted that he had more important business to conduct with Louise than a silly idea about Australia. He wanted some money. He had dreamed up a scheme that would improve their situation greatly. Louise resisted, protested, wanted no part of his hair-brained idea but he was like a terrier with a rat, he would not give up. Finally Louise made him sign a note for it and gave him the money as a loan. It was a worthless piece of paper for Rudi promptly loaned out the money at interest to people he didn't even know, people whose paths he would never cross again, and people who never paid it back. His career as a banker was brief and disastrous.

When the conference ended, only the single men among them had elected to go to Australia. Louise, tired of waiting for the British Government to decide their fate, began writing letters to attorneys in London to secure their release. Only one lawyer responded and after a short correspondence he secured the Hahn family's release, and arranged for their return to London. The four of them were taken off the Isle of Mann on a fishing boat loaded with kippers. The children swore they'd never eat kippers again.

The boat docked in Bristol where they were put aboard a train headed for London. From the train they were taken to another abandoned school which had been vacated for use by the London Refugee Committee. The school building was located near the rail yards, one of the areas most targeted by German bombers. Every night was hell. Air raid after air raid sent them scrambling to the only shelter available, the cramped space under the stairwells. To keep the Jews from fornicating in the dark, the men and women were separated and sheltered in two different areas. Louise raised the roof. If her family was going to die they were going to die together. No one was going to split them up again. Again she got her way, and the terror of the bombings was lessened a bit by their being able to touch, and hold each other close.

The refugees were only allowed to leave the school on important errands: visits to doctors, appointments with lawyers, trips to their respective embassies. Every day a prison wagon pulled up in front to take whomever wanted to go to the embassy scheduled as that day's destination. Louise went to the American embassy. The Americans listened to her passionate pleading, and within days the Hahns were released from the schoolhouse and turned out to search for their own lodgings. Finding lodging they could afford in overcrowded London was impossible. English families were not willing to shelter Germans of any stripe. The few places that would take them were too expensive. Finally, they located a widow in dire straits who had a second floor to let. The accommodations were as poor and cramped as the little rooms on the Isle of Mann had been, but it was the best they could do with what little money they had to lay out for shelter. In the middle of the first night there were air raids in that neighborhood which drove them out of the house and down to the underground shelters. It was far more reassuring to be underground than squatting under an open stairway. In the middle of the second night they were rousted out by the sirens again. In the middle of the third night, while they were safe in the shelters, the widow's house was hit and the second story caved in upon itself. From then on the four of them slept on the kitchen floor among the mice. The intensity of the bombings increased until every night became a time of terror. The whole city was going up in flames. Like thousands and thousands of other Londoners, Louise began to anticipate their deaths. She made plastic bags to hang around their necks each night when they went to the shelters, bags which held all their papers for the identification of their bodies if they were killed. In the midst of this unremitting nightmare word came that their number had come up. There was no road block left between them and freedom in America!

Louise wasted no time securing booking for the four of them on the first ship available. Their passage to St. Louis had been pre-paid while they were still in Germany but, without the affidavits, making reservations had been futile. In Frankfurt. Louise had purchased space on the Cunard Lines. When war broke passenger traffic to America was reduced to a trickle and space on the remaining ships in service was in high demand. Four berths were finally secured on a slow waddling vessel headed for Boston. It was highway robbery, but the difference in the price she had paid for first class fares was not refunded even though there were only steerage accommodations available on the ship. For once, Louise decided not to quibble.

Only desperation could have forced anyone out into the North Atlantic in November of l939. U boat packs were having a field day with British shipping. The winter storms set in early making sailing rough and dangerous even without German submarines. Their freighter traveled in convoy far to the north of the usual sea lanes to avoid the stalking enemy lurking beneath the surface of the sea. All the way across Louise found herself straining forward, urging the ship on its way. They had their first Thanksgiving dinner aboard ship and no one at table was more thankful than the Hahns. Never having heard of the American Thanksgiving before, they never celebrated the holiday afterward that they didn't remember that meal. It took ten days to reach Halifax, and only when they could see the land mass of North America could they believe they were safe. As the ship off loaded and reloaded before proceeding on to the United States they were not allowed to go ashore. The ship was tied up for several days before it pulled away from the dock and they were on their way to Boston harbor where their American saga could begin at last.

On the docks in Boston they were met by two well-dressed, well-fed ladies from the Council of Jewish Women. The ladies were effusive in their welcome, so effusive that the rest of the Hahns were ready to melt into their arms and do their bidding, but wary Louise did not let her guard down. They were told that a suite in a lovely hotel downtown in the heart of Boston awaited them. Louise had the wit to ask at whose expense had those reservations been made. The Bostonians were taken aback by the directness of her question. After some nervous hemming and hawing, they acknowledged that the Hahns would be expected to pay the bill. Louise dashed her family's anticipation of a luxurious bed, a good hot bath and a gourmet meal.

"Thank you," she said haughtily, "but we have friends waiting for us in New York and we have pre-paid for our bus fare. If you'll be good enough to call a cab for us to take us to the bus station we won't delay here in Boston but be on our way.'

Put off by her lack of appreciation for all the trouble they had gone to in her behalf, the now equally haughty ladies coldly secured a cab for them and sent them off. It was an exhausted, rumpled, tired, mentally worn out, pathetic little foursome of strangers in a strange land who turned themselves over to their friends in New York after hours on the bus. For the first time in so many many months they'd lost track of time they could let go of fear and be at peace. It was overwhelming. They enjoyed a few days of badly needed respite. Good food, good beds, clean clothes and the love of friends can do wonders for the soul. When they boarded the bus to St. Louis they thought they were ready to face whatever lay ahead.

In Indianapolis, they laid over one night in a hotel. They didn't want to arrive in St. Louis looking bedraggled and unkempt, like a bunch of down-at-the-heel refugees. That night, Louise packed Elizabeth's things into a separate suitcase. When they arrived in St. Louis she would have to go with the relatives who had sent the affidavits and who were offering her the best America had to offer. Elizabeth tried to keep a brave face but her chin trembled while tears, pouring down her face, ran into the corners of her mouth. She put her tongue out to lick the salty brine, catching her breath just short of a sob as she struggled to keep her eyes trained on her mother's face.

Louise resisted the urge to sweep her child into her arms and weep with her. The upcoming separation was killing her too.

"Darling," she said struggling to hold herself in check, "it's going to be lovely, really. They have a little girl just your age and they have a big house and they want you to have a good start in America."

"But I can have a good start with you," Elizabeth gulped. "A family should stay together."

Louise reached out and pulled Elizabeth to her so the child could not see her own tears. "Oh, my little one, I know, I know. And we will be together. This is just for a short time. Daddy has to find a job and we have to find a place to live and while we're doing all that you'll be so well off. You'll be settled."

"I don't need settled," insisted Elizabeth, "I need you."

Together, they cried as Louise rocked the two of them back and forth repeating over and over, "It won't be long, liebschen, it won't be long. We need you as much as you need us."

When the bus pulled into the dingy St. Louis depot a little knot of people who had probably never seen the place before were waiting for them. Elizabeth's host family, who had been such eager tourists in Berlin, so effusive in their invitation to come to America sometime, wasted few moments on the triviality of greeting the Hahns before whisking Elizabeth away in their big car. Brushing back her tears as she watched Elizabeth's little hand waving as long as could be seen, Louise turned, along with Rudi and Richard, to face their hosts who seemed to be distancing themselves as politely as possible from any real connection with them. This couple also had visited Frankfurt and also been guests of Louise's mother in Aachen. The best that could be offered relatives from America had been trotted out on silver platters. But the Hahns were destitute now, no longer able to meet these people as equals. They were dependent on their St. Louis relatives' largesse, and for how long nobody knew.

Conversation in the car driving to their hosts' suburban home was light, disjointed and impersonal. They pointed out places of interest as they went along, places that interested them but which meant nothing to Louise and Rudi at that point. They turned what few questions they asked on Richard, further avoiding dealing with Louise and Rudi. And then they were there, face to face in the living room, up against the reality of their mutual situation. After they were seated, the husband abruptly ended the empty amenities and laid it out for them.

"The servants wing will be yours," he said without preface, "and we think it best if both families live separately. The two wings are connected through the pantry so your meals can be brought in to you and you won't have to put up with us and we won't have to put with you." He chuckled nervously as though he had just made a joke, but their three guarded faces did not break into responsive smiles.

"Well," he said standing up, "Let's get you settled in. You must be tired."

With that he led them down the hall to the pantry and through a short connecting hallway to the small sitting room and two bedrooms that would be their quarters. They were never offered a tour of the rest of the house. As their host had laid it out for them their meals were brought in from the family kitchen, but Louise learned they were not eating at the level the family enjoyed. The cook prepared separate dishes for them that were a definite cut below the fare served in the dining room in the main house. Some days the paths of the two families did not cross at all. The Hahns no longer had any illusions that they were welcome, that the affidavits had been sent out of the goodwill these people felt for them. It was obvious that they were a responsibility the family would have ducked if they had had the guts to say no to the request for help. Within a few days after their arrival they learned just how unwelcome they were.

The host family came to the little sitting room for a conference and presented their plan for the Hahns. Rudi and Louise must find an apartment of their own as soon as possible. Their hosts would pay the rent for them, if it was modest, until Rudi could find work and take care of their own needs without help. They would give Rudi a letter of recommendation and help them enroll Richard in school. Then, having said all they had come to say, they left as abruptly as they had come. Louise and Rudi wasted no time in beginning their search for a place of their own. As for Richard, there'd be no school, he would have to go to work.

One morning while the apartment hunting was going apace, the woman came in to bring them the want ads from the paper and noticed Louise's bracelet.

"Is that platinum?" she asked in amazement.

"Yes it is." Louise replied. She handed it to her hostess to admire and told her the story of the bracelet. "It was the smartest thing we did, the only way we got any money out."

"I'll buy it from you." the woman said eagerly. "I'll give you ninety eight dollars for it."

"Ninety eight dollars!" exploded Louise. Then catching herself she said smoothly, "It's not for sale. This is Richard's college education."

"College education?" The woman lifted an eyebrow and smiled faintly handing Louise the bracelet as though it had become too cheap to consider. She turned on her heel and walked out. The apartment hunting picked up rapidly after that and within days the Hahns moved into a one-bedroom, sparsely furnished apartment where Richard had to sleep on a daybed in the dining room. They had found not temporary shelter as they thought, they'd found their home for years to come.

Louise took comfort from the thought that at least Elizabeth was living well. The rest of the family might be forced to live above a store abutting the sidewalk but Elizabeth was living in a big house being chauffeured to and from school, wearing fine clothes and eating well. So Louise thought, but Elizabeth was not telling her mother how things really were. She might be eating well, she might have "advantages," her surroundings might be a big cut above those of the rest of her family, but she was being wilted in her new surroundings. Never a moment went by that she wasn't reminded that she was the recipient of charity, even while being held up to the child of the family as a model of good behavior, good manners, and good hygiene. The child began to hate her, and in the privacy of their room she bit her and kicked her and messed up her clothes and upbraided her for being poor and dependent. Elizabeth never complained, never tattled, but the housekeeper knew what was going on. She went to visit Louise.

"How can you think of giving that beautiful child up for adoption?" she demanded. "You may be poor but so is that child. She's miserable. Haven't you noticed how she's losing weight?"

Louise went wild. "What do you mean adoption? My child is not up for adoption? Why would you think such a thing.?"

"You may not think she's up for adoption," retorted the housekeeper, "but that's what they're planning. Open your eyes woman, and see what 's going on!"

"They'll never get my child!" Louise shouted, grabbing her coat and rushing for the door. The housekeeper grabbed her coat sleeve and held her back.

"Don't be stupid! Don't do something rash. Think this thing through. If you go over there now as mad as you are and start a row they could cancel their sponsorship, go to the authorities and give you a bad name, and then where would you be? Out on the street, all of you. Your husband would never get a job. Calm down! Spring vacation is coming up soon and Elizabeth will be here with you for a week. Nothing's going to happen that fast. You've got to have a plan."

Louise stopped dead in her tracks, then flung her coat down on a chair and wept. She wanted to pull hair, to scratch, to scream, to tear the woman apart, but she knew the housekeeper was right. Trembling, she stared sightlessly out the window, breathing hard. Then she turned on the housekeeper.

"Was this their plan all along? Is that why they only sent an affidavit for Elizabeth and Rudi? Are they going to adopt Rudi too?" She was so wrathy she was fairly stuttering.

"I have no idea what they had in mind for Rudi, but I know they talked about the two girls going to college together."

"College! They aren't even going to go to the zoo together!" Louise picked up her coat but laid it back down without quite letting go of it.

The cook reached over and took her hand away from the garment. She pushed Louise down into a chair and stood over her. "Now you listen to me." she said sternly. "Don't you do one thing. Not one thing until you think this through carefully. You'll find a way. You'll work it out, but you have to do whatever you're going to do without arousing those people. They could really make things difficult for all of you. I wouldn't put it past them to try to get the government to send you back. Right now they hold all the cards!" Then patting Louise's arm she turned to the door. "I'm glad, at least, to know that blessed child is not going to be trapped there." She let herself out and Louise sat down at the table to cry her eyes out.

When she confronted Rudi with the news that night he brushed it aside. "That's a lot of hot air. They've never said anything to us about adoption. Your friend the cook has a vivid imagination."

"No!" Louise's voice rose. "It all adds up. Why would they send a split affidavit? Why have they not lifted a single finger to help us? They've got such a big house they could have given Richard a whole suite of his own. Why not him too?"

Rudi shook his head wearily, "If you've made up your mind that that's the way it is, that's the way it is. But the cook was right about one thing. You better think it through very carefully before you start trouble you can't stop."

Louise thought it through, she could think of nothing else. She plotted and plotted wildly at first, and then very carefully. By the time Elizabeth came home for her week's vacation her mother had it all worked out. She watched Elizabeth's joy at being back with them, even though she had to sleep on the floor beside their bed. She listened to her moan in her sleep at night while she was dreaming. And she saw how thin she was. And she saw that within days of being back in the bosom of the family Elizabeth began to fill out on their simple food, she began to sleep quietly all night on her hard pallet, and she chattered away nonstop, following them around as though she couldn't get out all the words she'd been storing up all these past weeks. But toward the end of her visit home she began to close down inside herself again. One could see her apprehension rising in the way she checked the calendar, sometimes twice a day as though she might have misread it the first time. Then the vacation was over. As Louise packed her clothes to go back, she laid her plan out before Elizabeth telling her exactly what to do.

"What I want you to do, Elizabeth, when you get back there, is cry. Cry all the time. Cry about nothing. Cry at the dinner table, cry in the middle of the night, cry every time that kid picks on you, cry when she messes up your clothes, cry when you leave in the morning and cry when you come home from school. Be as unhappy as you can be. But don't complain or explain why you're crying. Just cry."

When the big car came to pick her up Elizabeth began crying and was still crying as she pressed her face against the rear window of the car until they were out of sight. She arrived at her host family's home still crying and she kept on crying day after day, night after night. When asked why she was crying she only shook her head and refused to discuss it. The family called Louise in. When she left for the interview Rudi begged her not to lose her temper.

"Don't pick a fight." he pleaded. "Don't make trouble."

"Don't tell me what to do," she retorted, "these are your relatives, not mine. They're the ones trying to steal my child! No one in my family would do a thing like that!"

"They wouldn't?" mocked Rudi. "Your brother would let the Nazis carry you off."

Louise didn't answer, she flung herself out the door slamming it behind her. When she was ushered into the living room of the big house the couple didn't even ask her to sit down. Accusingly, they stood before her as stiff as two principals in a private school. Louise felt like she'd been called in for disciplinary action. They accused her of poisoning the child's mind against them. They denounced her for trying to subvert the child's attachment to their family. They talked about the great opportunity they could offer Elizabeth. And it came out that they had indeed intended to adopt her. That was too much! The row Rudi hadn't wanted exploded.

"Where did you get the idea that my child was up for adoption!" Louise's eyes flashed and that old toss of the head should have warned the woman that the waters were getting very dangerous. "Why in the world did you think I would turn her over to you!!"

"We thought you understood that when we offered her a home? Why would we bring her in and let our child become attached to her if we had to give her up when it was convenient for you to have her back? We've loved Elizabeth since we first met her in Frankfurt. We can give her so much! What can you give her?"

"What I can give my child is our business. If you want another child go to an orphanage!" Louise shouted. "My child is not an orphan and I didn't raise her for twelve years so she could teach your brat how to behave?"

"Do you know what you're saying?" The woman puffed up like an adder.

"I know exactly what I'm saying. This 'opportunity' is all for your daughter. My daughter is to be her teacher, her counselor, her role model and her servant. You've taken advantage of our predicament to steal my child!"

"Steal your child?! When what we wanted was to help her?"

"Yes, steal her! You don't want to help her, she doesn't need help. You want to help yourselves to my Elizabeth. But you won't have her and if you go to the authorities about this I'll tell them how you tricked me to get my child. We'll see what happens. Even refugees have rights! I'll go to the newspapers, I'll...."

White with fury the woman turned on her heel and left the room with her husband close at her heels. Louise was left standing clenching her fists at empty air. Elizabeth's things were packed, Elizabeth and her bags brought down by the housekeeper who was smiling broadly, and who, wordlessly, ushered them out of the house. But just before she closed the door she clasped her palms together like a boxer after winning a fight and winked at Louise. Louise took Elizabeth's hand and led her down the driveway with all the dignity she could command. During the long bus ride home Elizabeth nestled contentedly against her mother while Louise clutched her tightly to her. No one went to the authorities, neither the cousins nor Louise, but there was never again any contact between the two families. The Hahns were now completely on their own. Home again with the family, no matter how cramped things were, or how few pleasures life held, Elizabeth never complained about anything, never objected to anything, never let her parents know how keenly she felt that she played second fiddle to her brother, or how anxious she was to grow up.

Richard, approaching sixteen, extremely good-looking, made such an impression on people that he had no trouble finding jobs to help out. Employment was picking up in the United States in 1940 and it was not long until Rudi found a job selling lighting fixtures for a lighting equipment manufacturer. He was paid fifty dollars a month, enough for survival if little more. Louise handled the money Rudi earned and the family soon learned there could be NO extravagances. Every cent must stretch so that a few pennies could be laid aside for the shipment of their crates from the warehouse in Amsterdam. The fund had added up to only a few dollars when the Nazis overran the low countries in May of 1940 and immediately emptied all the warehouses in Holland sending everything back to Germany. When Louise read of the rape of Holland and realized that her last hope for quick success in America had evaporated, she broke down and cried as the family had not heard her cry through their whole ordeal. For the rest of that year and through most of the next she railled against fate as they managed merely to keep body and soul together. Then the United States entered the war and overnight anyone and everyone had a job. Richard at seventeen found steady work, Rudi's salary went up, and Louise waited tables part time in a little neighborhood luncheonette. Almost imperceptibly they began to pull ahead.

Early in 1944, when Richard was nineteen, the army sent him a letter. Louise couldn't believe it. They weren't even citizens, but Richard was being drafted. She'd never even thought about that possibility. She went to the draft board to protest but the draft board told her that the privilege of living in the United States carried with it the obligation to defend it. Richard was sent to boot camp in Georgia and Louise went along. Much to Richard's disgust she rented a room near the camp gate where she could cook meals for him when he could get away and where she could keep an eagle eye on his comings and goings. Elizabeth, at fifteen, was left at home to mind her mother's stove. When boot camp ended, the army sent Richard to England and Louise at last had to let him go. She went back to St. Louis and her drab little life for the duration.

Once Richard was in England the army discovered he had a fine musical talent so they handed him a horn rather than a gun and assigned him to the army band. There were American army installations all over England by that time and the band toured every one of them. Louise was happy. Army bands are not found in the front lines of war. But after the invasion of Europe in June of that year, the band toured base camps in France playing from flat bed trucks in all kinds of weather. When France was liberated Richard became even more valuable to the military forces. The army needed interpreters and few American boys could speak German or French both of which Richard had mastered as a child, one being his native tongue, the other heard everywhere in Aachen. He became a "hot property." He was part of the interrogation team that spent days with Admiral Donnetz when that German officer came to the Allies seeking peace. After V-E day arrived Richard was flown here and flown there to be present at all kinds of interrogations. It was during one of those flights in an unpressurized plane that he collapsed. At the hospital where he was taken they discovered he had an advanced case of tuberculosis.

Back in St. Louis, the Hahns received one of those terse telegrams the armed forces are noted for. They were told that their son was very ill. The telegram conveyed nothing to tell them what had happened or what the army intended to do about it. Three weeks went by without another word, three weeks in which Louise walked the floor nights. Then came a letter from the army saying that Richard was being sent to Fitzsimmons Hospital in Denver, Colorado where respiratory illnesses and wounds were treated. Louise went into action. She and Rudi loaded Elizabeth and themselves into the old car Rudi bought for his work and headed west. Elizabeth was taken out of school so Rudi and Louise assumed the role of teachers so she wouldn't fall behind in her classes. At Fitzsimmons the doctors told them it would probably be three years before Richard would be free of the disease and could be released to return to civilian life. Louise would not have it. She wanted him home now, and she meant to take him home. No one could take better care of him than his mother, she argued. She so fiercely barraged them with arguments and demands that he be turned over to her so she could nurse him back to health, the hospital authorities gave in.

In easier days, the army might not have capitulated but army hospitals were bulging with the casualties of war. There were not enough nurses, not enough doctors, not enough beds, and the country was moving on into post-war interests with a vengeance. Medical personnel were going back into civilian practice as fast as their enlistments ran out. They let him go with a medical discharge and Richard went back to the three room flat where Rudi and Louise turned the bedroom over to him and made it into a miniature hospital, study, and lounge. Elizabeth felt even more shunted aside by her parents' overweening interest in her brother's health. Louise was consumed with chicken soup, and fresh air, and exercise, and pills, anything to help Richard recuperate. And he did begin to improve. He filled out a bit, he slept better, he no longer looked like he might collapse at any moment, but his interest in resuming any kind of normal activity remained at low ebb. He didn't talk, he didn't read, he wouldn't go out into the fresh air as the doctors had recommended, he merely stared into space with the radio purring in the background for distraction. Louise and Rudi were almost at their wits' end when Louise tried one more thing.

As a child Richard had loved to draw. Louise went out and bought stacks of pads of drawing paper of all sizes, and colored pencils of every hue. She and Rudi urged him to sketch, draw anything. Rudi brought home lighting fixture catalogs for him to copy the illustrations. At first Richard listlessly copied to keep his parents off his back, and then he began to create. He created lighting fixtures for commercial lighting, space lighting, neon fixtures with elegant clean lines, all fresh designs. Rudi and Louise began to get excited. The functionality of his designs, his obvious gift of seeing light in space and setting, and the scope of his imaginative drawings of what could be done far beyond what was being done, gave birth to an idea. What if they went into business for themselves making lighting fixtures using Richard's designs? When she outlined her idea to Rudi he caught fire. When she suggested it to Richard he promptly enrolled in a correspondence course in electrical engineering.

They sat up late at night mulling it over and over. They calculated space requirements, they estimated costs, costs of starting up and costs of production once they were in business. One thing they agreed on immediately was that they would sell only quality merchandise. Forced to start out very small, they'd be able to hire only one technician, the rest of the work they'd have to do themselves. To begin with, they'd assemble parts and pieces they could purchase wholesale. Manufacturing from start to finish would have to wait. Established businesses were refurbishing now that peacetime production of equipment was beginning to make it possible to upgrade. It was the right moment to plunge in. Rudi would do the selling, Richard would do the designing, Louise would handle the finances and contracts, and they would all work in the shop.

They rented an empty storeroom across the street from their shabby little apartment and began. It was amazing how quickly Richard's designs began to attract attention. Rudi, one of the best salesmen in the market place now that he could speak the language, was able to get a contract with the Edison Brothers' Shoe Company which was expanding into the shopping centers of the new suburbs springing up around St. Louis. Every time they opened another store it featured Hahn Electric Co. lighting in its showcases and around its showrooms. That first contract sent them on their way.

The big trade shows resumed after World War II, and by 1947 the lighting companies were displaying their wares in the Chicago convention center. The Hahns couldn't afford the steep fees displayers were charged, nor could they afford a glitzy booth where they could show off their sleek designs. That didn't stop them. They loaded up their models of the best of Richard's creations and headed for Chicago anyway. Renting a room in a hotel near the convention center they set up their own showroom. Every day they would buy one entrance ticket to the fair and one of them would walk through the convention hall leaving copies of the glossy catalogs they'd had printed lying around in conspicuous places. The catalog was accompanied by an invitation to come to their showroom and see the models featured in their brochure. People came, enough people that Hahn Electric became known outside the St. Louis area. Orders began to come in. At that juncture it seemed wise to incorporate with Rudi as president, Richard as vice-president and Louise as Secretary-Treasurer. Then came their big break. The Edison Brothers' contracted with them to supply all their lighting fixtures in every one of their stores coast to coast. Hahn Electric had hit the big time.

Big time meant bigger production, production far beyond the capacity of their little storefront operation. They had to move, had to expand. But where was the money to come from for all this expansion.? Louise loathed debt. She lay awake nights trying to find a way to raise the capitol without going to a bank. Then, at that precise moment, the German Government passed its famous restitution law whereby people whose property had been seized by the Hitler regime would be paid full value for their loss. Now the receipts for their wealth that the Gestapo had issued in 1938 became valuable. They were worth plenty. Not enough to launch into a new building and buy all the machinery they'd need, but a goodly portion of it. Right on the heels of that bonanza, Louise got a letter notifying her that she would be restituted for all that her mother had lost to the Nazi treasury because she was the last member of the family who had cared for her the deceased. Altogether, the cornucopia of German Restitution poured enough wealth into their laps that they were in the first favorable position the Hahns had known since the day they were married. For investing her mother's restitution money, the larger part of their manna from heaven, Louise demanded additional stock in the company. Rudi never quibbled. He was almost salivating over the future on their threshold.

Hahn Electric Co. moved out to the edge of the city where more space could be had for less money and they began placing orders with metal and pipe and wiring companies for the materials they'd need to assemble Richard's non-standard designs. They had to hire additional help which presented them with another problem. There were no lunch counters or eateries of any kind in the area where the factory was now located. Their employees would have to brown bag it which was a detriment in hiring good people. Louise hit on the idea of fixing lunches all morning in her little apartment then taking them out in the back of her car to the employees as a bonus, a fringe benefit for making the longer trip to work by street car. Her mornings became frantic but it made for good personal employee-employer relationships which paid off in a more stable, contented work force. Soon they were producing to plant capacity and all without acquiring debt.

St. Louis was home to a sizable refugee group. Refugee Clubs were established which provided social outlets for these newcomers still handicapped by the language barrier. These clubs were also social service centers. Among the members of the clubs were many young people like Richard, young, talented, eager. Those clubs were the only place where young people could sit around and drink coffee while they talked the night away. As the refugees developed friends outside the immigrant group, they brought them to the club. English speaking visitors were always welcome. Through his contacts in the refugee club Richard met a very gifted young sound engineer with whom he became friends.

This young man was interested in the new sound equipment the electronic age was introducing. He and Richard talked for hours about amplifiers and stereo and tweeters and woofers and baffles, all the insider talk of the devotees of the new technology bringing the world of radio and records into homes and business places. It wasn't long until the two of them were approaching Louise and Rudi with plans to expand Hahn Electric company to include the manufacture of baffles and ceiling units for commercial sound systems. With canned music going into every elevator, every hospital corridor, every reception room in the country, it didn't take Rudi and Louise long to see the potential that lay in this young men's schemes. Hahn Electric stuck its toe in the water with some of the young engineer's ideas, and was inundated by additional waves of orders.

The young engineer was brought into the company as a protégé partner, given stock but no title, and Hahn Electric Co. spawned the fledgling subsidiary, "Soundolier." That meant further expansion and a still larger plant. This time Louise did not hesitate, she pressed her best suit and went to the bank. For almost a decade, Hahn Electric continued to exist, but more and more of the profits were coming from Soundolier. Enthusiasm for neon waned and shifted to indirect lighting. Hahn Electric struggled, then gave up. But what difference did that make? Soundolier was lining their pockets.

Without warning, in 1957, Rudi had a massive heart attack. It jolted everybody. What if he died? He survived, but it was obvious that he would never be able, with Louise looking over his shoulder, to lead the company as he had in the past. His charisma, his charm, his ability to sell ice cream to Eskimos was lost to Soundolier. The company would have to be reorganized. In the years since the young engineer had come into the business his role had grown and grown. His was the keen eye which could see where new business lay, the quick mind that more and more shared with Louise the task of watching the nickels and dimes to make sure they added up to dollars, the steady-on personality that inspired confidence in their customers once Rudi lured them in. He now demanded he be made a member of the Board of Three or he would leave. Without him, they'd be lost and both Richard and Louise knew it. Richard's role in the company began to fade. Together, Louise and the young engineer virtually ran the show.

For eight years Rudi remained an invalid while the company exploded in size. There was money enough now to relax a little. Elizabeth had married and gone years before, quietly slipping away from them at age sixteen into a home of her own. Rudi and Louise moved out of their little apartment into larger quarters and enjoyed some social life at last. They attended the symphony in the winter, and the Opera in Forest Park in the summer. They entertained and were entertained. They went out to eat in nice restaurants, maybe not the finest, but nice. They were the best times they had ever had together. Louise even made a trip to Europe during those years leaving Rudi behind for he could not travel. She wanted to see her

Father's house again, retrace some of the paths of her girlhood, look around. She'd been too busy for years to think about Germany, but now she had the time and before any more of the people who had made up her life died off she wanted to go.

In Aachen, staying at the best hotel in town, she immediately began searching for the servants, gentile Germans who had stayed on with her mother after the Nazis came to power and who had protected her and Rudi when they were driven to hide there while waiting to get out. She located the chauffeur, who was by then an old man. He came to the hotel to see her and when she stepped into the lobby from the elevator he clicked his heels and drew himself up as straight as he could in the style of chauffeurs of the l930's. Louise rushed to him and they threw their arms around each other while tears poured down their faces. They spent hours lost in memories of a past that had receded far enough to be talked about without excessive pain. After Aachen, Louise went to look for Babbet. There had been a lot of water over the dam for Louise since she left Frankfurt but Babbet's life had run a quiet steady course. She was still in her brother's home in the little village to which she had gone when Louise left. The whole population of the little community was thrilled when the American lady in her smart clothes and fur scarf showed up with a shower of gifts for one of their own. They threw a big party for the visitor and Babbet had more attention focused on her than she had ever enjoyed before. Louise returned to the United States satisfied. She could face the past at last.

A fatal heart attack in l965, and Rudi was gone. He had been a burden and a blessing, and he left a greater hole in her life than she expected. After he was buried another reorganization of the company took place. Richard became president, the engineer became vice-president while Louise continued as Secretary-Treasurer. When Rudi's will was read Louise had inherited his stock so that she was now the major owner, the controlling vote in corporate decisions. Richard was the president but Louise had more real authority than he. Richard wanted the power the title of President usually conferred on the holder of that office. He had ideas he wanted to try, new ventures he wanted to engage in, other subsidiaries he wanted to create, but he lacked the authority to put them into motion. Louise was not in an expansionist mood. The company was doing very well the way things were going, and she felt many of Richard's new ideas had little merit. Life behind the scenes became more and more strained as mother and son tussled over every question that came up.

Four years into the new situation and Louise had a heart attack, big enough to be a good warning. She was in Intensive Care for only a few days and when she was moved to a private corner room overlooking the park everyone who had not been permitted to see her before came to wish her well, or to pay their respects. Elizabeth and her husband Steve were there with their children, and so was Richard, but he left early. At the end of that first day out of ICU, after the last visitor had gone, Louise lay alone staring out the window looking at the sunset reflected on the clouds sailing over the city. Questions came and went, sometimes answers too, sometimes not. The beauty of the skies escaped her as she weighed and measured and discarded. Had it all been worth it? Rudi gone, Elizabeth absorbed in her husband and children, she and her son not able be in the same room together without the sparks flying, what did it all add up to? She found herself looking unseeingly at the glorious light in the sky and asking herself, "Do I want to see that sun rise again?" The sky turned mauve, then gray, and the stars came out before she could finally say with conviction, "Yes. I want to live."

The next year, when she was seventy, Louise began to cut back on her work. She had always poured her salary back into the corporation retaining only enough on which to live modestly well. She had not bought jewels and fancy cars, not even a home. The business, her first love, was where she'd invested her wealth as well as her time. She couldn't quite let go. For almost a decade she continued to put in half days in the office but as her 80th birthday approached she finally had to admit she was tired, too tired to go to business any more. She gave way to age, and in 1978 moved to Rossmoor where friends from St. Louis had retired. At that point Richard decided to sell the company. The classic battle between mother and son, which has been the stuff of so many novels about power, began. Louise could squelch any deal Richard produced - and she did - until finally there was a deal too good to pass up. In 1982 the company was sold. The money was fantastic, but money couldn't repair the emotional damage the struggle had caused. The estrangement between Louise and Richard was irrevocable.

She was very rich, but very rich didn't compensate for the void in her life created by the loss of her son.

From 1978 until 1993, for fifteen years Louise lived as one "the girls," participating in all their activities, yet holding herself a bit aloof. She was one of them and not one of them. Everyone conceded she was the best-dressed woman of them all, one of the most supportive of friends, a gracious hostess and an excellent dinner guest, able to converse in the native tongue of all but the Hungarians. Her friendships extended beyond their circle, however, and among the friends she made on her own was Frida, whose story has already been told. When Frida's heart condition confined her to her home, Louise visited her and took her soup. It was a new life for Lu, a life where she had time for female friends for the first time since leaving Frankfort.

In 1985, Elizabeth and her husband Steve retired from their own jewelry business in St. Louis and moved to Rossmoor also. Now Louise had family again. Elizabeth and Steve involved her in all their myriad of activities, as much as she would permit, and their children were the center of her being. 1992, May the l0th, Louise celebrated her 93rd birthday. The city of Aachen had invited her to attend a "homecoming" of Jews from that city who were victims of Nazism in the l930's and l940's. The gala was scheduled for April 29-May 4, but the trip was too rigorous for her frail health. It would have been a thrill to be back in the city of her birth for her birthday, but she could not make the trip. Instead, she spent the day in the lovely California coastal mountains outside Santa Cruz, sharing a picnic with Elizabeth and Steve in the redwoods where the bluejays stole her potato chips and the deer came close enough for her to talk to them. It was the last outing of her life. Confined to a wheel chair in a convalescent home outside Rossmoor's gates soon after, Louise lived for one more year and then followed Rudi to wherever he had gone and where the rest of us must go as well.

MIRIAM

World War I broke out in September, 1914, just as Miriam became nine years old. All her sisters and brothers were married or away at school and her father was in Germany on a business trip. As the German army began rolling over Polish Russia, Miriam's mother panicked. Gripped by hysteria she hired a gypsy wagon and driver and piling Miriam into it she fled east ahead of the Russian army which was reeling, retreating from the Germans. Mrs. Lewinsohn implored the driver to keep the Russian army between them and the Germans. Miriam was terrified. The two of them were cooped up in the house on wheels jolting over the countryside while the driver urged the horses on and on. At one point the wagon toppled over and Miriam had to be pulled out through the window in the top that was the only source of light in the interior of the shed on wheels. Then the tide of the war changed and Mrs. Lewinsohn ordered the driver to follow the advance of the Russian army and return them to Suwalki.

As the clumsy conveyance delivered them to their front door Miriam's father rushed out to greet them.

"Where in God's name have you been?" he demanded.

Tired, dirty and cross, Mrs. Lewinsohn. was in no mood to be questioned like a school girl. "I have been saving the life of your child!" she answered haughtily. "You weren't here to do it."

The rapid advance of the German army against the Russian front lines in September had cut her father off from a direct route home. In order to get back he'd taken a train through Sweden, traveled by stage to a port in Finland, then caught a steamer across the Baltic for home. By the time he reached a port north of Suwalki the country was back under Russian control in the first of the see-saws that would put first one power in charge of the area and then the other for three years. In December the Germans advanced again. Frightened by the reports of rape being perpetrated by the German army on the women in their path, her parents put Miriam and a sister who had come home from the University of St. Petersburg on a train and sent them back into Russia for safety. Exactly where they were to go or how long they would wait before their parents joined them Miriam didn't remember. What she did remember was being terrified watching her world disappear when the train pulled away from Suwalki. She wept inconsolably. It was days before, to her great relief, they were reunited with their parents in some big city inside the Pale, she does not know which one. What she did know was that the Pale was a safe place for Jews. For more than a century the corridor between Europe, the Ukraine and Russia, had been the oasis where Jews who could live, work and own land. Suwalki lay in that corridor. Once Mr. and Mrs. Lewinsohn were safely beyond the reach of the German army and had taken Miriam back into their custody her sister returned to St. Petersburg and school.

For months, Miriam and her parents took train after train through Western Russia going from one city to another, always a step ahead of the battle front, the chaos of war numbing the sensibilities of the Russians to the presence of Jews in their midst. Each time they left a city, directed by the ebb and flow of the war Miriam felt uprooted again. During those months in strange towns where streets were piled high on either side with snow, Miriam remembered going to school in the afternoon during the short winter days and coming home after dark. Each child carried a lantern, looking like so many fireflies as lantern light reflected off the snow. She never attended a school where there were morning sessions for most of the schoolhouses were used overnight as hostels for wounded soldiers. They stayed in every town where their journeys took them until the battle front threatened to overrun the place. In one town, one of the children called her a gypsy, for the child thought that Jews and gypsies were the same unsavory people. Miriam didn't know what a gypsy was any more than her accuser knew what a Jew was. Maybe it was in that town that Miriam was sent to stand in line to buy a loaf of bread. She was delighted by how shiny the bread was, shiny because it was filled with straw.

When the Russian Revolution broke out in the spring of 1917, Russia withdrew from the war. What had been a desperate flight from the Germans became an even more desperate struggle for survival in the chaos of civil war. Miriam's parents started for home. They were deep in Russia and the fighting completely surrounded them. They were truly refugees now. Though Miriam's parents were neither Red nor White, one of Miriam's sisters had become a flaming revolutionary and their angst over the additional danger she was creating for them gave her father an attack of what was possibly ulcers. Probably because of his autocratic bearing and his dress, in one of the towns where they sought refuge her father was arrested by the Bolsheviks and carted off ignominiously to a nearby jail. Frantic, dragging Miriam by the hand, her mother went to the jail to plead his innocence but the authorities would not release him. Next, her mother went to the Quaker Committee to beg for help. The Quakers were working hard to relocate displaced persons or assist them in returning to their homes. Successful in obtaining Miriam's father's release, the Quakers put the little family on a train headed west in the direction of Suwalki.

During the Civil War, civilians had to ride in cattle cars, packed in more tightly than the animals the cars were designed to carry had been. There were many children in the cars which made the whole trip one big adventure for Miriam. A train would take them a short distance, then the Army would commandeer the car. Everyone would be ordered out to wait for another train. There were no hotels, no dining rooms, no baths, no accommodations of any kind. They had to sleep wherever they could find shelter. At one point they were put into quarantine because of a raging typhus epidemic. When they finally reached the German front they were taken into custody again, this time by the Germans who were screening everyone entering any area they controlled in an attempt to prevent the spread of the frightful disease.

The camp was overcrowded with transients from all over the Russian Pale and the Baltic States. Food was scarce. The usual fare was bread and jam for breakfast and often nothing more for the rest of the day. One day Miriam and a few of the younger children climbed over the wire fence of the stockade and went to a nearby village to buy whatever food they could find for sale. It was their one reprieve from the ubiquitous potato soup for supper when there was any supper at all. The whole experience of camp life was exhilarating for Miriam. There were many children with whom to play, no lessons to learn, and a lull in the anxiety that had beset them for so long. But at last they were released, free to find their way home again. When her father abandoned their house in l9l5 he left ample funds with the employees and servants to maintain themselves in his absence. They found the house exactly as they had left it, neat, tidy and warm.

The closest most people have come to shtetl life is a trip to the theater to see *Fiddler on the Roof*. Miriam was born in one. Her shtetl was the enclave of Jewish employees who lived along the narrow streets behind her father's tannery. And Suwalki? Where in the world is Suwalki? Suwalki was a town of about 20,000 largely Russian Orthodox people city. Historically, Suwalki was first Lithuanian then Polish, alternately, depending on the rise and fall of those nations' destinies. When Miriam was born Suwalki was in the hands of Russia and had been since the days of Metternich. The Lewinsohn house faced onto the town square and behind the house was the shtetl of twisting lanes where Mr. Lewinsohn's Jewish workers lived. Most people have only the vaguest idea of what is a shtetl is. Shtetls were enclaves of poor Jews whose lives centered around the shul (temple) and ancient Jewish customs. Many shtetls were isolated villages where landless Jewish peasants huddled together, others were within cities surrounding a factory such as Mr. Lewinsohn's tannery.

Miriam's father's tannery accounted for a major portion of the economic life of Suwalki. Horse hides imported from Argentina were chemically softened in underground "vats" in a solution made from tree bark. The bark was brought to the factory where it was pulverized by large stone grinding wheels located in the middle of the factory yard. In addition to the dried imported horse hides, so stiff they could be stacked like huge shingles, the local farmers brought in their own animal hides to have them treated at the factory before they were sold to the shoemakers in the villages of the surrounding countryside.

Life in the close-knit Jewish community was intimate and dynamic. Energy was the outstanding characteristic of the social milieu. School for boys began early in life, but girls worked with their mothers in the house and in the garden as soon as they were old enough to hold a dish towel or a hoe. Children even younger roamed the narrow little streets, watched over by all the "Bubbes" sunning themselves on their stoops keeping an eye on the morals of the young people. These elderly women appealed to the little girl from the big house who came to soak up the vibrancy of the shtetl.

As the daughter of the owner of the town's major source of income, Miriam was accepted as the leader in the games the little children played. Because Miriam found the soldiers in the nearby camp so handsome in their uniforms, her father once found her dressed in bits and pieces of military regalia, leading her own army through the streets.

The part of "shtetl" life Miriam loved most was the Sabot celebration. No special attention was paid to Sabot in her home, however her parents did not object when she spent Sabot Night with one of the worker's families. She reveled in the soapy smell of the freshly scrubbed wooden floors and the special Sabot cooking, she was moved by the reading of the Sabot prayers, and she wondered at the reverence for the Sabbath the workers' families exhibited. She came as close to her Jewishness in that shtetl environment as she ever would again until Hitler came to power, disrupted her life, and forced her to see the world through the eyes of a refugee forced into flight because of Aryan antagonism toward all Jews throughout the world.

Suwalki centered around a large empty square that served as the town's market place. One whole side of the square was taken up by Miriam's family's house and the "Town Hall," the seat of town government. The other three sides of the square were lined with shops at street level crowned by living quarters above. A few other houses were mixed in with the store-dwellings, but not many. On Wednesday peasants brought in their produce and their chickens, ducks, geese and rabbits to supply the tables of the town folk. Miriam remembers going with the housekeeper to buy ducks or chickens from the farmers. The housekeeper would hold the birds out by the neck and blow on the feathers to reveal the thick skin beneath. It was so uncomfortable for the bird that Miriam protested.

"Why do you do it?"

"Because I want to see if the skin is yellow. If it's yellow it's ready to be eaten."

Behind their family home the streets of the shtetl extended for some distance. There was no electrical power to turn the grinding wheels of the factory so horses were used to pull the millstones around and around. Wherever there are horses there are dogs. Miriam loved to hang around the great vats and the sheds that made up the factory, to be near the horses, to be licked and loved by the dogs. The workers greeted the pretty little child with her good manners as a very special visitor which made her feel very proud. On market day, the peasants, coming to town to buy and sell, would often bring a little gift to Mr. Lewinsohn's little girl. When she walked around the square, idle shopkeepers would admire her and chat with her. In the world outside her house she was a personage. At home things were very different.

Her parents were well advanced in years when she was born, a little afterthought at the end of a large family. As with all her siblings, a wet nurse was secured the day she entered the world. One of her sisters was sent away to a nearby village to be wet-nursed for almost a year and a half before she was weaned and sent home. All of Miriam's brothers and sisters were l2 to 20 years older than she. Only one sister was still at home when Miriam was old enough to enter school. Miriam's mother had "standards" and those standards ruled her household always. One of her standards was that all the children, girls as well as boys, would have the best education available. For girls of any class, at the turn of the century in Russia, that was most unusual. Mrs. Lewinsohn hired the best tutors to be found and her children quickly learned that the tutor's authority was not to be questioned, When they were old enough they were enrolled in University, usually at the University of St. Petersburg. Being the little tagalong that she was did not exempt Miriam from this strict parental program.

Mr. Lewinsohn. was of a different mind about education for his daughters. He would have restricted their learning to the traditional female education. They would have learned to read and would have studied languages, learned to play the piano and studied painting. They would have been taught needlework, and they would have been tutored in all the social graces needed to be cultured, poised, charming women who could preside over a large household and make their way in society. As for the boys, he felt formal education was necessary, but its purpose was to prepare them to take over his business and modernize it, not to study the Torah. The second son, who was more pliable than the eldest, was sent to a technical school in Germany to study chemistry.

Miriam's father was a Russian Jew of the old Aristocracy but he loved his children with a warmth that contrasted strongly with his wife's cool attachment. She saw them as her progeny, he saw them as his beloved offspring. Miriam's mother was a pretty woman and a vain one. She spent hours on her wardrobe and "toilette" leaving her little time for the emotional care of the children. The servants received instructions on how the children were to dress and behave. By the time Miriam came along routines were well-established and order had long ago triumphed over the whimsies an imaginative child might create. Deportment, orderliness, and development of the mind were the cardinal virtues to be mastered. The others being away in school, Miriam would have been a lonely little waif indeed if it had not been for the children of the workers' families who welcomed her into their midst and gave her no quarter because she was who she was.

During their absence the Germans had overrun the town and were still there. The German language, now the official language, was used in the gymnasium. In 1917 the Lithuanians rushed in and took over the little province again. All the school children were turned out with little Lithuanian flags and Lithuanian folk songs to welcome the new occupiers. Lithuanian control of the area was broken in 1919 when the Treaty of Versailles made Suwalki part of the newly-freed Poland. Again the school children were turned out to welcome the new overlords with flags and songs. The Polish authorities were suspicious. They gathered together a group of the children of the leading families to interrogate them.

"Who taught you the Polish national anthem?" the Polish soldier asked Miriam.

"Our teacher taught it to us."

"And why did your teacher say you must learn it?"

"He said that if we were to live in Poland we should know how to sing her song." she replied, outwardly calmly while her heart pounded and her knees shook.

"But you sang the Lithuanian song not long ago!" he mocked.

"We thought we were going to be ruled by the Lithuanians then." Miriam had no notion of what this interrogation was all about.

"And would you have preferred the Lithuanians? Would your father have preferred the Lithuanians?" His voice was stern and Miriam became frightened.

"I don't know!" she wailed. "My father doesn't tell me what he would like or what he wouldn't like. And he didn't tell me what I should like or not like either. I don't know what to like." She was openly crying by then. "I can't speak to anybody in Lithuanian or in Polish. How would I know?" Shaking like a leaf, tears cascaded down her cheeks. He studied her tear-streaked face then said brusquely. "Dry your eyes and stop sniveling. What do you think we are, beasts?" It was Miriam's first encounter with politics and she never forgot it.

As life settled down under the new regime the Poles imposed their long suppressed culture on the rest of the populace. Only Polish musicians were allowed to perform at public concerts and only the compositions of Polish composers were played. Chopin was overworked in the schools, in all kinds of gatherings and in all the conservatories. All the schools were taught in Polish, a language Miriam scarcely knew and one she found difficult to learn. Only fourteen years old she was far too young to go to a University, and far from ready even for gymnasium. Somewhere her parents had to find a school where she could speak the language she knew in order for her to make up for the years lost while the family roamed. In Warsaw a group of White Russian intellectuals, fleeing the Revolution, had established a Russian-language gymnasium to teach the children of the émigrés pouring in out of the chaos behind them. Miriam's parents sent her there to board and to learn. The curriculum of the school was far too advanced for a child whose education had been as fragmented as Miriam's. She was woefully out of her element.

In addition to suffering from the stress of being in over her head at school, she was overwhelmed with loneliness in this strange city with its incomprehensible language on all the storefronts and signposts. She had never been away from at least some of her family before; now here she was among strangers with whom she had nothing in common. There was no shtetl to turn to for belonging. To make matters even more unbearable, war had so dislocated the economy that real want stalked the land. Food was so scarce in Warsaw that Miriam was hungry much of the time. Altogether, life was psychologically abusing the little lost soul who only wanted to go home. Once a friend of her parents came to Warsaw, and while she was there she visited Miriam as she had promised her parents she would. She was surprised at how thin and pale she was, and how immature she seemed. She asked Miriam about her menstrual periods. Had they started? Were they regular? Miriam had not menstruated for six months. When she confided that to her parents' friend the woman was horrified. She was sure Miriam was pregnant. Pregnant?

Innocent, lonely little Miriam who had never caught up with life enough to be close to a boy her own age, pregnant?! She was mortified.

The brother who went to school in Germany remained in Germany throughout the war. He married a German girl, a woman with "connections." Through those "connections" he went into the banking business and succeeded. By the end of the war he was a prominent citizen of Hamburg and a parent himself. When he was able at last to visit his parents he was stunned at how they had aged and how spiritless they seemed. The war had decimated his father's business. The tannery was still there taking care of local needs, but the shipment of hides from Argentina had dried up because of the disruption of shipping caused by the war. Miriam's father was too old to start over. Another of Miriam's older sisters had escaped the Revolution and returned to Suwalki soon after her parents got home. The brother from Hamburg resolved to take some of the burden off his father's shoulders.

"Come to Hamburg," he urged his sister. "There's no future for you here! We'll take care of you until we can find you a husband or until you settle on a career of some sort."

"Who says I want a husband?" She tilted her head to one side and stalked out of the room.

"Don't worry Papa." The younger man laid his arm around his father's stooped shoulders. "I shouldn't have been so blunt, but we will find her a husband, and we will take good care of her. I can afford to keep her better than you can."

Mr. Lewinsohn blew his nose into a large white handkerchief and cleared his throat. "A man should be able to take care of his own family." he said huskily.

"A man shouldn't have to live through what you've had to live through." retorted his son. "You took care of your family. Your country just didn't take care of you." Miriam's sister was carried off to Hamburg where she was married off so quickly that her brother decided to bring Miriam to his home to live. She was too young to marry off, but he could see to her education. Miriam put up no objection. Her brother had food in plenty, he lived in a big exciting city, and his young children would make Miriam feel she was part of a real family at last. But there were difficulties about getting Miriam into Germany. She was too young to be issued her own Polish passport when the rest of the family had obtained theirs.

Without one, the Germans, sticklers for protocol, would not allow her to come into their country. Her parents were forced to manipulate the local authorities and falsify her age in order to get the necessary papers for her to go. Now, she was officially two years too old to be allowed to enter gymnasium at the level of her educational development.

Her brother put her into a private school. Socially, the private school was a disaster. She was developmentally far behind the other students in her class. Very small for her age, painfully unsure of herself, she remained on the fringe of the life of the campus. She had nothing in common with the other students. While her classmates were growing up snug and safe in their sheltered homes, she was living through tumult they could never understand. To make her situation even worse, the passport she had been issued was only a temporary student visa to be retained only if she succeeded.

Her brother's wife was the soul of kindness, much loved by the rest of the family, but she was the epitome of German certitude. She could not understand this tiny little guest in her home who had picked up radical ideas somewhere along the way, ideas of wanting to be independent and earn her own living rather than marry and manage a fine house as she and her friends did.

"Miriam," she would lecture. "We want to give you everything we are giving own children. We want to make up to you for all you've missed. But, dear dear Miriam, you will have to give up some of these wild ideas you've acquired. It may be well enough for people like your sisters in Russia who have to make their way in a world where every civilized standard of society has been swept away, but you are not in Russia. You are in Germany, and in Germany there are certain restraints on women you have to observe."

Miriam's sister-in-law lived the life of the average well-heeled married German woman. She believed that if you fed children well, dressed them nicely, gave them love, and hired good servants to look after them, they would be happy and satisfied with the way of life of their parents. German women of her class oversaw the workings of their homes in the mornings, then went out with a friend to show off their fine clothes at the tea dances in the afternoon, while their husbands were at business. They went with women friends equally free to eat cakes and drink coffee and dance the afternoon away leaving the preparation of dinner to the maids at home. When Miriam's older sister had gone to Hamburg two years before she'd been in her mid twenties, eager to be part of the world she was entering. She'd had no radical ideas about making it on her own. Being bold with men, carrying weapons or shovels with men, working out-of-doors with men in all kinds of weather held no appeal for her.

The two sisters-in-law had a wonderful time together. It was easy enough to find the newcomer a husband in such circumstances. Miriam's sister-in-law knew all the bright young men in Hamburg, or knew someone who knew the ones she hadn't met. Miriam was too young to accompany her brother's wife on these afternoon outings. Her sister-in-law, looking to the future, continually preached to her about becoming more socially acceptable. But the more she scolded, the more she argued that such ideas made Miriam less than attractive to men of standing in the community who expected to provide for a wife and carry her around on their arm, the more Miriam stood her ground. It was an impasse. Miriam's brother was also worried about her lack of interest in the traditional life of the people around her, but he felt she would outgrow her notions after she'd been exposed to security for a time. So the contest went on. Though they fretted about her, they loved her and fussed over her just the same.

Miriam's eighteenth birthday was a very happy occasion. There was the usual family dinner, the usual cake and little presents, and after the candles were all blown out her brother demanded that she make a birthday wish.

"You tell me what it is and I'll see to it that it's granted," he said expansively.

Miriam hesitated only a moment, then said archly, "Anything?"

"Anything" he said stoutly.

"I want to go to Russia to visit the sisters." she said in as firm a voice as she could muster around her giggles.

"Russia!" her brother chortled. "Are you teasing? Didn't you have enough of Russia before?" But in spite of the laughter in her face he could tell she really meant it.

"I want to see my sisters again." she said quietly.

Sobered, her brother threw his napkin down beside his plate and proclaimed, "If that's what you want, then that's what you'll have."

The Civil War in Russia was over. Foreigners were encouraged to come in and spend their money. Lenin's New Economic Policy was in effect, and much of Russia's pre-war industry was back in private hands. One of Miriam's sisters married a man who managed a pharmaceutical factory before the Revolution, and now he was again in charge of production. They lived in the lovely villa near the factory. There were tennis courts, and carriages, and afternoon tea on the verandah, and dinner parties with the table set with crystal and silver as of yore. All the grace and charm of old Czarist upper class society had returned in their circle. The setting was perfect for a dreamlike interlude in Miriam's struggle with books and examinations. On a lovely April morning when the air was soft, and plum blossoms floated toward earth mingling their delicate fragrance with the moist smell of nearly turned loam, an April Easter Sunday in fact, Miriam left Hamburg by train. She had only two weeks between school terms but for that long she intended to be a fairy princess.

All the way into Russia her heart sang. She had seen this lovely landscape before, but under vastly different circumstances. It was sheer joy to see this mother Russia in all her spring glory. Miriam's sisters welcomed her with open arms and saw to it that those two weeks were an idyll to be remembered during many of the gray days ahead. She played tennis and drank lemonade seated in the green wicker chairs on the wide verandah. She went for lovely drives with her sisters and attended dinner parties, and everyone was kind to her. The two weeks flew by, and then it was time to go home. For months afterward she savored the memory of every hour of her visit. It was well she did, for Stalin seized control of the government in 1928 and the pharmaceutical house was nationalized once again. Her brother-in-law was sent to Siberia where he died and her sister was stranded in a now inhospitable country.

Back in Hamburg, she faced courses that would prepare her for matriculation exams. She slogged through book after book struggling to climb the mountain of new material that had to be mastered in order to graduate. One subject after another challenged her until she felt hopelessly mired in an assortment of studies she could not integrate into a comprehensible whole. Then came a letter. In Warsaw, she'd briefly had a close friend in the Émigrés' school, a girl who

236

was now studying chemistry at the University of Berlin. This girl had gotten Miriam's brother's address and wrote to her enthusing about the heady atmosphere of Germany's most prestigious University. Berlin was a city of brilliant society, of liberal intellectualism, of outstanding museums and theaters, she gushed. To be in Berlin was to be at the center of the universe. Miriam read the letter over and over, and every time her head swam at the prospects. Her friend had taken special exams in order to be admitted as an "extern" to the University. She told Miriam that the examinations were extremely difficult, but, with the help of tutors, Miriam could master the material. If she was accepted she could stay in Germany to continue her education.

If she became an extern she could not only choose her own field of study, she could get out of her brother's house and be on her own. Her brother was not for it. He was afraid she'd become too independent, maybe become a revolutionary and get involved in political activity like their oldest sister in Russia. He was afraid she'd get her picture in the paper like "Rosa Luxemberg," the German communist, and bring shame on his family. Nothing she said swayed him. He was determined that she would remain docilely in Hamburg, or return to Suwalki. Her father, that advocate of genteel education for women, came to her rescue. He offered to give her what support he could scrape together which would be little more than enough to grub by on. Miriam wasted no time. She passed her matriculation exams, then packed her bags and fled to Berlin. There, with the help of her friend, she secured private tutors to direct her studies for the entrance exams for the university. Latin, math, literature, foreign language, all had to be mastered to bring her up to University Level. She was soon working twelve hours a day.

In spite of being overworked, life became exciting. She was on her own, and she and her friend were inseparable. They ate together, they studied together, they told each other everything. When the time came to take the examinations Miriam went trembling into the great hall to meet her fate. Until the results of the exams were known she lived suspended in a sea of anxiety. When the results were posted she crowded to the front of the mass of students staring up at the long roll and felt skyrockets go off in her stomach when there it was, her name among those of the students who had passed. She had been admitted into the School of Medicine at the University of Berlin! She was no longer coming from behind. It took weeks for her feet to touch ground.

During her first year in medical school, she enrolled in courses required by the medical curriculum, but if there was to be a lecture by the popular Dr. Freud expounding on his theories about the subconscious Id which was given at the hour when she should have been attending a lecture on anatomy, she went to hear Dr. Freud. If Max Reinhard was producing a new play and she could come up with the price of admission, she went to the theater even if that day's reading went unread. Neither did she eat that day for she couldn't afford food and theater tickets too. There was nothing to worry about, she kept telling herself, after all she didn't have to take any exams for two years. She began to spend every cent she could scrape together on all kinds of tickets: concerts, the theater, lectures, anything intellectual. Never abreast of the reading, often absent from class, it wasn't long until she was falling farther and farther behind in her studies. Rather than study alone, she rushed off to join other students gathered in clots about the campus, engaged in heated discussions about life, or politics, or Art. Such pooling of ignorance seemed like the intellectual yeast of student life, but it wasn't adding much to her knowledge of the subjects in her chosen field. Soon money was so tight she was eating all her meals in her room. Maggi soups, frankfurters, bread and cheese - the rule was "cheap and quick." She lost weight. Her brother became worried that she was going to become ill, or that she might leave the gas lights in her room on at night, a breeze would blow out the flames, she'd die of asphyxiation. He and his wife pleaded with her to come back to Hamburg and finish medical school there.

Miriam gave in. She knew she wasn't cutting it, and she was tired of being hungry all the time. She went home to her brother, transferred to the Medical School in Hamburg, and buckled down. Entering at the third year level, her classmates had already spent two years together, their friendships were formed. She was the outsider, the newcomer. She felt like the little Match Girl with her nose always pressed against the window looking at life through a clouded pane. One student however, a gentile, the daughter of a military man from the Junker Class, also needed a friend. Her home life was so regimented she felt smothered. Whatever chemistry brought them together, the diminutive little Jewess and the tall Aryan girl, they clicked. Hildegard was not more bright than Miriam, but she had 'presence' which impressed Miriam. Hildegard and Miriam, Miriam and Hildegard, if you were looking for one you also looked for the other. In one class, the good-looking assistant professor began to single the two of them out for special attention. Though his true interest was in Hildegard, he never failed to include Miriam in all their conversations and outings. If he showed Hildegard how to handle an experiment, he then showed Miriam too; if he paid Hildegard a compliment, he complimented Miriam in the next breath. This went on until one day Miriam made a decision. He had invited them to a Sunday outing, and at the last minute Miriam called Hildegard.

"Hil, I can't go today. I've sprained my ankle. I can hardly walk. The two of you will have to go without me."

"Sprained your ankle?" Hildegarde's sympathy was genuine. "Why don't we just cancel the outing on the river and come over to spend the afternoon with you?"

"Absolutely not." Miriam insisted. "It hurts too much for me to be good company. I don't want to talk. I'll put ice on it and read and take a nap, and maybe by tomorrow the swelling will be down and I can walk again."

There was no sprained ankle, Miriam had come to the conclusion that she had to give them an opportunity to be together alone. From that day on, Hildegarde and the young professor included Miriam only now and then. By coincidence, within a matter of a few weeks, Miriam met a young man totally unlike any of the other young men who had crossed her path before. He was a 'dilettante.' He was not committed to a goal like the other male students in her crowd. He had dedicated his life to the pursuit of pleasure. He spent money most generously, something that didn't happen in the academic world. Altogether he was a marvelous new experience. His name was Hans Hirschfeldt and he came from a moneyed, old German-Jewish background.

Headstrong and impetuous, Hans was not accustomed to being denied anything. Adding to his attractiveness, having served in the war he was also older and more mature than the university crowd. Hans mother died when he was two and when his maternal grandfather died, he left money in several Swiss banks in trust for the boy to be turned over to him when he was twenty-one. He had received the best education available in pre-W.W.I Germany. Immediately following the war, he had even spent some time in England where he briefly studied Art. No one ever taught him how to earn a living. Father and son lived off a shipping insurance business his paternal grandfather had established which almost ran itself. The business received little attention from Hans father, and when it passed to Miriam's husband, he too left it to the care of employees. At war's end, the devaluation of the mark virtually left father and son broke. The shipping insurance business was all that remained of what had been a rather sizable fortune. Nevertheless, the insurance company produced enough income for them to manage. Father and son haunted galleries and auction houses and became collectors of Art.

A photograph of Miriam taken at that time shows an almost cameo quality, classical profile, long lashes over intelligent gentle eyes, a perfect mouth, hair pulled back simply away from her forehead, face in repose looking dreamily at something far beyond the camera's range. It is no wonder that with his eye for beauty Hans immediately wanted her for his own. Miriam was not convinced.

"What would you do with me?" she demanded. "Would you take me home and put an apron on me? Would you dress me all up and take me around to one showing after another? If you have any such ideas you are pursuing the wrong woman. I'm going to be a doctor."

"Of course you're going to be a doctor. I don't want a social butterfly or a house frau," he responded. "I just want you."

"But I have to study. I have to study long hours. I have to study uninterrupted. I can't fix your meals or see to your laundry. I don't have time."

"Who needs you to do those things? We have a housekeeper who will come to us. She's been with me since the day I was born. She'd be jealous if you did any of those things for me." He pulled her to him. "In fact, she'll take care of you too. You'll have more study time married to me with two people to take of your world than you have now." He kissed the top of her head which she had buried in his chest. "All you have to worry about besides your studies is keeping me happy."

Miriam pulled away far enough to look up into his face. "That could be more of a time killer than doing your laundry," she laughed.

Miriam's family was dead set against it when she told them she planned to marry this charming under employed young man. They argued that he was not the solid settled type, that he was a dreamer. He was a rich man's spoiled son, they said. She should wait until her studies were complete and her degree in hand before marrying. Miriam knew she was not madly in love with her lothario, but he was so gay, so romantic, so everything that had been missing from her life that she asked her mirrored image, "Why Not?"

They were married during mid-academic year vacation, even before Hildegard married her young professor. For three weeks at Baden-Baden in the Black Forest they were young, carefree, happy. Miriam had never been so happy. She came to believe Hans falling in love with her was a coup beyond her wildest expectations. He was "Mayflower German" while she was first generation Eastern immigrant. German Jews looked down on Sephardic Jews from the East, and she had married into the inner circle of German Jewish Aristocracy.

After they were both married Hildegard and Miriam continued their friendship, lunching together whenever their respective schedules permitted it, dining together with their husbands in little restaurants where dim lights made conversation easy and intimate. Both were pregnant at the same time and each gave birth to a son within weeks of the other. But Hitler came to power, and it was no longer safe for Hildegard to socialize with Miriam. They stopped seeing each other anywhere. Long years after Hitler died in his bunker under Berlin, Miriam got in touch with Hildegard again. Hildegard had given up medicine and become a renowned painter. Her works were shown in all the capitols of Europe and she was one of the founding members of THE GROUP who were revolutionizing painting throughout the western world. She and her husband left Germany at the end of World War II to go to Italy to make their home in a villa on the edge of a cliff with the Mediterranean below for a backdrop.

Back again in Hamburg after her honeymoon, plunged again into classes, Miriam was unaware of Hans' frustration as he cast about for something to which he could apply his considerable but undeveloped creative talents, something he could immerse himself in while she was so completely out of reach. He met an electrical engineer who was experimenting with the idea of changing and improving the dialing system of telephones by combining several numbers which are frequently used so that a special button would dial them for you. The idea was so exciting to him that he began to get involved in his new friend's experiments as a holder of tools and a procurer of coffee and sandwiches. At night, he read everything he could get his hands on about telephone technology and the transmission of sound. It was not long until they were partners, equal in knowledge, and equal in ideas. The experiments were expensive and required a constant flow of capital. The electrical engineer had no money, not even for his own support. He needed to cut back on the hours he spent experimenting and go back to work in order to earn a living. Hans drifted into supporting the engineer as well as covering the costs of materials. To meet these costs he drained money from the shipping insurance company without consideration for the health of the business. With his usual cavalier indifference to the mundane, he assumed that he would be much wealthier than he was once they perfected the device and sold it. He would be able to protect the Insurance business from under capitalization with the profits which would come pouring in from the dialing device.

Miriam, oblivious to all the financial machinations going on in their lives, had no eyes or ears for anything but her studies. She passed her final exams for a degree in medicine and entered an internship. For her Doctor's diploma she was required to write a dissertation on a topic chosen by the professor of her choice. Once her paper was finished and accepted it had to be printed at her expense and reprints submitted to an assortment of Medical Libraries. It was a very expensive process and it was only when she turned to her husband for the money that she learned that there was not enough left in the till to support her project. Sick at heart over this turn of events, Miriam had to take her problem to the professor for whom she had written the paper. He suggested that she send it to a Psychiatry Journal. If they accepted the paper, the Journal would provide the reprints which she needed. In 1932, a Journal of Psychiatry published her paper, provided the reprints, and Miriam received her M.D. degree from the University of Hamburg.

Clutching her precious parchment, Miriam came up for air and looked at the condition of her household. Arthur's invention had eaten into their income to the point where she would have to earn money and contribute to the household expenses, or they'd go under. It was her first sobering confrontation with reality since they'd been married. If she opened an office the equipment required to go into practice would cost more money than they could possibly lay their hands on. If she didn't open an office, how was she to parlay her degree into solid remuneration? One of her acquaintances, aware of her problem, suggested that she go to an unmarried middle-aged woman physician, well established in practice, for guidance. Maybe, her friendly adviser told her, this woman could give her tips on which would be most lucrative field of medicine she could enter without having to buy all that equipment herself. Miriam sought out the woman and Anita entered her life. Anita, almost twenty years older than Miriam, was the daughter of a wealthy businessman. She lived with her father and she welcomed Miriam into their home with an openness that put Miriam completely at ease. She found herself pouring out her tale of woe without reservations.

"My dear, there are few jobs in medicine where one can earn enough to live on." Anita told her. "There are some public service programs funded by the city where you can get invaluable experience, but the pay is abysmally low. The best they will afford you is supplemental income to what you have coming in from what's left of your husband's business. Those jobs don't pay enough for you to be able to save the money you'll need to get started in a practice of your own, even if you could put it all away."

Miriam's heart hit the pit of her stomach and lodged there. All her dreams of becoming an influential physician, an honored and respected member of her profession, were out the window? She was reduced to paying for the bacon or doing without. Her feelings must have been written all over her face for Anita reached out and laid a hand on her knee.

"My financial needs are few, living as I do." she said. "If there comes a time when you need money I'll be glad to lend it to you. I'm sure you'll be able to pay it back later on in life." Though touched, Miriam was not ready to go into debt. For the next two years she worked nights in the Emergency Police Service of her district. She was sent out on domestic violence calls or other emergencies that seemed to occur most frequently at night. It was challenging work, and the income it brought in was healthier than Anita had led her to expect.

Absorbed in her own career, always sensitive about any discussions of money, she was ignorant about the Nazis crippling Jewish businesses. A Jewish shipping insurance company could no longer issue new policies. The income her husband's company had produced was reduced to a fraction of what it had been. It wasn't poor management that was affecting her husband's company, it was government policies. Miriam's brother knew what was going on and tried to tell her but neither Miriam nor Hans would listen. Her brother forecast Hitler's meteoric rise to absolute power correctly, pulled up stakes long before the Nuremburg Laws were passed, and moved his family, his wealth, his household, everything to Holland before Hitler received the mantle of "Der Fuhrer."

As her brother was leaving for Holland, Miriam and Hans were off for England to sell the now perfected invention to a telephone company. Miriam was eight months pregnant, and for her, the main reason for the quick trip to England at that particular moment was to have their child born on British soil. They took a little English coastal steamer out of Hamburg so that if the child should make its entrance into the world enroute it would be on an English ship and thus be British-born at sea. In London they took a room in a boarding house in a middle-class section of London not too far from the Jewish maternity home in White Chapel where Miriam registered as a patient. The day their son was born, July 20, 1933, London experienced its first demonstration designed to force the government to take a stand against Hitler. Crowds gathered in Trafalgar Square to march on Westminster and demand that the government do something to stop this Hitler. Hans marched too. Exulting in the event, he marched while she delivered.

Some British telephone people advised him not to sell out his rights, but to improve some imperfections that still existed in the device, and wait for better offers in the future. Others urged him to sell now. While he vacillated, Hitler cut off their flow of money. No Jew could any longer receive moneys from home while outside the country. They were immediately in dire straits. No other course seemed open to them but to accept a British offer for far less money than the invention was worth, and return to Germany to salvage what they could. Their troubles had begun in earnest.

Back in Hamburg they were stunned to find that their lovely apartment had been taken over by a German family. In their absence, they had been declared enemies of the State for having been away so long. Their furniture had been put in government storage and it cost a small fortune to retrieve it. Forced to move into the "Jewish section" of Hamburg, they took a small apartment and crowded in. Now, at last, her husband put aside his dreaming, and put his shoulder to the wheel to try to keep the shipping insurance company solvent. It was hopeless. New restrictions and regulations applied to Jewish businessmen were issued and rigorously enforced by the government, frequently. They lost the company. Not only was her husband out of cash, and out of work, but Miriam's wings were clipped as well. Jews could still practice medicine, but they could only care for Jewish patients. She still worked for the city, and that work continued to bring in an income but so reduced it was not enough to keep their heads above water. Two years, then three went by while conditions steadily worsened and they tightened their belts tighter and tighter. Finally their desperation reached the point where they were forced to face the truth. There was no future for them in Germany.

In this crisis Miriam visited Anita again. There had been little contact between them since that first meeting but Miriam had never forgotten the kind offer of financial assistance. Anita was fully aware of the political situation and the persecution the Jews were experiencing. She encouraged Miriam to leave the country as quickly as possible and told her again that if she needed money she would be glad to lend it. She knew Miriam could not take funds out with her, but they might need money this side of departure: money for bribes, or for steamship tickets. Again Miriam refused her generous offer. She had come for reassurance and she had gotten it. If Anita agreed they should go, that this would not blow over, then they' would not be going out of foolish fear.

But where to go? The American immigration quota law required that applicants have relatives in the United States who would take responsibility for the immigrant until he/she could find work. Furthermore the German quota was full and there was a long list of applicants. Neither she nor her husband had any relatives in the United States. There was a man in Washington, D.C., who Miriam's father had helped to emigrate to the United States to avoid military service at the time of the first World War. A man from Suwalki was almost like family. Miriam wrote to him and asked for help. He gladly went to the consul in Washington D.C. to give an affidavit as a "relative" but since he made only fifty dollars a month the Consul did not consider him an adequate guarantor for the support of a family of three. His request was denied.

That option closed, they floundered around trying to think of other possible sponsors. Friends of her Hans' father, gentile friends, wrote letters to people in the United States whom they knew with standing enough to satisfy the immigration service. One of the people who received one of those pleas for help was a professor at Rutgers University. This professor had a speaking engagement scheduled for Paris so he wrote that he would come to Hamburg before going to Paris to meet them and assess their needs. Then he could decide how, or if, he could help. Determined to put their best foot forward, Miriam prepared a wonderful luncheon for the Professor and his son who was traveling with him. The luncheon impressed him, but what delighted him more was Miriam's little boy playing happily on the floor by himself. When the good professor returned to the United States he went to the Consulate himself to offer sponsorship. The Consul told him that since he was not Jewish and was not related to these people he could not be their sponsor. The professor was appalled at the callousness of such a ruling. A heated discourse followed in which the Professor beat the consul to the ground with his articulate discourse on the intention of the law rather than the language of the law. Affidavits were sent and October, 1938, the American consul in Hamburg contacted Miriam and her husband and gave them the coveted Visas.

Miriam promptly went to see Anita again to report the good news and to say Good-bye.

"We will be gone within the month!" she exulted. "The United States will let us in."

"'Good! Good!" Anita glowed with delight. "I'm leaving myself."

"You're leaving," gasped Miriam. "Why?! You're not Jewish, why do you have to go?"

"Because I've talked too much!" declared Anita. She seemed glad about this turn of events, not chagrined. "I opened my big mouth in too many places over this damnable Jewish policy. I had a 'secret note' slipped under my door the other night which said that my excessive sympathy for the enemies of the State, i.e. the Jews, would not be tolerated. I suppose," she said curling her lip in contempt, "that means that, if I don't get beyond their reach, if I ever open my mouth again I'll wind up in the bowels of that hellhole in Berlin where all detractors are held until they've been reprogrammed."

She turned her back on Miriam and stared out the window for a long while. Then she turned again into the silence that had settled over the room. "My dear, don't fret for me, I'm going out with all my money intact. I've been getting it out for months and there's little left, but there's enough to help you. Please! Can't I do anything?"

"There's nothing you can do," said Miriam dispiritedly. "We can't take out more than forty dollars each and we have that. We can prepay our passage to America, and we can do that. We can even prepay transportation costs on what things they will let us ship over, and we have that. To give us money would do us no good at all for we couldn't take it with us."

She rose to go but Anita held up her hand. "Wait," she said, "I have something to give you that I insist you take." She left the room and returned holding out her hand. On her palm lay a little gold coin about the size of a penny. It was an antique American one dollar gold piece.

"It's not German money. It hasn't enough cash value to be worth the attention of the Nazis, but I want you to have it. When you see it, think of me." Her lip trembled and unshed tears stood in her eyes.

Miriam took the precious little piece of metal and threw it into the bottom of her purse. In the hectic days that followed she forgot all about it. A little gold coin would do them no good in America. What they needed was to somehow get what little they had left to a safe place where they could tap into it later. Other people might know how to spirit money out of the country but not Miriam or her husband. Then came a letter from a Dr. Necheles in Chicago. Dr. Necheles had been one of Hans' boyhood heroes. When they were young they had been members of Blau-Weiss, a Jewish boys' organization, together. Dr. Necheles, being a few years older than Hans, had been a leader in their group. As a young doctor he had gone to China to work for the Rockefeller Foundation, teaching in a medical college out there. From China he had gone on to the

United States in the early twenties and settled in Chicago. Hans had contacted him by mail, asking for help.

Dr. Necheles was trying to bring members of his own family out from Germany so he could not offer sponsorship, he said, but he did offer advice. Bring out medical instruments. Germany made the finest medical instruments in the world. They were extremely valuable in the United States. If she brought out one of the new gastroscopes he'd buy it from them himself. Miriam bought as many medical instruments as they could scrape together the money for, all of which she hoped to use herself when she was allowed to take up the practice of medicine in America. They'd be good insurance in case something went wrong, but until that crisis they were not for sale. Since the Germans allowed exiting persons to take the tools of their trade with them, as a doctor she could crate the stuff and ship it along with everything else they were taking out.

Miriam packed, gave up her practice, and prepared to go. It was more difficult for Hans. All those antiques he and his father had collected, all those paintings, he couldn't leave them behind. And what about the graves of his parents? Who would look after them? Finally, Miriam accepted the inevitable and began packing the Art. ten to twelve crates of his "precious items" were put together to be taken out along with the slender accumulation of things she had packed. At last, on November l0, l938, they boarded a train in Hamburg bound for Amsterdam. November l0, l938! What a night to be leaving Germany. When they arrived at the Hamburg station to catch their train they were ignorant of what had happened in Paris just hours before. A gentile relative of Hans came to the station to see them off and told them

"A German officer, I don't know his rank or what he was doing there, but he was shot today in Paris by a young Jew! A young Jew! Can you imagine anything so stupid?
Every Jew in this country will get it now. Hitler hates all of you anyway, now he's got an excuse to turn the dogs loose on you. Thank God you'll be out of the way by tomorrow."

"What do you mean, by tomorrow." Arthur demanded.

"Oh, Hitler won't let this ride for twenty four hours. By tomorrow morning something will be in the works, you can bet on it."

No one felt like betting on anything at that moment. With hearts heavy for those they were leaving behind, Miriam's little family boarded the train and anxiously headed west. They would be out of the country before morning. Hitler's fury was already at work as their journey began. While they were on the train headed for Holland, all hell broke loose around them. Jewish homes were invaded and the occupants dragged out to be beaten. Jewish businesses were broken into and vandalized. Jewish synagogues were smeared with swastikas, their altar pieces stolen, some even burned. Thousands and thousands of windows in Jewish buildings of all kinds in every corner of the country were shattered. The streets of some cities were so full of broken glass that November l0th has been called "Crystal Night" ever since. And while all this was going on Miriam and Hans held their little boy between them and rode fearfully through the fury toward safety.

Miriam's husband's devotion to his Art was little greater than Miriam's attachment to her heirloom jewels. Though she knew she was forbidden to take them out of Germany she had been determined to try. At the last minute she slipped a few of her most precious pieces into her purse determined to carry them out with her. She did not tell her husband what she'd done, what a hazard she had created if she should get caught. She held the purse tightly under her arm as they rode across Germany, the jewels a firm lump against her breast. Shortly before the train reached Holland, rumor swept through the cars that all Jews were to be taken off at the border crossing, and God only knew what would happen to them. Panic swept over Miriam as she thought of the jewels that were bound to be discovered in such a situation. Shaking with fear, she ran to the rest room and frantically flushed them down the toilet out onto the tracks. Someone must have been amazed to find such a bonanza lying in the cinders or the weeds along the right-of-way.

At the border, all Jews were ordered off the train. There was no way to hide their identity for each of their passports was stamped with a red J. If they hid on the train and were discovered they'd be shot. All their belongings were taken from the baggage cars and placed on the platform beside them. Every woman was ordered to turn her purse over to the officials positioned there to check them through. As Miriam handed over her purse relieved that it contained nothing incriminating, she suddenly remembered that in the bottom of that purse lay Anita's souvenir gold coin. That tiny gift now had the potential of being the cause of their deaths. Petrified with fear, she stood holding her little boy's hand, almost in a stupor. What was she to do? How could she extricate that coin before the guards found it? Her mind raced, as her mouth went dry and her heart threatened to beat its way out of her chest. She watched the Germans working their methodical way down the line toward them in terror. Then it was their turn and the officials demanded that Hans turn over the keys to the luggage so they could go through it.

"They're in my purse!" Miriam blurted out hoarsely. "He doesn't have them."

Hans looked at her in surprise for he could feel the keys in his pocket.

"If you will let me have my purse I'll get them for you." She tried to make her voice sound steady and natural even though she was overcome with her own audacity.

The purse was handed over and Miriam rummaged in the bottom until her fingers closed on the tiny gold coin. "Oh, I don't think I have them after all," she exclaimed, turning to her husband. "Check your pockets dear, maybe I did give them to you."

She snapped the purse shut and handed it back as Arthur produced the keys. The moment attention was diverted from her to the luggage, Miriam pretended to cough, put her hand over her mouth and swallowed the gold piece that could have meant their doom. She did not get it back. As she watched the thoroughness with which everything was ransacked and pawed through, beads of sweat formed on her forehead. Just thinking about the jewels and the gold coin she might have had in her possession at that moment made her sick at her stomach. The guards even took the knob off her umbrella to make sure nothing of value had been hidden there. They slit open the tube of toothpaste in her cosmetic kit. They didn't spare a thing. When her little boy complained about being hungry Miriam took a sandwich out of her traveling bag, unwrapped it and broke it in half. She offered it sarcastically to a guard for inspection as further diversion.

"Would you like to examine this too?" she asked. "I may be feeding him diamonds."

Fortunately the guard chose to ignore her sarcasm and slammed shut the last trunk. He imperiously waved them through, never looking in her direction again. By the time they were seated in their compartment once more Miriam was exhausted. She gave little Michael the other half of the sandwich and laid her head back against the cushion. Michael happily swung his feet back and forth as he munched away, managing to kick the skirt of the seat with every swing of his small legs.

"Michael!" his father snapped. "Stop it! You're giving me a headache."

Miriam cocked her head and shot Hans a quizzical glance. Back there on the platform he had been the soul of elegant ease, urbane and unperturbed. Obviously, he had not felt what he projected. She shook her head. She had married a very polished man whose self control was remarkable. Miriam's little family was booked on the Holland-American Lines leaving from Rotterdam and they were among the first on board when the ship's gangway was let down. Gray skies, gray seas, and the gray spirits of the passengers made it a somber November crossing. The ship was half empty. Every night at dinner the half-filled dining room with so many empty chairs was a grim reminder of the pre-paid accommodations held by refugees trapped in the November l0th retaliation that rained down on tens of thousands of Jews for the death of one German in Paris.

Throughout their passage little Michael clung to his parents intimidated by the ocean that surrounded them, by the strange speech of the other people on board ship, and by the plethora of gleaming silverware around his plate at every meal. Miriam was so seasick during the wild winter crossing of the stormy Atlantic that she could not leave her bed. Her husband was so elated by their escape that he couldn't sit still in their cabin beside her. He took Michael for walks around the deck, he prowled around the ship poking into every nook and cranny of the vessel, he talked to the crew and drank with other passengers who were not affected by the pitching of the ship. The last night of their voyage he didn't go to bed. Bundled up against the fog, he spent the night leaning on the rail hoping to be the first passenger to catch sight of that revered symbol of freedom, the Statue of Liberty.

They disembarked onto the precious soil of America Thanksgiving Day, 1938 in a raging snowstorm. The earth was so buried under a white mantle that you couldn't see the ground. The fact that they had arrived on this most American of holidays was viewed by her husband as a good omen, but Miriam looked at the storm that made traffic come to a standstill and was filled with foreboding. New York intimidated her. They had heard of a hotel near Times Square where they could stay for one dollar a night, but how were they to get there? No public transportation was moving anywhere. Luck led them to a taxi driver who must have been in dreadful need of a fare. He agreed to try to get through the snow-clogged streets in spite of the abominable driving conditions. The crates of Art and antiques were left in storage at the pier to be delivered later when they had an address to which the stuff could be sent. Buried under all the various boxes and bundles they were taking with them they couldn't even reach the windows of the cab to rub a hole in the coating of frost that cut off their view of the city they were passing through. Miriam cringed to think that when they arrived at the hotel everyone who saw them schlepping all their hodge podge of belongings in with them would know immediately that they were refugees.

Snowflakes so big they looked artificial were coming down so fast the windshield wipers on the cab couldn't keep up. Twice the driver almost stalled out at corners where he had to stop for the lights. Now and then the vehicle got a little out of hand on the slick streets and they made half turns first one way and then the other. All three of them were straining, urging the cab forward every time the wheels spun in place with no traction. Safely delivered at last to the hotel they dragged their clutter of luggage and parcels into the lobby and piece by piece carried it back to the elevator in the corner. To their embarrassment they found that they and their belongings filled the elevator so full there was scarcely room for the door to close. In those days elevators had elevator operators and the operator on their elevator was a black man. Michael was mesmerized by him. In astonishment he blurted out, "Why is he so black?" Fortunately the operator couldn't understand German and Michael's grateful parents did not offer to translate.

Once all their things were crammed into their room they washed up and went to the dining room to eat. Cold, tired, hungry, they looked at the menu in dismay. It was Thanksgiving and holiday prices prevailed even in this modest place. They could not eat here. Miriam went back to the room while her husband took their son and ventured out into the streets of the hushed, deserted city to look for food they could afford. Father and son tramped along the sidewalks making new tracks on the fresh fallen snow. They listened in amazement to the sound of the wind roaring down street canyons walled in by tall buildings. They threw snow on each other and walked in the middle of the empty streets for the drifts in the gutters were above Michael's knees. His father kept brushing the snow off his head much to Michael's disgust. He liked his image in the store windows, all white on top. At last they found a street vendor who was rapidly being turned into a snowman, his shoulders and head covered with at least three inches of the white powdery stuff. They bought piping hot frankfurters in buns which they bore triumphantly back to Miriam. In their hotel room, seated on the bed, the three of them ate a very American dish for their first Thanksgiving dinner in their new country.

The day after Thanksgiving, Miriam phoned friends who had emigrated before them and with whom they had carried on frequent correspondence, but their friends were helpless to do more than cry "Welcome," and give them advice. The storm of the previous day had completely blocked traffic throughout the city. By Saturday the street cleaning crews had the sidewalks cleared so they could trudge off in the bitter cold to the Council of Jewish Women to register. The Council of Jewish Women, organized to assist refugees from Europe, told her husband, "We think we should concentrate on placing your wife since she has the more marketable skill."

Miriam's husband's grim silence revealed his inner turmoil, though he looked at the application in his hand and saw their point. Neither "Exiled shipping insurance business owner" nor "inventor" sounded very marketable to him either.

"We know that we can't place you in a position worthy of your background until you've passed the qualifying examinations of the American Medical Association," they said to Miriam, "but perhaps we can put you into a hospital in an assisting capacity of some kind as soon as your English is more perfected."

Miriam's silence was almost as expressive as her husband's. It hurt to sit here, hat in hand, a woman without a country having no status at all, being talked down to by some society woman volunteering to help poor immigrants. The portly woman on the other side of the desk, oblivious to Miriam's humiliation, went on talking.

"Until we can find something for you," the woman was addressing her, not her husband, "we'll give you an allowance of fifteen dollars a week. You may not know enough about the American economy to know that that amount is equivalent to the minimum wage guaranteed to American citizens. You'll have to find your own lodgings. Every home that has been opened to our agency is full. All I can suggest is that you buy a newspaper and begin with the want ads."

Miriam did some swift calculations. They still had about $120 of the money they had brought out of Holland and with the fifteen dollars a week from the Council they ought to be able to make it for awhile. She'd have to hang onto her husband's coattails to keep him from spending what they didn't have, but she was up to that. They left the Council office in silence while Michael chattered away between them as they walked back to the hotel. His presence was a blessing.

In the days ahead, while they waited for the Council to find work for her, Miriam's husband set out to find work for himself. To him it was a great adventure. He wandered through New York getting acquainted with America, and incidentally hoping he would trip over some kind of job he could fill. To Miriam, tramping through the city with want ads in hand, looking for a place where they could live, was no adventure at all, it was a nightmare. She plodded through the area between 120th and 150th streets West hoping to find someone with rooms to let who could speak German. Going up one street and down the next she finally stumbled onto a lady who had a sister living in Hamburg who spoke German well enough for them to communicate. She and her husband welcomed this little family into the one room with kitchen privileges they had for rent. The first gesture of kindness that came their way in America came through gentile hands. Meanwhile, her husband had walked into the path of the Lowell Thomas newsreels crews who were out looking for refugees coming to NYC from Hitler's Germany. They paid him for appearing on a newsreel that was to be shown throughout the country. It was a lark which he hoped would make him a celebrity, but nothing came of it. He went on looking for work.

The big obstacle to Miriam's taking any job was care for her son. They tried a day nursery, but since he could not speak the language the poor little boy spent every day, all day, crying piteously. The Jewish Council advised Miriam to place the child with some Jewish family who wanted to help the émigrés, a family who had a child near his own age from whom he could learn the language quickly. A member of the internationally known Warburg banking family was involved in helping Jews from Germany and she took an interest in the woman doctor with a child. She suggested a fine family who had two children, one of whom was the boy's age. They would take Michael to live with them for a few months until Miriam could get settled into something. It sounded perfect. It would free her to go to school herself to learn English. She took Michael on the street car to the house where he was to live, her heart aching at the thought of separation, while she chattered away about what a lovely home he was to have. Michael didn't hear a word she said. He was crying too hard to hear anybody. The parents of the little boy with whom he would share a room tried to soothe him but he clung to Miriam pleading with her not to leave him. She had to physically tear herself free from his clutching hands before she could walk away, tears streaming down her face. It was one of the most difficult moments of her life!

Since the turn of the century the public schools of New York offered classes for immigrants trying to learn the language. Classes for Hungarian-speaking immigrants, classes for Italian-speaking immigrants, classes for every known European language. Miriam was placed in a class designed for doctors where the language used in medicine could be emphasized. There were approximately forty students in the class, doctors from Austria, Hungary, Germany, and other countries around the world. Not all were Jewish refugees. Miriam eagerly dug in and began making good progress, but the arrangements for her son were not working. He couldn't adapt to his new family. Every night he cried for hours keeping the whole household awake until the host family was not only torn up emotionally, but exhausted by his anguish as well. They called Miriam and invited her to come to spend a few nights with him in the hope that with her present he would adjust.

That didn't work either. When she left for school each day he was wild with fear that she would not come back that night. There was nothing for it but to take him back to their tiny quarters.

The Council of Jewish Women came up with another solution. They recommended Michael be enrolled in the exclusive Babcock School. Though most of the students were day pupils there was a small number of children who boarded. From the moment Michael saw that school, for some inexplicable reason, he seemed to accept it. Miriam was told that he slept through the whole night, his very first day, and when Miriam visited him midweek he could already say "Okay" and "Well". When it was time for her to leave he did not cry, or cling to her, but smilingly waved good-bye as he held the hand of one of the teachers.

Relieved, her heart lighter than it had been since they left Holland, Miriam buried herself in her own lessons. She needed to overcome the language difficulty so she could find work and put her family back together. There were excellent teachers in the program and it was reassuring to know that the other pupils, prominent people in their own countries, were as humbled as she by their common language barrier. The teachers used articles in the Reader's Digest as reading materials. The articles would serve a dual purpose. In the process of learning to read they would also learn something about their adopted country.

One day, while chatting with other doctors from Germany, Miriam was dumbfounded to learn that Anita was in New York. She went immediately to the address she'd been given and there was Anita beaming and smiling in welcome. By the time she left Germany, Anita's name was on the Gestapo's list of subversive persons, an enemy of the state. Her citizenship had been lifted and a warrant issued for her arrest. Though she'd run at the last minute, she had no trouble about money for most of her wealth was already out of the country. They had a good laugh about the antique coin which Miriam had not retrieved. Again Anita offered to lend Miriam money, and again Miriam refused. If there was any hope they could make it on their own like everyone else, she and her husband preferred to do so.

As soon as her mastery of English permitted Miriam enrolled in classes to prepare foreign doctors to take the New

York State Boards in medicine. Medicine in America was more advanced in many important areas than in other countries and immigrants had much to learn. The older the students, the more difficulty they had cramming for tests, but Miriam was one of the youngest of the lot. Before taking the Medical Association Exams she had to pass an English language exam. The day she took the language test was the day Queen Elizabeth entered her "teens." There was no equivalent German word for "teen." Miriam learned a brand new word from the front page of the newspaper that day. After the language exam came the Medical exams which were exhausting. Both hurdles behind her, there was nothing to do but wait.

Before the results of the tests were known, the Council of Jewish Women informed Miriam they were moving her little family to Albany, New York. They had to clear some of the refugees out of New York City to make way for the constant horde of people coming in. The council felt Hans would have better luck looking for work in a smaller city. They left their son at Babcock and went to Albany. New York where Hans found part-time work as a salesman. Miriam went to work at the Albany Medical school in the physiology Department helping out in research - without pay. Somehow, she had to get her foot in the door. Volunteering had been the right move for soon an offer came from a hospital in a small city nearby. The job paid fifteen dollars a week so they were no longer eligible for Council assistance. They sent for Michael and when he joined them after six months at the boarding school he had forgotten German completely. He spoke English like any other American kid. He not only spoke like an American kid, he behaved like one too. Babcock had been the best thing that could have happened to him.

While they were still residing in New York Miriam and Hans received a letter from her sister in Hamburg pleading for help. Miriam's brother-in-law had been arrested, and, though he'd been released, her sister was sure he'd be taken again. They needed affidavits for themselves and their daughter. Her sister asked that they contact a lawyer living in New York who was originally from Frankfort and who was a relative of Miriam's brother-in-law. They went to the lawyer's office in lower Manhattan with her sister's letter in hand fully expecting immediate assistance. Instead, the attorney was surprised to learn that he had relatives in

Hamburg. Since he had already given several affidavits for other members of his family, he didn't feel he could do anything for them. Miriam broke down in his office and wept. The lawyer was helpless before her tears.

"Look," he said, spreading out his hands before him in a soothing gesture. "I'm honestly obligated to the limit of my ability to pay if it becomes necessary to help any of the people I've already signed for. But I'll look around. I'll find somebody. Don't worry about it."

Several days went by in which Miriam helplessly wrung her hands and wept. Then one day they received a phone call from a woman who said she wanted to meet them to talk to them about Miriam's sister. "My attorney told me about you," she said. "I think maybe I can help you. At least I'd like to try. When would it be convenient for you to call on me?"

Miriam's heart soared. It couldn't be happening this way. A stranger who wasn't related to any of them wanted to help? The woman gave them her address and by now they knew New York City well enough to know that this was a very chic address on the Park. They found their way by subway and bus and when the woman met them at the door of her apartment they saw before them the twisted body of a person deformed at birth. Awkwardly, they entered the apartment but within minutes were completely at ease. The woman possessed a quiet intelligence that reassured them and made her deformity recede into unimportance. She asked a myriad of questions about Miriam's background, about her sister, and her sister's husband. At the end of the interview she said,

"I am not without funds and I know many people in government. I'm not promising anything but if they can be brought out they will be."

Two days later the attorney called to tell them that his friend was being thwarted because she was not a relative. "She wants me to tell you not to worry. This only means delay until she finds another way to work it. I tell you, if anybody can spring your sister, it will be she."

Not reassured she called the woman herself. "If what I've been told is true, how do you expect to do it. When we couldn't get an affidavit from a friend who lived in Washington and was very willing to sign for us, the government wouldn't allow it. It took a show-down between the Professor who did sponsor us and an official of the immigration service before a non-relative could give us an affidavit. Do you propose to do that, to go to Washington for a face-to-face confrontation?"

"What I propose to do I cannot discuss until I know it will work. Now, don't worry, we will overcome this obstacle."

What she did was a gesture of generosity beyond Miriam's ken. The woman deposited money in a Swiss bank in Miriam's brother-in-law's name making him sole owner of the account, reserving no recourse to the money for herself. As far as the State Department was concerned, these were solvent people who needed no sponsor for they would never be a burden on the state. To Miriam's great joy, the hurdles they had not been able to jump were cleared away and Miriam's sister, her husband, and their twelve-year-old daughter were immediately booked on the German-American Steamship Line scheduled to leave Germany for the United States September I, l939. For the second time within a year, History and a date of departure collided. September I, war broke out in Europe and all American ports were immediately closed to German ships.

Before Miriam could sink into despair over this latest development their lady bountiful called to say in her gently adamant way, "We will overcome it." Using more leverage than most people could manage, she quickly secured passage for the little family of three on the Holland-American Lines to arrive within the week of their earlier schedule. Before September could melt into October Miriam's sister was in New York. Miriam was beside herself with joy. The Swiss bank account was emptied, and the money returned to their gracious benefactor. The destitute newcomers put themselves into the hands of the Council of Jewish Women. NYC was saturated with refugee Jews. Cities in the West were being pressured to help out, and Miriam's sister and her husband were lucky enough to be shipped off to San Francisco. When Hans heard the news he was wild with envy.

"San Francisco!? How can we go out and come back in again?" he demanded. "Can we get back on the list of newcomers? What if I break into their office and scramble their records so they have to place us all over again? How about getting a petition started? They petition everything in this country, why can't we? What a coup! We came a year too soon!."

There was no relocating in store for them, they'd have to make it in upstate New York. With her fifteen dollars a week they rented an apartment, bought furniture at the Salvation Army and acquired a big old refrigerator from the twenties with coils on the top. They entered Michael in the first grade in the public school nearby, and every day he went home for lunch all by himself. Miriam left sandwiches for him in that big refrigerator. He would rush in from school, grab his sandwich, pour himself a glass of milk, eat his sandwich and scurry back to the playground to play. Sometimes he would detour past her lab window to wave at her as he ran by. As for her own lunch, it was the moment of the day when her lowered status was brought home most forcibly. The hospital dining room was divided into different eating areas separating the doctors from the technical staff. Never could one of the lab people invade the holiest of holy places, the doctor's end of the dining room. When the chief of her department showed her around the hospital for the first time, he impressed on her as delicately as one can cut another person off at the knees, that she was must never act like a doctor, she must always remember that now she was a technician.

They put her to work testing urine samples all day long every day. She was a medical doctor doing the work of a lab technician. One day, while she sat at her worktable pouring solutions into test tubes, she looked up to see Hans standing outside the window with a rose in his hand. Laughing she went out to see what her silly romantic was up to now only to have him hand her a letter from the New York State Medical Board notifying her that she had passed the exams. At last she was a registered medical doctor in the state of New York. She could practice medicine in the United States and she could sit in the doctor's end of the dining room, see patients and be deferred to as befitted her station in life. Nothing was left standing between her and success, nothing but the silly American attitude about women doctors -- and the quotas most hospitals had regarding what percentage of the staff could be Jewish.

December 7, 1941, World War II exploded the "Good old boy" hold men had on the medical profession. With the departure of doctors for military service, the hospital's need for professional personnel became acute. Miriam's role expanded. She began teaching nurses and laboratory technicians, working nights and weekends in rotation with other registered professionals, doing whatever was needed in the pathology department. Her salary shot up from fifteen dollars a week to $2500 a year, far more than interns and residents received. Before long, she was assistant to the pathologist for the hospital. In 1943, she had an article published in a Medical Journal. Success was heady, and Miriam began burning the candle at both ends. Four busy years went by almost before she could catch her breath, four years of experience in anatomical and clinical pathology which made her eligible to take the Specialty Board exams in those fields. Thanks to the war, her horizons were expanding fast.

1945 rolled around, the war ended, a few of the doctors returned closing out some of her opportunities. Miriam's little family decided it was time to move on. Hans was not happy with small town life in upstate New York. He wanted to go west to see the country. Michael had made a full adjustment to American life and was doing well in school and he'd seen enough cowboy movies to make going west sound thrilling. Miriam registered with a national placement agency for Medical Personnel listing herself as a Board-Eligible Pathologist who would like to relocate west of the Mississippi River. Almost overnight an offer came from a hospital in Pueblo, Colorado. For some time she'd wanted to go to San Francisco to see her sister, this offer would make it possible to kill two birds with one stone. She'd stop in Colorado for an interview, then go on to the West Coast.

Naturally she took Michael with her so he could walk the streets of a western town where cowboys and Mexican desperadoes had once hung out. He fell in love with the romance of it all. He loved the towering mountains, the big sky, the ruggedness of a world which fired the imagination of a boy his age. Miriam was interested in the small hospital in this windblown place with its neat streets lined with modest bungalows. She'd be the chief pathologist if she was hired, something she'd never be in New York where men were heads of departments. When she and Michael continued on to San Francisco both of them left Colorado with their fingers crossed. In San Francisco she and her sister had a wonderful visit. Michael was almost as delighted with the Bay and the Ocean as he had been with the Rocky Mountains, but if Colorado was to be his new world he was ready for it. Then one day toward the end of her visit she received a letter from her husband.

"Take the job in Colorado if they offer it," he wrote, " you just failed your Pathology Board Exams."

Chastened, Miriam headed back for Colorado for the promised second interview holding her breath. When she arrived the administrator had a contract waiting, ready for her to sign. Miriam went to work immediately. She left the task of closing out their life in the East to him. He sold off everything he could not pile into their old car and headed toward the setting sun. He made a stopover in Chicago to attend a party celebrating the fiftieth birthday of his old friend, Heinie Necheles, and stayed on for a few days to reminisce about their boyhood in Germany.

Once in Pueblo Hans had no trouble with employment. He took a job with a real estate agency and for six months each of them reveled in what they were doing. Michael burrowed into the life of his new school like a happy little mole: not so little any more and not blind at all. But just as they thought they'd found their happy ending, fate turned her back on them. Within a few weeks after his arrival in that part of America noted world-wide for the recuperative qualities of the air for lung patients, Hans developed a cough. Not an allergic cough, not an ordinary cough, but a cough that wracked him until he was exhausted. Miriam was alarmed. She thought he had tuberculosis and rushed some of his sputum to the laboratory for analysis under the microscope. This was not TB. Thoroughly frightened, Miriam went to the chief oncologist at the hospital. That gentleman suggested she get him to Colorado Springs to a lung expert there at once. In Colorado Springs, they subjected him to a bronchoscopy examination and what they saw was cancer. Nothing had prepared her for this.

"Cancer?" Hans' voice was shrill. "I have cancer?" Miriam buried her face in her hands and wept. Mechanically he reached out and pulled her to him. "What are they going to do?" he asked hoarsely.

"They say surgery is the only hope." she whispered brokenly.

"What do you say?" he demanded holding her close to him so she could not see his face. "You're my doctor."

"Oh God," she cried. "I can't even save my own husband and you call me your doctor."

"You've answered my question." he whispered into her hair. "My chances are slim."

An operation was scheduled, her sister came from San Francisco to be with her, and Michael was boarded out so that he could go on with his classes. She and her sister took a room in a little hotel near the hospital where they slept at night, but their days were spent in the hospital corridor outside his room until he was out of Intensive Care and the doctors declared he would survive. When he slowly began to recover, her sister returned to San Francisco and Miriam took her husband home.

She went back to work walking on air. With a few weeks his color returned and his strength increased to the point where he too went back to work; but six months after the surgery, the cancer showed up again and the dying process took over. Michael was desolate. The end came Christmas Eve.

Now Miriam realized at last just what her husband had done for her. Never had she taken care of anything that smacked of business. In the past her father, her brother, her husband, each in his turn, had handled the boring details of business, taxes, public records of every kind, all the paper work that kept life in order. Through all the trauma of learning to deal with life on its own terms that followed, she continued to go to the hospital every day where she threw herself into work to escape. To help fill the void Hans' death created, at the end of every working day she took on extra work and began to train laboratory technicians again. Time slipped by, and before she knew it Michael was in High School. He became a major figure on the High School debating team and was often out of town at debates held across the state and beyond. The house was too often empty, too full of memories. She began to feel an urgency to move on.

Again she registered with an agency. She specified that she wanted a city west of the Appalachians where there was a good university. A call came from Michael Reese Hospital in Chicago inviting her to come for an interview. She went, she was interviewed, she toured the department, she met the staff, she assessed the modernity and extent of the equipment, she was satisfied. The Pueblo hospital offered her more money if she would stay, but money was not what she needed. She and Michael had to move on to a more intellectual climate and in Chicago was the prestigious University of Chicago. They moved in July of 1949. Michael took the University of Chicago Entrance exams and while waiting for the results went to classes at the Young Men's Christian Association to work on his High School graduation certification. If he passed the entrance exams he could forego his junior and senior years of High School to enter the University of Chicago's innovative program for bright students without graduating from high school but he wanted the diploma nevertheless.

Michael passed both sets of exams and began to study Art and Philosophy. Medicine was not for him. Miriam couldn't persuade him to even take the basic courses in biology, physics or chemistry that most college freshmen take. He had his own agenda. They found a good apartment with a nice view of the lake which would be home for the next four years. Miriam dived into her work and came up sputtering a bit. She was in the big league now, she had to stretch. She set to work with a will to take the Specialty Boards again.

Not only professionally but socially Chicago was good for Miriam. At last she had the time and opportunity to make friends on her own. She contacted the Necheleses who introduced her around their circle. Many of her colleagues were single and through them her number of acquaintances grew. She went to the theater, to dinner parties with new friends, she entertained occasionally, she spruced up her wardrobe, she had suitors. All in all she felt more like a woman than she had in many years.

One of the people who appeared on her horizon during that first year in Chicago was a Russian woman of wealth who, when she learned Miriam too was Russian, took the newcomer under her wing and introduced her around like a special protégé. Their association matured into a close friendship, so close that Miriam came to call her "Muti", the German word for mother. Her longing for family again manifested itself. "Muti" had two daughters. One of whom had written several books. The other was just receiving her master's degree and was about to marry a young professor whose field was Art. "Muti" didn't want an Art professor for a son-in-law, she wanted a doctor for her daughter. The daughter did as she pleased. After a stint in California the newlyweds moved to Massachusetts and it was in their garden that Michael was married years later. After two years, two years in which she passed the Specialty Boards and the State Boards in Illinois and gained more ground professionally, she came to another crossroads in her life. First, there was a man. Should she marry again or not? She decided against it and to separate from him, as well as to cut the umbilical cord to Michael, she quit her job. Within weeks she was offered an interesting position in Boston, Massachusetts at Boston's Lying In Hospital. They needed a woman physician with her qualifications. She took the job and headed back East.

Soon after leaving Colorado she began seeking out medical conferences abroad in order to travel. She religiously attended one every year. In Boston she followed the same pattern. Her first trip to Russia was to attend the first international cancer convention held in Moscow. Stalin was still in power, and all of the conferees were a little frightened at the tight security that surrounded them. Papers were presented, the receptions were elegant, the surveillance constant. She was determined to meet her sisters, surveillance or not, and she made it work. She had not seen her two sisters since her birthday trip in 1923. The sister living in Leningrad came to the home of the sister living in Moscow so that they could have a clandestine meeting with the little sister from America. It was like a Russian spy novel, the three of them meeting on a side street, Miriam dressed in clothing that would make her look like an ordinary Russian housewife right down to the shoes, especially the shoes. Nothing would give a person away faster in Russia than western shoes. They reminisced for hours, deliriously happy to be reunited, but Miriam was hurt by how poor they looked, and how old. When she inquired about how often they saw each other the older sister replied, "We don't get together very often. It's expensive to take a train, and there are all the papers to fill out. Then you have to register with the police that you're going and with the police when you get there."

"Besides, it's difficult to get enough time off from work." added the younger one sighing, "We write to each other more than we see each other."

Miriam reached out her manicured hand to cover the rough one lying on the table. "I'm going to make life easier for you both," she said earnestly. "From now on you will get more than a letter from me. You'll see."

When Miriam returned to the United States she learned through the Harvard Travel Bureau that in the future she could meet her sisters openly if they met beside the sea near Leningrad, and if she prepaid all their travel expenses, their lodging and their food. The Russians needed and wanted foreign currencies. Armed with that information, in ensuing years Miriam made three trips to the Finnish border area of Russia to see them, each time prepaying everything before she left the United States. Food was scarce in the rest of Russia but plentiful in this resort area. Her sisters reveled in the sumptuous meals they enjoyed at the hotel where Harvard booked them in.

Miriam heard stories of the grandparents she never knew, stories of their parents when they were young, stories which rounded out the personalities of her father and mother for her. There were anecdotes about life in Suwalki to make her laugh and anecdotes to make her wistful for the dear dead days of the past. But the true sadness woven into these reminisces was her sisters' matter-of-fact recitation of the grim facts of their own lives for the past three decades lived under the hammer and sickle. In their turn, the sisters relished hearing stories of her life in Germany and in the United States.

During those Boston years, though Miriam's life might be over-flowing, half of her attention was focused on Chicago. When Michael graduated with his Bachelor of Arts in Art he decided to remain at the University of Chicago to obtain a Master's degree in Philosophy. Always consumed with his life, wanting so much to have a major vote in what he did with it, she was not happy with his decision. What could he do but teach with such a background? Teachers never made money, she argued. She tried to discuss other careers with him but Michael followed his heart.

A year into his Master's program Michael came down with hepatitis B and was hospitalized for two weeks. That two-week stay in the hospital, watching doctors come and go, soaking up the ambiance of the medical world, persuaded Michael that he did want to go into medicine after all. Back in Boston with his mother to recuperate Michael entered medical school. Halfway through his internship war broke out in Viet Nam. Michael determined to get into the military immediately, get his military service over with as quickly as possible, and return to his studies. He requested duty assignment to Public Health. His choice was honored.

They made him a captain in the army and assigned him to the National Health Institute outside Washington, D.C., doing research in health problems. In research Michael found his niche in life. He loved the laboratory. The research in which he was engaged was of such complexity that it was accepted as the equivalency of a residency. In the army, he not only completed his medical training but his research led to grants for continued work in that field when he was a civilian again.

Miriam went to visit Michael and saw what Civil Service employment could offer. No personnel or budgetary problems, no administration, no charging of fees, a fixed salary. She decided to explore the possibilities of government work for herself. It took some months before she located just what she wanted, a job as a pathologist in a Veterans Hospital in New Jersey.

As she left Boston she crossed paths with Michael who was going to Harvard to continue the research he had been doing on the government payroll. He was to be paid through grants he received from medical foundations interested in his work. Harvard gave him space in which to pursue his research and the organizational support he needed. Once his work was organized he set out to also organize his private life. He was ready to find a wife. He set himself up in a Bachelor's Apartment, contacted old friends, and went to a party at the home of "Muti's" daughter and her husband. The professor of Art had become a big name in Art education in the Boston area. At the party Michael met Linda who was teaching both at Radcliff and Harvard, and was trying to write a dissertation in her spare time. She was part of the Art world he had once planned to enter himself. Her vivaciousness captivated him. Within four weeks they were married in "Muti's" daughter's garden.

Miriam came to the wedding and met the bride for the first time. She felt left out. It wasn't long until Michael's bachelor's quarters were too small for two people needing lots of room in which to spread out papers and books and who needed a room for a nursery too. They rented a larger apartment and six months later their first son was born. He was three months premature weighing only two pounds. The marvels of modern medicine saved him, but when a little sister was born eighteen months later, also three months premature, the marvel was not repeated. They lost her. Eighteen months later a full term child was born, a second son, and eighteen months after that a third little boy completed the family. Within six years Linda had given birth to four children. Miriam was appalled. She thought the flow would never stop.

Linda was submerged in pregnancies and diapers. Miriam couldn't understand it. Linda loved her work, but her dissertation was falling by the wayside, buried under the more pressing work of raising three sons while teaching full time. Miriam tried to do all her fretting by herself, but Michael and Linda knew she disapproved of such a big brood.

While Michael and Linda were being productive in their child-producing enterprise Miriam entered the most productive period of her career. She became assistant to the head of a department in the Veteran's Administration medical facility where she had been working as a pathologist. Six months later the director took a new job outside the government and his post was offered to her. She didn't want that much responsibility for detail, she'd shed such a job in the private sector and come to the government to escape. There was a great deal of travel involved as head of the facility, there were speeches to be made to Congressional committees, conventions to attend, medical personnel in training hospitals and medical schools to meet and inspire, and she was much in the public eye. Her myriad activities made her prominent within medical circles of the government.

Being close to New York City Miriam reestablished contact with Anita. No longer Anita's young "protégé", Miriam now stood as high in their chosen profession as Anita ever had. Anita was delighted for her and welcomed her into her circle of friends. Many of them were Quakers, most of them German immigrants like herself. They saw each other occasionally, and always on Christmas Eve. Every year Anita had a small Christmas party where they celebrated the Yuletide with all the traditional Christmas foods of Germany. Miriam always brought a special cake she baked for the occasion, an elegant creation of chocolate and nuts topped with whipped cream.

At sixty-five Miriam retired. She moved back to Boston to be near Michael and his family. She had achieved all she had set out to do, she wanted to try her hand at leisure for awhile, and she wanted to watch the boys grow up. She took occasional temporary jobs filling in for doctors on sabbatical or vacation, just to keep her hand in. Her savings from the big years when she'd been paid in fees gave her a comfortable cushion so she didn't need the money, but the extra work made her eligible for social security. Altogether, she was in good shape by the time she quit altogether. Occasionally she went down to New York to see Anita, and twice a year Anita came to spend a weekend with her. Seven years went by so pleasantly they became a blur, then Linda and Michael made a move that upset everything. They began closing down their life in New England to shift their scene to Illinois where Linda would teach at the University of Chicago. With them gone, what did Boston hold for her? Snow, cold, cars that didn't start or were sluggish, she couldn't think of enough good things to offset the deficits of muggy summers and frigid winters along Lake Michigan.

In 1976 Anita died and Miriam received a letter from two attorneys telling her that Anita had remembered her in her will. Several of Anita's other friends were also to be beneficiaries. The loss of Anita was a blow. Her last tie with Germany was gone. To have been remembered in her friend's will was touching, but Miriam didn't expect more than a thousand dollars or so to come since the estate was being divided so many ways. Probate, the lawyers warned, was a long process so she shouldn't expect to know how much she would receive for many months.

Miriam decided to go to California to see if that felt like a suitable nesting place for her sunset years. Anita's estate played no part in her decision. She telephoned her sister and told her she'd like to come for a month. She went, and they talked for hours but never came to any conclusions about Miriam's future. Then two days before Miriam was to return to Boston, she said to her niece who came to spend the day, "At Christmas I got a card from some old friends from Chicago who are living here in California somewhere."

Her niece laughed, "Northern California or down South?"

"I don't know," said Miriam, "I have the card right here. It says they're in someplace called Rossmoor. I don't suppose you know where that is."

"Rossmoor is right near here!" exclaimed her niece.

"Right here? You mean it's close by?"

"Sure. It's just over the hills behind Berkeley."

"How can I get there?" Miriam asked.

"Why, I'll drive you." laughed the niece.

Miriam called the Necheleses and invited herself out. Her niece drove her to Rossmoor and when the Steffie and Heinie learned she was going to leave New England they urged her to come to live near them. Hesitant to make a commitment too quickly Miriam demurred. Aside from the Necheleses and her sister's family, she wouldn't know a soul. She'd become a nobody, not be a somebody like she was in Boston or Chicago. To whom could she turn for intellectual stimulus? With whom could she socialize? She warmed to the task of finding reasons why Rossmoor might not be for her, in spite of the satisfying ambiance of the place. She left for Boston thinking she would not make that move.

The next day she was asking herself why she'd been so quick to back away. She hadn't really given the place a chance. Surely among all the professionals already retired there she could find companionship. What other place offered so much? She wrote to Steffie to see if it would be possible to rent for a month in Rossmoor to try it out. While she waited for an answer she heard from Anita's attorneys. She had not inherited a thousand dollars, her cup was filled to overflowing with over $30,000! It was incredible! Four times while she lived Anita had offered to lend her money, and four times Miriam had refused. In death Anita had given her $30,000, and Miriam couldn't refuse.

Still numb with wonder over her good fortune Miriam heard from Steffie. By coincidence someone they knew wanted a house-sitter for the month of March while they were away. If Miriam could come at that time the place was hers. Miriam returned, and during that month Steffie and Heinie toured her around the area until she had a clear picture of life in Rossmoor. They introduced her to some of their friends who in turn invited her for dinner. One of the first couples she met were the Schiffs, Ilse and Wim. Doctors gravitate toward doctors like flies to honey so she quickly belonged to the Schiffs circle like every other refugee who crossed their paths. Within two weeks Miriam knew this was the best place she could find for idleness. Heinie and Steffie put her into the hands of real estate agents and the search for a unit to buy was on. One day Miriam read in the Rossmoor News that a couple living up on Running Springs wanted to sell. She called Steffie as soon as she thought she would be home from work and finished with dinner. It was seven o'clock.

"Where is this Running Springs?" she asked. "Is it a nice neighborhood?"

"It's a very good location," said Steffie, "It's right near here."

"I suppose it's too late to see it today."

"It's only seven o'clock," said Steffie. "That's not too late. Let's call them to see if they'll let us see it tonight."

They drove up to the top of Running Springs, high enough on the hill to have a panoramic view of Mt. Diablo. When they walked in Miriam saw the mountain all mauve in the twilight, the aircraft warning lights blinking blue and red on its summit, and knew she had found her nest.

"How much?" she asked. And when they named a price she said without hesitation, "I'll take it."

Due to her fortuitous inheritance, her dear, dear friend, who had wanted to make her path easier in the past, had made both the present and the future secure. She called it "Anita's House." If Anita can hear across the gulf between life and whatever follows after she heard Miriam say with a full heart many times, "Thank you, my friend. I'm so proud to have known you and been remembered by you."

Closing out her life in Boston was a simple matter except for sorting through a lifetime of memorabilia. The greatest wrench was giving up her books. When she had culled and packed everything, the moving company arrived, and Miriam's possessions were on their way to their final home. When the last man walked out her door she locked it behind him, and went to take a long soaking bath to let the tension of the past week seep out into the warm sudsy water. She was immersed chin deep when the phone rang. Not even a bath mat remained in the apartment. She clambered out of the tub soaking wet, slipped, fell, and broke her left arm just below the shoulder. The pain was excruciating, she had to get help fast. Stark naked, no blanket or sheet to cover herself, holding a towel around her with one hand as best she could, she went to the phone. But what to do? To dial the number she had to let go of the towel.

Letting modesty go by the board, she started dialing. Her friends rushed in and found a cape to throw around her for the mad rush to the hospital. Because it was a major holiday there were no specialists on call. No one to decide whether the bone should merely be set or whether it needed to be pinned.

An intern put the useless arm into a sling and sent her home to wait for Tuesday when the orthopedic specialists would be back. A couple in her building brought her a cot to sleep on, someone else brought a floor lamp to give her light, and Lillian, dear sweet Lillian, daughter of one of Miriam's colleagues in at Michael Reese in Chicago, now residing in Boston, arrived with an arm load of loose baggy things she had scrounged from friends for Miriam to wear until she could get a slip over her head and fasten a bra. Every morning on her way to work she brought fresh rolls from the bakery, made hot coffee, and the two of them breakfasted sitting on the floor. At night she came from work with Chinese takeout and they again broke bread together on the bare boards. Until she could at last put Miriam on a plane for California, Lillian was there for her every day.

Out in California Miriam's car arrived but she was not there to receive it. Another friend of Heinie picked up the car and drove it to Running Springs Road and parked it in the carport behind her "manor." The furniture arrived. Again Miriam was not there to receive it, but Ilse and Wim were. They placed the furniture as they thought it fit the rooms and when Miriam arrived Ilse unpacked all the boxes under Miriam's watchful eye. It was quite an entrance into Rossmoor. There had been no stealing in unnoticed. She was well known in Ilse's and Steffie's circle before she arrived. Miriam spent the last twenty-three years of her life in "Anita's house," one of the oldest of "The Girls." She went to ceramics classes, played bridge, and all-in-all was as happy as Miriam could be.

In the end she became senile and had to be removed to a nursing home in New York where Michael, now at Columbia University, could watch over her. Fortunately, she never knew she was there nor how brief her stay.

ILSE

Miriam had a birthday party. A wonderful birthday party for a "big" birthday. She was eighty-five. Her very successful doctor son, Dr. Michael Field, and his equally successful professor wife, Dr. Linda Seidel Field, flew out from Chicago and gave a luncheon for her. Eighteen guests were invited. They filled her living-dining room. Miriam made up the guest list and planned the program. After the plates were gathered up she went around the group, one by one, explaining how each person present fit into her life. She started by saying that Ilse was the "mother hen" of the group. Ilse, said Miriam, had brought them all together. There's disagreement about how instrumental she was in the formation of "The Girls," but Ilse was the first of the refugees to move to Rossmoor. Her flight from Germany was quite pedestrian compared to the others, as fraught with danger as it was. She and her husband, Dr. Wim Schiff, fled Berlin early in Hitler's regime before Jews faced roadblocks set up to keep them from getting out.

Ilse grew up in the same grand apartment, in the same building, on the same block of the same exclusive street in the city of Berlin where her family had lived for generations. Around the corner from her home was the residence of an established surgeon. Typically, European doctors had their offices, their clinics and their residences all within the same suite of apartments. This surgeon was no different than the rest. He never went out in the rain to go to work. Successful, with a rich clientele, he was at the same time divorced, separated from his eight-year-old daughter, and very lonely. Then a bubbly girl of seventeen from around the corner crossed his path. Typically, also, European men did not marry until they were established, and usually chose younger women. When they remarried they assumed the dual role of being pater as well as husband. Ilse was twenty when they married, and Wim was thirty-five. The year was 1930. MEIN KAMPF had been published three years earlier. Few of the Jews of Germany took his book more seriously in 1927 than did the rest of the world. Many Jews were among the elite of German society and had reason to be complacent about their lot in life. Many even held positions in the liberal Weimar Republic. Among the few who read his book and took him seriously was Ilse. She read his blueprint for a world order from which

Jewry would be eliminated and began to demand that Jews "listen up."

Her family scoffed at her "alarums." Seventeen, they said, was the right age to be spooked by someone whose ideas were threatening, regardless of what a nincompoop he might be. At any age, Ilse was and is very vocal, only stopping now and then to get a breath, never long enough for someone to take the floor from her. Audibly, and at length, she gnawed over Hitler's ideas. When Von Hindenburg made Hitler chancellor in 1933 she began to shrilly urge her husband, her family, and all their friends to pack up and get out, but few would listen. Not until the Brown Shirts, the Nazis, began to march and to smear Jewish businesses with anti-Semitic graffiti did others begin to join her chorus. When none of the Aryan citizens protested the overt abuse of their neighbors, the Jews of Germany finally got the message. They were in the line of Hitler's fire and they had few allies. Jew-banging picked up tempo. First, the new chancellor nullified the right of Jews to obtain licenses of any kind. With the encouragement and cooperation of Hitler's government, Aryan Germans began muscling in on Jewish enterprises, taking them away from their owners. Jewish firms no longer received new government contracts, and if their business depended on existing contracts they saw their wealth wiped out overnight when those contracts were not renewed. The first anti-Jewish parade in Berlin occurred in April of 1933. Crowds lined the street and cheered and shouted "Heil Hitler," and not one newspaper editor protested. Ilse began having nightmares.

A month later, in May, one of Dr. Schiff's patients, a woman on whom Dr. Schiff had operated and with whom he'd formed a good friendship, a woman who was herself a member of the National Socialist Party, called to warn him.

"You have to leave." she said. "I'm telling you that someone is looking at your practice and you will be arrested. There's no time to waste. Get out quickly."

Though Dr. Schiff had brushed aside his wife's doom-saying before April, he didn't brush this aside. He heard his patient's terrifying warning and didn't hesitate. Within forty-eight hours he was out of Germany. Ilse was left behind to redirect his patients to other doctors, sublease the apartment since their lease had two years to run, then extricate herself. One thing she would not leave behind was the beautiful furniture designed by Rosenthal, the great German furniture designer, which had been made for their apartment. For a young woman of twenty-three, Ilse was exceptionally competent and clear-headed. She leased the apartment, furniture, dispensary and all, to the Brazilian Ambassador. Diplomatic immunity put the contents of the apartment, as well as the clinic, into Extra-Territorial Status, out of the reach of German hands. When the two years were up, according to the lease agreement, all their furnishings were to be shipped to San Francisco before the consul surrendered occupation of the Schiff's former home to the Nazi government. By the end of 1933, Ilse and her husband were in San Francisco where Ilse had relatives. By the end of 1935 the Rosenthal furniture and all of their possessions had followed them. *

The Shiffs arrived in America, like most who came after them, with empty pockets; but their story differed in that their household goods and family heirlooms were on their way, and they had plenty of assistance from well-established relatives. The greatest asset of all was that Dr. Schiff was a German-trained physician and surgeon. In the 1930's, Germany led the world in medical knowledge and surgical practices. German doctors had an "Open Sesame" entree wherever in the world they settled. Dr. Schiff started a practice in San Francisco in 1934 and enjoyed enormous success immediately.

In the beginning they rented a little apartment on Polk Street, but it was not long until they procured the services of one of California's most brilliant architects, Richard Neutra, to build a house for them in the Marina district on a narrow lot on Jefferson St., a block from the Palace of Fine Arts. "That house," Neutra promised, "will stand up under any earthquake." It did. The 1989 Loma Prieta earthquake brought buildings down all around their house but not a crack appeared in the foundation or walls.

After World War II, when the German government made restitution to the Jews for properties lost and income denied them, the same patient who had warned Dr. Schiff in time to save his life was still alive, and testified to the extent

---

* The Rosenthal furniture is now permanently placed with the San Francisco Museum of Modern Art.

of Dr. Schiff's practice at the time he was forced to flee. She also gave her estimate of the income he had been denied. She further testified that she had indeed warned him of impending doom and sent him on his way to safety. By that time, the Schiffs certainly did not need the money but Ilse's anger demanded satisfaction. Dr. Schiff had risen to preeminence as a surgeon in San Francisco; the Schiffs lived extremely well in one of the finest districts of 'The City.' Their great financial loss had been made up, but the loss in family left behind, family that refused to believe that the graffiti and the parades were anything more than a hubbub raised by a demagogue who wouldn't last long, could never be repaid. Some had gotten out but most had perished. The Schiffs received restitution as long as Wim lived and Ilse continued to be paid as his widow until she remarried.[**]

Her new husband was a Czech and their marriage made her ineligible to receive further payment. That Czech, Walter Gelnay, went through harrowing escapes and true travail before he was safely beyond the reach of Hitler or the British, they were as determined to block his escape as were the Germans. His story follows.

[**] Ilse has donated the money for a whole wing, twenty four rooms, of the new Jewish Home for the Aged in Danville, California, as well as the money for a whole floor for Alzheimer patients in the Jewish home in Tel Aviv.

WALTER

An American passport would have made all the difference, but Walter was not born in the United States as were his two sisters, Dita and Tilda. Having been born in the United States simplified Dita's narrow escape just as the Nazis invaded Czechoslovakia. Tilda had left Prague months before. Walter was forced to rely on his own wit and perseverance for salvation, not United States citizenship,. Born in Vienna a year after his parents returned from living in New York, Walter was an Austrian until he chose to become a Czechoslovakian. Walter's mother, the youngest of nine children, was an American by choice, not birth. In 1885, she had been carried in the arms of her mother to the United States as a six-months' old baby, the youngest of nine children. Walter's grandmother crossed the Atlantic in steerage trailing eleven children behind her: nine of her own and two orphaned nieces. Her husband had immigrated from Hungary the year before. The l880's were the decade when hundreds of thousands of Hungarians,citizens of the Austrian Empire at that time, came to the United States in search of a better life, .

The burgeoning railroads, busily lacing the American nation together through the eyelets of architecturally grandiose railway stations, offered instant employment to strong men eager for work. Recruited by a railroad on the docks in New York as he stepped off the boat from Ellis Island, Walter's grandfather located in Hoboken, New Jersey. He ached to be reunited with his family. Diligently, he saved his money toward the day when he could bring his wife and children over to join him. Steerage was cheap, and by living frugally and working double shifts, within twelve months he was able to go back to Hungary to make all the arrangements for his large household to follow him to America. Mary Gelnay was conceived during that interim while her father was at home with the family. Her forthcoming birth delayed their departure.

On United States' soil at last, the baby Mary in her arms, Walter's grandmother, followed by her gaggle of goslings, left Ellis Island, boarded a train and headed for their eagerly anticipated new home. Expecting to be swept up in her husband's welcoming arms, she was as excited as a young bride as she left the passenger car and stepped down onto the railroad platform in Hoboken. There were no welcoming arms. Instead, she was greeted by a delegation of her husband's co-workers, come to break the crushing news that her husband was killed in a train accident while she was steaming across the Atlantic enroute to the land of promise. Shocked and bewildered, stranded in a strange land with no one to help, she was frightened.

Determined to make a stand against the callous indifference of the railroad barons to their workers' safety and health, the Railway Workers Union secured for her a little insurance money which, at their urging, she promptly used to hire lawyers to sue the company. The lawyers took the money but there was no lawsuit to further compensate her, or to give the Union the victory they wanted. Now absolutely destitute, unable to speak the language, Walter's grandmother went back to New York City and opened a boarding house. Many Americans, as well as many immigrants, took their meals in boarding houses in those days. They paid by the week, not the meal, and they were regulars. If the food was good, and the place was clean and homelike, an enterprising boarding house operator could make a modest living from such an establishment.

The eldest son of the orphaned family had been told that in America all things were possible, that he would be able to go to Medical School. There was no medical school for him in their changed circumstances, instead he went to work along with every other child in the household above the age of twelve. The boys went to the sweat shops of New York City which relied on cheap immigrant labor for big profits; the girls went into domestic service in the homes of well-to-do, established Jews. Little by little, all pulling together, they rose from destitution to a minimal level of security and comfort. Little Mary, the baby, was put to work in the kitchen of the boarding house as soon as she was old enough to peel potatoes; and when she was tall enough and strong enough she was set to work serving table.

When Mary was fifteen, a young dentist, an immigrant from Austria who had made it into the ranks of the professions, came to board with the Hungarian lady. His name was Adolph Gelnay. He immediately fell in love with the pretty, vivacious girl who carried in the heaping dishes of food, and cleaned up the table after the meal. A year later, in l902, when he was twenty-five and she was sixteen, they were married. Mary escaped the endless routine of cooking, serving, and washing dishes that seemed to lead to nowhere. They moved into a comfortable apartment not too far from her mother and were soon blessed with a pretty little red-haired baby girl. They named her Tilda. Being the daughter of the youngest child, Tilda was the youngest among a crowd of grandchildren. For four years she was the apple of her grandmother's eye, then a baby sister, another little redhead, was born. The new baby's hair was even redder than Tilda's, titian red, and from the day she first staggered to her feet she dominated the household. Tilda adored Dita, the little sister who put flavor in her life for all her days.

When the Dita was two years old their father decided to go home to Austria for a year to visit his old mother in Vienna and introduce her to his family. The trip for a year turned into permanent residency. Mary fell in love with Vienna and Adolph had no desire to return to the hurly burly life on the Hudson. He opened up a dental office in the Hapsburg capitol and, with his American background, immediately attracted a large clientele. Adolph Gelnay was a brilliant, creative man but he was also perpetually restless. No career or place could hold his attention for long. Something in him always wanted to move on, to try something new, to make a fortune, to create large projects, and when they were complete to start over somewhere else. He made a lot of money and he lost a lot of money. His family never knew whether they were rich or poor. They only knew where things were at the moment. A year after they arrived in Vienna, Walter was born, a son for whom to build, a son to fill his father's shoes in time. To prepare for the boy's future, he said, Adolph launched into an ambitious project at a vital intersection in the heart of Vienna. He set out to build a total community modeled on projects he had seen going up in America. The project would consist of three large buildings built on the pie-shaped block bounded by Prater Str. on the west and Tabor Str. on the north in the second district of Vienna across the canal from the Old City. The buildings would house a hotel, a theater, and street-level shops with apartments above. The project was just underway when World War I broke out.

Adolph was conscripted into the Austrian army as soon as hostilities began. The Unit to which he was assigned was sent to Bratislava, not far from Vienna, in what was then Hungary. Not wanting to be separated from his family he bought a house at the edge of the town and brought them there to live. Their six years in Bratislava are better told through the life of Dita than the life of Walter. She was the Gelnay those years affected most. During their stay in Bratislava the children were tutored at home. Walter was 10, and ready for gymnasium, when the family moved back to Vienna in 1920. His parents enrolled him in the local school in the second district where the population was 85% Jewish. Part of a Jewish world, Walter grew up not knowing the meaning of anti-Semitism, but, as a Czech in Vienna, he knew what it was like to be an outsider.

When the Hapsburg Empire was broken up at Versailles in 1919, some of the territory went to the newly-formed Czechoslovakia, some to also newly-formed Yugoslavia, some to Italy, some to Poland and some to Rumania. Only a fraction of the former land area of Hapsburg Austria remained under the Austrian flag. All the citizens of the old Empire had to choose which of these new nations they would claim as their homeland. One could choose freely which citizenship he/she wanted, but there had to be some basis for the choice. Adolph Gelnay chose to be Czechoslovakian because the village from which his family had come the generation before him, lay within the new Czech boundaries. Adolph's mother resided in Vienna but his grandparents still lived in the little Czechoslovakian town where Gelnays had lived for generations. Having chosen citizenship, one did not need to move back inside the borders of that nation, but one was registered forever after in Vienna as a foreign national from the country one had chosen. As a Czech, Walter had to pay five times as much tuition as all but one of his classmates who was also Czech.

At school in Vienna, in the first classroom he had ever experienced, Walter was totally ignorant of the protocol of school life. Throughout his first day in his heady new environment his excitement knew no bounds. Having been dominated by Dita for so long, he practically wriggled with delight to be in a room full of boys. He was in trouble within five minutes of taking his seat. The teacher called the roll and when he heard his name Walter answered, "Yes?" He didn't bother to rise, or to even look up at the teacher, he was too busy taking stock of the boys around him. What they wore, what they had, what they were doing totally engaged him.

"Walter Gelnay!" the teacher called out sharply, amazed at the cheekiness of the new student. Again, without looking up, Walter answered, "Yes?" Only when the boys sitting near him pushed him to his feet did he stand sheepishly, embarrassed by the attention he had focused on himself.

Next, while collecting fees, the teacher ran out of small bills. "Can anyone in the class change a 20 shilling note?" he asked.

"Yes," responded Walter from his seat. Again the boys pushed him up to a standing position from which he transacted the exchange of money before taking his seat again.

More fees from more students, and again the teacher needed help. "Is there anyone else who can change a 20 shilling note? No one responded as the teacher's eyes swept the room. "Gelnay?" he inquired.

This time Walter rose and began silently digging in his pocket for his wallet.

"Yes, Herr Professor!" someone behind him hissed. Walter looked around found the other Czech boy in the class making little gestures toward the teacher mouthing the words again.

"Yes, Herr Professor." Walter said handing over four 5 shilling notes."

The teacher took the money frowning. "Do you always carry so much money, Gelnay?"

By now he had the routine down pat. "Yes Herr Professor," he said sitting down at his desk.

"Gelnay," the teacher's tone was less brusque than it had been in the earlier exchanges. "Students remain standing until I tell them they may sit. Is that understood."

Walter remained in his seat. "Yes, Herr Professor." he replied respectfully. The teacher threw up his arms in defeat as muffled giggles broke out across the room. Walter never forgot that day.

As the years passed, Adolph worked at a frenzied pace trying to run the hotel, operate the movie house, supervise the maintenance of the apartments, collect the rents, hire nothing done that he could do himself. It was giving him ulcers. In 1927, Adolph Gelnay's lawyer took him to task. "You're crazy."

he said. "You were in the war for four years, you've made enough money to live a good life without all this work, why are you killing yourself? You work 60 hours a day! Why are you doing it? Why don't you sell out?"

The lawyer knew that several times a group of men who wanted to buy Gelnay Enterprises had approached Adolph, but Adolph always refused. They offered him a million dollars, but he couldn't let go. Then they came back and offered him a million and a half. Still he refused. The price went to two million, then to two and a half. When he still wavered, his brother joined the chorus of voices urging him to sell. The business group offered to pay in U.S. currency, but still he hung back. When they offered him $3,000,000 he capitulated.

He kept the big double apartment that was home to his family, but the rest changed hands and he stopped running everything. Instead, he poured the same energy into becoming a big investor. With his usual plunger attitude he began buying foreign currencies. He bought French, Italian, American, Deutschmarks, Swiss, Austrian, whatever the banks could acquire for him. His timing was all wrong. No matter what he bought it collapsed. He finally lost the last of it in 1929. Undaunted, he started over. He went to America in search of a good business opportunity. Before he left he had a long talk with Walter, or rather he lectured Walter at length.

"When you finish at the gymnasium I want you to go to the University. In these times a gymnasium education is only the beginning for a man with ambition. You should get a profession like I did. If business fails you can always fall back on it."

Walter had no interest in going to the university, he'd never been a student. He wanted to become an auto mechanic. An older friend had secured an agency which sold spare parts for the Austrian Steyer Automobile. His friend urged him to come to work for him. He wanted Walter to run the office, to dispatch the parts to the customers as the orders came in, and to operate the warehouse. That would free him, the boss, to go out to sell to garages and service stations in Vienna and the surrounding suburbs. As a special lure to get Walter to come in with him, his friend promised that when he was away on business outside Vienna, Walter could use his car on weekends. Walter leaped at the opportunity. He could be involved with cars without going to mechanics training school. He could drive an automobile to all the dances on the weekend. He took the job and, eager to make his mark on the world, he worked hard. He studied the catalogues, kept a close eye on the inventory, and was becoming an expert on spare auto parts when his father came back from the United States. Adolph had negotiated the exclusive distributorship throughout Europe for the Dayton Tire Company of Ohio.

Deciding that Vienna was no longer the energetic hub of the central European business community, Adolph saw Prague as a much more promising center of manufacturing and industry so he established his offices there and sent for Walter. Like it or not, Walter had to give notice to his friend and go to work in Czechoslovakia for his father. Spare parts were more to his liking than tires, but he was still involved with cars. Adolph found rooms for them in a hotel on the main square of Prague near the office. There they were joined by a representative of the Dayton Co., a Mr. Newman, who also took up residence in their hotel. The hotel sported a bar with a dance floor where many of the men of industry, and the women who search out such men, spent their evenings drinking and dancing. Walter was a bit slow on the drinking, but the dancing was his specialty. His sisters had insisted he take lessons so he could escort them to tea dances. He'd become one of the best ballroom dancers in Vienna. The three of them, father, son and Mr. Newman, lived it up. Adolph could drink continually, drink after drink, and never get drunk; nor did it affect his capacity for work the next day. Walter, on the other hand, would be worthless on the job if he mixed alcohol and dancing, and he'd rather dance than drink any time. As for women, his father, now liberated from his marriage, had never been too restricted by the mores of society. An iconoclast to the core, Adolph Gelnay could never be limited by someone else's notions of right and wrong. Wine and women for the father, women and dancing for the son. Or so his father thought. In truth, off the dance floor Walter was too shy to succeed with women. A man about town doesn't let his playboy father know that, however.

The Gelnay Company was beginning to cover the Czech market with Dayton tires when complaints about the quality of the tires began to flow in. Adolph Gelnay was not a man to deal in shoddy goods. He insisted on quality in everything he touched. He and Mr. Newman went from place to place checking out the complaints and found that the tires were indeed constructed poorly, made of second-rate rubber. The display and demonstration models they received were high quality, but the tires shipped to fill their orders were inferior in grade. Indignant, Adolph went back to the United States to straighten out the matter. Unable to receive satisfactory answers to his questions, he took the Dayton Co. to court, and the case kept him tied down in America for the next four years. Walter was left in Prague to shut down the business until the matter was settled to Adolph's satisfaction. With the office closed, Walter was out of work.

Both his sisters were married and his sister Dita was the wife of an exceedingly rich textile manufacturer in Reichenberg, Czechoslovakia. Tilda and her husband, who had lived in Reichenberg also, were back to Vienna. For the first time in her life, Dita was without members of her own family around her. Dita's husband Otto stepped into the breach and offered Walter a job.

"Walter," Dita's voice came over the wire insistently. "You must come to Reichenberg! You must! We want you to. Otto wants you to work for him. You can work in the mill or you can manage the garage or you can work a little in both places."

"But..." Walter started to protest.

"No But! Papa's left you high and dry. You don't have a job. You come here. We'll give you a car of your own, and you can have your own apartment. Now don't argue with me!"

"What will you pay me?" he demanded. He couldn't give in too quickly though the offer couldn't have pleased him more. It was like a raft being pushed out to someone trapped in a strong current. He hadn't known what to do.

"Pay you!? What do you mean, what will we pay you? We'll pay you what you're worth and nothing more." Dita retorted. "Now pack your things and get out here. We'll talk about what we'll pay you when we decide what you're going to do."

She hung up before he could put up any more phony objections. He left Prague and headed for Reichenberg the next day. Not every young man his age in Europe could have his own place and tool around in his own car. He felt like Don Juan, or a leading man in the movies. And the car did make him popular with the girls. That little Fiat roadster was his ticket to social success. Walter plunged into the life of Reichenberg and had a fine old time until Otto brought him to heel. His brother-in-law was hard on him, made him toe the mark. Walter had to arrive at work on time and Otto expected a good day's work for a good day's pay. No coming in whenever he got up, hung over. It was time for Walter to grow up. Walter's mother always said Walter had a memory like a sieve, that if she sent him to the store for three things he forgot four. Otto would not excuse or make light of forgetfulness. If a thing was to be done it was not to be put aside until later, and in the process forgotten, it was to be accomplished, completely, on time. That kind of direction was what Walter needed. For three years he worked hard, saved his money and tooled around Reichenberg in his little car, but he could see no future for himself in such a little town. Becoming involved with a girl, he was afraid he'd wind up being forced to get married. Everything seemed to point to a dull life in a dull place having a dull career as his brother-in-law's employee, and that would never do. He was, after all, Adolph Gelnay's son. He gave notice. He was going to Paris where a big-city boy like himself belonged.

In Paris, his old friend from school, the other Czech in his class, was an agent for a foreign company. The only way an alien-national could be employed in France was to represent a foreign company. Walter went to work for his friend. Jingling the money he'd saved in Reichenberg in his pocket, driving around Paris in his car, with no Otto around to curtail his comings and goings, he lapsed into his old lackadaisical habits and had himself a first-class fling. His car and his bulging wallet soon brought him a sizable circle of new friends. His new friends loved to play poker at night, and not to be left out, Walter joined in though he couldn't concentrate long enough to remember the cards that had been played or what he should be building in his hand. He lost a lot of money.

And he spent a lot of money. He loved the theater so he saw all the shows, he haunted all the best clubs, and if one is to be a man about town one needs a big wardrobe so he acquired one. Then he decided to go into business for himself. He rented a small office and set himself up as an exporter of fine women's clothes. He bought big lines of stock like Schiaperelli, never on credit, always using his own money. He bought retail, paying handsomely for the clothes but he couldn't sell them for enough more than his investment to make ends meet. When he couldn't pay the rent on the office, and couldn't pay any of his suppliers, his creditors confiscated all the clothes he had in stock, including his own elegant wardrobe, and put him out of business. He was broke. He was down to buying day-old buns from Samartaine, buns so hard he had to dunk them in order to eat them. Walter walked the streets looking for something to do. He couldn't go back to Reichenberg, a failure, and face Otto. For a month, he found coolie work ironing shirts in a sweat shop in the heat of August, but where was the future in that? Within eight months of leaving dull little Reichenberg, high flier Walter had no prospects for the future, and was forced to throw in the sponge. Rather than go back to Dita with his tail between his legs, he sought haven with his sister Tilda in Prague where her husband Stasch had relocated her.

Back in Prague he applied for dozens of positions and was called in for interviews several times, but nothing permanent came of his efforts. One day he was called in by a malt company with whom he had interviewed earlier and was hired. At the malt company, the lessons Otto had provided back in Reichenberg produced results. Walter buckled down and was pleased with himself and so was the company. No sooner did he hit his stride, however, than he got the measles. Little Norli, Tilda's child, brought them home from school. The measles flattened him, though he was never as ill as Dita had been when she'd gotten the measles and had to leave Paris, nor did his recuperation take so long. But he was out of circulation just when he most wanted to be in the thick of things.

Soon after he recovered and returned to the business of malt production he received a letter which was a reply to an even earlier application, made when he started reading the Help Wanted columns in the paper when he first arrived in Prague. He had seen a solicitation for someone who could speak several languages, especially French, to go to Beirut. Beirut was a French mandate and the Beirut branch of the Skoda Corporation needed a salesman to sell spare auto parts throughout the Middle East. No one in Europe ever thought of the Near East, as the Middle East was then called, as a place to seriously pursue a career unless that career was in oil, but the Skoda Corporation was a big company with branches everywhere. If he could make it big with Skoda in Beirut, then transfer back to some capitol in Europe, the world would be his oyster. What interested Walter most was "opportunity" and this opportunity was too attractive to pass up.

"I'm driving through to Trieste," said the man from Skoda, "Why don't you go that far with me? I'd like your company. That way I can take you to the ship for Beirut?"

Walter was delighted by the prospect, but he couldn't leave Europe without saying good-bye to his mother. "Oh," he replied, "that would be good! But I have to see my mother in Vienna before I go."

"Great. I've never been to Vienna. You'll give me an excuse to stay over there for a day or two. I'd like that." He stuck out his hand. "You've got yourself a ride."

Grinning from ear to ear, Walter took the man's hand in both of his and shook it vigorously. "This job sounds better all the time. You begin employment with a vacation!"

It was March of 1935 when the two young romantics set off. They had two days in Vienna, days in which Walter had a wonderful visit with his mother while his traveling companion saw the town, then from Vienna they drove like a couple of tourists through beautiful, hilly Yugoslavia. There were gorges, and valleys, and waterfalls, and picturesque landscapes such as Walter had never seen on the plains and low hills of northern Europe. They took so much time sight-seeing along the way that it took a month to get Trieste where Walter would take ship for Lebanon. It was another month before the little freighter he had booked nosed into the dock at Beirut. There was hardly a port between Italy and Lebanon they hadn't explored along the way.

With his cosmopolitan background of Vienna, Prague and Paris, Walter arrived at a camel-transport crossroads in a part of the world familiar to westerners only through the pages of travel books. Everything was strange and pungent and wonderful. The sounds of Beirut were the most stirring part of the new experience. From the towers of the mosques, four times a day, came the Muslim calls to prayer; tinkling bells around the necks of camels, goats and donkeys were heard on every street; vendors called from the entrances of their tiny shops, hawking strange wares. The air was full of melodious sounds charming to his European ears.

In Lebanese society he was thrown with Lebanese Christians, Muslims, and a pot-pourri of Arabs, a melange of people only Hollywood could have imagined throwing together for fraternization. He got along swimmingly well with them all. During the little more than a year he was there before his father returned from America, Walter made a place for himself in Beirut. For four years Adolph had kept the Dayton Tire Co. in the courts, only to lose in the end. First Adolph went to Vienna to start over; but, estranged from Mary who still occupied the family apartment, life with his mother was dull. Vienna, too, was stiff and boring compared to the life he'd been living in America, so he headed for Beirut to be near his son. He didn't bother to consult Walter to see if Walter wanted him there, he just came. While in the United States, he had purchased all manner of dental equipment with which, as soon as he arrived, he began a specialty in dentistry. He rebuilt malformed mouths through oral surgery and then made dentures to fit his reconstructions. There was good money in it, and he had the field to himself.

The hotels of Beirut were the social gathering places for foreign visitors There were businessmen and travelers from all the Mediterranean countries as well as the Middle Eastern countries inland from Lebanon. Walter was surprised at how many Europeans were in residence in the city, and they too hung out in the bars of the hotels. Adolph could always be found in the watering holes wherever they were. In these hotel oases Adolph met some wealthy Arabs from Baghdad who wanted to build that city into a showplace. They needed building contractors, and they were willing to pay for them. After a scant twelve months in practice, Adolph gave up dentistry immediately, and became a contractor. After all, he'd built Gelnay Enterprises, he knew how to lay out such projects. He went to Baghdad and began making big money again by building grand houses for wealthy Arabs. A year later when the *Anschluss* came, March 15, 1938, Adolph Gelnay, Man of Action, Big Contractor in Baghdad, called Walter in Beirut.

"I'm going home," he shouted over the long distance lines. "I'm going back to get your mother and grandmother and bring them out here."

"No! No!" Walter shouted back. "I will go. You stay there and make money for the rest of us. Find a place for the women, and I'll bring them out!"

An argument followed that Walter knew he had to win. His father's meteoric temper would surely land him in jail, at the very least, or in a concentration camp at the very worst. The first time a Nazi pushed Adolph around he'd take a swing at him and the rest would be history. Caught up in the heady smell of success, he had more work than he could handle, Adolph gave in and let his son enter the lion's den in his stead. Walter took ship and went back. The crossing to Athens was terrible, but three days after landing in Greece Walter was in Prague with Tilda and his mother. Tilda had just returned from Vienna, the last place Stasch had put her down. At her insistence, Stasch brought Tilda out as soon as the Nazis marched in. Mary Gelnay had left Vienna when Otto cleared the path for her, insisting she leave the old grandmother behind for Adolph's mother refused to leave. So, unless he could play the rescuing knight in shining armor for his grandmother, Walter had come home for nothing. He managed to get a call through to Vienna, but his grandmother stubbornly assured him, just as she had the others, that nothing could make her budge from her home.

"I will not be pushed around by a bunch of bully boys!" she shouted over the phone. "This is my home and I'm going to stay in it!"

When Walter offered to take Tilda back to Beirut she was indignant. "Do you think Stasch and I could have a better life there than we can in New Jersey? I'm not going to raise my child in a heathen place like that! I'm going to America. I'm an American citizen you know, I was born there."

He had no better luck with his mother. "I'm going to my sister in New Jersey!" she said stoutly. "It would take more than the Nazis to get me to go to live with that man again."

Walter had put himself in jeopardy for nothing. Neither he nor his father had given a thought to how he would get out of Czechoslovakia once he was back in. Since he had no American roots, he could not secure an American passport. Having given up his job with Skoda to make the trip, he couldn't get an exit visa for business reasons. He had to cross Nazi-controlled soil if he was going back to Beirut, and without an exit visa issued by the Czech government, his Czech passport would not be enough. Unable to figure out how he was going to escape, he needed a job to survive while he was there. He went to work for a Jewish firm, Markus Werner, the largest private Importer in Czechoslovakia. By December of l938, however, Markus had cleared out for the United States, and Walter was out of work again. Also by December, Tilda was in Paris and Mary was safely in New Jersey. While Markus was still in Prague and while Walter still had work a letter came through from his father.

With his usual cavalier response to reality, brushing aside Walter's dilemma as though it didn't exit, Adolph wrote that Walter should bring back all the books he could lay his hands on about brick making. There was a sheik in Baghdad, Adolph said, who wanted to build a brick plant and he, never side-tracked by ignorance when he smelled a killing, had secured the contract to build it. All Walter had to do was get out of Czechoslovakia and get to Baghdad, and the two of them would make a larger fortune than the private homes' contracts could yield. As usual, the son had been grafted onto the father's schemes without a by-your-leave. Walter got the books, he did the reading, he became as informed as he could be about the process of making bricks without ever visiting a kiln, but he was still faced with the riddle of how to get out of Czechoslovakia so that he could get to the building site.

When Hitler took the Sudetenland on March 29, l939, Walter was still there. Hitler made protectorates out of Bohemia and Moravia, the industrialized portions of Czechoslovakia that he needed. Slovakia was not only totally agricultural but populated almost entirely by simple peasants. The poor rural folk spoke a regional dialect unintelligible to people speaking Hungarian, German or Czech. They possessed only a tiny smattering of proficiency in those languages, barely enough to carry on trade. Hitler didn't want these undeveloped peoples in his Third Reich so Slovakia became an independent nation. However, the major cities of the remainder of Czechoslovakia were dependent on Slovakia for food. For centuries these peasants had brought their produce into the cities to the farmers' markets to feed the urban dwellers. With the national boundaries re drawn, something had to be done about passage for the farmers back and forth across the various new borders in order to continue the marketing system in existence.

Batches of transit cards, none made out to individuals, were given by the Nazis to village councils to be distributed to whomever needed them to get to market. The bearer of one of those cards had free passage into and out of all the countries under Hitler's control. Walter had an inspiration. If he could get his hands on one of those cards he would be able to get out of Czechoslovakia in any direction he chose and on through any country in his path since the cards were not designated for any particular border. During his previous days in Prague, when the malt business introduced him to the farmers of the areas that supplied the grain needed for the malt, he had made many contacts. Now, one of those contacts paid off. In late March of l939 Walter secured one of the priceless bills of passage.

In the tumultuous, chaotic days that followed the reorganization of Czechoslovakia, regulations had been established at the borders about who was to be let out or who was to be let in or what they could carry with them. Quickly, before the usual Nazi proscriptions could be put in place, Walter bought train tickets to take him out of Czechoslovakia, across Austria, and all the way to his father. He even secured transit visas with his little card which would guarantee his being allowed to cross all the countries that lay between Austria and British-held Baghdad, including Lebanon. Then he set to work to convert all the money he could lay his hands on into salable merchandise - watches, tools, leather shoes, - - two trunk loads of it which he shipped to himself at the railway station in Trieste. If it never got there, he wouldn't lose anything for he couldn't take the money out with him. If it did go through he could convert his investments back to currency once he was in Baghdad. Having dispatched the trunks he wasted no time dispatching himself.

Encountering no difficulty at all he took the train to Trieste. There were plenty of uniforms traveling first class, but few in the coaches. Keeping his face averted to avoid any untoward contact that might get him into trouble, he rode through the countryside pretending to be bored with the need to travel. When the train pulled in to the Trieste station two days before the ship was to leave for Beirut he hurried to the baggage area with his fingers crossed. If his clandestine wealth had not arrived he wouldn't dare try to trace it. But lo and behold, there were the two trunks waiting for him, sitting right in the front of the office where he could see them as soon as he approached the baggage storage area. Fate had looked kindly on him after all. Walter didn't believe in miracles, but from then on he believed in his own good fortune. He pulled the claim checks from his pocket, got the trunks out of the railway station and went directly from the train depot to the ship. Once he saw his worldly wealth safely stored in his cabin, he went up to the top deck to look out over the docks of Trieste, exulting in how cleverly he had maneuvered events and how his karma had produced his escape. He was free! He had money. He was on his way. Overflowing with satisfaction with himself he remained in a state of euphoria all the way to Lebanon.

On board was a congenial bunch of businessmen going out to make their fortunes buying raw materials for Hitler's burgeoning industrial enterprises. The air was full of the heady talk of profits to be made out of this or that scheme, or this or that bonafide contract already in hand that had sent them eagerly to the land of camel caravans and Bedouin rubes. Walter, relishing every word, began to feel expansive and experienced, ahead of the pack with his background and contacts. When the ship docked, all the men flocked toward the gangway eager to be off the ship and on their way about their individual concerns, none more loquacious or hearty than Walter. He casually handed over his passport and visa to the ship official at the head of the gangway who was letting passengers disembark. That worthy checked every name against an exit list made up by local authorities.

"Sorry Gelnay," he said handing Walter's papers back to him. "Your name is not on this list. I can't let you off."

All his new-found confidence drained away. In dismay he watched the ship empty out, even the crew go ashore for leave, while he stood off to the side cooling his heels and stewing. What had gone wrong at this late date? How could he get this straightened out?

When there was no one left to go ashore Walter went back to the disembarking officer and demanded an explanation. "Why won't you let me down? My papers are in order. Look at them again!"

"I know they're in order," he argued, "But I don't make the rules. Your name isn't on that list and if it's not on that list I can't let you off."

"Well, you could double check. It has to be some mistake!"

With bored indifference the official called down to the guard on the dock.

"Go call the French and find out why Walter Gelnay's name is not on the list of people who can disembark! Find out why he is to be sent back to Europe."

Sent back to Europe! Walter couldn't believe his ears. Sent back to Europe?? It was unthinkable! His heart threatened to burst through the walls of his chest. Many anxious minutes later the dockside guard returned from making the phone call and shouted up to the officer and Walter waiting at the rail.

'They wouldn't tell me anything, they just said 'Ship him back where he came from.''

Frightened, stunned, Walter's usually fertile brain was momentarily frozen in disbelief - but not for long. Seeing a man loitering on the dock below he called down to him "Will you carry a message for me?" he yelled, "I'll pay you well."

"Okay," the man called back, "Throw down the message and the address and the money and I'll go."

Hastily Walter wrote a note to Frantisek Schoenmann at the Office of the French High Commissioner, wrapped the note around some bills and threw it to the feet of his waiting courier. Frantisek was a good friend from Walter's previous stay in Beirut; if there was any help for the situation Frantisek would know of it. Then a horrible thought struck Walter. What if the idle fellow on the dock took the money, pocketed it, and went off to the coffee bars to while away the morning chortling to his friends over his windfall?

He called down again to the man, "When you deliver this note you'll get the other half of your money." It would cost him double but this was no time to be cautious.

The note read: "Walter Gelnay, with proper entry papers, is being detained aboard ship in the harbor. Can you do something?"

With his heart in his mouth, Walter watched the man set off at such a shambling pace he feared the fellow would never deliver the message. There was nothing he could do but wait for he had no other avenue of hope open to him. He strode nervously up and down the deck, keeping an eye glued feverishly on the entrance to the little lane leading down to the ship from the street above. It seemed much longer, but within the hour he saw Frantisek come running down the cobbled lane, scanning the upper deck anxiously, looking for him as he ran. Walter leaned over the rail and hailed him.

"Frantisek, Here! Here!" he called.

"Why are you not allowed to come down?" Frantisek shouted when he saw him.

"I don't know why, my papers are in order. I have a transit visa to cross Lebanon to go to Baghdad, but they won't let me go."

"Throw me down your passport and your visa and I'll see to it." Frantisek ordered.

Walter threw down the precious papers making himself temporarily a man without a country with no papers to prove he had a right to be anywhere. More than two hours passed, two hours of trembling fear, before anyone showed up. Just when Walter began to despair that he would never get off that ship short of Trieste, a messenger from the French Authorities arrived with orders to let him go. Walter went limp with relief.

The messenger handed over Walter's papers at the foot of the gangway and Walter wasted no time getting himself and his trunks out of Lebanon. He took one of the desert taxis that carried six or more passengers and their luggage across the trackless landscape. There was no road. A taxi driver simply took off and with an unerring inner compass found his way across the empty terrain. The taxi had no shock absorbers, no air conditioning, and the padding was so thin on the seats they were as hard as boards. It was a long, dusty, exhausting trip, and while the other passengers sweated and complained Walter blessed the ancient machine and every mile it covered. He was not in Hitler's hands. He was off the ship. He had his goods with him. None of the family except his old grandmother were in any danger. He was on his way to his father and the future. He again thanked his lucky stars or whatever beneficent power watched over him. That was May of 1939 and the world still deluded itself that a general war might not come.

Reunited in Baghdad, he and his father went to work on the brick factory. There was no skilled labor to be had, the only workers available were Bedouins and illiterate Arabs who were not accustomed to working like Europeans work. They were neither industrious nor competent. The brick plant, which was to be finished in a matter of four months according to the contract, was obviously going up at a rate that might see it completed in a matter of four years. The sheik began to suspect that Adolph Gelnay was flying by the seat of his pants and not soaring very high. In other words, the sheik was suspicious that Adolph didn't know much more about building a brick plant than he did so in August he fired him. While Adolph and Walter were still pondering what to do next it was September and the long-feared war broke out in Europe. Immediately Walter rushed to join the British army since Baghdad was part of the British Mandate covering that part of the Middle East. The British, still imbued with their chauvinistic sense of invincibility, would not induct foreign nationals into their service at that time.

Thwarted in his attempt to get into the war immediately, Walter bided his time and went to work for C. Ades Ltd., a company owned by a Jewish Arab from Damascus. Ades, Ltd. imported spare parts for cars of every make and model in the United States. Ades also handled every other technology they had any reason to believe that the oil sheiks wanted for the modernization of the region, especially air-conditioning equipment. It was a big firm, big enough to serve the whole Arab world. Walter worked for them traveling everywhere but to Lebanon until he learned in December that Britain's allies, the French, were beginning to recruit Czechs, Poles, and Yugoslavs from among the refugees in the region. Beirut was chosen to be the recruiting center for these men without a country so Walter left Baghdad immediately to go back to Beirut to get into the war. He would risk anything to get into a uniform, any uniform in which he could fight the Germans. The borders between the Arabs and the Lebanese were unguarded in those days of European control. Only at the seaports did one run into difficulty. He went into Lebanon unchallenged this time.

Once in Beirut he went directly to the French Army Recruitment Office. Again he met with frustration and disappointment. This time a Lieutenant Colonel, Dr. Reichenthal, decided that Walter's eyesight was too poor for the first wave of recruits and classified him as a "B", a member of the Reserve List. He was forced to stand by helplessly as the first contingent left for France without him. What was he to do? He wouldn't go back to Baghdad, there was nothing for him there. His father had returned to building houses on small contracts which would not provide Walter with any future, and it was not likely that Ades would welcome him back following his abrupt departure after so short a stint with the company. Because of his eagerness to join the French forces the police issued him a work permit so that he could remain in Lebanon until he was called up. Casting about for something to do in the interim he learned of an opening as *"chef de reception"* at the Hotel St. Georges. The St. Georges was a very swanky hotel for such a drab little city. The dusty little streets and the rickety little shops that surrounded the place made the building look incongruous, but anyone who was anyone stayed there. Hotel St. Georges was in the same class of ranking hotels in the region as was the Shepherd Hotel in Cairo. It was the best place in Beirut to keep one's ear to the ground and follow events in Europe, especially for someone who spoke several languages.

In June of 1940, when France capitulated and all allied personnel still in Beirut were evacuated to Palestine, Walter and his father, who had given up on becoming a millionaire in Baghdad and reestablished himself as a dentist in Beirut, packed their bags and headed south. But at the Palestinian border they were brought up sharply.

"Get out of line," the border guard bawled. "You Gelnay, both of you, get out of line!"

Walter's stomach plummeted. It was like being stopped from getting off the ship.

'What do you mean, get out of line!" Adolph's voice took on a tone of belligerency that made Walter's hair curl.

"Tell us why we have to get out of line." Walter hoped his more level tone and outward calm would defuse the verbal bomb he feared his father had hurled into the proceedings.

"I don't know why!" shouted the Palestinian. "All I know is that it says here you can't come in. Now get out of line!"

"But we're Czech citizens," Adolph protested. "And the British said the Czechs were to be removed from Lebanon. Now don't tell me we can't go through!" He started forward.

One guard rushed forward with his gun butt raised over his head just as another shoved Adolph in the chest so hard he lost his balance and sat down hard on the sand. "Get out of here!" the guard snarled, "before you get your head split open!"

Walter pulled his father to his feet and dragged him back away from the border. Panic set in. What was it in the stars that kept stonewalling him at borders when his life was in danger? Unable to leave, Walter went back to the St. Georges, but life had taken on a heightened sense of immediacy. For how long would he be able to continue there? With France fallen to the Germans, what would happen to Jews in Lebanon when the Vichy government took over? Walter felt like a sword hung over his head. Then a great sigh of relief went up all across the city. It was learned that it would be an Italian Armistice Commission, not the Germans or their Vichy underlings, who would be in control of the Lebanon Mandate now that France was out of the war and the Germans occupied Paris. No one feared the Italians.

The members of the Italian Commission naturally took up residence at the St. George's. Every day they came down about l0:00 a.m. for a leisurely breakfast, then left for the offices of the French High Commissioner for a leisurely day's work. Around five they returned and settled down to leisurely drinks in the public lounge before dinner, engaging in friendly small talk with other guests staying at the hotel. All of the hotel staff were privy to every nuance of German planning that fell from the lips of the chatty Italians. Important conversations might well be extended into the dinner hour on the terrace where candlelight gleamed off crystal goblets and silver table service. Discreet waiters hovered close enough to be able to hear above the sounds of the surf below. Tidbits pieced together later in the kitchens were sent along the human network so quickly that by daybreak everyone knew all the information gleaned from the Italians the night before, and so did the British on Cyprus. If one was to judge by the atmosphere created by the casual Italian Commissioners, there was nothing of imminent danger being set in motion anywhere in Europe. In this relaxed environment, Adolph Gelnay tried again to leave for Palestine by himself and, unencumbered by Walter, he was successful.

When Rommel began advancing rapidly on Egypt in l942, the German high command decided on a pincers movement on the British forces in North Africa ranging from Tunisia to the eastern borders of Palestine. German planes and supplies began arriving at Aleppo in Northern Syria, a development that did not go unreported at the St. George's. Great anxiety began to build among those French residents of Beirut who were not pro-Vichy, an anxiety that rose considerably higher when the High Commissioner's Office notified the St. Georges that officials from Vichy would be stopping at the hotel within days. The best accommodations the hotel could offer should be prepared for them for an extended stay, so said the memorandum. With mounting fear Walter followed developments closely.

Twenty-four hours later two men arrived, one a Mr. Girard who was tall and thin, and about forty-five years of age. As he approached the desk he pulled out his diplomatic passport and handed it to Walter so that Walter could complete the registration. As Walter bent over the register he felt a sharp kick in the shins administered by the hall porter standing beside him. He looked up to see the porter staring at the other gentleman accompanying Mr. Girard. Walter shifted his gaze and went rigid with fear. The other man slipped a passport back into his right-hand inner coat pocket just as Walter turned in his direction, a passport bearing a gold-embossed swastika on its gray cover! Blood rushed to Walter's head. His hand trembled over the register. He struggled to control himself enough to complete Mr. Girard's registration before turning to the German to receive his identification. Not trusting himself to speak he wordlessly held out his hand for the dreadful passport. Reaching into his left breast pocket, not the right, the man pulled out a French Diplomatic passport just like Mr. Girard's. Stiffly, keeping his eyes lowered to the register before him, Walter entered the phony name and identifying numbers into the ledger and returned the French passport. He motioned discretely for bellboys to take the considerable luggage of the two officials up to their suite.

When the two men had been sent off Walter turned to the hall porter as he wiped the sweat from his brow. "What do you think, Cristo?" he said under his breath, "Who are they really?"

"They're Nazis," hissed Cristo. "That tall one must be a decoy."

"I'll bet the tall one doesn't have a thing to say about anything." Walter whispered hoarsely, "It's the other guy who's in charge."

"I agree. I agree," Cristo nodded vigorously. "But how can we be sure? You can't tell the British that we just "feel" something. We've got to know who they are and what they're up to."

"Tell the chambermaid to find out!" Walter urged.

Christo called the chambermaid on the floor where the two new registrants were lodged, and in Arabic asked her to find out all she could about them. At the first opportunity, he urged, she was to report back to him. While the Vichy men were at dinner that evening the maid went in to turn down their beds. Skillfully, from long practice, she searched through their things. Her report to Cristo was that this must indeed be a very important mission. Unable to read German, she could not tell what any of the papers she had seen were about, but there were stacks and stacks of documents in the room ready to be signed, and many, many papers. All of them were imprinted with German Swastikas. In the linen room she told the other maids that one of the gentlemen had the finest silk underwear she had seen in months. Cristo, a loyal British subject from the island of Cyprus, immediately telephoned the British consul on Cyprus and reported what they'd learned. Knowing that the British knew put Cristo at ease, but Walter was not reassured a bit. After all, it was the British who had refused to allow him to evacuate to Palestine. They wouldn't do anything to protect him if the German commissioner found out he was a Jew.

With the new officials in residence life around the hotel immediately took on a charged atmosphere of efficiency. Unlike the Italians, they left for the High Commissioner's offices every day promptly at a quarter of eight. Every evening they returned promptly at seven, too late for any socializing in the public rooms. Dinners, which had taken an hour and a half when the Italians were in charge, now were served and eaten in thirty minutes. The two men never exchanged a single greeting with any of the other guests. During the day, the old casual gossiping and loitering about continued but in the early morning hours and after the new "residents" returned at night all was spit and polish and timed to the minute. Like all secrets, in time it came to be known that the German was a Mr. Reinhard, and that he had come to Beirut to organize a fifth column which was to be infiltrated into every country throughout the Middle East.

Life became super charged for Walter. How long could he hope to be safe with the Germans now invisibly in Lebanon? He found himself continually looking over his shoulder to see if anyone was watching him. He tried again to get into Palestine to join the British army there. This time he obtained exit papers through a Hungarian Orchestra Leader who was taking his musical group to a place called Surabaya. The orchestra had been at the St. Georges the year before on this same journey. The orchestra leader had 25 travel visas to the Far East by way of Palestine. One of his musicians had not caught up with them so he had a surplus visa which Walter coveted. Walter went to the man's room soon after they were checked in.

"Please," he whispered earnestly from the hallway, "Let me come in, I must talk to you."

Surprised the leader admitted him. "What's this all about?" he asked. "There's nothing wrong with our reservations is there?"

"Oh no," Walter assured him. "There's nothing wrong for you but there's everything wrong for me."

He poured out his dilemma, "So, you see," he concluded, "I have to have that extra visa you have. I'll pay you for it."

"You don't need to pay me!" the leader exclaimed. "One Hungarian should stand by another, don't you think?" He smiled as he passed the precious document into Walter's trembling hand.

Now all Walter needed was an exit visa from Lebanon, he had the document from the orchestra leader for the other side of the border. Among Walter's many acquaintances was a Mr. Thoreau who had at one time been a Lieutenant in a French Tank Regiment. Because he would not return to France with the army to fight under the Germans the previous spring, he had resigned from the military and was now a member of the High Commissioner's Staff. Walter went to see him. He told him everything he knew with certainty, and all of what he guessed about the Germans in residence at the hotel. Several more had arrived in recent days who gave themselves away by telling the hotel desk they had come from Aleppo. No Frenchman would ever say Aleppo, for them it would always be "Alep." Mr. Thoreau asked many questions and was grateful for the information concerning these newcomers, so much so that when Walter asked for an exit visa Mr. Thoreau ordered it prepared immediately.

Within just a few days after that visit, Walter had the document he needed to get across the border from the Lebanese side. His elation knew no bounds. This time he was sure he'd cross the border without incident. The British had issued neither of his papers so he wouldn't have to deal with the list on which his name appeared to be marked Persona Non Grata. He wasted no time in putting Lebanon behind him, he hoped.

Bidding good-bye to his friends at the hotel he gave notice and booked a seat on one of the taxis which were running every hour from Beirut to Haifa. The other passengers were all Arabs traveling on business.

It was almost high noon when they reached the Lebanese border at Ras En Nakura check point. Border guards had to inspect their luggage and check their papers before they could cross. Everyone handed over their permits and the guard disappeared with them into the guardhouse. While they were waiting for the permits to be returned and for them to be waved across the border another taxi arrived from Beirut. That taxi was routinely checked and waved on in a matter of a few minutes. Walter and his fellow passengers began to grumble. Why were they being held up? The taxi driver went off to the guardhouse to inquire and returned to say that the guards had not finished the passport checks with Jerusalem. Fretting to be gone the other passengers were in no mood to wait when the guard returned with everyone's passport but Walter's.

The official told him that the authorities in Jerusalem were still pondering his transit-visa. The others could go but he could not. Walter thought he'd be sick. The driver suggested that Walter wait for another taxi, that he and the rest go on without him. Reluctantly, Walter agreed since the mood of the group was growing ugly over being already delayed excessively long by this one problem. He told the driver to deliver his luggage to the taxi depot in Haifa where he would pick it up later, then he sat down to wait again.

Two hours passed before the border guard came out a third time. "I'm sorry," he said, "but this travel visa is no good." He handed Walter the transit-visa he had secured from the Hungarian. It had already been marked 'canceled.' Shaking his head in sympathy he said, "I really am sorry, but you can't go."

Walter was horrified. How could it be? Here he was in Lebanon with nothing to his name but the clothes on his back. Right in front of him, only a few hundred yards away, was Palestine where all he owned was now on deposit in Haifa. In Palestine lay his chance to escape the Germans. In Palestine, his father was in residence waiting for him. In Beirut, he now had no job to go back to. He laid it all out before the border guard pleading with him to let him through but to no avail. All he could elicit from the man was the uninformative fact that the Immigration Department in Jerusalem had instructed him to cancel Walter's transit-visa, and the very explicit fact that he was not going to let Walter go across that border no matter who was waiting for him. Furthermore, he was not going to call Jerusalem again to try to pry an explanation out of them about why the transit-visa had been canceled. Nor, in exasperation he added, did he have any suggestions as to where Walter could turn for information on other ways he might be admitted into Palestine. Above all, he was not about to get interested in where Walter was to lay his head that night.

What a pickle. To all intents and purposes he had become a hunted man, and he didn't know why. He was faced with the very real prospect that, if he couldn't get out of the country quickly, his identity would be betrayed and he would be captured and sent to Germany to be interned in a concentration camp, or worked to death in a labor camp. Either way, he was in deep trouble. Sick at heart, he slipped back into Beirut just at dusk and found his way to the home of a friend, Dr. Joseph Krauser. He knew that there he could find temporary sanctuary. It would be too dangerous for his friend to harbor him long, so he <u>had</u> to find a way out of this deadly country as quickly as possible. The probability that the Germans at the hotel would now learn of his identity and ferret out his whereabouts if he hung around the city, was too great to be shrugged off. Beirut was really a small place with grapevines extending into all its alleyways. No one would be able to hide him for long.

"What you ought to do, Walter," said Dr. Krauser after they had explored idea after idea, "is find someone who knows the border well who would take you to an unguarded spot and you could just slip across in the middle of the night. Once you got into Palestine there'd be plenty of Jews to help you, and I don't think the British would throw you out even if they caught you. Besides, they might never know you were there."

Walter was delighted with the idea. He set about to find such a guide the first thing in the morning. A young peasant from near the town of Saida (Sidon) was unearthed who ran an underground railroad of people back and forth across the border all the time, a smuggler of human beings for hire. After haggling over the fee he would receive once they reached the border he agreed to take Walter to a place where he knew

Walter could cross safely. They set off on foot that very morning, Walter lagging far enough behind Hamid, the guide, so if they were seen it would not appear they were traveling together. He had no disguise, he would have to go as he was in the clothes he was wearing. He was not dressed for hiking.

The young peasant took off in a southeasterly direction toward Jebel Yarmak. Progress was slow for Walter was wearing leather street shoes, and the rocks in the road cut through the thin soles bruising his feet. By nightfall they reached a small Arab Village where the only place they could find to sleep was in a stable. Walter was so tired he could have slept on the bare ground. The Arab huts of the village were little better than the stable anyway so it was as good a place as there was to bed down. Dinner was only bread and cheese which Hamid scrounged for them, and for which Walter paid handsomely but he was in no position to argue about price. At dawn they started out again while the air was still cool. Day was just breaking when they heard the sounds of approaching troops coming down the secondary road along which they were then traveling. Hamid quickly climbed up into a tree along the side the road motioning Walter toward another a few yards away.

Like a member of Robin Hood's band Walter hid among the branches of the tree as the marching unit passed along the road below. His pulse sounded so loud in his own ears he was sure the soldiers could hear it above the noise of their boots on the roadway. He was scared to death he'd sneeze. He and Hamid remained roosted like guinea fowl until the squad was out of sight. Only then did Walter realize that his chest ached from holding his breath. Coming down from their hiding place they wasted no time in abandoning the road and struck off across the countryside. Neither had any desire to risk meeting other military units that might be patrolling the area. Keeping a furtive eye out for farmers or stray travelers they scrambled across rocky gorges, climbed hills, scrambled down slopes, kept moving without rest. The journey became an endurance test for Walter. His ankles began to swell out over his shoe tops while his feet cried out for relief. All day they walked without food or drink and when night fell they had to sleep in a deserted mud hut Hamid found for them. There was no supper that night but Walter didn't care. He dropped to the dirt floor and was instantly asleep. Before dawn the following morning

Hamid shook him awake. They set out again, shivering in the cold, desert, night air. By now Walter was stumbling along, his shoelaces untied to give his feet more room in the sweat-drenched shoes which were killing him..

By the time they reached the Litani River he was barely keeping up. At the river's edge Hamid motioned to him that they had to swim across, there was no other way. He gestured to Walter to undress and hand him his clothes. Walter was to wait before entering the river until he, Hamid, reached the other side. Wading into the water with their clothes in a bundle on top of his head Hamid struck out for the other shore swimming strongly. Walter watched as the guide climbed out on the opposite bank and disappeared into some bushes. Only when he was fully dressed did the peasant emerge from the brush and signal for him to follow. Walter plunged into the swift-flowing stream and with long even strokes came out on the bank almost where Hamid stood. Using his shirt for a towel Walter got dressed and their weary march continued. About noon they reached the top of a fair-sized mountain beyond which lay a long, narrow valley. Hamid explained that the boundary of Palestine ran along the center of that valley floor and that this was as far as he would go. Walter would have to make the border crossing on his own.

Two days earlier, when their journey began Hamid had provided Walter with a kafir, the flowing headdress of the Bedouins. Hamid now wanted his kafir back and refused to sell it. Walter had been grateful for that headdress every sun-drenched step of the way, he hated to part with it. Some Arabs were working in a field on the slopes of the mountain where they stood so Hamid suggested that it would be wise to make the crossing after dark, to stay right where he was until the farmers went back to their village. By now Walter's ankles were swollen so badly he looked like he had elephantiasis. Any excuse to lay down between two boulders out of the sun for a few hours where he could see without being seen was welcomed. He dozed like a lizard in the warmth of the rocks for several hours but by 4:00 he became impatient to put Lebanon behind him. Skirting along the fields where the Arabs were working he started down the mountain. Distances are deceptive on a clear day and the terrain he thought he could cover in half-an-hour took two-and-a-half hours to cross. It was 6:30 when he entered Palestine. About 500 yards beyond the border ran a road which paralleled the boundary line of Lebanon and while Walter hesitated not knowing whether to take the road or keep to the rough ground a jeep load of soldiers came along. There was no place to hide.

The Jeep immediately stopped and one of the soldiers called out, "Ta'ala Hon"

"Ta'ala Hon" in Hebrew means "come here." Walter stumbled as fast as his poor feet would carry him across the 500 yards that separated him from the soldiers. They kept their guns trained on him as he approached which was unnerving. When he was close enough to see their insignia and knew they were Jewish soldiers he was nearly giddy with joy. Before they could begin any kind of interrogation he poured out his story

"I want to go to Kibbutz Kfar-Giladi," he ended his monologue, "I can get help there."

"We're from Kfar-Giladi" said the sergeant in charge. "Hop in." Walter began to cry. Tears of relief poured down his face. "You are like angels," he choked over the words, "I don't think I could have made it any farther."

He was worn out. He was dirty, thirsty and hungry. He'd been under such duress for so long his nerves were raw. At the kibbutz they turned him over to the director of the community, a man in his early fifties Walter judged. He gave the man his passport along with the canceled visa. While the director silently studied the documents Walter began going over his history again. He gave him a brief outline of the events of his last three years, he told him about his father already in Haifa and he ended his recital by asking if the people of the kibbutz could help him get to Adolph. The director scrutinized him intently throughout the recitation. An imposing man, big of chest, with a mane of thick gray hair scraggling over beetling eyebrows, he exuded confidence, Walter was so inspired by his quiet strength he found himself pouring out his anger against the British.

"I don't know why they don't want me here! I don't know what I've ever done that would get me into this fix with them. Some blind stupid mistake and they won't try to clear it up! They won't even talk to me themselves, I only get to talk to Lebanese or Palestinians who keep saying it's the British who are blacklisting me!"

There was a long pause at the end of Walter's recital, a pause in which the director drew deeply on his pipe exhaling a smoke cloud that encircled their heads. Walter was too tired for more words. He sat silent waiting. Then the director rose from his chair and went to lean against the frame of the open door looking out into the fading twilight.

"We won't do anything until you've had a bath and some dinner and then we'll take you by car to Chalsa and turn you over to the British police." he said flatly without turning around to face Walter.

"The British! How can you call that helping me," Walter cried. "They'll arrest me."

"It's the only way," the director said turning to look at him as he spoke. "We don't want trouble with the British. We can't afford It." His gaze was steady and his tone final. He took a step toward Walter and laid his own hand on the younger man's shoulder. "But not to worry," he said comfortingly. "Lots of people are coming in illegally these days and the British aren't sending any of them back. What they'll do is take you before a magistrate who will put you on parole."

"Parole from what?" protested Walter. "You have to be guilty of something to be put on parole!"

"Parole only means that you have to report to the authorities every few weeks so they can keep track of you, that's all" the director's voice was steady. "Whether they come in legally or not, all newcomers are on parole until they get clearance and are situated. Now go get a bath and something to eat, you'll feel better. If you don't report to them now," he called over his shoulder as he walked away, "you'll be hiding out all the time."

Not convinced at all that there was no other way but bowing to the unquestionable authority of the director, Walter forlornly followed one of the soldiers to the mess where he wolfed down the first food he'd eaten in two days. After the meal he was given a towel and soap and led to the shower which was little more than a small wooden shed with the sky for a roof. The water was bracingly cold. Fed and clean, his aching body somewhat refreshed, he returned to the sheltered walk outside the door of the mess hall and sat down on the bench built onto the wall. Another soldier sitting there offered him a cigarette. Walter smoked in silence staring out into the compound. He had hoped for harbor, had trusted that Jews would protect Jews, and now this. He felt betrayed no matter what the director said. He didn't like it. He didn't like it at all. Twice the British had done him in, why should he trust them now? For some reason they didn't want him in their territory and damned if they would tell him why. A stray dog couldn't be more unwelcome. He wanted to shout his fury to the housetops and refuse to go, but, if he didn't go voluntarily the director would report him to the British who would hunt him down, or the soldiers would forcibly take him to Chalsa. He crushed the cigarette butt out under his foot and sat listlessly waiting.

It was long after dark when the jeep pulled up in front of the kibbutz cafeteria and he and the soldiers piled in again. At Chalsa they turned him and his papers over to the British Police and with a cheery "Shalom" left him to the mercy of the merciless "Raj". The British booked him without any explanation and threw him into a cell with about 30 Arabs representing two small tribes which had been trying to kill each other off. Walter squatted on the bare floor with his back against the wall staring around him in disbelief. From Prague to this? After all that struggle to get to freedom here he was jailed with a bunch of wild Bedouins. He spent a miserable night with the bedbugs and his fellow cell mates. Dawn came and nothing happened. When by nine o'clock the next morning still nothing happened, Walter lost patience with the whole affair. Angrily he rattled the gate to the cell shouting in English, "Let me out of here! Let me out of here!"

A British guard came to see who was making such a ruckus and Walter told him that he wanted out of there, he wanted to be fed, and most of all he wanted to see the magistrate. The guard disappeared without a word and in a little while returned to let him out. He was put into an almost bare room alone to wait for the Sergeant to get around to his case. To his amazement, they brought him a wonderful breakfast of ham and eggs. Walter began to feel better. This was more like it. Maybe it would be all right after all. They had even put a pack of cigarettes on the breakfast tray so he had a leisurely smoke with his coffee and felt a bit expansive. An hour later the sergeant showed up and when Walter was brought before him and asked how he happened to be there he poured out his story again. The non-com listened without interrupting his face offering nothing. When Walter stopped talking the sergeant looked directly at him for the first time.

"Immigration will have to straighten this all out," the sergeant said quietly. "I can't see that this is a police matter. We can't put you on parole until Immigration says you can stay." He handed Walter's papers back to him. "I'll get a guard to take you to Metullah where the Immigration Office is located."

"Another hand off." he told himself. Another delay. No resolution still of this maddening impasse. Dumbly, he followed the attending soldier to the waiting car and they headed out of Chalsa leaving a cloud of dust hanging in the air behind them. When he and his escort arrived in Metullah they didn't take him to the Immigration Department at all, they took him to another police station. What was this all about? Again he was interviewed by a sergeant, and again he was told to wait, that he would see the magistrate in a little while. He no longer cared, he was emotionally exhausted. Another two hours went by in which he sat without moving. waiting to have them call his name. When they did call his name he rose and approached the counter to which he had been summoned.

"Follow me!" a young non-com ordered. They did not proceed to a magistrate, they went to a small armored car waiting outside. Something was terribly wrong, terribly, terribly wrong, but what was it?

Every nerve of his body became taut with fear. Prodded in the back by an accompanying policeman, Walter climbed into the back seat of the vehicle. The armored car drove straight to a Lebanese Customs border crossing and stopped in front of a small building. Two Lebanese customs guards came out and had a brief exchange with his British captors loudly enough for Walter to overhear. The British intended to send him back to Lebanon! This comedy of errors had become an incomprehensible nightmare. An argument between the Palestinian British police and the Lebanese border guards broke out. The Border Guards became increasingly officious. Walter began to follow the verbal battle. The Lebanese insisted that they wanted to see Walter's entry visa granting him permission to go from Palestine into Lebanon. Without such a visa they told the British they would not allow him to cross back into their country. Walter's hopes began to rise. Silently he began cheering for the Lebanese, hanging onto every word of the hot argument trying to find hope in the exchange. The two groups grew more and more heated in their debate as the Lebanese became ever more obdurate.

The argument turned into a yelling match between the British sergeant and the Lebanese guards. Walter was not going into Lebanon without an exit visa from Palestine, not across the border at that point anyway, and that was that! By now the Lebanese guards were shouting with exasperation. Forced to back down, the British sergeant climbed back into the car and roared back to Metullah in a rage. At the police station Walter was again thrown into a cell where again he waited for the Gods to decide his fate. It was nearly five o'clock in the afternoon before the curtain opened on the next act. During all those hours of waiting he kept going over and over the events of the past week trying to find the key to why the British had singled him out for exile from safety. Nothing came up, he couldn't solve the riddle. He hadn't crossed swords with any British official that he could think of. There were other Czechs and other Jews who had been granted asylum in Palestine without question. Why not he? What had he ever done? Who was nailing him to a cross and for what reason?

At five o'clock the sergeant and an Arab auxiliary policeman came to the cell and let him out. The sergeant told him that the Arab was going to take him to the no-man's-land between the border of Palestine and Lebanon at a point where he was to cross on his own returning to Lebanon as illegally as he had come into Palestine. Walter tried to argue, to protest, to demand that this order be canceled, but the sergeant turned away and left him alone with the fierce Arab in whose hands his fate now lay. Walter gave up, this Arab would not think of helping him find a way out of this. They walked to the border in silence and once they reached the line of demarcation between freedom and absolute jeopardy, the Arab pointed toward Lebanon and gave him a little shove. There was nothing for it but to go. He started out steadily enough but halfway there he looked back over his shoulder and saw to his relief that the Arab had turned around and headed back into Palestine without waiting to watch the returning refugee go all the way across the no-man's land between the two borders. Walter dropped down in the weeds out of sight. About 8:00 he rose, saw that the path was clear and turned back toward Metullah. It was still daylight and Arabs were still working in the fields. When they saw him they started yelling and running toward him. Swollen ankles or no swollen ankles Walter ran as if his life depended on it, which indeed it did.

As he approached the Metullah gate it was well guarded by British soldiers who rudely refused to listen as he tried to brazen it out. With studied indifference, they took him back to the police station where he was again put into a cell and left for the night. Long hours after the lights had been dimmed, as he sat huddled against the wall so miserable he couldn't sleep, a Jewish auxiliary policeman came to the cell and whispered through the bars in English.

"Ssst! You there. If the sergeant sends you tomorrow again into no-mans-land, don't worry. Stay there and I will come out and bring you into Metullah."

Walter felt like crying. Those were the first kind words he'd heard since he'd come to this dreadful country. When the sergeant reported for work the next morning he saw Walter first thing.

"So you're back?" he jeered, "Well, we'll see about that."

He picked up the phone, made another call to the Immigration Department in Jerusalem, and Walter overheard him say: "No, no, let me try, let me try. I will get rid of him."

All morning they let him cool his heels, but that afternoon they replayed the scenario of the previous day. Walter was marched again to no-man's-land and forced to cross over into the weedy field. Again the policeman did not wait until Walter was in Lebanon before turning back, so again Walter fell to the ground among the weeds and waited and waited and waited. Night fell, a moonless night with only the stars to illuminate the world around him. A light breeze came up and cooled off the world. Walter shivered as the day's sweat on his body was dried by the night air. He began to despair, to fear that he had trusted in vain, that the night messenger had been a hoax.

About l0:00 he heard a faint "Hello."

"Hello" Walter called back joyfully, but keeping down in the weeds fearing a trap.

"Hello." came the response, closer now. Walter wanted to believe so badly he stood up so he could be seen by whoever was looking for him. On his feet he nearly fainted. Three rifles, held by three men kneeling in the field in a circle around him, were trained on his breast. Again the order, "Ta'ala Hon."

Walter came on trembling knees, sure that this time his number was up. Approaching close enough to see in the dim light of the stars, he saw with relief that the men with the rifles wore the bandoleers of a special corps of the French Army, the Tcherkessen. It was not the British, it was not the Jewish auxiliary, it was the French. When he was within arm's reach Walter held out his passport which the British had returned to him that afternoon explaining in their language as he did so that he had the necessary exit-permit issued by French authorities. Silently, they took his passport and rising to their feet led him uphill for half an hour until they reached their bunker. There they gave him food without comment, leaving him to one side to eat as they examined his papers. Satisfied that the papers were authentic, when he finished his meal they let him talk. By then the story seemed to spin out of him like a Victrola record going endlessly around and around.

"How did you know I was there?" he asked after finishing his recital.

"We were watching from up here." one of them answered. "You were marched out to the edge of the strip by an Arab in uniform, given a shove and then before you had taken ten steps he turned around and walked back. If you're trying to expel someone from your country you don't give him a chance to double back on you."

"We thought you were a spy!" broke in another. "We thought it was all a ruse to make it look like they were getting rid of you as a cover."

A British spy! Walter laughed hysterically. It was the first funny thing he'd found to laugh about in days. "What are you going to do with me now?" he asked.

The sergeant major in charge pushed his beret back and scratched his head. "I don't know what we can do with you, or for you. We're a border patrol, military. This whole thing is screwy but it's not in our bailiwick. The only thing I know to do is to send you to Chiam and let the commander figure it out."

There was general assent. Walter himself didn't have any ideas, he was on the wrong side of the border and going back to Metullah would probably get him strung up this time.

Meekly he obeyed their orders to stand up and follow the detail that would escort him to Chiam.

Walter stubbed along for a few steps then sank down on the wet grass. "My feet." he said.

The sergeant major bent over Walter's legs and grunted. The ankles were swollen out over the shoe tops. Turning to the others he said, "This guy can't walk. Look at him. How are we going to get him there?"

Silence reigned for several minutes then the quiet one, the one who had said nothing before, spoke up. "Send him on that old horse we've got. We can't spare the jeep."

An escort of one guard and one soldier were ordered to take him to Chiam. They were a strange trio silhouetted against the black sky as they moved toward the old sun-baked town: the tall thin Czech on horseback, the short Lebanese, and the stocky Frenchman who led the horse walking beside him. At Chiam, the French unit's headquarters was billeted in a schoolhouse. Brusque, and unsympathetic, the commanding Lieutenant ordered him forwarded to Merjayoun, this time by motorcycle sidecar since he literally could not even shuffle any longer. It was close to 1:30 a.m. when they left Chiam. At 2:30 a.m. the guard, the driver and Walter were thrown out of the motorcycle when it didn't take a curve in the road and overturned in the dark. The cycle was completely destroyed. They had to make the last mile on foot no matter how slowly Walter could move. Walter could only walk by stiffly lifting one foot off the road and setting it down flat a few inches ahead of the other. All the action was taking place in his knees. He felt like a mannequin in a puppet show.

They arrived at Merjayoun about 4:00 a.m. The night duty personnel didn't know what to do with him either, so he was thrown into the worst possible prison of the whole area, for holding until the office force came in the next day. The cell was nothing more than a hole in the wall of the fortress, a hole about four feet by eight feet with no window. It was solitary confinement at its most uncomfortable. The cubicle had only a bare concrete floor and a small opening for light high overhead. A wooden stable door which bolted him in from the outside covered the entrance. About 8:00 a.m. they came to release him and lead him back to headquarters where he was shown into the office of the commander. Miserably tired, miserably dirty, and miserably hungry he showed no interest in what was going on around him. He no longer protested his treatment nor demanded to see higher authorities nor asked for food. He dully waited.

When the commander arrived Walter looked up without rising and stared at him refusing to believe this turn of events. Cdr. de Hebrand, who had repeatedly visited Beirut with his wife in the days when Walter was Chef de Reception at the Hotel St. Georges where they always stayed, looked down at him. There was no sign of recognition on the Commander's face though he knew Walter well. After one of the Hebrands' visits to the hotel the chambermaid had brought Walter a small ring she'd found in the rooms they had just vacated. Walter had written the commander a short note telling him that the ring had been found and that he had locked it up in the hotel safe until the Commander directed him as to what he should do with it. The next time the family came to Beirut, Walter returned the ring to them personally. The ring was not intrinsically valuable but it had been in the commander's wife's family for generations and she was thrilled to recover it. At the time Commander de Hebrand had thanked Walter profusely like one gentleman to another. Here, in Merjayoun, the two men faced each other in a very different situation. The commander went to his desk and sat down. Walter rose and limped over to stand in front of him. Cdr. de Hebrand looked up quizzically, a slight frown of puzzlement on his face.

"Do I know you?" he asked.

"Of course you know me," Walter said. "I was the chef de Reception at the Hotel St. Georges."

The commander rose from his chair in amazement. "What in the world are you doing here like this?" he demanded.

Trembling with relief at finding a sympathetic ear in high places Walter poured out the whole story for yet another time. The commander listened with growing indignation.

"You're free to go back to Beirut." he declared. "I'll send you in a staff car immediately."

"But the Germans are coming in. If I go back to Beirut they'll send me to Germany." The full impact of Walter's dilemma sank in.

"Then you'll go to Palestine. I know that sergeant at Metullah, I'll deal with him."

He ordered one of his men to take care of Walter. "He is a gentleman, treat him like one!"

They gave him a meal, they allowed him to shower and shave in the officers' quarters, and when he was ready, Cdr. de Hebrand led him to a staff car where a major from the General Staff waited. The four of them, Cdr. de Hebrand, the major, Walter and the driver, proceeded to the border. They drove along a road that paralleled the boundary for some distance before they stopped the car. The major from General Staff pointed out some buildings on the other side of the invisible line that separated Palestine and Lebanon.

"That is Kibbutz Dan." the Commander told him. "Go across this no-man's land and when you're inside Palestine again wait in the bushes until the farmers of the kibbutz come out to work the fields. Find out from them whether there are any soldiers or policemen at the Kibbutz,and, if there aren't, go on in. If there are, wait. The people of Dan will get you to Haifa, I've talked to them on the phone."

There were some Arabs working in the fields on the Lebanese side of the no-man's land so the two officers walked with him to the middle of the neutral zone. The Arabs seeing the French officers accompany him over neutral ground let him cross unmolested. Walter did as he was instructed. After he had crossed into Palestine he hid among some shrubs and waited. He felt like Moses in the bulrushes. In a short time a small group of young men and women carrying hoes came from the kibbutz to work the fields. They passed close to where Walter was hidden. Using the only two Hebrew words he could think of that fit the situation Walter called out softly, "Shalom! Chawer!". Startled, they came to him. They listened as he poured out the story of de Hebrand's instructions. There were no visitors to the kibbutz that day so they walked him openly into the community without fuss or bother, as naturally as if this was an everyday occurrence. They fed him, they gave him a bed in the home of a young couple who welcomed him, they made him a part of Kibbutz life. After a day's rest during which his ankles returned to normal size, they sent Walter into the fields where the project for that day was picking up stones, rocks and boulders and loading them into carts to carry away in order to clear the fields. Walter pitched in as though he was a permanent resident. For over a week he reveled in the life of the Kibbutz. He played with the children in the evening, sang and danced in the firelight with the young people at night, and learned a few more Hebrew words.

It was eight days before they could make contact with Haifa and arrange for Walter's safe passage to his father, eight days in which his faith in the future returned. One last hurdle to be faced was the check point at Rosh Pina. Walter was put on a bus with about eight men from Kibbutz Dan who were going to Tiberias. There was the usual banter as they bounced along the road until they approached the crucial moment at Rosh Pina. The driver stopped the bus before a small cafe just short of the check point and all the passengers piled off to get a coffee. When they were safely inside the cafe, out of sight of the border guards, the bus driver and a man named Yankel drove on to the guard hut to clear the vehicle and its passengers for the crossing. From the cafe, the passengers watched through the fly-specked window as the driver and Yankel came out pass in hand, climbed into the bus and drove on across the border. There the driver pulled off the road and Yankel got out, cupped his hands around his mouth and bawled: "Okay, you guys. Make it snappy, we've got a long way to go!"

Running as a group with Walter in the center, the men crossed the line and piled onto the rickety old conveyance which had become Walter's chariot to freedom. When the check point lay in the dust behind them Walter let out a howl of triumph. He was on his way at last! He was free! He couldn't stop talking and laughing, his relief was so great. At Tiberias, his father was waiting open-armed. Walter wept to see him. Never had he felt more rescued, more saved, more protected. Adolph took Walter to Haifa and after days of just eating and sleeping and letting his frayed nerves recuperate, Walter tried again to join the British army but still the British stalled him. They were not ready to induct refugees at this time, they said, particularly Czech refugees. Walter's impatience was choking him. This war was going to pass him by, he was never going to get into it. He was becoming downright bull-headed about it. A panicky feeling would wake him in the middle of the night, or grip him when he was walking the streets. First, they had rejected him because he was an alien national, now he was rejected because he was a refugee. Couldn't these damned British see how much he wanted to fight, and fight on their side? Walter, along with the local authorities, was told that he and they would have to wait for a directive from London about the Czechs. In London there was fear that some refugees might be spies, and since Czechs represented so many different national backgrounds they were more suspect than any of the other refugee groups. Walter tried to swallow his impatience and find a job. There was no question any longer about his remaining free to live and work in Palestine without harassment.

Civilian jobs were plentiful because of the military drain on manpower. He found a job working for a company which operated a group of bonded warehouses on the waterfront. For a year he supervised the loading and unloading of the ships which crowded the piers. Most of the merchandise coming in was military supplies of one kind or another purchased from any country with whom the British could do business. Haifa had been made a supply depot for the British forces in No. Africa. He was making a contribution of sorts, but he yearned to don a uniform and be a soldier. At last he got his wish, he was called up by the British army. At last he would get into the serious business of retaliation. Every new revelation about what was happening to Jews back home made it more imperative that somehow he could fight back. Supervising the distribution of war goods was not on a par with having a gun and going off to battle.

He was assigned to a Czech regiment which would serve under British commanders. The men were given three weeks of training before being sent out to the front lines of North Africa. On the day Walter was scheduled to head for the battlefields, military trucks pulled up to the camp and all enlistees were ordered to line up. As their names were called they were to throw their gear into a truck bed and climb in after it. Walter's name was called, and with great elation he tossed in his gear and threw one foot over the tailgate ready to hoist himself in only to be stopped in mid air when he heard his name called again. Thunderstruck, he heard himself ordered to retrieve his gear and step out of line. Walter was not going to North Africa, he was not going to fight, he would have no need for a gun. He was being sent to British headquarters in Jerusalem. Because he could read and write French, German, Czech and English they needed him in the procurement office to handle requisitions for supplies. Bitterly, he cursed his language skills. No matter how well they had served him in the past, no matter how well they would serve him in the future, they had cheated him out of the war he wanted and relegated him to an office where he'd push paper and never kill a German. Psychologically, he was back at the Lebanese border all over again, wanting in and being kept out.

In Jerusalem he was billeted wherever he could find rooms. There was no mess hall so he was given a ration allowance with which he could eat wherever he chose. He might as well have been a Civilian except for his uniform and his Post Exchange shopping privileges. He found a lovely room in the home of a Dr. Strauss, a German Jew who had lived in the Holy City for years. Civilian Gelnay, he called himself, but for three years he lived better than a civilian for he not only had PX (Post Exchange) privileges, in addition to ordering supplies they made part of his duty running the PX itself. What made it even better, the British were paying the Czechs overseas pay, five times the pay of the British soldiers assigned to the same area. He was making more money than officers in the field. He was a wealthy young man. Being a civilian soldier was a pathetic way to fight a war, but the assignment carried plump bonuses even if there was no glory attached to it.

Walter didn't miss out entirely on the North African War. In the line of his duty, when a convoy of trucks loaded with supplies was sent to the front in that arena, Walter was put in charge of the mission. When the supply trucks rolled in, the drivers were very popular. Walter was a corporal. As a corporal he wore two "pips" on his collar The Czechs didn't wear stripes on their sleeves as the British did. Officers in the British army wore their rank identification on their collars, enlisted men wore them on their sleeves. For all the world those Czech "Pips" looked like officers' insignias. The British sergeant in charge of the depot to which the shipment was consigned, wherever that might be, would inevitably snap to attention and salute as Walter's lead truck pulled in. Only when Walter signed for delivery would the British non-com realize, to his chagrin, that he'd saluted a mere corporal. It tickled Walter every time it happened. The snooty British who had refused to have him in their army for so long were paying him handsomely now for services rendered, and showing deference to boot.

One night a friend of Walter's fixed him up with a blind date for the movies. Walter hadn't been too enthused about the idea, blind dates were hard work, but his friend insisted. Walter gallantly showed up with chocolates from the PX for both of the young women. In December of l943, anywhere in the world a box of chocolates made quite an impression, but especially so in a backwater like Jerusalem. His blind date was a pretty girl named Sara, which means in Hebrew, "fruit of the cactus." She was a Sabra, someone born in Jerusalem, child of an old settled family which had been there for six generations. The blind date turned out to be a small miracle. Sara and Walter knew that night that something special had happened to them both. Sara's family were less than overwhelmed by her attachment to someone they regarded as a foreigner. They wanted her to marry someone with roots in Palestine who would not take her away when this dreadful war was over. Nor did they like Walter's lack of Jewish piety. Her father was orthodox to the core. He wore a long beard, clapped his yarmulke on his head the minute he got out of bed in the morning, attended synagogue every Saturday and treated his family like the patriarch he believed himself to be. Walter's lackadaisical attitude toward religion, his indifference to his own Jewishness, his easy relationship with women offended Sara's father.

Adolph didn't like the prospective marriage either and for some of the same reasons. He wanted Walter to marry a Czech, a princess of a woman, not a provincial girl like this one with her simple ways and old-fashioned values. Adolph wanted his son to "marry up," to rise in society as it had been possible to do in the dear dead days of Vienna before this Nazi nonsense had engulfed the sane world. With less than enthusiastic acceptance then on either side, they were married in June of l944. Once they were married, Sara's family enjoyed the PX privileges of their new son-in-law which did wonders for his acceptability.

Sara was from a large family of 8 children. Her father was a watchmaker and jeweler in Jerusalem, a man of position and modest wealth. Sara worked for her father as a designer, and as an artisan made many of the pieces herself. Because jewelers' supplies were difficult to come by during the war they made new pieces of jewelry from old pieces they bought at auctions, or which were brought in by people needing money badly enough to sell their treasures. One of the creative things Sara did was take apart the old silver chain purses women once carried and make exquisite new pieces from the links. She was so gifted she made her father a comfortable little fortune, but she never let him pay her anything for her work. When her father died he left each of his two daughters an apartment in Jerusalem, but only on condition that they come back to Palestine to live. Neither girl went back so both apartments went to their brothers who also inherited the jewelry business.

October, 1945, Walter reentered civilian life. When Walter was issued his dogtag in 1940 he had turned to a friend and pointed to the last four of the eight digits on the back of the metal disc which identified him. The first four numbers, 2500, meant he was Czech. The last four digits on Walter's tag were his own identification, 1945.

"That will be the year the war ends for me." he declared.

Prophetic? Who can say? When Walter was discharged he went to work for the Armed Forces Broadcasting System which continued broadcasting as long as the men who had fought the war were still in uniform. The job was fun, though it obviously had no future. Life was good, very good, then it got better when Sara got pregnant. They moved out to the suburbs and Walter went into business with Sara's brother-in-law, a Hungarian Jew from Romania who had become a Palestinian. The two young men got along famously, and with Walter's severance pay from the army, plus the brother-in-law's savings from his prosperous photography studio, they entered the import-export business. All of the contacts with suppliers Walter had made during the war while he was procuring military and PX supplies could be tapped for foreign goods to be sold in peacetime Palestine. It started off well, and for over a year they were in clover, but one day a man came into the office and made a little speech.

"I've come to introduce myself." he said. "I'm a doctor engineer, and I'm the only man in this country who can make DDT. I'm willing for you to be the sole agent for my product and peddle it for me for I'm only interested in the manufacturing end of the business. You won't have to do any thing to sell the stuff, everyone wants it. My only stipulation is that you make immediate payment when I deliver the DDT because my funds are limited."

At first Walter was put off by the pomposity of the man, but he talked it over with his brother-in-law rather than turn such an opportunity away too carelessly. Certainly DDT would be one hot item in a fly-blown land like Palestine. Pharmacies and drug stores would snap up such a product. The doctor engineer left them bottles of the liquid to use for demonstration. Their salesman would walk into a store whose windows were swarming with flies, get everyone's attention through a prepared spiel about how he could wipe out all those flies in one swipe of spray across the glass, then dramatically fire off a generous blast and everyone could watch the flies land on their backs on the floor. Orders invariably stacked up before he left the premises. The engineer delivered, Walter paid, the salesmen sold and the engineer delivered again.

For six months they couldn't stock it fast enough. Then came the beginning of a series of complaints. Flies weren't dying any more, people were angry. Walter and his brother-in-law couldn't believe it. They went to the storeroom and opened several bottles taken at random from the shelves in order to see for themselves. Some bottles worked, some didn't. Some of the stuff would kill a fly in mid-air, some of the stuff wouldn't kill a fly sitting on a table covered with it. Indignantly they called the engineer to tell him what they'd found.

"Impossible!" he shouted over the phone. "You take it to the University and have them test it. You'll find out it's a solution of 5%."

They took it to the University but it wasn't five percent, it was .05 percent. They called him back. He promised to come down to see for himself but he didn't show up. Walter and his brother-in-law took an army friend of Walter's with them and they went to the village where the engineer lived. He was not at home and when they said they would wait his wife, backed up by two big shepherd dogs, refused to let them in. They went out to the street to wait. About 4:30 they saw the engineer coming jauntily down the street carrying his briefcase. He saw Walter's brother-in-law who was over six feet tall, veered off quickly and started to run. He ran right into Walter. Walter jumped him and started beating him about the head. The engineer started screaming and the whole village came running. The villagers called the British police who ordered Walter's party out of town and back to Jerusalem.

In Jerusalem, they instituted proceedings against him. When the day of the trial came the guards brought the engineer into the courtroom in handcuffs accompanied by his lawyer. Walter's lawyer decided it might be wise to speak to the other attorney before the judge came in. Professional courtesy, he said. The two attorneys had a brief conversation and then their attorney came back to tell them that the engineer was offering them l/3 of all they claimed he owed them. Their lawyer told them they should take it. He said he was sure the other attorney had gotten to the judge in advance and if they didn't take that, they might get nothing. Walter refused to make a deal. His brother-in-law preferred to take the money. It was the end of the partnership. Later they learned that the engineer knew nothing about making DDT, he'd gotten fifty bottles from an army sergeant who was pilfering supplies, and the rest of the bottles contained nothing but kerosene.

The whole affair left such a sour taste in Walter's mouth he decided to go back to Czechoslovakia. It was l947, and Czechoslovakia had not yet disappeared behind the Iron Curtain. Leaving Sara and little two-year old Ben to follow later, he packed up and headed first for Switzerland where he had friends. He intended to visit there for a few days, then go on to Prague, but his friends had a proposition for him. American army surplus was being thrown onto the market, almost for the cost of hauling it away, and in goods-starved Europe a guy could make a fortune peddling it. The Americans didn't want to cart any of it back to the United States with them. What if four of them, they said, joined together, pooled their savings, and had a go at being peddlers? Walter fell in with the idea with his usual enthusiasm for something new. They went to Frankfurt, bought all they could pack into an automobile, and headed for the small towns of Germany. They had salami and fruit, toilet paper and soap, all kinds of marvelous stuff. The people of the first town stared in wonder at this plethora of things they hadn't seen for years, but they had no money. It was heart-wrenching. No one seemed to have any money. There were the goods to be had, cheap, and there were the people dying to buy them, and there was the absolute absence of any medium of exchange. Walter decided to go to

Prague and open an army outlet store there. Purchases made in Frankfurt could be shipped to Czechoslovakia where they'd be even more in demand, and where some people could still be found who did have money.

Walter walked into Prague, a man of relative wealth, rented a little store and the apartment upstairs over it. Then he sent for his family. With a two-year-old baby in her arms, Sara made her first trip outside her native land, all alone. That was the first time she followed Walter to a new life in a strange place, but it would not be the last. When she joined Walter in Prague they settled in and she began trying to learn the language. For a few short months, Walter reveled in being home again, being back in Prague, back where he still had connections and where the streets were all familiar. Prague had not been bombed. Things were pretty much as he'd left them except there were no Jews in the shops, or on the streets. The old ghetto was a ghost ghetto. His elation at being back ended abruptly at the end of February, 1948. The Communists forced the legitimate government out of power and took over. Walter had been loudly indiscreet in his denunciations of the Communists, and had frequently spoken out to whomever would listen, about the political instability building up around them. Knowing how records were kept on dissenters, it seemed expedient to leave as quickly as possible. Communist retaliation against detractors was occurring openly around them. People disappeared, or you saw them scooped up and carried off. He'd been trapped in Czechoslovakia once before, he saw no reason to repeat his own history.

Leaving everything behind - car, furniture, everything they could not carry with them - they took off for Basel, Switzerland, arriving with only fifty Swiss francs in their pockets. All the money which he'd converted into Czech currency was worthless for when the Communists came to power they changed the monetary system without recompense. Walter and Sara spent 15 francs on breakfast the very first morning. It was a wonderful breakfast, the best they'd had since they left Jerusalem - pancakes, fruit and coffee - but it left them with no more money to be spent for food that day. They went to the Jewish Travelers' Aid at the railroad station, showed their passports, and asked for help in getting to Bern where Walter had friends. The clerk took the passports, disappeared into an inner office, and in a few minutes out walked an old school chum from Vienna.

"I knew there couldn't be another Walter Gelnay," he cried. "How in the world did you get here?"

There was back-slapping, and laughing, and war stories, and the result was that he gave them 100 francs, the maximum amount he was allowed to issue to anyone at one time, enough and more to get them to Bern. The central offices of the Jewish Travelers' Association were located in Bern, and Walter's local friends told him that was the place to go for help. In spite of an excess of refugees, and a scarcity of jobs, probably through the intercession of his Basel friend Walter was given a seasonal permit to work. No permanent permits were issued to people without jobs or money. Walter could work to support them, in other words, while The Traveler's Association tried to locate some other country to which they could immigrate. That temporary work permit sent Walter back to the hotel business.

He found a position at a resort hotel that was open only for the winter season. To keep them from taking root in Switzerland, refugees were not allowed to rent apartments, they had to stay in hotels or hostels. Sara and little Ben were left in a hotel in Bern while Walter went to the mountains to be the procurement officer for his new employer. When the manager of the hotel learned that Walter had to be separated from his family he offered to let Walter bring his wife and child to live in the employees' hostel behind the hotel which was the living quarters for the staff. Every day the manager had the chef send dinner over to Sara and Ben. It was an idyllic interlude. If it had been possible for them to stay in Switzerland, Walter might have continued in the resort business but they were there on borrowed time and knew it.

Getting out of Switzerland, as they must, proved very difficult. One of the guests at the hotel tried to help him get a visa to Argentina but that didn't work. They could find no exit open to them. They were still there when another season rolled around. A second job for the second season on an extension of his work permit took Walter to a hotel located in Lucerne. He was hired as cashier, and this job paid handsomely. Lucerne so pleased them and the job paid so well, they longed to become Swiss citizens, but when the season ended Walter was unemployed again. Being a "temporary" was a no win situation.

Between seasons they had to use up all the money they had saved on the last job. Walter wanted an end to this suspended state, he wanted real life to begin again. He went to Geneva where the International Refugee Organization created to assist people who were stranded in countries other than there own was headquartered. He reasoned they might have more clout than the Jewish Travelers' organization in Bern. He made application for a visa, any visa to anywhere: Paraguay, Canada, South Africa, Sweden, anywhere where he and his little family would be welcome. They took his application but they promised him nothing. Walter returned despondent to the little house he had rented outside Bern in defiance of the regulations. Hotels and hostels were too expensive.

One morning Walter saw an article in the paper about a recruiting team from Australia which was in Germany interviewing refugees for immigration to the land down under and the article said that the team would come to Switzerland next. Walter promptly sat down and wrote a letter applying for a visa to Australia, a poignant letter laying out the story of all they'd been through. He told them he was an ex-serviceman in the British Army, that he had many skills all of which he itemized, that he'd make an ideal immigrant. Sealing the letter he mailed it to the office where the newspaper said the interviewing team would be located. In response a week later a letter came which read,

"Dear Walter,

Your letter to the immigration commission was passed on to me because I'm a deputy of the International Refugee Organization and I'm in charge of their actions. I have just passed on the list of refugees to be sent from Switzerland, but there will be another list and I will let you know when it will be."

The letter was signed by another old school friend from Vienna, a man who had gone to the United States as an immigrant, enlisted in the American army, served with the Americans in Europe, married a girl from Luxembourg who did not want to live in the United States, and was now in charge of the selection board for the IRO, the International Refugee Organization. Walter's network of old friends seemed to span all of Europe. A few weeks later he received another letter from his friend telling him to come to Wangen, Switzerland to see him. Eagerly, Walter made the trip to Wangen and learned that his friend had found work for Walter that might put him in the right spot where he could draw attention to himself and thereby win consideration for immigrant status to Australia. Walter was to be an interpreter for the Australian recruiting commission. Walter's language skills would be invaluable to them. Eagerly, he took the job. To his sorrow, however, he quickly uncovered one criteria for entrance into Australia that automatically disqualified him. They would not issue visas to married Jews. Single Jewish males, all right, but not married men with families. They had such a surplus of unmarried women in Australia due to the loss of men in the war that they were seeking single men from everywhere. Walter was crushed. The job immediately became merely a temporary job, not a solution. The commissioner, however, was so impressed with Walter's work that when he realized he had an abundance of visas he gave Walter the necessary entry papers for his whole family. Walter felt like he'd passed check point Rosh Pina again, that he was free and on his way.

To repay their passage each of the men leaving Europe had to promise to give the Australian government two years of labor at government wages before launching out on his own. When the ship docked in Melbourne, the male immigrants were taken directly to the vineyards north of the city to harvest grapes. Australia had tons of grapes hanging lush on the vines and too few agricultural workers to harvest them. It was stoop labor, physically exhausting. Heavy bunches of grapes hung close to the ground. At 39 Walter was almost twice the age of his fellow immigrants, but pride forced him to try to keep up with them. By the end of the first day he was in agony That night he devised a strange contraption to make the work easier. The next morning he reported to work with a ten gallon can attached to his rear. He had cut holes in the sides of the can and strung rope through the holes which then went around his waist. To roars of laughter from the others he tied the rope so that the bottom of the can rested on his buttocks. He would sit while they stooped. From one vine to another he moved, plopping himself down on the can to save his legs. When he had filled the big container into which he gently laid the bunches of grapes as he cut them free from the vines, he would take them to the waiting trucks loping along with his can wagging behind him. Then he would lope back to his place along the row and plop down to cut some more. He was a ludicrous sight to see. For four months this comic routine continued six days a week. Then the government hauled him out of the vineyards and returned him to employment more in line with his past experience in industry. They put him in charge of the parts department for Jaguar Automobiles, Inc. There he served out the remainder of his two years.

Several jobs followed until he found the niche in industrial management that occupied him for the remainder of his years in Australia. Sara became a member of the community, happily made a home for them and sent Ben off to public school. Walter wanted Ben to learn French since both he and Sara were fluent in the language and they felt that proficiency in the elitist French language could give him a handsome advantage when he was older, but Ben would have none of it. He only wanted to learn Australian English and talk like the other kids. The years flew by, 15 wonderful years and then Walter received a letter from Tilda.

"Your mother is growing old," she said. "You must come to see her."

Walter thought Tilda was telling him that his mother was near death. He dropped everything, took a leave of absence and headed for New York.

"I don't know how long I'll be gone," he told his boss and his family. "If my mother is dying..." he spread out his hands in a gesture of uncertainty.

Sara and Ben saw him off, comforting him as best they could, trying to be optimistic about what lay ahead.

"Don't worry about us," Sara assured him. "We'll manage just fine. Stay as long as you feel your mother needs you. Just be sure you write!"

Ben's grandmother meant next to nothing to him, she was just an old lady in some pictures his aunts, whom he'd never met, sent them. But to have a grandmother die you've never seen is still to have a grandmother die. Walter went east with a heavy heart. When he landed in San Francisco he was met by Dita's daughter who seemed surprised at his concern for her grandmother. When he showed her Tilda's letter she laughed. "I'll bet you anything this was Mom's idea. She's been pawing the ground over the fact that she's been separated from 'her baby brother' so long. So far as I know, Granny's fine."

Vivian insisted that he linger long enough for them to get acquainted and long enough for him to see San Francisco. He thought the whole Bay Area was wonderful. It whetted his appetite to see more of America. If there was no urgency about getting to New York, if this was just another piece of Dita's manipulation, he decided he might as well take the Greyhound Bus across country and get as much out of this trip as possible. Two days of riding and he had only reached Cheyenne, Wyoming. The country was so beautiful but it was so vast! Going across America by bus was like going from Sydney to Perth that way. If he continued on all the way to New York he'd be another four or five days getting there. He couldn't take it. He made a phone call.

"I can't do this bus business anymore." he told his mother, who sounded quite well on the phone, "my back aches, my legs ache, my head aches. I'm flying the rest of the way."

Years had passed since he'd seen his sisters. Would he know them? A lot of water had spilled over everyone's dam since then. Time had changed him, it must have altered them too. But when he walked down the steps from the plane he saw two redheads waiting just outside the entrance to the airport and knew they had to be his sisters. With them was a white-haired lady much smaller than he'd remembered. What a reunion! 26 years! Everyone babbled at once. They laughed, they cried, they hugged and kissed, and as they were leaving the airport he chuckled sheepishly and said, "I wasn't sure I'd know you."

"That's what they said," snapped his mother. "But I told them that if they didn't recognize you I'd introduce them because I'd know my boy anywhere."

It had been a ruse. His mother was not ill, Tilda's letter had been deliberately misleading. They wanted to see him. They wanted to pry him out of Australia after all this time. Year after year, he'd promised he would come for a visit but he hadn't. That night after dinner Dita took it one step further. "Walter," she lectured, "why should you stay out in Australia? You haven't got anybody out there and neither does Sara. You belong here near us. Why don't you look around and see what you can find? There won't be any of that difficulty with visas. We'll all promise the U.S. government we'll feed you. You won't starve. Bring your boy back here where he has some relatives. Australia is a back water. It's no place for him to grow up"

Walter thought of Australia and Sara and Ben and asked himself, "Why Not." Ben could go to architectural college here as well as there. Sara didn't have a life she'd find hard to give up. He decided to look around to see what was available, then write to Sara. He looked around, but he didn't like New York. He didn't like the hectic pace of business. He interviewed for jobs so he could see some of the inner workings of American firms, and the high level of energy and competitiveness he saw appalled him. His world was far more personal than this. He didn't like it but he wrote to Sara anyway, she had a right to be in on the decision. She wrote back and told him that if he didn't like New York why not go to Toronto where she had relatives and see if he liked that better. On the map Toronto was only a couple of inches west of New York. She thought they could drive over for the weekend.

Walter stayed with Dita and Tilda for three months and New York did not grow on him. He went to Toronto and he called the home of the relative Sara wanted him to contact. There was no answer. He called every day at all hours of the day for almost a week with no answer. Three days into his stay he wrote a letter and posted it to the relative telling him where he was staying and when he had reservations to leave. While he waited to hear from the relative he wandered all over the wonderfully clean city. There wasn't one single beggar on the streets. The people were conservatively well-dressed, everything looked prosperous and promising, and the pace of life was much slower than New York City. He read the Want Ads. There were 20 pages of positions being offered! He made no effort to interview for work, if he and Sara decided to come back it was obvious he'd have no trouble finding a job.

The day he was to leave Toronto he checked out and seated himself in the lobby as he waited for time to catch a cab to the airport. He was chatting with the drunk in the next chair when a tall, distinguished, gray-haired man in well-tailored clothes walked in. Walter couldn't help but notice him, his bearing was rather proud and regal. The man stood in the middle of the lobby scanning the room. When he spied Walter he made straight for him.

"Are you Gelnay?" he asked.

"Yes" said Walter. "Who are you?"

"I'm Pock, the cousin of your wife." he said "I got your note."

"I called and called," said Walter a little accusingly.

"I know. I wasn't home. When I went to pick up my mail today I found your note and came right over. In fact I'm not living at home right now." He cleared his throat and for an almost imperceptible moment seemed to hesitate. Then he said, "My wife died about three months ago and I've been staying with my sons, going from house to house like a lost soul which I guess I am."

Walter made sympathetic sounds and shifted from one foot to another. He didn't know how to respond to this stranger's need.

"Come with me," Pock urged. "They're saying 'kaddish' for my wife at Temple tonight. When it over we'll go to one of my son's for dinner. I've already told him."

Walter hadn't said prayers for the dead, ever, but he decided it wouldn't hurt. "Let me call the airport first," he said, "and cancel my reservation. And I'll need to get my room back for the night here at the hotel, then we can go."

They went to Kaddish. Walter found himself wandering mentally from face to face trying to size people up rather than concentrating on the Rabbi. He didn't know enough about the liturgical order of worship to follow it without effort, and he didn't even know the person being mourned. After the service they went on to Pock's son's for dinner where he was very much alive to everything said around him. The family was obviously very wealthy. Father and sons were in the business of making accessories for cars: hood ornaments, special paneling, all the extras kids were buying to stylize their "hot rods." Walter judged that car accessories was apparently a very good business to have. Mahogany paneling on the walls, inviting leather furniture, oriental rugs on the floors, all the accouterments of wealth quietly shrieked at him. They assured him he'd have no difficulty with immigration; after all he was a British Army Veteran and he was a citizen of a commonwealth nation. Canada needed men like Walter. Walter went back to NYC the next day. He wanted to talk it over with his sisters. In New York he wrote to Sara. "Pack it up and come. It is good." He saw no reason to spend the money to make a round trip to Australia, Sara could handle everything.

As usual Sara willingly accepted his decision and threw herself into closing out their life in Australia. Ben had a year and a half left of his three-year architectural degree program and he didn't want to start over in another country. There was much correspondence back and forth between Sydney and New York until it was finally agreed that Ben could remain behind. While Sara packed, Walter went back to Toronto and found a very nice apartment for her to come to, then started looking for work. Jobs were easy to find and he found a few, tried them on, quit and went on to the next, before he found the one that suited him. He settled in as office manager for Lady Manhattan, the American clothing company. Six weeks after his return to Toronto Sara arrived after a long flight from Australia. That day, Toronto was socked in by fog thicker than any London can produce. Standing on the curb, Walter literally could not see the street cars running down the middle of the street. He went to the Railroad Station to catch the bus to the airport only to be told that nothing was coming in, nothing was going out, and no busses were going to the airport until the driver could at least see the stoplights. When finally the fog thinned out enough for traffic to move safely, the bus went to the airport with Walter on it. The place was empty except for one lone woman standing in the middle of a raft of luggage, fighting to hold back tears. One plane had come in through the fog, disgorged its passengers and then was towed to the hangar. All the passengers were met by someone who whisked them away, except Sara.

A year passed and then, unhappy with Lady Manhattan, Walter decided to go into business for himself. He came up with a unique idea. He bought second hand clothes from individuals and sold them via mail order. He put out a little catalog, a simple little piece that listed the garments, material, color, size and price. There were no frills, no pictures, no descriptions. Just lists of the merchandise. But the clothes was so inexpensive that people didn't mind buying a pig in a poke. The garments were in good condition and clean, and if they didn't fit you the price was so low you could pass them on to someone who could wear them. He'd just gotten his feet wet in the business and showed his first monthly profit when he got a call from Exquisite Form Brassieres, the parent company of Lady Manhattan. Exquisite Form wanted him to take over the job of Production and Inventory Manager. Walter's second little experience as an entrepreneur had proved to him that he much preferred a career in a large company to the work of a rags merchant, or any other kind of shop keeping. He took the job and remained with Exquisite Form for the next decade.

Sara had been in Canada a little over a year and a half when she developed breast cancer. In the 60's, radical mastectomies were the only procedure known, or at least in service, to combat the disease. Mortality rates during surgery were high. Walter cabled Ben who was in Italy attending a summer institute in architecture before coming on to Canada. Ben dropped everything and flew in in time for the surgery. The Toronto relatives were wonderful to them. When the surgery was over the doctors could assure them of nothing more than the fact that the operation itself had been successful. They thought she was free of cancer, but for how long they wouldn't even hazard a guess. For several years Sara was well and they were happy. In 1976 Walter retired. The first thing they did was get into their car and drive to Chicago. From Chicago they drove to Denver, from Denver to Arizona, and from Arizona on to Dita and Tilda who had both moved to Rossmoor in California. They covered a lot of miles on that trip, enough so that Walter was satisfied that he had seen some of America at last.

Six weeks after their return, Sara started bleeding. Walter rushed her to emergency where she was examined first by the doctor on duty, and then by a specialist who told them she now had cervical cancer which also required immediate surgery. Walter was stunned. It couldn't be, not a second time. The doctors opened her up and closed her up. The cancer had penetrated into the lining of the uterus and they feared that if they tried to remove it they would only hasten the spread of it. Walter wouldn't accept a verdict like that. Sara was not terminally ill, they were mistaken! He took her to other doctors in other towns, to anyone who had a reputation in the field of malignancies no matter what kind. But none of them gave Sara any hope. Finally she called a halt to it. She wanted peace.

Medical costs were astounding, so astounding that he had to go back to work. He took a job in a small town about 35 miles from Toronto, a town so small it was like living in the country. For two more years they lived from one day to the next holding each other close, and then Sara became very ill. They gave her morphine to control the pain and each day she wasted away as he watched, but would not believe. If she said she was fine he believed it because he wanted to believe it. Finally, she had to be hospitalized. One day he was standing in the hall of the hospital listening to the doctor who was in her room.

"How are you Sara?" Walter heard the doctor ask.

"I'm fine," she answered clearly enough for Walter to hear and rejoice.

The doctor came out of the room and said quietly to Walter, "She's dying."

"How can you say that!" he cried. "I heard her tell you she is fine."

Wordlessly, the doctor turned and walked back into the room with Walter at his heels. By the time they reached her bed, Sara had quietly slipped away.

Walter was lost. He ate his meals in restaurants, he showered and shaved as soon as he got up in the morning and kept himself presentable, but he took no interest in anything. Dita and Tilda called and wrote and insisted he come to California for a visit until finally he gave in and went to put a stop to their pleading. Obediently, he did everything they told him to do for as long as he was there, then he went back to Toronto and did everything his friends back there told him to do. The days slipped by silently, the nights were filled with dreadful dreaming, the season changed. Life went on, but without Walter. Most of the time he was too numb to be interested in the world around him. Then one morning he woke up and said to himself, "I've got to hang those pictures."

When he'd brought Sara back to the city from the little town where they'd been living, the essentials for housekeeping had been unpacked but the things that always made Sara's house a home were still in boxes. The simple task of putting the apartment together the way Sara would have done it was the starter button for Walter to reenter the world. He found a little job of no consequence, just enough work to fill his days, and a year later he found a lady friend with whom to spend his evenings. He went to California every year for a visit with his sisters. Time passed, but there was no real forward movement to Walter's life. He was marking time.

In 1985, Dr. Wim Schiff died. Walter had met the Schiffs through his sister Tilda, and he and Tilda had even vacationed once with them in Palm Springs. Now he began to correspond with Ilse, take her out when he was in California, call her long distance on the phone. In 1988, he shut down his life in Canada and bought himself a studio unit in Rossmoor. He hadn't been here three months before he and Ilse were married. He retains his little manor where he goes every day to make long distance calls, read his mail, leaf through old records, keep new ones, and follow the stock market. His absence leaves Ilse free to do her own thing without him underfoot. Ilse has her own tastes, he has his. She has her own agenda, he has his. They respect their differences and make way for each other, but Ilse is their social secretary and she keeps him busy some afternoons and all evenings. Happily, they attend the theater with friends, play bridge all afternoon or evening, and give dinner parties.

Walter kept Tilda's books and paid her bills, did her income tax, and watched over her as long as she lived. Independent Dita has her own accountant and handles her own affairs. She doesn't need her baby brother to do those things for her. What she needs, and what he provides, is that sense of being surrounded by "family."

DITA

The pile of soggy Kleenex on the table beside her kept getting larger with every fresh outburst of crying. Every time she thought she had herself under enough control to put through the call to Germany she choked on tears again. Fifty years! Fifty years since Greta had risked her life for the four bedraggled Jews whose need was so great. Fifty years! It was like going back three lifetimes getting that letter this morning. She hadn't been able to do anything but bawl since it came. Over and over she read it with dear Greta's face leaping off the written page, passage after passage. Greta had been so young, so passionate, so vulnerable, she had refused to look at what her actions in behalf of these Jews could mean to her own life. "I am going with you." she'd said, her blue eyes solemn and defiant. "I can't leave you now, not like this."

She had gone with them. Nothing they could say, no warning about what could happen to her if she was caught, deterred her. Through the black-out that quenched all the street lights in Reichenberg as they fled ahead of the air raid expected any moment, through the weeks of waiting hidden out in Prague, all the way across Germany on the train where one's heart stood still every time a German official strode through the car, in the face-down with the Gestapo at the border, and into Holland where they were stranded for months, went Greta holding little Peggy in her arms. As the daughter of a German stalwart and the fiancée of a storm trooper, Greta could have gone anywhere by herself without fear, and with dignity. But she'd gone with them, her life in as much jeopardy as their own, all the way to the ship for America.

Dita tried to see through the tears that kept welling up in spite of herself, and looked at the envelop again. The letter had been forwarded twice! How in the world had Greta found an address for her after all this time? Even an old address. What was most humbling was that she had remembered, that she had wanted through all those years to know how it had been with "Frau Dita!" Why hadn't she, Dita, ever tried to find Greta? She owed the girl so much! Her only excuse was that so much had happened since then that she hadn't had time to think about the events that made up her life before America. The cup of her life was always running over. There'd been so much to learn, once she was safe in the United States, so much to do to get their heads above water financially, and keep them going. Overnight, once they arrived, the past became the past, the sooner forgotten the better one slept. Guiltily, she admitted to herself that there was also the fact that Greta had been lost in the hatred and resentment that engulfed her every time she thought of what Hitler's maniacal plans had cost them, and every member of their families. 100 relatives gone up in smoke.

Yet the moment she received the letter this morning, Greta's perfume, Greta's laughter, Greta's lullabies sung to the children in the small flat in Amsterdam, were as clear and as fresh as when the girl had been her only friend, her nurturing nursemaid, her helper in all the details of life a pregnant woman faced. Obviously, Greta had never forgotten. That was what was so overwhelming. The thought of Greta loving her and remembering her, and wondering about her for half a century, broke her heart! Finally, momentarily running out of tears, Dita felt steady enough to get the international operator on the phone. She gave her the number that Greta had hopefully sent her,and she listened to the two little staccato rings, then the pause, then two more staccato rings that told her she was connected with a European phone number. The phone only rang twice before there was an answer.

"Goot Morgen" Time alters bodies but not voices, she would have recognized the lilt of that voice anywhere.

"Greta!" she cried over the phone. "Oh, my darling Greta!"

There was a sharp intake of breath on the other end of the line and then Greta's joy sang out over all those thousands of miles. "Frau Dita?! Oh Mein Gott, is it really you?"

They began laughing and crying and talking all at once. Across all those years they reached out to touch each other, to embrace each other with words that tumbled over one another. "Oh Greta, I was so glad to get that letter. I've wondered so often if you and your family lived through the bombings."

"I lived! I lived! My babies, did they live?"

Dita choked and couldn't speak for a brief moment. Then she answered. "They lived, thanks to you, and they kept on living. They're living right here in California. But they're middle-aged women now, Greta darling, and they have grown children of their own. Oh my dear, my dear. How I wish I could see you."

They talked for over an hour, an hour in which the fateful days before and during the Strauss family's escape were relived. The German girl, now a senior citizen herself, and the Jewish woman whom she had helped flee from "Der Fuhrer", reminisced and told each other stories of what life had been like for each of them since 1938, and repeated themselves over and over until they were emotionally exhausted. When they hung up, Dita lay back in her chair and let the letter slip from her fingers. Her mind wandered where it would, she was too tired to control the direction of her thoughts.

She and Otto had been so rich when Greta came to be their baby's nurse, and they had been so close to being absolutely impoverished when she'd kissed Greta good-bye at the gangway to the ship. All the years came tumbling back in memory, bits and pieces of disconnected times and places that made up the collage of her life. It was as though that letter had pried the lid loose on a store of images like faded photographs found in an attic trunk. The realization that she didn't have a single picture of Greta made for one more damp Kleenex. She didn't have any pictures from the pre-America past. Portraits, snapshots, newspaper clippings, had all been left behind when they'd run with nothing more than the nightclothes they wore, and two little overnight bags packed in haste.

Dita was christened Edith, but she never liked her name. At the first opportunity she changed it. She chose a new name when she entered school in Vienna at the age of twelve. For the first six years of her education, she escaped the confines of classrooms. There was another Edith in her new class in her hated new school which gave the saucy, red-haired little elf reason to rename herself. She chose the name "Dita" and defied anyone to say her nay. She was Dita from then on, and rarely does anyone say her nay about anything yet today. Because of the curious twists of her father's life Dita spent the most precious days of her childhood in Bratislava, then a part of Hungary, now a part of Czechoslovakia. Her Hungarian odyssey began just as the opening salvos of World War I were fired. Dita was not quite seven.

The schools in Bratislava were taught in Magyar, a language her parents did not want their children to learn, so Tilda, Dita, and Walter were tutored at home. With Dita's disposition and the tutor's indifference both at work, lessons were no more serious than the child chose to make them. The one whip over her head was that every summer the three Gelnay children had to go into the heart of Bratislava to the Board of Education offices to take their year's end exams which would establish their educational placement in the Vienna schools when they returned. A quick study, Dita waited until late spring to buckle down and learn; she could always pass the exams without putting out real effort. For her, education began outside their door and the books she loved were not printed on paper, they were found in nature.

For six years she lived in an idyllic community of houses set far from each other among the trees. There were no other little girls nearby from whom she might have learned the "sugar and spice" nuances of being a girl child, and Tilda was too much of a house mouse to be a model for such a vivacious being. Instead, there were ten boys near her age to play with. Ten boys who accepted her as one of them because of her capricious imagination and her willingness to try anything just to keep up with them. She honed all her plentiful skills at handling men on those ten boys. She climbed the hills at their heels, she skated with them on the ice-covered ponds and streams near their home, she swam with them in those same waters in the summer. She joyously struggled to match or exceed their feats, to be the first to find the birds' nests they were looking for, to do her part in building forts among the trees, to skip rocks across the ponds. Sometimes on her own, disregarding her petticoats, she hunted for berries and nuts, or prowled along the little stream not far from their house learning to love passionately the lessons of nature. They played Indians -- even European children were entranced by the Indian lore of North America-- and she was always the Indian cook. Her culinary efforts as an Indian were a far cry from what was going on in her mother's kitchen. That Dita left to Tilda. Tilda was learning to sew pretty samplers and dolls' things and even make clothes for herself. Tilda might be the dearest sister in all the world, but her domesticity did not rub off on Dita. Walter was her pal, her confidante. When the war ended Papa left them in Bratislava and went to Vienna alone to get his project off the ground financially before disturbing his family. Dita's time in paradise was extended for another two years.

In Vienna Adolph worked at a feverish pace. Too much money was being sunk into his project as his dreams expanded the scope of it. His theater would be as fine as any in Vienna. It would have a cantilevered balcony, something quite new in construction techniques. His would be the first hotel in Vienna with hot and cold running water in all the rooms. On the top floor of one of the apartment buildings right on the corner of Prater Str. and Tabor Str., he combined two apartments into one to provide a grand home for his family. Everything was to be done yesterday, by the best workmanship to be had. Fortunately there were veterans, skilled workmen not yet settled into the economic life of the city because of the postwar depression that gripped the country, whom he could hire at fairly low wages. The apartment for his family was ready in 1920. Mary and the children were forced to leave their suburban world and move to one of the busiest intersections of the capitol of Austria.

The second district had been the Jewish ghetto which was created in the 15th century by the House of Hapsburg at the time the Inquisition was started in Spain. Franz Joseph had ordered segregation of the Jews ended in the eighteenth century, and made Jews legally free to move to wherever they wanted to live after that. Most, however, remained in the old ghetto among familiar scenes and sights and sounds. The area teemed with life. The streets were jammed with people and dogs and carts and vendors, and now and then a belching motor car. Old people sat in doorways and children scuttled in and out among the pedestrians. Overhead, telephone and power lines criss-crossed the sky providing excellent perches for the multitudes of pigeons which were a nuisance to the crowds below. Only on the boulevards was there grass and trees and flower beds and space to see the clouds above.

When they returned, Dita was enrolled in the finest girl's school in the city, and at last was herself cooped up in classrooms, where, like Walter, she was forced to follow routines, required to observe protocol, made to stand when the teacher entered the room or called on her to recite, constantly entreated to behave like a "young lady" of twelve should behave. Gone were the days when she could outwit the tutor, ignore the lessons, create her own world out of her fantasies. The free bird was caged. Forced into a private school run by Protestants who revered form and order above all, life became heavy and repressive. With tears streaming down her face, in those first months, she went up to every tree along the boulevards and hugged it. Slowly, painfully, she adjusted to the new life which had been forced on her, but never did she quit testing the limits of propriety and straining to take back control of her life.

The only portion of her urban education that pleased her came in the form of her lessons after school, lessons in piano and dancing. The music spoke to her and the dancing lessons freed her from the constraints life had wrapped around her. For four long years she remained in the prim and proper girl's school until she had completed the equivalent of a U.S. Junior College education. Then, at last, relieved of the need for any more book learning, she was off to the " Academy of Music and Interpretive Dancing " for advanced instruction. The Academy was a much happier milieu for her than any she had known since Bratislava. At the Academy, her expressiveness could have free rein. Graduation came all too soon, but its compensation was that she received a diploma which was also a certificate for "Teacher of Physical Culture." That certificate gave her the power to fly away. She wasted no time in flying away to France to revel in the freer air of Paris, to escape the strictures of Viennese society, and hopefully be launched into a brilliant career in the theater which would keep her on the Left Bank forever.

Paris! In 1928! The city on the Seine was completely seductive. She just missed being there when Magda was touring the major theaters of Europe, and was booked into and out of Paris frequently. Dita embraced Parisian life with all her usual ardor for new things. Overflowing with exuberant self confidence, she advertised herself in the newspapers as a teacher of Dance and gathered together enough private students of her own to pay for the lessons she needed if she was to break into the world of dance in this sophisticated city. After a few weeks of being handicapped by her inadequate command of the language she decided that she also had to go to the Sorbonne to improve her French and perhaps take a few other courses. Education became important at last, Paris had forced her to face how ignorant she was. She found herself working night and day with little time left in which to enjoy the very things that had lured her to the cultural capitol of the world in the first place. Two years went by like the surge of wind. She made friends at the Sorbonne and in the dancing classes in which she enrolled, and she was just beginning to be invited out, to feel quite the Parisian, when she came down with the measles. One of her pupils had come to class with a fever, and Dita had comforted her. The child recovered quickly, but Dita almost died. She lay abed burning with fever for days, and when the fever passed she was limp as a cat. She had to give it all up, everything, her studies, her pupils, her ambitions, and return to her parents in Vienna for several months of recuperation.

As usual, in the life of Dita Gelnay, what looked like adversity turned into opportunity. Fate, in the person of her sister Tilda, opened the door of her Vienna captivity when she was well again, and redirected her path into a much more enchanting future than even Paris had offered. Fame, she did not achieve, but fortune poured into her lap. Tilda had been married for some time and was living with her child and husband in Liberic, known in the Sudetenland of Czechoslovakia as Reichenberg. Reichenberg was a town of about 35,000 people. It was not a culture capitol in any sense. Nor was it even as sophisticated as Vienna. Dita had no inkling when she saw the little town that here lay her destiny. She was there because one day while she was recovering from the measles she got a call from Tilda.

"Dita!" Tilda cried over the phone, "You've got to come to Reichenberg. You've just got to. There's the most wonderful opportunity here for you."

"Opportunity to do what?" demanded Dita.

"Don't sound like that." Tilda scolded. "I know Reichenberg is not Paris but they need another exercise-dancing school here. The mayor's daughter just told me!"

"A dancing school in Reichenberg." Dita laughed scornfully. "Who would take dancing lessons in Reichenberg."

"Oh Dita," Tilda pleaded. "Don't be so superior! What have you got to lose? Mama is not going to let you go back to Paris without a fight and you know it. Come here and be near me. I want you here."

Dita sighed as she hung up. It was true that her parents had no sympathy at all with her desire to go back to Paris. And the further truth of it was, that she had been homesick in Paris in spite of all the excitement. Secretly, she was glad to have family around again. She didn't fare well without them. To be near Tilda in provincial Reichenberg, though, would be little better than staying here in stodgy Vienna. But for a short spell, what did she have to lose indeed? At least it would be a bit more like going back to Bratislava than staying here. If she couldn't have Paris she'd at least have the beauty of a small town where houses were surrounded by trees, not facing concrete sidewalks squished in, wall to wall with their neighbors. She went to Reichenberg and she opened up a little school. Within a short time she had a very respectable number of students and was making enough money to be on her own, beholden to nobody. One day, her fledgling pupils put on a show for the employees at the local textile factory where many of their fathers were employed. It was the largest textile factory in the whole of the Sudetenland and was run by a handsome bachelor in his early thirties whose father had turned over management of the factory to him. He had expanded it and now lived richly off the fat of the land from his share of the profits produced by the family business. His name was Otto Strass, and he was used to having any woman at whom he crooked his finger fawn over him.

Out of courtesy to the entertainment committee that arranged these cultural events at the factory, Otto dropped in to watch the children of his employees strut their stuff. The children were mere beginners, not at all interesting, but the teacher who led them in the dance was all fire and fluid motion. Her big blue eyes and brilliant red hair were ablaze as she performed the simple routines with the children. He was enchanted. He wanted to know her right then, but he couldn't betray his personal interest in the teacher to the committee. Reichenberg was not very big. It would be all over town before nightfall that Herr Strass was out for another kill. He would have to bide his time. He'd find out who she was soon enough. Not long after the recital he saw her one day as she walked along one of the major shopping streets of the little town, and again she ignited something in him. Discretely, he made inquiry about where she lived. He promptly wrote her a letter. The letter was poetic, carefully crafted like a form letter, and more than a bit arrogant. His invitation to her to have dinner with him was seductive and enticing, which put Dita on the alert. He gave her a phone number to call if she was interested. What kind of man made such a proposal? If he wanted to see her why didn't he call or come around to ask.

Dita read the letter aloud to Tilda. "Can you imagine?" she declared, "The nerve of him. Who does he think he is?"

"The richest man in town," Tilda answered calmly. She looked at her sister shrewdly. "You ought to think about it."

"Think about it indeed!" Dita tossed her red hair back from her face and threw the letter into a drawer.

She didn't answer the letter nor did she make the phone call, but that didn't mean she didn't think about it. Two weeks went by with no further word from him. Piqued, Dita took the letter out and read it again. She went back to Tilda to talk it over some more.

"What do you think?" she asked Tilda, "Do you think I should call him?"

"Look,' said Tilda, "You're not missing anything. You can call and you can meet the fellow and if you don't like him you don't ever have to go out with him again. What have you got to lose?"

Dita made the call and Otto came like the true beau brummel in his wonderful car bringing flowers and flattery to whirl her away for what he hoped was the beginning of an "arrangement." He let her know early in the evening that he was not the marrying kind, that he found her exciting and attractive, and that he'd like to enter into a non-binding relationship with her if she would settle for that, but no more. Dita was wildly indignant. She would not settle for that! Eyes blazing she let him know in very clear, cold language that she was not available for such an arrangement, and, what was more she would appreciate it if he took her home immediately and didn't bother her any more. Once inside her own door she burst into tears and threw the flowers into the wastebasket.

The next day the phone calls began, but she wouldn't come to the phone. He took to writing but she wouldn't answer his notes. Then one day a woman approached her on the street, a beautifully dressed older woman of about sixty, possessed of great dignity.

"Aren't you Miss Gelnay?" she inquired.

"Yes I am," said Dita.

"I thought so," she smiled. "My son is very much in love with you."

"In love with me?!" Dita was startled. "Who is this man who is in love with me?"

"Otto Strass." replied the woman proudly. "And you are doing exactly the right thing. Marry my son. I want you to. Don't give in to his escape from responsibility. He has played long enough."

"But I don't see him," protested Dita.

"You will," smiled his mother. "He's too much in love with you to hold out."

Otto didn't hold out. As his mother predicted, it was not long before a contrite Herr Strass was on her doorstep, openly paying serious court. For eight months he showered her with flowers, wonderful dinners in fine restaurants, evenings at the theater, and no suggestions again of taking trips away on their own. He finally capitulated and asked her very properly to be his wife. So they were married. It was 1932.

There were few portents yet of the dangers that lay ahead for Jews, especially for very rich Jews who lived in Czechoslovakia. Even if there had been, Dita was too engrossed in her new life to be aware of the world outside Reichenberg. There was the great estate in the country to look after where they spent their summers; there was the magnificent townhouse in the city for the fall and winter seasons; there were servants to command, and parties to give and attend, and charities to administer, and all the trappings of the life of wealthy young women in Europe. She reveled in all of it. They went to Italy for long weeks at the seashore in summer, they skied at the best resorts in Switzerland in the winter, and if Otto was worried about what was going on around them in the wider world he did not burden her with his concerns.

Walter came to Reichenberg to replace Tilda when Tilda's husband took a new job and carried his wife and baby off to Vienna to live with his mother-in-law, Mary Gelnay. Walter was footloose in Prague. Dita, never wanting to be without some of her own family around her, prevailed on Otto to give Walter a job. As usual, Dita's wish was Otto's command. Walter was offered a job and Walter came, which rounded out Dita's life. But he stayed only a little over three years. When Dita got pregnant Walter left. One thing had nothing to do with the other, but it made his departure seem normal and to be expected. Dita was creating her own family. It was 1936 when Dita had her baby, a little girl whom she named Peggy. The whole family doted on the little darling, and a young German girl named Greta was found to be her nursemaid. With a baby in residence the Strass household achieved that perfect image of what the best of upper class families in Europe were like. No wonder Dita was unaware that things were going sour for the Jews of Germany; nothing of that kind of information intruded into her world. She wasn't in Germany nor was any member of either of their families. They were insulated in Reichenberg against the stresses of the wider world of Nazism and international treaties.

By 1938, however, when she found herself pregnant again, the ugliness growing in the world was intruding on her halcyon existence, like it or not. There could be no further looking at the world with provincial blinders on. World events stared them fully in the face. Hitler moved into Austria in March, and some of her family was now in his path. Her parents were permanently separated by then, Mary having vowed she would live the life of a gypsy no longer. She still lived in the family apartment on Praeter Str. and Tilda was with her. Walter was off in Lebanon on his own, having gone to work there the year before. Their father was in Baghdad where he was prospecting for another fortune to replace the one he'd lost in international currencies. Three Gelnay women were closed in behind the new boundaries of the Third Reich, Dita's mother, Dita's grandmother and Dita's sister.

Dita's reaction to the Anschluss was to want to fly immediately to Vienna to rescue at least her sister and her mother from the Nazis since her father's mother refused to leave, but before she could move there was a phone call from Tilda who had already fled to Prague. Their mother was still in Vienna, which was a great worry, but her mother wanted out. Dita and Otto drove to Prague immediately. After that family counsel with Tilda, neither Dita nor Otto fell back into their former complacency. How long would Czechoslovakia escape? Watching what happened in Vienna that spring made every Jew is Eastern Europe uneasy. Tilda and Dita had less to fear than Otto and Stasch; they had been born in America. Once Otto extracted Mary from Vienna, she and Tilda were determined to put Europe behind them and go to their relatives in the United States. Tilda was the first to go, leaving Stasch behind in Czechoslovakia doing whatever it was he was doing that kept him there. Then it was Mary's turn. Tilda got only as far as Paris, initially, but Mary went straight away to her sister in New Jersey. Otto had smoothed the way for Mary and as soon as

Mary was packed and on her way, Otto ordered Dita to get her own American passport reinstated, "just in case." She had lost it as Tilda had lost hers, by letting the deadline for filing for dual citizenship go by.

Dita and Otto began wrestling with their dilemma. Tilda had had nothing to leave behind, the Gelnay properties in Vienna were already gone. But they, the Strasses, they had so much to leave behind if they decided to go. Otto's father wouldn't hear of selling the mill, or the garage. He practically tore his hair out at the mere suggestion of such idiocy. He was as convinced as most of his class of Czechoslovakians that Hitler was appeased by the annexation of Austria, that "Der Fuhrer" had no territorial ambitions that would lead him to turn northward. Whenever the senior Mr. Strass was reminded that the Sudetenland had belonged to Germany before the Versailles fiasco, he grew even angrier and pounded the table.

"Austria never belonged to Germany! He didn't take Austria! The Austrians wanted unification! They're Germans, we are not!"

"Plenty of Czechs feel German!" retorted Otto. "And plenty of them think the Germans know how to run a country."

Otto didn't share his father's convictions, but his father's adamant opposition immobilized him. All spring and summer the only thing Dita and Otto did was anxiously watch the course of events in Austria trying to find any signs of reassurance in the slightest turn of events that fate would not turn Hitler loose on Germany's southeastern neighbor. There were no such signs beyond the torrents of words coming out of Hitler's mouth which no gentile in his right mind would any longer trust much less a Jew. For Jews, every word coming out of Hitler's mouth was another nail in their coffin. One day they were convinced they had to get out while there was still time, the next they said it might not happen in Czechoslovakia after all so why not wait and see. They were as traumatized by indecision as many another Czech Jew with non-liquid assets.

To add to their confusion about what to do there was the baby Dita carried in her womb which was scheduled to be born in late September. Surely it was best to wait until the child had been delivered to make up their minds about the future. When they should have been converting their wealth into gold and storing it away in Switzerland, they procrastinated, took no action in their own behalf. Then came Munich and their world was in upheaval. After Chamberlain betrayed the Czechs in September and the British awarded all of the Sudetenland to Hitler, no rational man or woman could continue to hope that somehow, some way, the Allies would hem Hitler in. Otto, and all the other Jews of the Sudetenland, stood exposed and knew it. Now he began to make serious efforts to salvage something, to find some way to ferret some of his wealth out of the country, but it was too late. There were no buyers. All the Germans had to do was wait and take it, whatever it was: Jews' businesses, Jews' professional positions, Jews' homes.

From the moment Chamberlain stood under his umbrella on the steps of his plane back to England and proclaimed to the world that there would be "Peace in Our Time," the people of the German-speaking sector of Czechoslovakia began air raid drills and learned how to don gas masks. Dita struggled to keep panic at bay and her wits about her as she tried to make a game out of teaching her two-year-old to walk around in a gas mask without being afraid of suffocating. Not wanting the child to be frightened, she showed her pictures of other children in gas masks, pictures that appeared daily in a defiant press. Wanting desperately to present Otto with a smiling face each night when he came dragging home, she did her best to choke down her own fear and play the light-hearted gay companion. Her dissembling was almost pathetic in its artificiality, and Otto grew impatient with the pretense that everything was as it had been.

The household became so tense the child within her quit moving. Day after day there was no sign of life in her belly. That added to the terror that now stalked her through every waking hour, the mounting fear of a stillborn birth. She would awaken in the middle of the night and find herself straining at her pillow as though trying to pull a heavy load through deep snow. Meanwhile, Otto was becoming desperate in his efforts to find a way that they could leave without being bankrupt. Futility stalked his every scheme. Lest one of them betray the fear that festered within and increase the weight of fear that beset the other, they had little to say to each other when they were together. Then came the night to be remembered forever.

It was one o'clock in the morning when they heard a pounding on the wall of their bedroom coming from the elevator shaft beyond. Startled awake they could hear the muffled voice of their chauffeur.

"Herr Strass!," he was calling, "Herr Strass!

Otto leaped out of bed and ran to the hall door with Dita lumbering along at his heels. The chauffeur, a Czech of German heritage, had climbed up the elevator shaft to avoid being seen by the concierge and was now clinging to the grillwork of the opening in the hallway.

"You must go," the chauffeur whispered hoarsely through the grate as he saw them emerge from their apartment. "You must go immediately. We are expecting an air raid from Germany any minute and in Frau Strass's condition," he nodded toward Dita's huge belly, "there is no time to waste. The car is ready."

They opened the grillwork door and let him out onto firm footing, then ran back inside their apartment motioning for him to follow. Waddling into the bedroom as fast as she could move, Dita threw a robe on over her nightgown and began wildly tossing things into a bag. With the barest number of necessities they would need packed, she rushed to the nursery where she wakened the baby's maid.

"We must go." she urgently told the bewildered young fraulein. "Thank you, thank you, dear Greta, for all you've done for us. You've been wonderful. But we must go right now!"

She bent to pick up her sleeping daughter but the maid reached out ahead of her.

"I'm going with you," she said calmly, gently pushing Dita aside. "I won't leave you in this condition."

"But, it could be dangerous," Dita protested trying to take little Peggy from her.

"I'm going with you!" the girl stubbornly repeated, holding the sleeping child close to her breast. "Now you pack the things Peggy will need and I'll get her ready. Go on. Get ready." she made a shooing motion with her free hand.

Twenty-three years old, practically engaged to a storm trooper who would have killed her if he had known she was helping Jews escape, a dutiful daughter of a patriotic German citizen, without notifying her family or her boyfriend, Greta dressed the sleeping child quickly, then threw on her own clothes. Carrying the baby she followed her employers, still dressed in their night wear, out of the apartment and down the hall after the chauffeur to the car waiting below. Lights dimmed, the big powerful car purred through the blacked-out city, threading its way among the tanks and milling soldiers that filled the streets, on out to the Motorway where they headed for Prague. The Strasses couldn't leave the country without a visa for Otto, and the necessary visa could only be obtained in the capitol.

The four of them traveled in silence as though they were afraid to leave their words hanging in the air behind them to betray their departure. Fortunately, little Peggy, in Greta's arms slept soundly through that wild ride. Once in Prague, they took Greta with them and went to stay with friends to keep their presence in the city as secret as possible. They sent the chauffeur back to Reichenberg with the car just as the dawn was breaking hoping their absence would not be noted. Day after day, while Greta cared for little Peggy in the home of their friends, they hounded the American Embassy for the precious Visa they needed. Otto had once been a force in the business community of the capitol, known by politicians and businessmen alike. Now he found that doors once thrown open to him in welcome were closed, almost sealed against him. Strass, the Jew, had replaced Otto Strass, the wonder boy of the textile world. No magic of personality or commercial power was his any longer. During those long frightful days the child in Dita's womb lay unmoving like a lump below her breasts.

In a twinkling, the fear of losing everything was replaced by the knowledge that their material possessions were already lost. The fear now was of being trapped themselves, of not getting the Visa in time, or maybe not at all. Otto must have that visa if they had any hope of escaping in time to get out ahead of the advancing armies. At the very last minute the invaluable document came through. It was issued just days before the Nazis closed the borders of Czechoslovakia to international travel, an act which would have entombed them. They immediately left Prague by train, traveling second class in order to keep a low profile, and headed for Holland. The faithful Greta still carried little Peggy in her arms as she constantly watched anxiously for Frau Strass to go into labor. The borders between the Third Reich and Czechoslovakia were still open as they crossed into Germany so they were not forced to show identification until they reached the borders of Holland. All the way across Germany Dita stretched out prone on a wooden bench with her hands clasped over the dead weight of what she believed was a dead child. Greta played games with little Peggy, read her stories, and kept the child happy. Otto, sunk down in his seat until his head barely cleared the window frame, stared morosely out the window. Only when some train official came through the car did Peggy's parents sit up and take notice.

The abrupt invasion of Czechoslovakia had caught even the German Civilian government off guard. None of the rigidity which would mark Nazi control of Europe in months to come was yet in place at the Dutch border. As the train came to a halt at the platform of the last station inside Germany the usual customs officials came aboard. With military smartness they went from car to car demanding to see passports. Officiously, they checked baggage with their usual vaunted air of authority intended to awe passengers. When Dita presented her American passport and the maid presented her German papers they were stamped and returned to the two women which left only Otto's fate hanging in the balance. Unceremoniously they were all hauled off the train like ticket-less stowaways.

"You," barked one of the inspectors pointing to Dita, "may leave Germany, and you may take your child with you." Dita reached for Peggy but Greta stood rooted in place, the little girl held firmly against her breast. Peggy locked her arms around Greta's neck and began to whimper.

Coldly the guard stared into Greta's face but her gaze did not waver. For a long moment there was a silent contest of wills, then the inspector retreated angrily. "All right Jew-lover. Go with her if you wish," nodding toward Dita's huge belly. "Be a handmaiden to an American Jew brat and its Jew mother if you can stomach that." "But you," he turned toward Otto snarling "must go back."

"Why?" demanded Otto in the best tone of outrage he could muster.

"Don't ask, Jew," the customs official thundered. "You just may not go!"

Dita flung herself at Otto shrieking and screaming. Arms outspread she threw herself across the front of Otto to face the startled Nazi. "You cannot keep him!" she cried wildly. "You cannot! I will throw myself under the train if you do not let him go! I will lie down on the tracks and not move! I will kill myself right here! He must go with me! I will not leave without him!"

The uniformed representative of the Third Reich was unprepared for such an outburst from a Jew. The unborn child in her belly, her flashing blue eyes and dazzling red hair, the dramatic gesture of protection spread out over her husband's chest, the unseasoned official was shaken and unnerved by the theatrics of it all. He'd received no instruction on how to handle hysterical pregnant women, nor had any official pronouncements about the fate of Czechoslovakian Jews been issued. If he held the Jew with his Czech passport but also an American visa, what about the woman with her American passport? There might be a mistake. What would happen if this American creature carried weight in Berlin? American Jews had a way of causing all kinds of trouble. And if these were just ordinary Jews why would a good German girl be traveling with them? It was too confusing. Not knowing what to do, he let them go, all of them, into the sanctuary of Holland.

It was a miracle not to be believed! Trembling with spent emotional energy, and a sense of triumph, Dita hauled her heavy body up the train steps with Otto's help and sank into a seat next to the window. For over an hour after the train was underway again, the three of them sat in stunned silence, no one spoke. Otto clasped and unclasped his hands in his lap as Dita shook with suppressed laughter and relief. Even little Peggy was subdued as she nestled in Greta's trembling arms.

Once they were in Holland out of harm's way, they were face to face with the enormity of their poverty. Everything had been left behind, they were penniless. They didn't even have passage money to America. The only wealth they had at hand was Dita's jewelry. They had not been so foolish as to try to bring it with them, they had known they could never get it across the border. What they had done was a stroke of genius on Otto's part, the only sensible thing that had been accomplished the summer before. To prepare for such exigencies as they now faced, he had conceived the idea of getting Dita's jewelry out of Czechoslovakia and into a bank vault in Amsterdam. In Berlin, Dita had a German friend with whom she had gone to school in Paris, a woman named Louise who was a very close friend whom they could trust. The previous July, Otto had casually suggested to Dita that it might be smart for her to turn her jewelry over to Louise and ask her to take it to Holland where she could put it into a safe deposit box and send them the key. As a gentile, Louise could do that without question. Dita emptied out her jewel cases and went to the bank vault to clean out the rest of it, then carrying her small ransom in a little cosmetic case, she had gone to visit her old school chum using her American passport to get her into and out of Germany. Louise had gladly taken on the assignment, and had carried the jewels personally from Berlin to Amsterdam where she made the deposit and forwarded the key as planned. It had been a very smart move for the jewels could easily be converted into instant cash.

Besides the jewelry, there was one other possibility. In Amsterdam was a carpet company which was one of Otto's largest accounts. Payments were made by their clients on a quarterly basis, not monthly. If the quarterly payment had not already been sent to Reichenberg, Otto might be able to intercept it. As soon as they were checked into a modest hotel in the city of canals, Otto went to the carpet firm and luck broke their way. The treasurer of the carpet company was a little late that month with his accounts, the money was still there, and Otto succeeded in intercepting it. Luckily, that quarterly payment was big enough, along with the sale of the jewels, to see them through all the weeks of their enforced stay in Holland, to pay for all the hospital expenses they unexpectedly faced, not only for the baby's delivery, but also for its hospital stay when it developed bronchitis, and to give them an adequate stake for America. They might not be rich any longer, but at least they were solvent. All they could see ahead of them, in late September, was the waiting time required for the affidavits from Dita's cousin in New Jersey to arrive, and for the baby to hurry up and be born.

They waited through the remaining days of September and they continued to wait until late October before little Vivian decided to enter this world. Day after day Dita dragged herself around sure that she no longer carried a live child within her, and through all the days of waiting the German maid kept to her self-appointed post. Greta kept the household emotionally stable with her wonderful cheerfulness. She did the marketing, cooked the meals and shielded the family as best she could from the mundane tasks of life. There was certainly plenty of disorder in their world to keep her busy. In early October Otto had to be admitted to a hospital in Amsterdam because of kidney complications. While he was having his problems, the new baby finally made its exit into the world. It was not still born, nor was it damaged in any way. Vivian might have given her mother heart failure with her two-month quiescence, she would give her greater anxiety as a young adult. Dita had not given birth to another Tilda. Once born, the baby fell victim to bronchitis. For three months they were forced to linger in the Netherlands spending precious money because of one illness after another. It would have taken someone more heartless than their German fraulein to leave them in such straits. Only when she knew the little family was well enough to travel and about to depart for America did she make plans to leave her beloved "Frau Dita".

When Dita paid her for the last time she presented Greta with a dowry large enough to establish a home for herself and her storm trooper, enough to set them up in a three-room apartment completely furnished. In the face of such beneficence, the storm trooper forgot the maid's betrayal of Nazi principles. That marriage proved to be a most unhappy union but Dita would be long retired in Rossmoor before she received the precious letter that put her in touch with Greta again. From subsequent correspondence she learned the details of her courageous young friend's failed marriage and the world she had created for herself out of the ashes of World War II.

The trip across the Atlantic was an endurance contest for Dita. Alone with two children to care for, no Greta to take over when she was frazzled and tired, she learned what motherhood was all about. Otto's patience was her salvation. They were met at the docks in New York City by her cousins from New Jersey, and whisked away to her Aunt's home until they could find a place to rent. It wasn't difficult to find housing in early 1939 for America was still in the grips of its Great Depression. They rented a large house so they could bring Mary and Tilda to live with them. The American relatives had done enough, and neither Mary nor Tilda was faring too well where they were. The culture shock of American family life with its strident individualism was intimidating. The best thing to do was to gather all the Europeans together under one roof.

As soon as they were settled into their new home near Dita's aunt in New Jersey, they began to write to Otto's parents every week offering affidavits, pleading with them to come out while there was still time but their offer was constantly refused.. The senior Strasses still believed that Otto had been foolish to leave so much behind when he was a Czech citizen. They still believed that the Jews of Czechoslovakia would escape the fate of the Jews in Germany and Vienna because, they said, Czechoslovakia was not Germanic in philosophy or personality like those two countries. The family in Czechoslovakia continued to stubbornly refuse their offer until Hitler marched into Poland and they had to admit that the fate of the German and Austrian Jews would also be theirs. World War II was declared and the escape hatch slammed shut. The Nazis pulled down the curtain between east and west allowing their captive peoples no further contact with the outside world. Rumors, and reports from escapees, were terrifying, but nothing Dita and Otto could imagine approached the magnitude of what was happening to their loved ones who had clung to vain hopes.

Long after the war was over they learned from a new friend in New York who had lived through Bergen Belsen, and who had been a friend of Otto's sister in that infamous camp, about Otto's aunt who received a package in the mail and upon opening it found the ashes of her son. From survivors of the camp where he died, they later learned that the son's skin had been used to make lamp shades. As for the Aunt, they could learn nothing. She disappeared late in the war. Otto's sister died in Bergen Belsen of typhoid, her husband died in the gas chambers of Auschwitz. One of Otto's nephews was shot trying to escape the extermination camp where he was interred at the age of sixteen. His brother, a namesake, another Otto Strass, locked up in yet another concentration camp, met a girl there named Dita and married her. After the war they were among the lucky few who were rescued by Allied soldiers. The younger Otto and Dita Strass now live in Israel, the only survivors besides Dita's Otto of the entire family. Young Otto has written a book entitled, THERE IS NO GOD, a philosophical proposition quite understandably coming from a person with his experiences. That man, then only a boy, saw with his own eyes his father and one of his brothers put into the ovens while he was kept alive to work. If there is a God, he asks, how could it all have happened? Altogether, 100 members of the Strass and Gelnay families died in the Holocaust because they waited too long or because there was no loyal Czech chauffeur to spirit them away in the night. All had believed that they were safe in their rational homelands of Austria and Czechoslovakia, untouched by the Aryan racial superiority madness that was vilifying life before the world. Austrians and Hungarians, they said, were a different breed from those Teutonic Huns. By the time they were willing to concede that Hitler's ambitions were monumental in scope, and that the Final Solution meant all Jews within his reach, that it was Hitler who would determine their fate, not their neighbors, there was no longer any way out.

Tilda and her mother came to live with Otto and Dita in Hoboken, in January, 1939. Otto began his search for employment scouring the textile factories of New Jersey and New York for something he was qualified to do. The whole world was on the verge of war and many people in high places on both sides of the Atlantic knew it. All things necessary for the successful prosecution of a long titanic struggle were being openly organized and developed on a large scale by industrialists in Britain, but very grudgingly and secretively in isolationist America. Here, the man in the streets was not willing to accept that which was as plain as the nose on one's face. He continued to see the whole Axis aggression as a localized affair, whether it be in Russia, in China or in the nations bordering Germany. One thing was obvious though, if war came, fibers would be in short supply and badly needed. The textile industry in America was just beginning to awaken to the prospects of the volume of production that would be consumed when Otto began his search for work. For someone with his background, there was unquestionably a job to be filled. He quickly found employment with the New York firm of Strausser & Eineiger, a manufacturer of woolens. The former manager of the largest textile mill in Czechoslovakia, went to work earning the humiliating sum of eighteen dollars a week as a research specialist in the laboratories of Strausser & Eineiger.

The research plant was so far from Hoboken that Otto decided to move the family to Long Island where he would have a decent commute. Of course, Mary, Tilda and her little daughter Norli went along. They couldn't make it without him and he couldn't afford to set them up in their own quarters. Eager to move up the ladder, Otto poured himself into the business and in no time at all had developed a process for making cashmere, that luxury leader of the woolen trade. A patent was taken out by Strausser & Eineiger and the partnership was reorganized to include Otto among the partners. But Otto, who spoke no English when he arrived in the United States, was handicapped in legal matters. He did not realize that the new contract with the company excluded his widow from sharing in the income the company would derive from his patent should he die and leave his family without income. When Otto did die a decade later, Dita was left with only the life insurance money that came to her at his death and the social security benefits for the children.

When the United States entered the war, Dita joined the Red Cross with her friend Lisl Scadron, and wore her uniform with pride. She was an ambulance driver, a job for which there was little call in Forest Hills, Long Island, but she looked marvelous in her Sam Brown belt, her Overseas cap, and her military style single breasted jacket with brass buttons. An oil portrait of her so attired hangs in her Rossmoor home today. Her children were in school, and she was far too active a woman to spend her days at a bridge table even if she had learned the game. She became involved in the PTA, the Girl Scouts, in various charities, and most of the cultural auxiliary groups in their community. To all appearances, life was serene and secure again. But the fear aroused and imbedded in her subconscious during the wild days of their escape was always there waiting to pounce. Every day, when Otto left for work, the old anxious gnawing premonition of danger was in the pit of her stomach. If one of the children came down with a fever she found herself holding her breath, afraid it was more serious than it was. She hovered over the sick bed of any member of the family who was ill until she was sure that person was on the mend. She could never take life for granted again, never.

The war years slipped past like a dream. The fighting ended, and after one wild burst of tumultuous joy, America went back to its peacetime pursuits. Affluence such as the country had never known filled the land. God seemed to have returned to his heaven and all seemed to be righting itself in the world. But in 1950, Dita's wonderful new world came crashing down around her ears. After only eleven years in the United States Otto developed a brain tumor and before she could get used to the fact that she *might* lose him, he was gone. She was inconsolable. They had been through so much together. Never had Otto failed to support her through whatever she had to face. Her whole life had been woven around him. How could she go on alone? The big house had to go. Expenses had to be cut back, way back. And with only the insurance money and Social Security payments for the children in her pocket, Dita had to go to work to help support the family. Tilda and Norli had gone out on their own several years before, but there was still her mother as well as her children for whom she was now responsible.

They moved to a smaller place on Long Island so the girls could stay in their school. Her mother kept house and Dita found work as a medical technician in the hospital where Otto had died. While in Paris, Dita had toyed with the idea of becoming a doctor and had taken three terms of pre-medicine at the Sorbonne. Now it paid off. She had enough education to pass the qualifying exams for the kind of work she was employed to do. She liked the hospital environment, and her salary, added to the government checks for the children that came as promptly as the months rolled around, made ends meet. Fear of failure subsided. The only trouble was that there were too many long hours in the evening when she felt the loneliness of widowhood. She missed Otto's presence in the house at night. She missed his bringing in the news of the world when he came home after work. She missed him in her bed.

She took a second job. Dita makes friends easily and she had become friends with the head of the microbiology department at the hospital, a female doctor who had an independent evening practice of her own. Dita became the receptionist in her evening office. Medical technician by day, receptionist at night, she was burning her candle at both ends.

At least she was too tired to think about what ate away at her all the time. Her hours with the girls were limited to waking up time in the mornings and weekends. She knew she was missing some of the best days of their adolescence but it couldn't be helped. Under this rigid scheduling life was workable even if it was flat and incomplete. Months went by in which she was too busy to allow herself to even be aware that down underneath she was becoming restless again.

While Otto still lived, they met a couple in their neighborhood named Dalton, a couple who were having serious marital problems. Otto liked the Daltons and so did Dita. From time to time they ate together or stopped to gossip when they ran into each other in the shopping mall. They saw enough of them to have some sense of what was going on. They talked about their neighbor's problems like all neighbors do, but they didn't allow themselves to become entangled in them. They were friendly,but they had no intention of becoming involved in their messy situation. Just as Otto was dying, the Daltons began a long court battle over a property settlement preparatory to obtaining a divorce. Mrs. Dalton had found someone else to love whom she wanted to marry. In his pain Ernest Dalton turned to freshly widowed, lonely Dita for comfort. He would invite her out for dinner, then pour his troubles all over her throughout the meal. Or he would drop by after she came home from work and pour them out again all over her living room. Dita didn't mind, Ernest's troubles were a welcome diversion from her own. Soon they began "seeing each other" for the sake of seeing each other, not merely for the purging of his grief and wounded ego.

Ernest Dalton was a romantic man, a man who hated being alone. Dita might be less romantic, but she too couldn't abide singlehood. He began to fill his days and nights with romantic visions of Dita, while on her side, Dita was ripe for the kind of attention Ernest was showering upon her. The fact that Ernest was still married rankled, for his protestations of love seemed presumptuous in the face of that safe barrier. Frustrated by what she considered to be an impossible situation, she left town. She took a vacation and boarded ship for Britain where her old friend Louise now lived. Eight days after she arrived in London she received a cablegram from Ernest proposing marriage. He was free at last, his divorce papers had come through. He urged her to come home immediately. Dita packed her bags and flew back the next day. Her friends told her she was crazy, absolutely crazy.

"One year," they said, "and you'll be a widow again. Dita, the man has already had a series of heart attacks. What do you want? To have to go through this all over again?"

Dita can be obstinate, she refused to listen. "I'll take the risk," she declared, tossing her head. "One year of happiness with a man you love is worth whatever follows."

Dita and Ernest were married 22 years, and during those 22 years Ernest had eight more heart attacks. The fourth heart attack was so severe it forced him to give up his coffee import business and retire. His health began to decline after that until at last he was on oxygen, dragging a little gray tank behind him wherever they went. Dita decided it was time for them to give up the house and move to a more friendly climate. Both Peggy and Vivian were living with their families out in California, Vivian in Tiburon and Peggy in Hillsborough. Dita had been to Berkeley where they first lived many times to visit, most often without Ernest for whom travel had become too difficult. She and Ernest decided that if they were going to relocate they should go out there where they could be near the girls. Leaving Ernest in Tilda's care Dita came to the Bay Area to have a look around. Through a network of relatives and friends she was put in touch with Ilse and Wim Schiff in San Francisco. Ilse and Wim, who took a shine to Dita as soon as they met her, took her around to look at many locations, but they pushed Rossmoor where they had a weekend place. Dita weighed everything in her mind, all the pros and cons of each locale as she saw them, always asking herself how they would fit Ernest's limited range of activities. Rossmoor would do, she decided, if Ernest was as pleased with the environment as she was. Returning to Long Island with all the pictured brochures about Rossmoor that were available and floor plans from their sales office she presented him with enough data to override any objections he might raise about not knowing enough to make such a decision.

The day after Dita returned, Ernest called Peggy and her husband, Fred, and told them to buy one of those manors for them, whichever one would be available first. Peggy and Fred chose the unit, Ernest sent the money. The Daltons moved to Rossmoor in 1973. It was pouring rain the day they unloaded their furniture and there had been no rainy pictures in any of the literature. Nevertheless, Ernest loved the community. In 1974, one year after coming to California, Ernest had one heart attack too many, and Dita was widowed for the second time. In her grief she sent for Tilda to come out to console her.

"I'll stay a month," soothed Tilda. "Mother can watch over Walter that long by herself. But then I have to get back."

"What I need," Dita cried when Tilda arrived, "what would make my world complete again would be to have my sister near me. Go home and get Walter and come on out. Why do you stay back there in all that weather? Come on out and let's be a family again!"

Tilda went home but before they could come out, Walter's illness took a drastic turn for the worse. Operated on over a year before for brain tumor, the doctors had given him ten years to live. Walter didn't live a year. Now Tilda, was buried under the business of closing out his life in Connecticut. Left on her own, Dita buried her grief over Ernest's death in activity, any kind of activity that would keep her distracted. She resolved she would never marry again, never. Two men had loved her very much, and she had lost them both. That was that. She buried herself in Rossmoor affairs, she corresponded with friends she'd neglected, she spent hours with her mother who came out in Tilda's stead. How long she might have kept up her frantic pace is a guess, for a friend from New York unwittingly interrupted her life. She dropped Dita a note telling her that a couple of dear friends were looking for a place to retire away from New York, and she had recommended Rossmoor. Would Dita please show them the community?

Characteristically, Dita graciously invited Mr. & Mrs. Edward Von Westerborg for lunch. She extolled the quality of life in Rossmoor, she told them of her activities, she described her many friends, she made much of Ernest's joy in being there, she became eloquent about the congenial ambiance of the place, and along with her sales pitch for Rossmoor some impulse made her add a long discourse on her determination never to marry again.

"Never in a million years!" she declared dramatically. "Never."

The Von Westerborgs did or did not believe that she would never marry again, but they did believe that Rossmoor was an exceptional community. They bought a manor up the hill from Dita, then left for a short vacation in Hawaii. Tan and relaxed, they went back to New York to sell their house and ship their things. Their furniture made it to California in good shape, but their own trip was filled with tragedy. As the von Westerborgs were enroute to the west coast by car, their only son piloted his plane into the Bermuda Triangle and was never heard of again. Before they could recover from that loss, their only daughter, age 53, died of lung cancer. If that wasn't enough, three weeks after the daughter's death, Mrs. Von

Westerborg collapsed with a heart attack and died. Within the space of three months, Ed von Westerborg had lost his entire family. Lost, bewildered, he huddled in his unfamiliar "manor" alone with his grief. He had nothing to do. He had sold his publishing firm back east before coming out to California so he had no work to fall back on.

He was as totally alone among strangers. He belonged to no organizations, he had no friends in this community where life had stranded him. Dita's big heart took him in. She consoled him, cooked for him, took him around with her, and as soon as she thought it was appropriate, she began introducing him to every eligible woman she knew. She invited widows near his age for dinner, and she kept the conversation going all evening. When he took a trip back east, she gave him names of friends in Chicago and New York whom she urged him to contact. He didn't contact any of them. Ed had already made up his mind about a woman for his life. If he was going to remarry it was Dita he wanted, no one else.

Dita tried to stick to her avowed intentions, insisting that she was not interested in another marriage. She tried to talk him out of it, and wound up talking herself into it. Ed had a wonderful sense of humor, he was good company, he was clever with tools, he was imaginative with words, and he played a good game of golf. When he proposed that he keep his place up the hill so that he could retire there every day to work and leave her time free for the activities she had enjoyed since Ernest's death, Dita capitulated. She was seventy when they were married, he was a decade older. In 1989 Ed died at the age of ninety, and at last Dita made her peace with being alone. Vivian is dead, but Peggy comes once a week to spend the afternoon and showers her with gifts of orchids and books. She is the reigning queen of scrabble, playing the game in three languages, and no one beats her. She has her Tuesday morning French group, which she organized, From her living room window she can look out at Mount Diablo and she spends hours sitting in her chair with the mountain for inspiration as she keeps up her voluminous correspondence. At 93, she is still chic, charming, gregarious, and playful. Tilda is gone but Walter and Ilse live just down the hill and her circle of friends is made up of people of all ages. As always, her life sparkles as much as she has the energy to handle.

TILDA

Stasch took her to Vienna from Reichenberg and dumped her at her mother's. No "by your leave" about it. The new job he had taken, he said, would require so much traveling that she and Norli would be alone too much. Her grandmother lived not too far away so she'd have plenty of family around even though she was separated from Dita. Humiliated, Tilda believed Stasch couldn't stand to live in the shadow of his new brother-in-law. Otto had tried to be his friend but Stasch was so stiff and formal with the older man, Otto could not win him over. The truth was that Stasch felt overshadowed by Otto, Dita, and a good part of the world. Tilda was chagrined by the abruptness with which they left Reichenberg and unhappy about being thrust upon her mother, but what could she do? The timing could not have been worse. Unwittingly, Stasch had left his wife and child in the path of the Germans as they marched into Austria in March, 1938. Tilda's paternal grandmother whiffed the Nazis off with a wave of the hand.

"Poppinjays!" she snorted. "Like some Wagnerian opera!"

Mary Gelnay did not take the Boche so lightly and neither did Tilda. Tilda was so frightened she was reduced to hysterics. Poppinjay or not, Hitler meant business and she was convinced his business with the Jews of Germany would instantly spread to the Jews of Austria. All the German laws against Jews would be put into effect as soon as the Nazis had the gates closed and all Jews were corralled. She knew it! She knew it in her bones, and she was scared. She wanted out. Out of Austria, out of Hitler's reach, out of Europe! Norli had been home from school for days running a high fever but hysterically, Tilda threatened to pick her child up bodily and run just the same. It was a rather ludicrous idea considering little Tilda's diminutive size and Norli's long-legged eleven-year-old frame, but no one laughed. Tilda's fear suffocated them all. She tried all day Saturday after the tall barbarians marched in to get Stasch on the phone.

No one ever knew where to find him these days. The itineraries of his work week he left with her every time he came home were never accurate. He was a salesman, a traveling salesman with an appointed round, but when she tried to reach him at any of the places where his itinerary showed him to be, someone always told her that he was out, that they'd have to track him down. Tilda tracked Stasch down on her own this time, calling number after number, checking off one town after another, praying fervently each time she dialed the phone that this call would be it. If anyone promised to find him for her she hung up. She didn't have time to wait. She didn't trust anyone to get on with the search for an elusive salesman on a Saturday afternoon. Finally, after hours of nerve-wracking futility, Stasch's voice was on the other end of the line.

"Stasch, you have to come right now and get us!" she shouted as though the telephone service had been crippled by the Nazi invasion, "I won't sleep another night in Austria, I won't!"

"Whoa! Whoa! Hold up! Why the panic? What's the matter?" he asked.

"Why the panic?" she cried. "What's the matter with you, Stasch? Don't you pay any attention to anything going on anywhere in the world except in your account books? The Germans are here! They marched in this morning and they're taking over the city!!"

"Tilda, I know." His tone was level and his words deliberate like someone patiently dealing with a distraught child. "I heard it on the wireless. But what does that have to do with you not sleeping another night in Austria?"

His question was like kerosene on a fire. "Your wife and your child are here right under the noses of the Nazis and you don't know why I won't stay?" By now she was practically shrieking. "Do you think they won't know that we're Jews, or that we're here?"

"They won't know tonight, Tilda. Now, calm down. Don't get so upset. They'll be weeks getting anything sorted out." He paused to give her time to take in what he was saying. "They've got bigger problems right now than finding out who's still in Vienna and who's Jewish. There's plenty of time to see what they're up to and then we can decide what we'll do. Until then, relax. Don't do anything rash that will call attention to yourself."

Tilda heard only what she considered a roadblock to her intentions. "Decide what we're going to do? I don't what you're going to do!" she cried angrily, "but I'm leaving and I'm taking

Norli with me. Tonight! Or tomorrow if I have to wait that long. Whatever they decide I won't be here to hear about it."

"Where will you go, Tilda?" A little edge of impatience crept into his voice which made her burst out in tears.

"I don't know,' she sobbed, "but I'm not staying here. I'll go to Prague."

She heard him sigh, and then there was a long pause which told her he was thinking. "All right, Tilda." he said at last. "I'll come as fast as I can get there."

Stasch came the next morning, the first full day of Nazi occupation, and found Tilda all packed ready to go. Mary stood silently aside as together they took their feverish daughter between them and headed for the railroad station. When they were inside the great vault of a building Stasch set down their bags. "Wait here," he told Tilda, nodding toward a bench in the waiting room, "I'll go buy the tickets."

Tilda sat nervously on the edge of the bench her hands twisted together in her lap. The waiting room was full of Nazi uniforms, and every time one came within fifty feet of her she clutched her purse and turned her eyes toward the ornate ceiling. Norli lay stretched out on the bench in a feverish half sleep. Her fever was still far too high. She ought to be in bed, bundled up against the chill of March. Instead she was running like a fugitive with her mother out of the present into a fearful future. Things were so chaotic railroad personnel were making no effort to determine who was buying tickets or who came and who went, Jews or gentiles. All anyone needed to get on a train headed out of Vienna in any direction was a valid passport and a ticket.

Stasch showed the trainman at the gate their tickets and passports as they walked casually around him as if they were making a routine business trip out to the countryside. All the way down the platform, Tilda's heart beat so wildly she was sure the other passengers could hear it thumping like the boom of a bass drum.

Once they were safely aboard, and once the train began to move, she took a deep breath and sighed a long sigh. Caught up completely in her own fear she'd paid no attention at all to Stasch's reactions to anything. Now she turned to gaze at him. Usually loquacious he'd had almost nothing to say from the moment he arrived in Vienna until now. Tilda had talked enough to fill the airwaves that surrounded them until this moment. She was startled by the strange detached look on his face. It was as though something in him had been suspended. As though the action had been stopped on a film in which he had a role to play and the image on the screen was frozen there. Someone needed to set the reel in motion again.

Surprised and alarmed anew, she sat silently staring at him. Catching her gaze, he moved slightly and smiled a bleak little smile. Then he winked at her. That wink, something he did playfully when things were good between them, threw her off. The rest of his face did not reflect the action. She could think of nothing to say and he was speechless. They rode in silence for some time as the miles flashed past the train window. Keeping her eyes fixed on his expressionless face she pondered his aloofness, his distance and his silence. Then he stirred in his seat and said abruptly, "I'm getting off at Bruen. I think I can do some business here before getting back on schedule. You and Norli can manage without me from here to Prague. You're safe now."

She couldn't believe her ears. "Business? At a time like this?" She sat back and looked at him in amazement. If that wasn't just like her father!

"Business!" she exploded, leaning across the space between them as they sat facing each other. "What kind of business is so important you can't take your own wife and daughter to find a place to live? Where are we to stay in Prague? How will you find us? What are we supposed to do?"

"Tilda," he interrupted her as she kept on repeating "Business?" over and over again, "you'll have no difficulty finding a place to stay. Go to some of the places we've been before. Just take a taxi and choose which place you'd like. Then you can drop me a note, or leave word with your mother and I'll be able to find you." Stasch looked at her as a soberness so unlike him filled his eyes and was reflected in his voice. "Tilda, we have to eat every day, not just the days it's convenient for you for me to work. You're safe. You don't have to change trains. You have plenty of money. I came when you called, now I have to go back to work."

She felt lectured, punctured, reprimanded. Tears welled up behind her eyes but she was determined not to cry. If he wanted to abandon her that was up to him, she wasn't going to beg. The train slowed down for the little village just inside the border of Czechoslovakia and Stasch reached up to the rack overhead for his bag. Then he moved out into the aisle as the train came to a halt. Quickly he bent down to kiss them both, a little peck on the cheek of each. "Take care of Mama for me. Make her believe how much I love her" he told Norli reaching across Tilda to ruffle the child's hair. Then without looking back he was gone.

Was Stasch already part of the Underground? Had much of the persistent travel that had kept him away from home for weeks at a time all this past year had been about this Hitler? Tilda knew nothing about an underground. She didn't even know one existed. Even if she had known she wouldn't have dreamed that Stasch, fun loving Stasch who clowned around with other men and spent money much too freely, could be involved in secrets and plots and espionage, wearing the uniform of a German general. With his blond hair and blue eyes he could easily pass. Though born in Krakow, Stasch spoke German fluently and without a noticeable accent. Thinking this to be one more example of Stasch's unpredictability Tilda cuddled Norli against her inwardly fuming, feeling utterly abandoned and unloved.

Once in Prague, it was a simple matter to find a good pension, she knew Prague well. She unpacked, settled Norli into bed trying to keep her fears in check until the child fell asleep, and then she hysterically called Dita and Otto in Reichenberg.

"I'm going to immigrate" she wailed over long distance. "I'm going to get out!"

"Where are you?" demanded Otto.

"I'm in Prague! I made Stasch come and get me out of Vienna. Mama is still there and Grandmama wouldn't come!"

Otto didn't question the wisdom of anything. He knew Tilda and he'd been following the radio broadcasts all day switching from one station to another. "Where in Prague." he demanded.

Tilda gave him the address of the pension.

"Stay right there. Don't go out. Let the porter run any errands you need. We'll come as soon as we can." he told her sternly.

They came, as late as it was, and by the time they arrived Tilda had worked herself up into incoherence. She threw herself at them babbling about Stasch's indifference, about her mother trapped in Vienna, about the old grandmother who said she wouldn't be driven out of her home by a bunch of rough-necks drunk on power, about how scared she was, about where she would go. Patiently, her brother-in-law listened as he sat her down and seated himself before her. He held her hands in his while Dita dabbed at her red, swollen eyes and put a cold cloth on her forehead. When she was quiet enough to hear, Otto began to talk.

"It will never happen here, Tilda," he said soothingly. "Hitler will never come here. You are safe now. Stasch is right, life has to go on. We'll get Mama and Grandmama out of Vienna and the four of you can live in Prague in comfort. There's no reason for you to immigrate. You have us. We'll see that you have everything you need. You're all right." He rubbed the backs of her hands with his thumbs as he spoke, trying to soothe her.

Tilda would not be soothed. She sobbed and the tears flowed as Dita shushed and Otto repeated what he had said over and over. Nothing helped. She refused to be persuaded that there could be safety for a Jew anywhere on the continent of Europe. They talked long into the night, and when Dita and Otto were convinced that gentle little Tilda was intractable this time, that she was going to leave Europe no matter what anyone said, they began to explore possibilities with her.

"Australia! That's the place. We'll go to Australia," she declared. "The country is nearly empty. They'll have room for us."

"But Australia won't take in a woman with a child. They want men who can work the land." argued Otto. "Don't think about Australia. Think about America! You can go to America, you were born there."

"But I didn't fill out the paper," she wailed. "I should have but I didn't. I never thought I'd care." When she was 21 she should have filled out papers requesting dual citizenship, for that option was hers, having been born in the United States, but she had failed to do it. Now she was Czech, and she was Austrian, she'd lost her American citizenship by default.

"Don't worry about it." Otto said sternly, weary of the tears and lamentations. "The Americans will let you fill out the papers now I'm sure. They may not be willing to get involved in the politics and wars of Europe but they're sympathetic to the plight of Americans trapped anywhere, and you have a right to American citizenship. They won't have to bend the rules to let you in. Go on down to the Embassy tomorrow and find out how you can rectify the mistake. Make sure they know you never intended to give up your American citizenship, that it was just an oversight on your part."

Light was breaking over the castle above the city when Otto and Dita climbed wearily into their car and ordered the chauffeur to take them home. Otto had been talking to himself as well as to Tilda all night and he knew it. What did this takeover of Austria mean for Czechoslovakia? He was too tired to solve riddles right now, riddles that were being analyzed all over Czechoslovakia at every level of society, and by persons with more expertise in foreign affairs than he had. The newscasts had been full of speculation. He put his head back against the deep upholstery and went to sleep. Tilda went the very next day to the American Embassy. Thank God, she thought, if they gave her an American passport there were plenty of relatives in the United States to send affidavits. When she walked into the Embassy offices everything was in an uproar. People were coming and going, telephones were ringing, clerks were frantically trying to process all the requests coming from the press of people who shared Tilda's sense of urgency. When she finally got in to see the ambassador, having refused to talk to a lesser being, to her great relief he was reassuring.

"I'll tell you what the rules are," he said. "You have lost your citizenship by not filing for it when it came up, but I think we can almost guarantee that you'll get reinstated without any problem. It should be an easy matter. I'll send your papers to Washington and when they see that you were born in New York I'm sure they'll give you a passport. There's just one hitch though, your child will not be able to go with you except on a visitor's visa. When you gave up your citizenship before she was born you deprived her of any claim on the U.S. government."

Tilda caught her breath and stared blankly at him for a full minute before she recovered. "However I have to take her I'll take her. She doesn't stay behind, she goes with me."

The whole experience at the embassy convinced her even more that she had to move out of Hitler's reach as quickly as possible. All those Jews desperately pleading for visas couldn't be wrong. They must feel the way she did, that any place in Europe was a dangerous place. Nothing Otto said about

Czechoslovakia not being Austria carried half the weight with her as did the desperate tension she had seen and felt waiting in the lines at the American embassy that morning. She suspected Otto himself was not all that confident. In the days that followed, she became convinced that her brother-in-law was going through turmoil himself over what to do. He immediately sent his mother-in-law and the old grandmother word that they were to come to Prague, and he put Dita to work getting her own American passport reinstated. The old grandmother still would not leave Vienna, but Mary came when Otto insisted. She moved in with Tilda and Norli and her presence had a calming effect on her daughter. She was there when Walter arrived from Beirut, ready to cart both his mother and his grandmother off with him to safety in the Middle East, but no one was going.

"I should go out there and eat sand the rest of my days?" his mother asked indignantly. "I can't live with that man here, why would I go to live with him out there? No! I'm going to my sisters in America!"

"Well, I'm not going," Tilda tossed her head disdainfully. "I'm not going to go anywhere where I have to walk around with a rag over my face!"

Walter, who had no American birth to fall back on, had put himself in jeopardy for nothing. Without an exit visa which could get him across Austria, and without an American passport with which to obtain an exit visa his big problem was how was he to get out of Czechoslovakia himself. At that point Stasch showed up. Tilda laid out her plan to go to America before him, urging him to come with her. They could both go on her American passport once she had it. They'd told her so at the Embassy. He was her husband and he was as entitled to travel on his wife's passport as a wife was to travel on her husband's.

"Quit your job, Stasch. Please! Go see your folks and say good-bye. We can be free in America!"

"I'm free right here, Tilda." he argued. "I won't tell you not to go. Go ahead if you'll be happier there. But I'm not going. What would I do? How would I be able to support you? I don't speak the language, I don't know how to do anything but sell and you can't sell stocks and bonds to people you can't talk to. Maybe it's a good idea for you to go over there until you're convinced that this is a safe place to be. You can always come back!"

"But I want you to come with me" she wailed. "Why won't you go? I don't care what you say, you're not safe here."

"I'm not?" he queried. "Why do you persist in saying that? Is Otto going?"

"I don't know what Otto's going to do." she cried. "I know he told Dita to get her American passport reinstated. Maybe he's coming out too and maybe he's not. That's their business. But you're my business and I want you to come. Oh Stasch, what will I do without you?"

Gravely hunching his shoulders up under his ears he turned and with his hands thrust deep into his pockets went to lean against the window frame where he stared out at the street below. He was always peering out the window these days, pulling the curtains back just a fraction, peeking furtively at whatever was in his line of vision. What did he expect to see out there? Turning to face her, he folded his arms across his chest and leaned back against the wall. The sadness in his face hurt her. Unsmiling, he shook his head slowly but firmly in the negative

"I have a job here, Tilda. I make good money. There's a depression in America just like there is here. If I go over there I'll be a burden on your relatives and I'd hate that."

"I can't believe you, Stasch!" Tilda protested. "In America you'd be safe, job or no job. So you accept a meal or two until you find a job. Is that so terrible?"

"Let's do it this way," he finally said, "you go on before me and if you like it you can send me an affidavit and I'll come later. Maybe by that time I can learn something about how they do business in America."

"Business!" Tilda cried furiously. "What's business? We'll eat. We'll live! Come with me," she pleaded. "If you don't, I don't think I'll ever see you again."

They kept it up for hours with Tilda weeping and pleading while Stash remained unmoved. As sick at heart as she was at the idea of leaving him, she still couldn't bring herself to believe that they had nothing to fear, that their lives were not in danger. Stasch seemed resigned to their impasse and stopped protesting. He never said another word to discourage her. In fact, once he seemed to accept the idea that she was bent on going, he actually seemed relieved. That night, before going to bed he re packed his bag ready for departure and very early the next morning, just before dawn, he slipped quietly out of bed, dressed quickly and let himself out the door without ever lighting the light. She pretended to sleep, pretended she didn't know he was leaving because she didn't know how to say good-bye, but when he was gone she wept into her pillow. A few days later she went back to the embassy. At the embassy there had been no progress. Nothing had come through from the United States Again she was told that the process was not simple, that such things took time.

"The government is working as fast as it can," the young clerk waved his hand toward the clusters of people around every desk, "but there are so many of you it will take weeks. Washington, D.C. is deluged. Not just from this embassy but from every embassy in Europe. Even the English! It will be awhile, Mrs. Eisner. It can't be helped."

"Awhile?" To Tilda every hour was "awhile." She made up her mind to go to Paris and wait there for her applications to be approved. She had a Czech passport that would get her that far and she was as eligible for American citizenship in one capitol as another. In Paris, she had a cousin who owned a very exclusive lingerie shop where she sold only hand-made brassieres, slips, girdles and nightgowns. Tilda was sure her cousin would take her under her wing and somehow provide for her. Without waiting any longer for the passport to come through, brushing aside all objections from her mother or her sister, she and Norli left Prague within the week. Stasch came to be with them for the last two days and there was a final searing moment at the station when she pleaded again with him to go while there was still time, but it was a perfunctory performance on her part. She was numb inside. Years later she would learn that Stasch did have a hidden agenda, an unalterable rendezvous with fate. Her worst fears were solidly founded, she was saying Good-bye forever. Stasch couldn't come with her.

Tilda's nature was to mother, to take care of people. Tilda was little mother to the two younger children until they moved to Bratislava, but once they "took to the woods," she stopped being their little nanny and began to explore the possibilities of her own personality. She learned to sew. She learned to cook. She learned that she loved to be at home. She liked parties and dressing up. She loved making beautiful hats that she loved to wear. While Dita was out roaming the countryside with the boys, Tilda was happily engaged with the world in her lap. She took French lessons, piano lessons, ballroom dancing lessons, any lessons available in Bratislava to prepare her to be a social success once they were back in Vienna. But she took no lessons that would prepare her for the day when she desperately needed to know how to do something to earn a living.

She was seventeen when they returned to Vienna in 1920, too old for gymnasium. She was regarded as a "young woman", and a young woman from a substantial family had no need for a University Education. Adolph Gelnay would never have been able to see the wisdom of preparing girls for work, they were to be prepared for society. Tilda's dreams of the future were all romantic fantasies in which she was found by the handsome prince who climbed the vine that led up to her turret and carried her away with him. Her life was full of parties and friends and good times, and on the whole she was happy. When she was eighteen she met a prince, an older man who seemed to love her as ardently as any fantasy Prince Charming could. His experience and her naiveté were a perfect combination to create illusions. Her parents were not romantics and they did not share her enthusiasm for this man. His inability to tell the truth infuriated them to the point where they finally set a trap for him and forced Tilda to see him for what he was. She broke off her engagement to him, but her heart was broken in the process.

She was left with only boys her own age with whom to dance and to play. The custom in Europe was for women to marry older men but her flirtations were now restricted to the group of young people she and Dita were thrown with. No Prince Charming was likely to come her way again. Or so she thought. Broken hearts are one of the easiest of all maladies to survive. All you need is a replacement part, a new face, a new voice, a new vibration and when you're only nineteen replacements turn up frequently. She found one within six months of her tragic farewell scene. He was an old friend, Stanislaus Eisner, someone she'd known for years. Stasch, they called him. Stasch was a little older than Tilda but not enough older to be glamorous. He was a funny old shoe of a friend who made her laugh, but she never thought of him romantically. However Stasch thought about her along those lines and had for some time. He was shrewd enough to know that she was ready for a shoulder to cry on, ripe for the plucking. If he loaned her his shoulder for weeping she might discover it could also be a good shoulder to snuggle into. Stasch never made her laugh more heartily than when he declared that he was her fate.

"Go away," she chortled, and shoved him out the door. "Never in a million years." The Gelnay girls measured time in grand sweeps.

She thought he was kidding, so when they drifted into being a twosome at all the parties and picnics she never gave it a thought that they were drifting into more. Stasch spent happy evenings at the Gelnays. He liked her parents and they liked him. Sometimes the two young people went alone to the movies playing at the theater her father owned. It was happening almost behind her back, this attachment Stasch was planning. She was twenty when they became engaged. Stasch was three years older. He was a bright young man, restless, energetic and romantic. In short, except that Stasch had a lovely disposition, he was more like her father than Walter was. They became engaged in 1923 and in 1926, when he was financially secure enough to please her father, they were married. Nine months later their only child was born. Tilda hadn't wanted a baby so soon but she didn't know how to prevent it. She thought of aborting but nineteen-year-old Dita was absolutely opposed to the idea. She pleaded with her not to do it and Tilda was never been able to stand up to Dita.

"Don't Tilda, don't do it. I'll work, I'll help support it. Please don't do it."

Dita overrode her and Norli was born. The course of Tilda's life was set. She was to be a wife, a mother and a nest maker. Wherever Stasch put her down she made a home for them even if he wasn't in it very much. Her husband's search for the perfect job took them many places within Austria and Czechoslovakia. One of his short-lived jobs had taken them to live in Reichenberg. That job required lots of traveling and in his travels, earlier than most, Stasch became aware of the intensity and fiendish design of the Nazis' intended Jewish pogrom which went far beyond anything the Jews had ever experienced in Russia. The Nazis' projected plan for the Jews was far more sinister than mere uprooting. Soon Stasch was away for longer periods of time, he was less playful when he was around, he was lost in thought for hours on end. Tilda had Dita to put sparkle in her life so she hadn't noticed then, but in looking back over those years Tilda felt like the parade passed her by when she let Stasch take her to Reichenberg from Prague.

In Paris, she found a room in a pension near her cousin's shop for herself and Norli. Her cousin gave her a job as an apprentice corsetierre and she learned to make girdles and brassieres. Because of her long experience with a needle she mastered the art very quickly. Soon she was putting lovely piping and embroidery on the exquisite garments custom ordered by her cousin's clientele, while Norli sat beside her making miniatures of her mother's creations. Tilda was delighted with herself. When she got to the United States she'd be able to earn a living doing this, maybe. Maybe she could even open a shop of her own some day like this one. She made a complete line of samples to take with her. While her fingers flew over the work in hand her mind errantly focused on America. She knew that all her daydreaming about America was her way of not thinking about Stasch, but it was too painful to think about Stasch. She wanted to blot out the memory of the sad, enigmatic look in his eyes that last day at the Prague Railway Station. They had stood with their arms around each other, Norli tucked between them, and looked long into each other's eyes as though trying to faithfully record in memory every emotion reflected there. But she hadn't been able to read his emotions. Sadness was all she could see in his face. Without fail, she wrote to him every night and posted the missive every morning, but his letters came to her in batches mailed from here or there or somewhere else. Some reached Paris in three days, some in three weeks. But never did he mention joining her. She gave up asking.

Aside from working at the lingerie shop, she spent much time badgering the American Embassy in Paris. She'd had her paperwork transferred from Prague to Paris and was now hounding the French for news they couldn't supply. American identification was a handy thing to have but a bona fide passport was better. She became so well acquainted with some of the clerks at the embassy that they greeted her by name when she came in. It was six months before the precious papers arrived. The moment they came she wrote joyfully to Stasch,

"We can go to America now. I have the affidavits from New Jersey and I am now once more a proud American citizen. I can take you with me to America."

His answer was the same as it had always been. "When you have a job for me in the United states I'll come."

So far as she knew Stasch was still in Prague with Walter when, on a wet December day in 1938, she took Norli by the hand and boarded a ship headed for her relatives in New Jersey. She was on her way to an uncertain future but one she anticipated with great hope. Behind her, like a great black sorrow that could engulf her at any time, was a husband for whom she was beginning to grieve as though he was dead. Her mind became a battleground for these two disparate forces: hope and grief. In spite of all that, when she didn't fall into the trap of dwelling on Stasch and the world she'd left behind, she felt ten pounds lighter knowing that she and her child, her sister and her mother had all escaped. Her mother was already in America and by phone from Paris she'd learned that Dita was out of Hitler's reach in Holland. All of the members of the various families they'd left behind them, except Walter and Stasch, thought they were mad to go, but mad or not, the path into the future looked bright to optimistic little Tilda.

On the boat, a customs' inspector, checking the luggage of all passengers, found her little bundle of samples.

"What's this?" he demanded.

"Those are samples," Tilda said proudly, "I'm a corsetierre."

"Samples?" he said, "If they're samples we'll make sure you can't sell them" and with that he took his scissors and cut a swath into every piece. "Here," he said, " now they are really samples." Tilda took her precious work back to her bunk and cried. Her first encounter with the unbending American law was crushing.

All of Mary Gelnay's brothers and sisters had remained in America, had established themselves and raised their families. Of the nine children she was the only one who had turned back to the Old World. Every one of them had been glad to send affidavits, but it was her sister in Washington, D.C. who also offered shelter when she arrived in the summer of 1938. In Pleasantdale, New Jersey near Newark, Mary had another sister who operated a summer resort. She had no children of her own and when Tilda arrived at the end of that year she invited Tilda and Norli to come to live with her. She needed help. Tilda could stay in a little servant's room near the kitchen and she could earn her keep at the resort until she found other work to do. There was no way she could find other work for her days were filled with what her Aunt expected of her in return for a miserable little room, adequate food, and no school for Norli. Tiny little Tilda, just barely five feet tall, staggered under the heavy trays of food and dirty dishes that she had to carry to and from the dining room. Norli was put to work assisting in the kitchen or folding napkins and table cloths. Norli was quick at fetching and carrying, and fetch and carry she did. Life at that resort was miserable for them both. They not only were the poor starving relatives thrust into the chimney corner, but they were made to feel like it.

All through January and well into February this state of affairs continued, then Dita and Otto arrived. The Strasses immediately rented a big house in East Orange, New Jersey, and gathered the whole family under one roof, Mary, Tilda and Norli, plus the four of them. Their ties to the Aunt in Pleasantdale were forever frayed by those months of drudgery. Otto was out of work, Tilda was now also out of work, and Mary was too old to get a job. With two small children Dita was exempt from the workplace. Her major assignment she felt was the keeper of the diaper pail. It was up to Otto and Tilda to bring in the money. One of their cousins had a very nice dress shop in East Orange which drew in a wealthy clientele. Tilda turned to her. The cousin put her to work making girdles and Tilda's Paris designs were an immediate success. She began making custom things so exquisite she always had a backlog of orders. The accolades were heady but the pay was too small to be anything more than auxiliary income to the household. Certainly it was not enough for her and Norli to go out on their own.

Otto's search for work landed him in New York City. The commute was impossible. He and Dita decided to move the family to Long Island. Since Tilda couldn't survive on her scant income, without the shelter Dita and Otto provided, she and Norli would be out on the streets if they didn't move to Long Island with the rest of the family. She gave up her job and went with them which made her feel like she was totally engrafted on her sister and brother-in-law again, a situation she detested. No one ever made her feel like she was a burden, but she knew how hard Otto was struggling. At night she lay awake mulling over how she and Norli could make it on their own, to be a family in their own right. Dita's pediatrician needed an au-pair for his children so Norli, who was not yet twelve, went to work as companion to his children. She had to live with the family and go to school along with her charges. After school her life belonged to them. From the moment they all returned in the afternoon until the Doctor's children were in bed for the night Norli was their "Nanny." Tilda agreed to this when she thought she'd have work within a few weeks and they could move out on their own but a whole year went by before Tilda could get her head above water enough to allow Norli to quit and come home to be a child again. It was Norli's second job before she was even a teen-ager.

Of all the things that had happened to her since she and her mother fled the security of her Grandmother's home in Vienna, that year with the doctor's family was the most psychologically damaging of all. Norli felt set aside, unimportant, disposable. In the doctor's household she was treated like a servant at a time in her life when she needed all the love and nurturing she could get. Once Tilda went to work again, Norli came back to Dita's and took care of her Aunt's two small tikes after school, but at least once dinner was on the table her chores ended. Norli was a full member of a family here. and there was plenty of love and acceptance. Tilda had a job in a little dress shop in Brooklyn which meant taking the subway to and from Forest Hills every day, seeing little of Norli except on weekends, still beholden to her brother-in-law for their shelter and to her mother for child care. Life was emotionally exhausting and humiliating in spite of protestations from Otto and Dita that they felt enriched by her presence. Over and over they told her that they were all in this together, that she should quit fretting about things for which none of them had solutions. She believed them, but she longed to have a home of her own.

Dita's sensitivity to Tilda's plight made her look around for something more remunerative for her sister to do than sewing in a girdle shop. In her salad days in Paris she had acquired two friends, twins, daughters of great wealth whose family had left France as soon as Hitler came to power in Germany bringing all their money out with them. One of the twins, Lisl Scadron, lived in Forest Hills near the Strass-

Eisner-Gelnay household. An energetic woman endowed with tremendous mental drive, Lisl Scadron hated housework, she found her greatest joy in organizational activities of all kinds. The other twin, Trudy Jarno, lived in Arlington, Vt. Trudy was the philosophical twin, someone who communed with the world around her. Both of them sought leadership roles in community affairs. Trudy had need of a housekeeper for one month in the fall of 1939. The girl she'd had, had gone back to Europe when the war broke out in September and the girl she was to have, would not arrive for another 30 days. She called Dita to see if Dita knew where she could find help for such a short time. Dita turned to Tilda.

"Why don't you leave that awful job of yours and go to Trudy's for a month." she said. "She needs you and you need a vacation. Something else will turn up before the month is out. I guarantee it. It's beautiful up there in Vermont and you deserve a break. School's started. Norli will be all right here with me and mother."

Tilda's job was indeed awful. She didn't need much urging to get her to leave Norli to help Dita as she went to Trudy's. It was more like going on vacation than taking a job. In Vermont she and Trudy had a wonderful time together. The trees were breathtaking in the riotous color of their foliage, and since Trudy loved to wander about the little villages of New England scuffling through the fallen leaves browsing away an afternoon with Tilda in tow it was a heavenly respite. Tilda dreaded the arrival of the new housekeeper but the hand of fate was at work while Tilda reveled in her lovely interlude. Back on Long Island, Lisl became an ambulance driver for the Red Cross. She'd been itching to do something for the war effort from the moment Hitler marched into Poland and England declared war. She loved being out and about in her uniform, attending meetings and planning Red Cross activities for overseas. Lisl could forget everything for a passion, whatever passion gripped her at the moment. The day-by-day life of a housewife had never held any appeal for her and at this juncture, when her war work filled her days, she longed to turn the full responsibility of the domestic scene over to someone else. She'd had a young girl from Vienna keeping her house and caring for her little boy, but the young girl was restless and yearned for city life. Just as Trudy's girl arrived from Europe, Lisl's girl gave notice. Dita saw another opportunity for Tilda. She now suggested to Lisl and Tilda that it would be a good arrangement for everyone concerned if Tilda went to the Scadrons to do for them what she had done for Trudy: keep the house, take care of Lisl's little boy, and become a part of the family. The only alternative Tilda had was going back to the dress shop in Brooklyn. Going to work for the Scadrons as housekeeper and surrogate mother was far more appealing than the long commute to Brooklyn, and it had the advantage that she could have Norli with her. They offered her the job and she grabbed it.

There were three floors to the Scadron house. The first floor was given over to the usual family rooms of any home, the second floor was where the Scadron family bedrooms were located, and on the third floor were two bedrooms and a bath that could be given over to Tilda and Norli as their private quarters in the house. It was perfect. Tilda took over with relish. She supervised the cleaning woman, the gardener and the cook. She was there for Lisl's little boy when he came home from school and wanted cookies and milk and someone to listen to him. She saw to it that Walter's cleaning went out on time and that the milkman, bread man, and every other delivery man fulfilled their appointed rounds on time. Otherwise, they heard from her by phone. She planned menus and served Lisl's overlapping committees cakes and coffee at the drop of a pin. She became indispensable to the family.

Her uppermost concern, however, was Norli's education which had been too long a matter of what she could get when she could get it. She wrote dozens of letters of inquiry to schools where her friends thought Norli could fit in and catch up for all the time she'd lost in their travails. But every school she contacted charged incredible tuition, tuition far beyond the salary she earned at the Scadrons. Finally, there was a letter from the Mother Superior of a convent in Scranton, Pa. who had been touched by her plea, a lovely letter inviting Norli to come to the convent at a very minimal cost. Norli had had no religious education - they never went to Temple, she never attended religious education classes, they were Jewish in name and cultural identification only - and all their Jewish friends warned Tilda that the Catholics would try to convert the lonely susceptible child if she turned her daughter over to them. Tilda thought long and hard about it but decided a good education was worth the risk.

"Promise me one thing," she told Norli, "When you go there, if they try to convert you, don't do it. If you feel that's the right thing and you want to do it, wait a while, wait for a year after you come out of the school, and then if you still want to do it I'll have no objection whatsoever."

No one tried to convert her. The nuns were wonderful to her. They went out of their way to tutor her and help her overcome her educational handicap, but the well-to-do Catholic girls with whom she lived made life miserable for the poor little Jew in their midst. Every month Tilda sent her a little money but she was still the poor child in the school. She was there for two long years. At the end of her second year, just when she seemed to have caught up with the other girls her age, she startled her mother by declaring that she did not want to return to the convent. As kind as the Nuns had been she didn't want to return to them, and what was more she didn't want to go to any other school either. What she wanted, she said, was to go to work. She was fourteen-years-old, and with parental permission in those days in the State of New York she could get a work permit which would allow her to go into light work such as retail selling.

Her uncle Otto told her that if she really wanted to work rather than go on with her education, that she should take the subway in to the City, get off at 57th St. and, starting at Bergdorf Goodman, go from one department store to the next right down Fifth Avenue and make application at every one of them. By now America was at war, help was in short supply, and he thought she just might pull it off. Tall for her age, and matured by life beyond the maturity of girls much older than she, she landed a job in the handbag and costume jewelry department at the very first stop - Bergdorf Goodman. She worked there for six years. When she was sixteen she began going to night school. Working days, studying on her one day off per week, going to school at night, she finished High School and continued on into college. The long train rides to NYC and back again to Forest Hills late at night gave her additional study time.

Once she and Norli were secure at the Scadrons, Tilda's letter writing increased. It had never been a matter of "out of sight, out of mind" where Stasch was concerned. Not in Paris and not in America had Tilda given up hope that she could get him to move across the Atlantic. She wrote letter after letter to the last known address she had for him pleading with him to use the affidavit she sent and come to her, but the rare letters she received before the outbreak of war in September, 1939 which closed the borders to mail going in either direction, continued to put her off. His reasons were always vague and frustrating. To Tilda none of his reasons seemed adequate, but he never offered fuller explanations nor did he explain why his letters were mailed from here and there, rarely from the same place twice. After the war in Europe broke out her letters were returned or simply vanished unanswered, but she never stopped writing. It was a whole year after the war was over before she had any verification of the fears that had haunted her for so long about what had been the true anchor that held him in Europe. He had joined the underground to resist the Nazis, and only when he became ill in the middle of the war did he attempt to make a dash for it. She was told that he succeeded in getting as far as England, then he disappeared. Passage had been booked for him on a liner to New York but he never showed up. It was as though a hole had opened in the earth and swallowed him. After seven years of silence she had him declared dead.

During five of the six years Norli worked at Bergdorf Goodman Tilda ran the Scadron house. No one could have gentle Tilda around for that long and not love her. Both Lisl and Walter came to think of her as one of their family. Walter Scadron came to her with his troubles as readily as did Lisl, or the child. It was an ideal arrangement and could have gone on indefinitely except for Tilda's desire to give Norli a home of her own. When Norli was nineteen Tilda decided it was not fair for her to continue to live in servant's quarters. She deserved a place where she could entertain young men and have more privacy. Tilda gave notice. The Scadrons were stunned.

"Please, don't leave us," they begged. "Don't leave us. Anything! We'll do anything! You're going to be outside in the rain. You're not used to it."

"Then I'll take an umbrella." Tilda said firmly. "My daughter is old enough to have young men call. She deserves a place to do it."

"You're going to sleep on a park bench." Walter threatened. "What are you going to do?"

"I'm not going to sleep on a park bench, I'm going to get a job. Don't worry about me."

There were tears and there were sleepless nights, it was scary. But she found a pleasant little house to rent not too far away, a nice sunny little house which she and Norli could call their own. Bloomingdale's opened up a store in Flushing Meadows, one of the modern small suburban branch stores that were springing up all over America in the late 1940's. It was a nice store, bright and lovely in decor, all cheery and new, and Tilda went to apply for a job.

"Oh, Mrs. Eisner," she was told," you're just what we're looking for, but you have no experience. We can't hire you without experience, it's company policy."

"But how do I get experience?" Tilda protested, "if no one will hire me?

"Why don't you go to a small shop and get some experience and then we can hire you," they told her. "Really, just a few months of experience some place else would be enough."

Disappointed but resolute, Tilda found a small lingerie shop in Forest Hills where she sat in a tight little corner doing alterations. She hated it, there was nothing creative about it, the customers carped and there was no elbow room in her workspace, but it was a job that kept her independent, and gave her "experience," and that meant everything. Her miserable job lasted only a few months for true to her word, one day Tilda came home to find a letter in the mail from the lady at Bloomingdale's. When she responded to the woman's request that she contact the store she was invited to come in to discuss a proposition Bloomingdale's had for her. The company had decided to add a corset department to the Flushing Meadow store and they wanted Tilda and two other widows to come in and create the department, even to the counters and dressing rooms. They told her that a buyer would come out from New York on a regular basis and the three of them could tell the buyer what lines they wanted the store to carry. Nothing they ever suggested was questioned.

Tilda loved the job. Being on her own and making a decent living without the aid of relatives or friends fed her ego. Norli no longer sold jewelry and bags at Bergdorf's, she was working for a dentist which gave her shorter hours, more time for study, and a sense of dignity she hadn't gotten from dealing with the public from behind the handbag counter. She was still going to night school but now she had some time to play too. She began to have friends, go to parties, meet people her own age and have beaux. Having a place of their own to which she could bring young people made all the difference in their outlook on life. Tilda and Norli were both happier than they'd been for over a decade. Then one night about 2:00 a.m. Norli opened the bedroom door and whispered into the dark,

"Mother, are you awake? George would like to talk to you."

George was a young cousin of the Scadrons Norli had known for years and someone she'd been seeing a lot of lately.

"Now!?" Tilda exclaimed. "Do you know what time it is?"

"Never mind the time," Norli whispered, "it's important."

Tilda threw on a robe and went in to the living room where George sat nervously on the edge of the couch. When Tilda came in he stood and began pacing the room while he talked. "I've got this wonderful opportunity to go to California to work for awhile." he said, "It's a super job and I want it very much."

"So, take the job!" said Tilda. "What does that have to do with me?"

"I want Norli to go with me," he said. "I don't want to leave her here in New York."

"No!" Tilda interrupted him. "It's out of the question. She will not go with you on a trip when she is not married to you. There's no point in discussing it."

Norli took up George's arguments about them being two adults but Tilda refused to listen.

"Consenting adults my eye," she snapped. "There's nothing adult about running around the country like two brats, unmarried. Norli's not going to California, and I am going to bed." With that she stalked into her bedroom and shut the door firmly.

George went off to California alone. No sooner did he arrive in Los Angeles than he called long distance. "Norli," he asked, "Where does the sun rise?"

"In the East, of course" she said in surprise.

"Well, that's where I'm headed" he said. "I can't be out here without you."

George came back and he and Norli announced they would be married in two days so that he could get back to

California and his assignment before the company gave it to someone else. This time he would take Norli with him. A wedding in two days!? How could it be done? Frantic, Tilda called Dita and together the Gelnay sisters were equal to the challenge. It was a small wedding held at Dita's but it was lovely. The bride and groom left immediately after the reception and went west for four months before returning to live in Forest Hills near all the relatives. They were there when family problems at the Scadron house boiled over. Lisl and Walter were getting a divorce. Lisl had flown the coop and there was no shooing her back in. She moved into their lovely lake home in Danbury, the Scadrons' "weekend place", leaving Walter to rattle around in the big house in Forest Hills alone.

Months of mourning went by before Walter regained his balance, months in which he monopolized Tilda's life, pouring out his sorrow over lovely dinners in fine restaurants, in walks through the park, over the phone several times a day. She found him waiting for her when she emerged from Bloomingdale's in the evening. He became a fixture. Then suddenly he decided he wanted to take a trip to Europe and he wanted Tilda to go with him. The shoe was on Tilda's other foot. This was Norli and George all over again.

"No!" she said firmly. "I don't want to go to Europe or anyplace else with you and us not married."

"Then marry me." he retorted.

Without a moment's hesitation she shot back "All right," daring him to retract his proposal, but he didn't.

As though it was pre-ordained, Tilda fell, almost literally fell, into marriage with Walter Scadron. They had no surprises for each other. It was like putting a marriage on over a comfortable old relationship. They had all the same friends, Walter's son loved Tilda and Norli loved Walter, Lisl was delighted for them, and so it was done. They went to Mexico on a honeymoon after which Tilda returned to the Forest Hills house as its mistress, not as a servant-guest. Tilda's mother came to live with them, and for sixteen beautiful years they divided their lives between travel and family activities. During those years they gave up the big house and moved to the lake place at Danbury when Lisl sold out to them. Mary Gelnay came to live with them when Dita and Ernest moved to California, and was with them still when Walter Scadron died.

Widowed again, Tilda closed out the house in Danbury and headed West. Taking their mother with her, she went to live on the same street down the hill from Dita in Rossmoor. Mary Gelnay died there years later, but while she lived she was the center of the family and always included in all of Tilda's activities. Friends of Tilda and Dita to this day refer to her as "Grandma." Walter came to Rossmoor to stay long after his mother was gone, but his coming brought the number of Gelnays in residence back up to three. Life had taken them on vastly different paths but they were assured there would be no more separations in the future.

SUZANNE

Under the dexterity of her long slender fingers the clay responded like living membrane, it seemed to draw energy from her touch. Suzanne's hands knew form as intuitively as waves curl when they touch the underlying ocean floor. Firm and supple, her fingers could produce graceful shapes in clay though her body had refused long ago to glide and leap and bend to the images of her imagination. Once she had danced to express the emotions for which there were no adequate words. Now lumps of gray clay were the means through which her creativity could find expression. Across the table from her Miriam was intent on her own piece of art. Her scientist's fingers, schooled in the use of fine instruments to do delicate work requiring the greatest precision and patience, grasped the scalpel-like tool with which she worked at the intricate design she was putting on a bowl. There was little conversation between them, a companionable silence had settled over their corner of the room.

Suzanne held the little figurine out at arm's length to gain perspective. Something in the stiffness of the pose made her flash back to the day she started to school in Budapest. She had held back rigidly like that forcing her mother to drag her along as they went to take the trolley cars from Pest where they lived to the hills of Buda where the "wonderful" new school stood. If this school was so wonderful Suzanne thought why wasn't her mother going instead of her? Rarely did Mama have a good idea and fight for it, and though she had fought hard for this one, Suzanne was certain it was not one of her better ones. She wanted to go to the public school where she could walk with her friends. Papa had thought that a capital idea. But no, Mama wanted this school for her and for once bested Papa.

Margaret Madaiy Zahler wanted the new school for her trying child. She refused to argue about it. Once you gave Suzanne an opening there was no end to the discussion. Margaret bit her lip and kept walking. The baby at home with the governess was as docile as this child was rebellious, and he was a boy. It was as though some mischievous force had switched personalities of her children. This Montessori School had to work. Her daughter must have choices later in life; she must never be forced to marry someone because there was nothing else she could do, and she must be independent enough to make up her own mind as to a mate if and when the time came to choose one. To make her independent, to give her what Margaret herself had not had, was what lay behind the bitter fight over the Montessori School. But she couldn't tell Michael any of that, the distance between them was greater with each passing year.

She hadn't loved Michael when she married him, and she didn't love him now. Her mother had chosen him, he had wooed her mother in order to get the beautiful shy daughter who didn't seem to enjoy his presence. No formal matchmaking had taken place, no yentel had been hired, no dowry had been provided, but she'd had nothing to say about the matter. Her mother had chosen her husband, like her grandmother had passed her mother off to a man she didn't want either. It was like a chain with links one couldn't break. How much further back it went than her grandmother she didn't know. Suzanne's grandmother had been forced by her mother to marry when she was eighteen, marry a man much older than she who had several children by a deceased first wife. Within nine months of becoming a step-mother, Suzanne's grandmother became a mother as well. The old man died within a few years leaving nothing but the restaurant from which he'd never been able to support such a large family. The young widow had worked hard, had kept them all together, and she'd made the restaurant pay. She curried favor with regular customers, she flattered people, and she was a good cook. It was a combination that worked. People came again and again to the widow's place, one of those people being Michael Zahler. He was handsome, he was charming, he was energetic and ambitious, and he was in love with the cook's daughter Margaret. So what if he was a Jew? Who cared?

"What in heaven's name do you want?!" Margaret's mother had shouted. "He's got no babies for you to raise. He'll give you a good home. He could have any girl he crooked a finger at. Don't stick your nose up at the likes of him, they don't come around very often."

"But I don't love him!" wailed Margaret. "I don't want to get in his bed."

"I don't love him!" mimicked her mother, sashaying around the room like a little flirt. "'I don't want to get in his bed.' What do you want my pretty one? Love doesn't last! Love is for books and for fairy princesses. Bread on the table, that's what counts!"

There was no resisting her. In the end she'd given up and given in, and Suzanne had been born within that first awful year. When Suzanne was a baby she'd had to do everything herself - cook, clean, wash, iron - but when a son was born, a fraulein came into the house. There was only one bedroom in their apartment, one bedroom for five people, so the fraulein and the children got it. Michael wouldn't move to bigger quarters, he said he couldn't afford it, but he could afford fine clothes and lots of going out... alone! They had to sleep in the great room, the room that was the gathering place for everybody. They ate in the kitchen for there was no dining room, only a hallway the children used as a playroom and the three rooms. But Michael could boast that he had a son and his wife had a fraulein to help her.

The fraulein was useful, no doubt about it, Margaret did not want to give her up. They lived in the only apartment house that was near the mill where Michael worked as a grain buyer. All the mill hands who lived around them were forced to live in little low houses that were not much more than sheds. There was no place in the neighborhood where children could play. The fraulein took the children on the trolley to the park every day except in the worst of weather, and while they were out of the house Margaret could read. Michael couldn't understand all the reading but books were her salvation.

"Always reading!" he would cry. "Why don't you do anything but read? Why don't you go out and promenade with the other women?"

What women he was talking about was a mystery to her. They had no friends with whom they spent their social hours. She had nothing in common with any of the women around her. Michael, disappointed with life, was a tyrant at home. He thought that playing the autocrat was the way to keep a family in line. He was charmingly affable out in the world but at home he displayed little good humor. With other men he was genial, open, enthusiastic. With women he was winsome one moment like a young boy and the next moment he exuded primal animal magnetism. His older brother Emil was rapidly becoming known as one of Budapest's foremost men of medicine and the contrast ate at Michael. In America, he had half brothers he scarcely knew but who were reputed to have "arrived" over there. He had a younger half brother living in Rumania who was a big success as an entrepreneur, the sole distributor of English publications throughout the country. Of all the family, he felt the greatest failure was his and he burned under the burden of that.

When he was eighteen, he'd been forced into military service and for two years marked time while his brothers forged ahead. Once free of the army he'd wasted no time on the university as Emil urged him to. Business was for him, not books and fancy ideas, he said. He had no time for the cultural things his brother and his wife thought so important. Margaret read voraciously. She'd read anything. She was filling her head with liberal ideas, ideas that she didn't try to force on him but kept to herself. He knew what she was thinking just the same and it infuriated him. The silent war between them sent him out most nights to look for company. Not for women, he had no time for that, but to the theater, to clubs, to anyplace where light-hearted people were gathered and he could escape all the "high-mindedness" at home. To go to those places and hobnob with those people took money and a man had to dress well which cost more money. He didn't earn enough to move to a better neighborhood where Margaret might find friends more to her liking unless he changed the patterns of his life. When he let himself feel guilty about that, or selfish, it made him even angrier at home.

When Suzanne was two Margaret got hold of a new book written by some crazy Italian woman named Maria Montessori on how to educate children a new way. Margaret had talked of nothing else for days until he yelled for silence. She'd tried to enroll little Suzanne then but they said she had to wait until the child was older. Now that it was time for the child to go to regular school she'd brought it up again. She might shut up but she never gave up.

"Spend good money on a hare-brained kind of school where they don't study they just play? Never!" He'd used his most towering voice but Margaret hadn't quailed at all.

"She will go to this school even if I have to work as a charwoman to pay for it!" The idea of his wife out working was humiliating! He was beaten and he knew it.

Suzanne held the little figurine in both hands gazing quizzically at it. She'd need to take a pinch out of the skirt here and there and create folds to give it motion. A smile played about her lips as half her mind was still fixed on that day when she was six and acting like a brat about going into one of the greatest things that ever happened to her. When they left the cars to climb the long drive leading into the villa that housed the school Suzanne stopped holding back. It was like a park with flowers and grass and trees, not like a school. And when they entered the room to which they'd been directed she let out a whoop and darted away from her mother to plunge in. There were toys everywhere, things she'd never seen before. And the kids were all busy and talking and making believe. The chairs and tables looked like they'd been made for dwarfs and were painted in colors like those in her paint box at home. The room was bright and cheery and there were pictures on the wall. If this was school she was in heaven. Bless Mama for this!

As they had taken the cars over the bridge from Pest that morning and made two transfers along the way her mother had told her that the fraulein would bring her and come to get her, but when she was bigger she could go by herself. Going home that evening Suzanne vowed to get bigger right away. She loved the school and she didn't want the bigger kids to see her coming every morning with a fraulein like some baby kid. Within two years she was making the trip alone which gave her plenty of time to day dream wonderful fantasies about the things she saw along the way. What Margaret derived from books, Suzanne received when she delved into her own imagination.

The same year Suzanne was introduced to school she was also enrolled in dancing classes. Not wanting her child to compete with her rich cousin, Magda, Margaret enrolled her in a school taught by a pupil of Raymond Duncan, brother of the famous Isadora. Suzanne's teacher had studied the free-flowing classical dance of the Duncans in their School of Dance in Paris. With her usual zest Suzanne threw herself into dancing lessons quickly, quickly becoming one of the star pupils. The angry ugly duckling she had been for the first five years of her life became a happy cygnet full of grace and charm. Knowing that her father had resisted the two things she loved most in all the world, dancing class and the Montessori school, Suzanne turned all her affection on her mother, and made her the most important person in all the world. For three years life was filled with the excitement and the joy of being a child, but when she was nine all that changed.

The Great War had ended the year before and at Versailles the "Big Four" Powers proclaimed the breakup of the Hapsburg Empire. They separated Hungary from Austria and forced the Emperor to abdicate. In the vacuum left by his abdication the Communists seized power and put an end to class privilege. From that day on, all the institutions of the country would be open to all people alike regardless of class or gender. That included the University. No one was more thrilled than Margaret Zahler. The year before Michael had taken a new job in Bessarabia as a grain broker. He was working hard trying to make a fortune out of the commodity market. For months on end he didn't even come home. With him away there was no one to stop her so Suzannne's mother was among the first women to enroll in the University.

Margaret went to school at night leaving the children safe at home with the fraulein. She took classes in Political Science and History. Not many women were interested in such things. She was the sole female in her section. In political science classes. Margaret read Karl Marx and tracts by Lenin and everything she could lay her hands on about the new politics coming out of Russia. She was particularly interested in the Marxist theories about the equality of women. Communism was theoretically fascinating, but she remained skeptical about it as a political order. Her interest certainly did not extend to party membership. Margaret was as euphoric about her school as Suzanne was about hers, while it lasted. The bubble burst in less than a year.

In November, 1919, Admiral Nicholas Horthy, and the right-wing forces of conservatism who backed him, wrested control of the government from the Jew, Bela Kun, whose ideas were running amuck. Kun had tried to nationalize everything. The communist assault on traditional morés came to end. Privilege was reinstated, women returned to their rightful place in the home, and University education again was the preserve of a wealthy elite. No such expensive "whim" was allowed Michael Zahler's wife. He had no money for any more fancy education than Suzanne's. Margaret was bereft. As devastating as it was to have to give up school though, Margaret faced even greater repercussions from the new government. Admiral Horthy, acting as regent for the deposed King became virtual dictator of Hungary. Coming from a long line of Protestants as he did, his right-wing regime unleashed a Fascist-style pogrom aimed at the communist left that netted all kinds of people, especially Jews because of the strident advocacy of communism over aristocracy by some Jewish intellectuals. All Jews who were members of the Communist Party, or even those Jews who had paid court to Communist ideals, were rounded up. Margaret, a Protestant married to a Jew, a woman who read Marx and studied political science at the University, who was reported by the concierge of their apartment as espousing radical ideas, was scooped up along with wild-eyed activists whom her timid nature would never have allowed her to take to her bosom. The most daring thing she had ever done besides enter the University was march one time with the suffragettes when Rosa Lagerdoef was there.

The police came for her on the morning of Suzanne's ninth birthday. Already awake, shivering with delighted anticipation of her mother's coming in to wake her with a birthday song, Suzanne bounded out of bed when the pounding on the door reverberated through the apartment. They didn't even let her mother say good-bye. They simply led her away by the arm while the Fraulein stood and wept. As their descending boots echoed through the stairwell, doors on every floor opened cautiously, then their apartment was filled with people wanting to know why Mrs. Zahler had been taken away. The fraulein knew no more than they did but she meant to find out where they'd incarcerated her mistress. Drying her eyes she threw on her coat and tied a babushka under her chin. Then she left Suzanne's brother with neighbors upstairs after pleading to no avail with Suzanne to also take shelter in someone's apartment. The first place she intended to look was at the police station downtown.

Suzanne could not be coaxed to leave the apartment all day, nor did she eat the lunch one of the neighbors brought in to her. She sat huddled on the floor in a corner refusing to be comforted, convinced she would never see her mother alive again. While Suzanne crouched in fear at home the fraulein did the rounds of government offices until she learned where Margaret was being held. Then she sent Michael a wire to tell him what had happened. Suzanne lay awake that night listening for footsteps on the stairs. It was late when Michael Zahler, leading his wife by the arm, strode into the courtyard of the building. Planting his feet astride in the middle of the paved square he threw back his head and shouted his fiery indignation at the closed windows rising on all sides above him.

"This is Michael Zahler," he bellowed. "I've brought my wife home! If anyone ever again dares to bring charges against her, or in any way jeopardizes my family, I will do more than cry out. You will deal with me, whoever you are."

Lights went on in several apartments but no one raised a window to welcome Margaret home. Fear of the new regime, or fear of Michael, was too great for anyone to openly deal with her arrest. Suzanne rushed out into the frigid hall to stand barefooted at the top of the flight of stairs leading up to their floor, shivering as much with joy as with the cold.

Miriam laid her work aside, rubbed her eyes, and broke in on Suzanne's reverie. "What is it?" she asked, pointing a finger at the female form in Suzanne's hands.

"If you have to ask," laughed Suzanne peering through her thick lenses at the diminutive woman across from her, "then it's nothing."

"Well, it's a woman, of course," Miriam said sarcastically, "But is it a nun, a peasant lady, a peddler, or what?"

Suzanne laughed again. "We'll have to wait and see. She hasn't told me yet."

Miriam pursed her lips. Sometimes Suzanne's levity was a bit too much.

Suzanne's "levity" had been a problem lots of times. When she was at the gymnasium it had gotten her into a heap of trouble. She hated gymnasium. Coming out of the personal, intimate atmosphere of the Montessori School where she'd spent eight of the best years of her life into a public gymnasium with its rigid rules and hide-bound traditions had been a shock. Much to her parents' disapproval,.she gave the teachers "fancy" names which she used at home in referring to them, Her father talked to her about respect at such lengths that she learned to keep her own counsel about anything associated with school. But she didn't do well academically, and spent most of her time day-dreaming about what life would be like once she was free of the place. One of her favorite daydreams was planning her own home when she had one. Mentally she drew floor plans, chose furniture and fabrics, created a beautiful nest that was spacious and light and beautiful.

Five years of good harvests and her father came home from Bessarabia with enough money to buy a membership in the Grain Stock Exchange and open his own grain exporting business which he called The Contaxport Corporation. Feeling expansive he moved the family away from the grain mill area and out of the shoe box apartment where Suzanne and her brother were born. He put them into a lovely villa surrounded by gardens in the suburbs of Buda. That had been a wonderful change. They were able to spread out in six rooms, plus a large elegant foyer and a glassed-in solarium. And to make it especially luxurious,they had a second toilet. It was wonderful. There had been a bad side to this new affluence as well. Moving up in the world was expensive so she'd been forced to leave her beloved Montessori and go at last to public school. It was a big penalty to pay for growing up and being "rich." Rote learning was a new, horrible experience which she neither appreciated nor embraced. Only dancing classes remained of the good life she'd known before.

At gymnasium however, Suzanne discovered boys and that was exciting. Tall and striking, with wide-set doe eyes and a classic nose, Suzanne exuded the same animal spirits that emanated from her father. They were a lot alike in a lot of ways, she and her father, and it was not long until there was trouble again. Her mother found her indifference to learning deplorable, and her father thought she was far too young to be flirting with boys. There were scenes, sometimes bordering on the theatrical, and more scenes, but on the whole they managed, the three of them, to keep their conflict from rupturing the family completely. Suzanne itched to be out and away. Fraulein held her in check better than her parents since the two of them continued to share a room and she saw far more of the young girl than did they. Then, as if to add insult to injury, Michael Zahler overextended himself and lost the business. That meant that they lost the villa and had to return to cramped quarters where there was no privacy for anyone. The crabbing and carping and struggle for power increased. If she'd experienced success at school things might have been better at home, but she hated math and detested science which she found incomprehensible. She didn't fit in with the other students who had come up through the public schools and had never known the energizing atmosphere or a non-structured classroom such as she had developed in.

During her years at gymnasium Suzanne went every summer to Germany to study orthopedic exercise, a new field that had not yet reached New York. Each summer she chose a different part of Germany and a different teacher. Those summers convinced her that she wanted to teach, not perform. Her plan was to put in a year after graduation from gymnasium at the Dance Academy as a full time student in order to receive her certificate for teaching. With such credentials in her pocket she could open her own school. It was well that she could present her plan as a practical matter of getting ahead in the world, it was the only way her father would pay for those summers in Germany.

"Papa," she screamed during one of their confrontations over those trips. "Do you want to support me for the rest of my life? If I'm going to make a lot of money I have to have more to offer than other teachers!"

"Support you for the rest of your life?" he bellowed. "Ha! At the rate you're going we'll be lucky if you finish gymnasium. You're going to get yourself married to some pimply kid."

"And then you'll have to support us both!" she interrupted.

"Support you both?" he glared at her over the top of his paper. "I'll turn you out on the street."

"Then I'll go to Uncle Emil," she shot back.

Throwing his paper down and reaching for his coat he roared. "Then go to Germany. Go anywhere. And don't come back before fall term!" He stomped out of the house while Fraulein biting her lips to keep from laughing left the room hurriedly.

In the middle of her final year of gymnasium with her precious diploma almost in hand she had a skiing accident that laid her up for weeks. She was in traction for what seemed eternity, an eternity in which to worry about whether or not all her dreams were down the drain because of this injury. During one of the lowest points in her convalescence a friend of her mother's came from Italy for a visit. The woman was a translator and was working as an interpreter for Mussolini. Through the office of "Il Duce" she had contacts all over Europe. Thinking how to divert the bored, depressed girl on the couch she asked Suzanne, "If you could have one wish right now, what would it be?"

Suzanne didn't hesitate. To while away her invalidism she was reading a book about Sweden. "I should like to go to Sweden," she said.

"That's my gypsy for you," laughed Margaret. "Suzanne would roam the world if we had the money and would let her."

"Well, if what she wanted was a world tour I wouldn't be able to help, but just maybe I can do something about this wish." said her mother's friend. "We'll see."

Suzanne recovered fully, returned to school and forgot the whole conversation, but the friend of her mother did not. One day a letter came offering Suzanne the opportunity to teach exercise classes for six weeks after matriculation in a private school housed in a grand schloss in the mountains at Vexo, a small village in Sweden. It was a wonderful opportunity and the moment her school year ended Suzanne headed for Scandinavia.

The mountains surrounding Vexo were breathtakingly beautiful. There were not too many students in residence during the summer term so Suzanne had plenty of free time to haunt the little town tucked under the shadow of the castle. She became friends of the shopkeepers who found her feeble attempts at Swedish highly amusing, and she visited with the local people along the streets using a combination of her limited command of their language and her facility in German which was a second language for many of them. One of her tasks at the school was to roam the hills around the castle with all twelve of the headmistress's dogs on leash. The tall girl with the long stride, her hair blowing in the wind, endeared herself to the villagers, among whom was a young doctor and his wife who had five small children of their own. When the six week session in the castle came to a close the doctor invited Suzanne to remain with them for a month and give their children additional instruction. Though the doctor's wife was frank enough and honest enough to tell Suzanne that she had an anti-Semitic bias, they treated her like a VIP.

They took her to Stockholm on weekends, they gave parties in her honor, they asked her to dance for their friends, and they shared their family life unreservedly. It was the most delightful vacation Suzanne had ever had. She was the exotic, the glamorous Hungarian. She loved it. The oldest of the doctor's children, a girl, was eager to practice her German. Suzanne suggested that one thing she could do was to correspond with Suzanne's brother who was the same age as the girl and who had been studying German for years. Through correspondence she could learn to write and she could learn something about Hungary in the process. The correspondence that began that summer developed into a deep friendship that spanned eleven years without the two of them ever meeting. In l940, two years after Suzanne fled to America and Michael had gone to Romania, Suzanne's mother invited the doctor's daughter to visit her and her son in Budapest. What Margaret prayed for happened. The two fell in love and planned to marry. But when the girl returned to Sweden to make wedding preparations her mother squashed the whole affair. That marriage could have saved Suzanne's brother's life.

When Suzanne returned from her magical summer she entered the Dance Academy as a full-time student and a year later received the all-important, officially stamped document that gave her the right to teach exercise and dance whether in an established school or as an independent teacher. In one room of the family apartment she held late afternoon classes for gymnasium girls, and in the evening more classes for working girls. All morning she went from one home to another for private lessons or physical therapy. When summer came she went back to Germany to the Laban School of Dance to learn the new methods coming out of the Martha Graham School in New York. When she returned from Germany she integrated some of what she had learned into her own curriculum.

Five days a week Suzanne lived and breathed dance, but on weekends she partied. The era of the vamp, the l920's and early l930's, did not belong to America alone. The same youthful revolution was also going on in Europe. Cafes were filled with single people of all ages, and weekends there was always a house party somewhere where the "new woman" danced and drank and smoked with all the dedicated hedonism of the "flapper" in the United States Suzanne's supple dancing and her sparkling personality made her a hit wherever she went. At one of those parties she met handsome young Ernest Kenley who didn't dance well at all, but who decided upon meeting Suzanne that he'd like a dancing teacher in his life permanently. Unfortunately, the object of his admiration did not share his enthusiasm. She wanted an older husband, not a young ex army corporal not yet settled in a career.

Ex-army corporal Ernest was born in upper Hungary in 1909. The political aftermath of World War I reduced the Hungarian Empire to Hungary which was 1/10th the Empire's size. Out of her lost northern territory and Germany's southeastern corner Czechoslovakia was created. As the political boundaries changed, Ernest's roots technically were no longer in Hungary, but in the this new country not yet unified in loyalty or language. When the Czech government was formed in 1919 pressure was applied to the Hungarians living within its borders, forcing many to flee. It was a traumatic experience for Ernest, a boy whose father had served in the Hungarian army, who had been wounded on the Russian front and who was never able to work again. In addition to being refugees, Ernest and his siblings, along with the invalid father, were reduced to being dependent on the meager income his mother could earn. It was humiliating in the extreme. To support the family after they found their way to Budapest, his mother sat at her kitchen table and made suspenders for men on order. An excellent student, at thirteen, Ernest began tutoring other students, but he earned so little his additional income didn't help appreciably.

Ernest dreamed of becoming an architect, but there was no money for the education he would need to become licensed by the government. Upon graduation from gymnasium he went to Business College for two years. Then he was drafted! Ernest was assigned to the artillery where the officers still rode horses. Horthy, old aristocrat that he was, never mechanized his army until it was too late. He perpetuated the imperial trappings of 19th century military organization. Feathers in your helmet and gauntlets on your hands may make you ever so handsome and swashbuckling, but they were not enough to assuage the loneliness of Ernest's situation. As the only Jew in his unit, Ernest was subjected to a constant barrage of open anti-Semitism. Once, when he walked into the non-commissioned officer's mess the others all walked out. After two years of boring peacetime service, made more onerous by his personal situation, he vowed he'd never put on another uniform, ever. The humiliation of his military experience was fresh in his belly when he met Suzanne.

To be young in the very early thirties in Budapest meant wonderful parties on the Danube - if your parents were modern enough to allow it. Luckily, Suzanne's mother trusted her and wanted her to drain her cup of youth dry. Groups of young men and groups of young women would rent adjoining farmhouses for a Saturday night, one for the males and one for the females. They'd have a big party at one or the other of the houses that night and then on Sunday they'd pair off in rowboats for a trip upstream on the river. The men would row against the current facing the girl in the prow of the boat who acted as navigator. At noon they would all gather along the riverbank for a picnic then, having eaten, they would continue on upstream until it was time to turn the boats loose to drift downstream on the current. They lashed the boats together to make a solid flotilla and had a wonderful time climbing in and out from one to another literally rocking the boats as they shifted places. The phonographs they'd brought along played the latest music from America and someone always had a ukulele to whose accompaniment they sang all the latest love songs. They told jokes and laughed at nothing at all until dusk fell. Then they pulled into one of the restaurants along the river's edge for dinner.

Suzanne had a cousin, a very handsome cousin who had a friend, he assured her, as handsome as he. The cousin invited Suzanne to go along on one of the outings for he had a new boat, and he and his friend would be delighted with her company. Suzanne was sure the invitation came because the whole family knew she was suffering from a broken heart. For three years she had been in love with a Jewish doctor whom she had expected to marry but who had dumped her to marry a girl with a lot of money. She was crushed and her parents were indignant, but there was nothing to be done about it. Half-heartedly Suzanne agreed to go. As it turned out, her cousin's friend was young Ernest Kenley whom she'd met some time before. The young ex-army captain was attentive, he was eager, and he was very nice, but Suzanne was not impressed. Then on Sunday night, when they pulled into the shore for dinner, a man who was a newcomer to the group decided that Suzanne was for him. When she spurned his offer he said something insulting to her and her cousin's friend leaped spiritedly to her defense. For the first time Suzanne looked at Ernest Kenley, really looked, and saw him not as someone too young, not as someone not settled, not as a romantic young ass, but for what and who he was. Romance bloomed immediately. Within months they were talking of marriage.

"One thing you have to be willing to do if you're serious about me," he told her "you have to be willing and ready to emigrate."

"Emigrate? Emigrate where? Why?"

"America if we can. If not, Australia."

"But why must we emigrate?"

Ernest leaned back in his chair and twiddled his glass in his fingers. "I read this Hitler's book. I know he's serious. Now that he's been appointed chancellor he'll have the power to carry out his plans. There won't be a Jew left alive in Europe if he has his way."

"Oh Ernest," she laughed in protest, "You're not serious. He's just a strutting like comedian with a funny mustache. No one takes him seriously."

"I take him seriously!" Ernest's face was somber.

"Well, I don't" Suzanne laughed, "but I love the idea of going to America. It would even be fun to go to Australia, but I'd rather have America."

All of the family on both sides of the aisle were there for the wedding except for cousin Magda who was out in Java. Both sides of the family meant a lot of people. Their wedding photograph shows the two of them in the middle of a five rank tier of relatives of all ages. Emil & Michael Zahler still looked so much alike that it would be easy to mistake one of the brothers for the other. Tall, distinguished, sure of themselves, they were impressive men. Ernest and Suzanne made as handsome a couple as could be found. It was a gathering of obviously very middle-class people, obviously cultured and obviously sure of themselves. A decade later most of the happy crowd would be packed into cattle cars headed for extermination camps, or be already dead.

The newly-weds went to Italy on their honeymoon, soaked up the sun and each other, and upon their return moved into a large modern apartment which Suzanne's parents spent a fortune furnishing. If the Kenleys had any serious thought of emigrating it was not apparent. An interior decorator was hired who won a prize for what he did to one of the rooms in their apartment. The apartment was the most spacious place in which she had ever lived, the home she'd been dreaming about since she was a little girl. One large room was set aside as her Studio, and at last she really had the space in which to develop a school. Before she married Ernest, Suzanne had over 100 pupils and after her marriage, with the new space available, she quickly expanded to 200. Ernest had a good job and between them the money rolled in. They continued to party, to do the town, and to live the good life. But the idyll was abruptly broken when the Nuremburg Laws were passed in Germany in 1935 and some of them put through in Hungary. Ernest suddenly came out of his honeymoon bliss like a bear emerging from hibernation.

The old sense of urgency to get out while there was time consumed him. He had to find a place of refuge for them as quickly as possible. America seemed impossible. The Hungarian quota for the United States was full and the waiting list a yard long. Australia seemed the most likely haven. He quickly filled out application forms at the Australian embassy. The Australian government required that new immigrants have on deposit $2000 per member of the family before their requests would be processed. How could they get $4000 out of Hungary when already the law prevented any Jew from leaving the country with more than ten dollars in his/her pocket? $4,000 was a lot of money. The good times came to an end. Ernest set up a bank account in London. Every cent they could scrape together went into that account, carried there by friends traveling on business or vacationing there. Their couriers were necessarily gentile, free to carry as much money as they chose.

But they were some time away from actually filing an application. The money had to be accumulated first. Suzanne had a cousin named Clara who the year before had married a Russian and gone off with him to Moscow. Clara sent back glowing reports about life in the East, and the high places in the government held by Jews. They wrote to Clara about possibly emigrating to Russia. Clara's answer was illuminating. They would probably have to settle in Siberia if they came, she said, that was where new émigrés were being sent to colonize. It was not difficult to see that cousin Clara was saying, "Don't come."

At first Suzanne's parents thought this silly talk of emigrating was some more of their daughter's perpetual day-dreaming, but once Michael sounded out Ernest and realized they were serious, the battle began.

"Where is your head?" he demanded. "You're living in cuckoo land. Look at the life you have here. What about

Suzanne's school and your job? Are you going to throw all that away? What's the matter with you?"

"The matter is that all of this is an illusion." Ernest cried. "The reality is that it isn't going to last. Can't you see what's happening?"

"I don't know where you get these crazy ideas," shouted Michael. "This is Hungary! Hungary doesn't have a madman."

"Hitler has plans for all of Europe." Ernest's voice was icy. "Why don't you read something besides those stock market reports? If you think this is going to last, you're the one with the crazy ideas."

They learned to live in strained silence, the four of them, polite but on edge in each other's presence. It was taking a lot of time to save $4,000, and in the meantime they had to find level ground on which the four of them could meet. Then in 1938 the impossible happened in Austria. Hitler marched in and within weeks Margaret was insistently urging the young couple to go. Ernest urgently pleaded with Suzanne to get out of Hungary to safety while the doors for migration were still open. He would wait alone in Budapest to hear from the Australians. They were close enough to the $4,000 that they could sell some things and fulfill the financial requirements if only their number came up. Suzanne contacted the doctor and his wife with whom she had lived in Vexo hoping they would take her in. Sweden was a neutral country, the safest place in Europe to wait. The doctor and his wife would not take her themselves, but they found a family who wanted an au-pair for their children who were glad to have her. For four months she was in Sweden waiting hour by hour for word from Ernest that they had found asylum.

While Suzanne waited and worried, Ernest haunted the libraries of the various embassies looking for something in the fine print of Emigration Law that might spring them from the trap he felt rapidly closing shut around them. Every day he also went to the Australian embassy to check, and every day their names were not on the list of those being granted visas to enter the Land Down Under. Then one day, in the American Embassy library, he found a nugget in the fine print he had not seen before. The golden bit of information sent his pulse rate skyrocketing. It said that since Czechoslovakia had not existed as a nation when the quota system was being written by Congress at the end of World War I, that 3,000 persons from that country would be admitted annually into the United States. Hungary was allocated only 800 people and there were thousands waiting. There was no waiting list in Czechoslovakia, too few people knew the law. Ernest, born in Czechoslovakia, and later forced to leave his country, had never renounced his citizenship. It was a miracle! He could go to America instantly and, of course, take his wife with him. Jubilantly, he phoned Suzanne in Sweden to break the good news.

"Come home as fast as you can," he shouted over the wire, "we're going to America!"

Suzanne left Sweden on a cloud. Not since the day they moved into their apartment had she been this excited. Ignoring the German law that Jews could not ride trains without special permits, she headed across Germany with her heart in her mouth. When she purchased her ticket in Sweden she did not identify herself as a Jew. Hungarian passports did not yet carry in the infamous red J that would soon be stamped on every identification a Jew carried with them. Since her point of departure had been from a neutral nation and her destination was in an allied nation she was traveling across the Third Reich in defiance of the law as an international tourist. That train ride was one of the most harrowing experiences of her life. Midway across the country the train was sidetracked for days in order to make way for troop trains carrying the German army west to the borders of Belgium and Holland. Every moment she was on German soil seemed like an eternity. She found herself not breathing when someone in uniform passed through the car. She kept her eyes riveted on the dreary scene outside the window so as not to attract attention to herself. She spent as much time in the lavatory as she dared. What would they do if they found that this good-looking, young Hungarian woman was a Jewess? From time to time she dozed off, but she could not sleep. Her nerves were so taut she'd dream she was stepping off curbs and wake herself with involuntary jerking motions. When the train began to move again Suzanne was so relieved she cried. Had she known that she was on the very last train that would be allowed to cross those international borders controlled by Hitler whose passengers were not interrogated as a matter of course, she might not have been able to hang onto her composure as long as she did. Luckily, she didn't know until after she was off the train in Budapest. While she was enroute, Hitler closed all German and Austrian borders to all but passengers on government business.

When Ernest found the key to their escape in the American immigration laws, Margaret became as excited as he at the prospects.

"I'll write to the relatives in America right now," she cried. "They'll send affidavits."

In a clan that stretched from New York to Chicago surely someone would sponsor them. In Chicago, Michael had a nephew, Julius Zahler, president of the Hoffman Cheese Co. When his mother brought him the request he refused to even consider it.

"I don't know these people." he snorted. "How do I know if I'd even like them? I'm not going to start sending affidavits to anybody and everybody who asks for one. Just because she's a Zahler doesn't make me want to take her in off the street."

"They're not asking to be taken in off the street." his mother retorted. "They're not poor. They just can't get in over here without the affidavit and it has to be given to them by a relative. Now don't be such a snobbish boor. Do it!"

"All right! All right. I'll send the affidavit," he said. "But they're on their own when they get here. I'm not going to support them." Julius sent the affidavit and it arrived even before the exit visas had been issued.

Hitler's order to close all international borders with Germany and Austria hit the Kenleys like a bombshell. They had some money in the bank in England to make a start in the United States, they had the precious affidavits from the United States, they were expecting the all important U.S. visas any day, they even had their exit visas from the Hungarian Government. They had packed all the things they were allowed to take with them and those were ready to be shipped. Now this! They couldn't leave Hungary to go in any direction!

In the midst of their panic fate took another turn, grossly malevolent for the future of Europe, but in the very short run the break Suzanne and Ernest needed. Chamberlain went to Munich and gave the charlatan of Germany the Sudetenland plus the illusion that there was no end to the concessions the West would make. In a euphoric moment of elation over the ease with which he had gobbled up two of his neighbors, Hitler opened all the borders and let international traffic flow freely again. It wasn't long until his territorial greed closed all the escape hatches again, but they were open long enough for Suzanne and Ernest to slip out. Michael howled his protests all the way to the station to see them off while Margaret fairly trembled with relief and excitement.

"When you get there, send for me." she pleaded.

"You know we will," Suzanne assured her.

"You're going to be sorry!" Michael warned them, "America is a crass place and you'll wish you were back."

Ernest shook his head hopelessly and handed Suzanne up into the car. With heavy hearts they started off on the trip across Austria and Switzerland to France. As their car crossed the Hungarian border Suzanne leaned out the train window and spit on Austrian soil. As the miles flew by they began to notice that Ernest was the only man not in uniform on the train. Where had all the men gone? Were they all conscripted into Hitler's army? Would someone become curious about this civilian in the cars filled with women and children? Would they pull him off the train and throw him into some labor battalion which seemed to be the fate of every Jewish male in Austria? Even crossing the Swiss border did not make it easier to breathe. Only when they had safely crossed into France and left Germanic efficiency behind could they believe that they were really free, really safely on their way to a new life in America.

Paris! The war fever that gripped the world behind them was hard to comprehend in the city on the Seine. Here, the old carefree atmosphere of Paris still held. The cafes were all open, the theater was going full blast, people walked and talked in that careless way free people have which had been missing from Budapest for some time. They stayed with artist friends from home who were in residence on the left bank and they had such a wonderful time they almost thought of truncating their journey and becoming French citizens. But some somber sixth sense Ernest could not completely bury kept them from making that fatal blunder. After days of partying to all hours every night and sauntering along the river front by day, they boarded a train for London. In London lay the money with which to book passage to New York. In 1938 a dollar was worth five English pounds and they could live quite well on a one dollar a day. They rode the double-deck busses all over that wonderful city, went to the theater, ate reasonably well, and waited for sailing time. Suzanne even had two evening gowns made to wear in the salon on the ship going over, thinking to prolong the party until they hit the shores of their new country. By the time their fortnight in London ended and the tickets and gowns were paid for, they had a wee bit over $1000 left for their new beginning. As it turned out they could have saved the cost of the gowns, Suzanne was seasick all the way across the stormy Atlantic.

In America life was good for the Kenleys from the start. Poor they were, but lots of people were poor in the United States in 1939. The depression still held the country in thrall. A dance studio was out of the question. First, too few people could spare the money for dancing lessons. As for exercise classes or physical therapy, most of the techniques that were widely accepted in Hungary had not yet been introduced into the United States. Second, Suzanne's dance styles were not in vogue over here. Tap Dancing was all the rage and those children whose parents could afford lessons wanted their little darlings to be little Shirley Temples. Suzanne's one salable skill was Swedish massage which she had studied years before. She charged one dollar an hour which was almost three times the minimum wage established in 1937. Her clients were rich Europeans who loved the pampering; Americans could not yet condone such licentious hands-on intimacy. In her first two weeks she made twenty five dollars which was equal to the pay of clerks and service industry workers. Ernest had a more difficult time finding work but with what Suzanne made they weren't destitute. They could live on her earnings. At last an ad in the newspaper turned up a job as shoe salesman for the Botto Shoe Co. Ernest had to have a car for the job which bit into their savings, but he bought an old one which didn't cost too much money. In order to save what Ernest earned for a store of their own as soon as the economy picked up, they continued to get by on Suzanne's income.

The breezy energy of life in Chicago was infectious, they became optimistic about the future and began to relax into their new surroundings. Open to new relationships and experiences, they quickly made friends among other immigrants who had found their way to the Midwest. One day, a few months after they had settled in, when the spring air was exhilarating and the sun sparkled on Lake Michigan, a day when one ached to be out in the clear air of the countryside, they went driving into the farm area west of the city. They were with a couple they'd met recently. The four of them had decided to have a picnic. On a shady hillside with a long view of the hills on the other side of the shallow valley below they saw a lovely spot. To reach it they had to get through or over a four-strand barbed wire fence. Crawling carefully between the stretches of wicked wire thorns they spread out their blanket on the young spring grass. Hungry by then, they immediately opened their picnic baskets and set out their fare. Lolling back in anticipation of a sun-drenched lunch followed by a lazy nap, they fell to eating and talking. Just as Ernest lifted the first forkful of his dessert to his mouth the other woman gasped and pointed up the hill.

"Look!" she whispered hoarsely.

They all turned to stare at what had caught her eye.

"Here, too!" whispered Ernest.

Nailed to a tree above them on the hill was a sign which read: "No dogs or Jews allowed."

Somberly, all joy in the fresh breezes and warm sunlight gone, they picked up the rest of their lunch and the rest of their paraphernalia and returned to the car. The drive back to Chicago seemed longer than it had when they covered the same miles that morning.

Suzanne sighed a long sigh. Miriam looked up inquiringly. "I was just thinking," Suzanne said, "about the time we saw a sign on a farmer's tree that said 'No Jews allowed.'"

"Why think of that now?" Miriam's voice was curt. "It's too long ago. I think you'd better forget such things and make up your mind about that woman you're making before you go any further. She still looks like a nun to me, a nun without her head covered."

"Maybe she's a missionary." Suzanne saucily retorted.

"Missionary, huh." grunted Miriam turning back to her bowl. Suzanne looked at the feet of the figurine in her hand. Should she put shoes on her? Shoes, always shoes.

By 1940, they were ready to invest what was left of their thousand dollars and what they had saved in the past year and open a store of their own. They had to borrow another thousand dollars from Suzanne's cousin to do it, but they succeeded. Proudly they took over a rented storefront and contracted with a Czechoslovakian Shoe Manufacturing Co. that made shoes for the cheaper trade, shoes for the kind of district where they had been able to find a reasonable lease. Suzanne gave up giving massages by the hour to work in the store by the day, however long that day might be. Almost from the beginning the Kenleys were working 60 to 80 hours a week doing everything themselves from sweeping the walk out front to hauling their own merchandise from the warehouse. Suzanne learned to drive the car so she could take over all the errands and leave Ernest free to mind the store. He was a better salesman than she.

Things were just coming together, the business was becoming sound enough that they could worry less about making ends meet, when the United States entered World War II. Even here in America Hitler could crimp their lives. There were no more Czechoslovakian shoes for the American trade. Also the United States slapped rationing onto the populace and issued ration books. The infamous #l7 shoe stamp which limited Americans to one pair of shoes per person until---. No one knew "until" what. The whole rationing system was so chaotic in the beginning that there was no certainty that Americans would get more of a lot of things for a long, long time to come. People hoarded their stamps. Business fell off at a frightening rate. It was months before the government could get a clear picture of how many boots would be required for the armed forces, and until that need was met the public could get by or go barefoot. Added to America's own need was the desperate need of Britain. Britain could no longer supply military demands of any kind. The British soldier was dependent on the United States for the clothes on his back and the food in his mouth to say nothing of the weapons in his hands. The United States had to become the arsenal and quartermaster for all her European Allies, maybe even Russia.

Leather was confiscated by the War Department and shoe manufacturers without government contracts were in straits as dangerous as retailers selling to the civilian population. Ernest and Suzanne tightened their belts and lay awake nights again. But at last the government announced that the game of "catch-up" had been caught up, and that additional stamps, including shoes, would be issued soon. Now Americans could indulge in a maximum of seven pairs of shoes a year. Seven pairs? During the Depression they'd been lucky to have three. Furthermore, the government said, stamps would be issued on a regular basis for everything from rubber tires (which were almost impossible to find, stamp or no stamp) to butter. The amount of gasoline one could have was limited to one Sunday afternoon drive a week unless one could get extra issues like small businessmen or car-poolers. It meant more paperwork for the Kenleys which kept the midnight oil burning more frequently, but business picked up immediately and the fund for a second store began to grow. By 1944 things were humming along.

With the end of the war in sight, talk everywhere was about what was to be done for the boys when they began coming home. Post-war planning almost obscured the final effort to win the war. Suzanne and Ernest did a little planning of their own. They decided to have a baby. Suzanne was now 34 years old. If she was to be a mother it was time to do it. In those days there was no way of knowing the sex of the child in advance so Suzanne was surprised and delighted when the doctor lifted his head so that she could see him above her knees and said,

"You got what you wanted! It's a girl!"

When the nurse handed her the little bundle for the first time Suzanne's joy knew no bounds. She had to check her out for herself to make sure that everything was there that was supposed to be attached and in good condition. Once satisfied she held her close to her cheek and whispered to Ernest, "I wish mother could see her."

It hurt to think of her mother. Margaret Zahler had wanted to come to America as fervently as she had ever wanted anything. Suzanne had only to close her eyes and she could still hear her mother's voice as clearly as she had heard it that last day in Hungary.

"Go!" her mother had urged. "Go! Don't listen to your father. Go! Get on that train and go." She had even pushed Suzanne toward the waiting step. "Go, and as soon as you get there you send me the papers and I'll come too."

There had been such a quarrel the night before. Michael had made a last ditch effort to talk them out of going as though somehow they were deserting him, spurning his life, leaving him behind.

"Why are you throwing up lives that have so much promise to go a brassy place filled with boorish people who have no culture?" he'd shouted.

Wearily Ernest had given the same answers he'd given over and over. "Because we want to live. If you had any sense you'd come with us."

To everyone's surprise Michael, for once, had not snorted in derision, instead he'd demanded heatedly, "To do what? What could I do in America? I don't speak the language, I don't know anything about grain markets outside Europe. What shall I do, be a door opener at the Hungarian Embassy? Or a porter in a railway station? What good would it do for me to go?"

At first they'd argued with him that with his business experience he could find many things to do but he had ended it, they thought, by shouting at his wife, "All right. Let them go and go yourself. They can send you the affidavit when they get there and you can go to America." He paused and then added more quietly, "If you like it then maybe I'll come too." It hadn't been a full capitulation but it had made them think the argument was over. Then his final parting shot at the train station had seemed to negate the promise.

They'd wasted no time sending affidavits to her mother. It had been a real challenge for them to prove they were settled enough to sponsor anyone, but they persisted until the sacred document was on its way to Budapest. They'd had to list her as an Austrian - she had been born in Vienna - to accomplish it, but everything was in order when the packet was mailed off. Margaret Zahler wasted no time in delivering all the papers from America to the American Consulate. The precious exit visa would only be issued when the Hungarian government received proof that she was indeed entitled and authorized to go to America. At the consulate the application and the affidavit were checked and found to be in order. All that was required was for her number to come up on the Austrian Quota and she would be on her way. It was almost a year before she received word from the Americans that her number had come up. Trembling with excitement, flushed with joy, she went to the offices of the Consul. That worthy welcomed her and shook her hand.

"Mrs. Zahler, it's my pleasure to be one of the first to wish you "Godspeed" on your journey to America. Everything is ready." He smiled broadly at the demure little woman who stood before her. Taking his pen from its stand on the desk, he removed the cap, and pulled the paper toward him to sign it.

411

Before pen could touch paper, a clerk came running over from a nearby desk, consternation flooding his face, and spread his hands out over the paper to stop the action. The consul, poised to sign, looked up inquiringly.

"Don't sign it, sir. Please don't sign it, it's a mistake. She's here six months too soon. She has to wait."

Margaret went chalk white and reached out a hand to his desk to steady herself. The consul looked from the agitated clerk to the stricken woman in front of him. Slowly he put his pen back and returned Margaret's papers to the envelop in which she had brought them.

"I'm sorry, my dear," he said awkwardly, handing her the packet. "I know it's a disappointment but don't take it too hard. Be patient. Six months is not so long when one is pulling up one's stakes for a lifetime."

Numbly, the timid little woman took the proffered papers, and shaking like a leaf, walked away. Six months later it was too late.

Late in 1939, after the war had begun in Europe, doctors discovered that Margaret had cancer. The required surgery was a success but the convalescence was long. Through it all Michael nursed her and cared for her with such tenderness that Suzanne's mother at last fell in love with the complex man she had married. It was almost like falling in love when one was young. From then on his fate was her fate. When Suzanne held her treasured child close on that most special of all days in 1944 she did not know what that fate had held for her parents. Only when the war was over and mail flowed freely again did she learn what had happened to them, and to her brother.

After Margaret was well enough for Michael to pick up his own life again he went back to Rumania. For years his brother Darvush had a lucrative business in Rumania where he was the sole distributor for all English papers and periodicals coming into that country. Early in 1940, before Hitler made his move against Russia, Darvush, like Ernest, saw the handwriting on the wall. He began preparing his affairs in order to emigrate to England. When Michael learned that Darvush planned to sell his business Michael pleaded with his brother to turn it over to him, promising to pay for it as he could. The deal was struck and at this final hour Michael at last became the big entrepreneur he had always longed to be.

Margaret remained behind in Budapest in a little apartment where she lived with their son. As he had more than a decade before, Michael traveled back and forth as best he could under the chaotic conditions of wartime travel that prevailed throughout eastern Europe.

Then came March, 1944, and the Germans marched into Hungary. Immediately their son was scooped up by the Nazis and thrown into a labor battalion to be sent to the German army in Russia. Alone in Budapest Margaret made the fatal mistake that cost her her life. As a gentile she was safe in Budapest, she could have remained out of harm's way, but once their son was gone, she packed up everything and went to be with Michael in Rumania. As the German army retreated before the Russians late that year the Nazis finished off the last of the Jews in their rear. In their path of retreat were Michael and Margaret Zahler. All that is known of the circumstances of their deaths was learned from a postcard Margaret threw from the train, pushing it out between the slats of the cattle car in which they were being transported to an extermination camp. Among the inexplicable things that happen in a maelstrom of war, that postcard found its way to Ernest's mother in Budapest.

It was Ernest's mother who also received the news of the pitiful ending to Suzanne's brother's life. When the war was over a young man, who had been taken along with the brother in the raid on Jews in Budapest when the Nazis came in, appeared at Mrs. Kenley's apartment. He told her they had been sent to the German army but the Russians had captured them, and as prisoners of war had marched them off to Siberia. Suzanne's brother had contacted cousin Clara, then V.I.P in the Communist party, but to no avail. Hungry, cold, exhausted, the Labor Battalion marched day after day with so little to eat they could scarcely keep to the road. One day Suzanne's brother's will gave out. He refused to go on. He sat down beside the road and froze to death. The young man who brought the news made it to Siberia and survived the brutal conditions under which they lived and worked, but he had promised his friend that he would let them know back home how it was for him when he died, and he had come to keep that promise.

In all the Mother's Day rhetoric, and in the countless reams of the Hallmark Greeting Card Company's schmaltzy poetry honoring the day, is a shadow of Ernest's mother. Not well-educated, always a little baffled by her gifted son, she was above all someone you could count on. When the Germans marched in that raw spring day in 1944, and began rearranging the lives of the Jews of Budapest, Ernest's mother had a guardian angel, a gentile neighbor. They had never been close friends but they were on friendly terms, stopping to chat amiably as they came and went from their apartments. On the day a German squad appeared in the courtyard of their building and ordered all Jews to pack what they could carry and congregate below in thirty minutes, her neighbor rushed across the hall and threw open Mrs. Kenley's door.

"Don't' go," she cried. "For God's sake don't go."

" How can I not go?" whimpered Mrs. Kenley.

"Come over to me!" insisted her neighbor. "If you go down they'll take you away."

"If I don't go they'll come to look for me."

"Not unless someone tells them you're not there. The concierge won't tell. He hates them.

Mrs. Kenley, trembling so hard she could scarcely walk, grabbed a few things and closed her door behind her. Like a hunted animal which she had become, she went to the refuge offered. They did not look for her that day, and before another day passed her friend had found a hiding place for Mrs. Kenley over in Buda with a gentile friend of hers. She went out and bought a cross for Mrs. Kenley to wear around her neck, and like two old friends going out to visit or to shop, arm in arm, the two of them strolled down the street to the streetcar. The ride to Buda seemed an eternity as her neighbor kept talking and talking keeping up the charade of innocent errands until she handed Mrs. Kenley off to the safety of her friend. These two gentile women passed her back and forth between them for eight long months.

When the Russians occupied Pest, Mrs. Kenley was on the Buda side of the river. It was reported that the Russians were handing out food on the Pest side and one of the greatest chores her two ministering angels had to contend with was getting enough food for Mrs. Kenley too for she had no Nazi-issued food stamps. Mrs. Kenley made up her mind to go home. The Danube was choked with ice floes but, like Eliza in "Uncle Tom's Cabin," she braved the danger of being ground between two floating ice islands and clambered across to return to her own apartment. At first the Russian food distribution provided enough to keep body and soul together, but before long the Russians quit distributing food. Living by her wits she was clever enough to keep herself alive until war's end when the parcels from Suzanne and Ernest began to flow in. The first day the Chicago Post Office would accept parcels for delivery to Hungary the American Kenleys mailed 25 packages. They didn't arrive all at once. Only one came through on the first post. Mrs. Kenley opened the box and was thunderstruck by the contents. It was full of things she could trade for food: needles, pins, thread, adhesive tape, combs, all kinds of light-weight notions Spreading it all out on the table she walked around and around this incomprehensible wealth unable to take it in that all of this belonged to her. And that was not the end of her plenitude. The boxes kept coming with everything her American family could lay their hands on that postage restrictions allowed them to send.

Early in l946, when the troops were mostly all home, the U.S. government began opening the doors to immigration again. The first mother of an immigrant to come through was Mrs. Kenley. Suzanne and Ernest had pushed the paperwork through in a miraculously short time. Having her with them was a blessing. She took care of little Katherine leaving Suzanne free to work in the store again with Ernest. With both of them on the job again they decided to expand by opening the long planned second shoe store. Mrs. Kenley took over the cooking which meant a return to the heavy Hungarian food Ernest no longer loved and could happily do without. But who was to tell her? Mrs. Kenley spent her days looking for ways to be more helpful until sometimes Suzanne wanted to scream, but her mother-in-law's eagerness to please left Suzanne mute.

The tension was reduced when the Kenleys bought a beautiful townhouse on Lakeshore Dr. on the North Side. Mrs. Kenley had her own apartment upstairs. There she could cook all the sour cream and paprika dishes her heart desired. She made many friends among the mothers of the Hungarian members of the Chicago Symphony and the ladies visited back and forth, chattering away in Hungarian as they strolled together along the parkway. They spent hours in Hungarian cafes drinking strong, rich coffee, they went to matinees in downtown movie houses, they kept themselves out of their families' way as much as possible, but for Suzanne there was still too much togetherness. No plans could be made without taking Mrs. Kenley into account. There was never a sibling to send her to for respite. She would never take a vacation without them, and in good conscience, they could not take a trip without her. She was there every day and every day and every day.

Katherine, Suzanne decided, was what fate had sent her to make up for all she'd lost and all she had to endure. For a sixteenth birthday gift Suzanne took her to Europe. In truth Suzanne was making a pilgrimage. Like many other Jews who had escaped in time to live rather than die with the millions who perished in the Holocaust, Suzanne had to go back to walk the streets of Budapest with the ghosts of all those who had vanished. "She should see her roots for herself," she told Ernest. "I want to show her where I went to school, where you and I lived after we were married, where Uncle Emil lived. I want to take her to the graveyard to see all her family's names on the wall. I want her to have some roots."

"Suzanne, it's all right with me if you take her, but I don't want you to be disappointed. She's going to see it all through the eyes of an American child. It's not going to feel like homeland to her, it's going to be that funny place her parents came from."

They left Chicago on a hot, humid day in June, Suzanne perspiring from the weather and from her excitement. All the way across the Atlantic she had a hard time sitting still. In her mind she retraced her steps along the main thoroughfares of her life in Budapest, rode the streetcars across Buda to her Montessori school again, danced before her students in the little parlor of that last apartment she'd shared with her parents before she and Ernest were married, and floated down the Danube on a late Sunday afternoon as the shadows reached across the river from shore to shore. But when they were finally in Budapest Suzanne knew her pilgrimage was a failure. The Budapest Katherine was seeing was alien to the world she herself had known. The roots she had wanted Katherine to cultivate were forever lost for them both. Suzanne was communing with ghosts Katherine could never know. Even the graveyard had been destroyed. She and Katherine were tourists, American tourists too well dressed among the shabby citizens of a Russian-controlled second-rate country. Suzanne came back to the United States an orphan. The enormity of it all finally sunk in. The United States was all the home she had.

Suzanne went back to work and Katherine went back to school where she discovered boys that fall. Academics took a second balcony seat above the center stage of young love. In her senior year Katherine stumbled over a classmate who had been under her nose all along. He was headed for Yale. They became inseparable. In spite of her preoccupation with the social whirl, she luckily had the necessary GPA for Barnard, which was a train stop away from New Haven on the railroad that ran from Boston to New York. Katherine went East that fall and some of the life went out of their townhouse. At Barnard she majored in Sociology during the school week, and a boy in Connecticut on weekends. La Bell Telephone kept Suzanne abreast of all the unfolding events going on in Katherine's life.

After Katherine left for college Ernest and Suzanne went into partnership with an investor to buy another store. Ernest was back to working sixty to eighty hours a week. It was too much. In 1965, he had a little warning heart attack, and then a big one. HE WAS GONE. At 56 the handsome young corporal who had come to her defense on the Danube left her defenseless by Lake Michigan with a daughter in college and an ill mother-in-law upstairs. Suzanne was bereft. But there were too many responsibilities, too much to do, there was no time for her own grief. Ernest was buried, Katherine went back to Barnard, and Suzanne went back to work alone. She came home from whichever store she had been in that day and climbed up to her mother-in-law's apartment to check in. For some time they had talked to Mrs. Kenley about a home for retired German Jews that her doctor had recommended, but no decision had been made by the time Ernest died. His mother never went to the home. Three months to the day after her son's death the valiant lady who had walked across the ice from Buda to Pest crossed the river of life into death. An autopsy showed that her heart had literally burst open. They had known she was ill but not how ill. They had known she had a weak heart, but not how weak. So Suzanne buried them both, mother and son, in one year without ever having had time alone with Ernest since the day his mother arrived in the United States nineteen years before.

After the second funeral, and after Katherine returned to Barnard for her senior year, Suzanne sat down and sized up her life. She knew she was in over her head with two stores on her hands. Before Ernest died they had sold the original store. Neighborhoods change and the location of the first Kenley enterprise had become too dangerous for either of them to feel safe on the property. Now she sold the new store to the partner and kept only one. Ernest had loved the stores and Suzanne had loved Ernest, but Ernest was gone and Suzanne hated every day she went to work. It didn't take long for her to throw in the sponge and sell out entirely. For the first time in her life she was idle. What had looked so good at a distance - time to do all the things she had not had time to do before - produced ennui. She played bridge, did volunteer work, went to ladies' luncheons, went through all the activities that usually fill the days of widows, but it was unfulfilling. She was too young.

One day she went to have lunch with a friend who worked in the Mayor's office at City Hall. As she waited for her friend to clear her desk so they could leave she watched the hustle and bustle going on around her and knew she had to go back to work. Over lunch she poured out her dilemma to her friend. She was floundering, she said. She had to be productive some way but she had no skills, she wasn't prepared to do anything but sell shoes and she'd had enough of that. If she had pondered all this before hand Suzanne couldn't have found a better person to whom to express her restlessness.

"You're a Godsend, Suzanne." her friend declared, "A real Godsend. We've wanted to start a program for sometime that we can't fund. You could afford to work part time and you've got the kind of smarts we need."

Wary about the part-time pitch Suzanne waited, not wanting to expose herself until she knew more.

"This society is growing older and we haven't done one thing to prepare for it. We've got elderly shut-ins who have no family to look after them and no public agency committed to doing anything about it."

Suzanne thought of Mrs. Kenley and her interest was piqued. "Are you thinking of putting up homes for these people?"

"No! That's the trouble with Americans. They always want to build a building and have that solve a problem." Suzanne's friend filled her mouth, then talked around the salad. "We want to keep them in their miserable little rooms, or apartments, or shabby hotels, not because we think that's best for them but because they think that's the way they want to live."

"All people want to be independent," said Suzanne remembering how her mother-in-law clung to her apartment resisting the "home" the doctor argued for.

"Exactly! But some of them are so crippled, or blind, or sick, or timid, or whatever is the matter, that they never get out, they never have company, they don't eat well, they don't get their welfare or social security checks cashed, they don't get their bills paid. We need to be able to go to them where they are and do for them what they need to have done."

"You're talking about a visiting nurse kind of program?" Suzanne began to feel excited about the direction this conversation was taking.

"Exactly. Except the visitor would NOT be expected or allowed to play nurse. If medical care is needed the visitor should get in touch with county hospital or visiting nurse's associations. But the other assorted dysfunctional aspects of their lives could be addressed by someone with a little training and a big heart."

"Are you offering me a job?!" demanded Suzanne.

"Yes!" said her friend. "Even without the mayor's approval I'm offering you a job. I've given this a lot of thought. You could work out of Hull House so someone would always be available for consultation. You could be a junior Jane Addams. Think about it."

"Think about it? What is there to think? When do I start?"

Suzanne had found her niche. Soon she was working far longer hours than she was being paid for. When she turned the key in her latch in the evening it was with a lovely tired feeling of accomplishment, not with the vague unrest she had felt ever since Ernest's death. She was doing something worthwhile, she was making a difference, and it was far more satisfying than fitting shoes to feet too small or too large. But the situation was too good to last. Richard Nixon came into office and cut such social programs out of the budget. Indignant at the callousness of the Federal Government's approach to the care of the elderly poor, Suzanne rolled up her sleeves and organized a program funded out of the Mayor's office with moneys from the City of Chicago, rather than a program dependent on federal moneys under the supervision of the city.

Her program relied on human talent that was going to waste. She organized the elderly poor into a one-to-one program to benefit the elderly ill and helpless. Healthy elders were paid the minimum wage to assist the lame and the halt and the blind. They took the house bound shopping. They tidied up the homes and apartments of the blind and feeble. They did whatever was needed to make life easier for the physically handicapped. And they stayed awhile to visit. It was a wonderful program, a program to be proud of. As coordinator, every day for her was hectic, funny, exasperating, educational and rewarding. Altogether life was good for almost a decade.

But not good enough. Katherine no longer came in and out, she was living in Berkeley near Rossmoor. She, Suzanne, was sixty-seven years old with a lot of miles left in her. Out in California were Kathy and Magda waiting for her to come out and play. Work lost its luster. It was time to throw in the sponge and call it a day. There were a lot of things to consider before Suzanne seriously made up her mind in 1976 to leave Chicago to move out west. When she did decide in February of 1977 she rented a manor up on Skycrest at the top of Rossmoor for two months to use as a base while she found exactly what she wanted. She and Ernest had worked like dogs to get started when they arrived in Chicago but once on their way, though the business demanded careful bookkeeping, they had fulfilled the American dream of affluence and security. She could afford the good life on a modest scale. She could afford Rossmoor. She chose an agent and after several discards when he took her through the front door of the house in which she lived until the end, she knew it was for her.

'If my dining room table fits I buy it." she told the agent. The dining table fit.

EPILOGUE

Because of Social Security, retirement communities like Rossmoor have sprung up as popular depositories for the elderly. Once, isolated from society, elderly people of modest income were hidden away in the solitary confinement of a little apartment, a relative's back bedroom, or--in the case of the desperately poor -- on poor farms, those pre-Social Security rural dormitories where counties housed the homeless, the dull, and the poor elderly. Poor farms were a staple of American Society until Social Security came into existence and allowed their inhabitants to live independtly in their own quarters. Every county had one. The farm was supposed to be self sufficient. The residents were to live off the produce of the farms, chickens, and livestock raised on the farms to feed them. Poor farms were hidden away off main roads, far from the sensitive sight of the general citizenry.

In today's retirement communities most of the elderly of modest income are free from the shame of being old or being a burden. They are affluent enough, because of Social Security, pensions, and/or accumulated savings, to maintain their independence, to enjoy relatively good health, and to live with self respect. In affluent retirement communities, the wealthy live among people like themselves who no longer want the burden of houses too big and too empty. Tired of maintaining expensive property, they welcome turning over the maintenance of their surroundings to a Community Board of Directors. While comfortably sheltered, they are often as lonely as less affluent retirees in walkup apartments on busy streets. All communities, no matter what level of spend able wealth their residents enjoy, provide a companionable environment and a variety of entertainments that keep their residents stimulated and interested, a social climate not accessible to senior citizens in the wider community.

Which community to choose depends on a panoply of reasons. Foremost is matching income to costs. Second is the wish to be near one's children, not under their feet. Or they may have other relatives and/or friends in the area with whom to keep in touch. After those reasons comes flexibility of life--the freedom to travel without concern for the property left behind. The fourth choice is desirability of climate. Most of the retirement communities in the United States are located below the forty-fifth parallel. Lastly, some are keenly concerned with perceived "fit" of personality with the lifestyle of the community in question. There are, of course, other reasons. It does not happen often, but neither is it rare, that a person(s) did not choose that community but was placed there by her, his or their child, or children, who, looking for a safe environment, deposited their elderly parents in that place and then went home. The "children" may live hundreds, or thousands of miles away and almost never come to visit.

Through this removal of the oldest segment of the population from their former neighborhoods, society has lost one of its most valuable assets. Retirement communities are unrecognized for what they are in fact: reservoirs of talent, cul de sacs of bright minds, deep pools of experience, and "libraries" of the kind of wisdom that in yesteryear was handed down in extended families. Un-mined by scholars, what is being bottled up in these gated communities, buried under the euphemism of "retirement" - as though the mind goes on vacation and memories of the past are buried under indifference and neglect - is much intellectual wealth of the world of ideas, stored in the brains of society's former movers and shakers. Retirees are an inestimable lode of rich source material for future corporate managers, educators, scientists, politicians, et al. Most of that treasure is going to waste because modern society worships immaturity and gungho opportunism. Generation X, like the Boomers before them, are too impatient, too in love with a "brave new world" of their own, to see they are throwing away inestimable accumulations of knowledge.

Contrary to popular mythology about the elderly, they never stop thinking. On the average they have about fifteen years after their active work-a-day lives are over in which to remember, to cogitate, and to reassess the past and realign their ideas about the future of mankind. They hunger to break bread with their replacements and plum the depths of technological change and social reorganization. They have the leisure to study and cogitate about tomorrow. Shut away from the energy of the engines of enterprise, they lapse into remembering the past when they were in charge.

As a rule after the first decade or so of retirement, their search for pertinent memories of the past takes longer. They change subjects because there is so much stored in their heads they get distracted by unbidden memories or ideas that pop up during conversation. Yet one finds nuggets of exceptional wisdom or insight among their fragmented snippets of information. In the repetition of old material, something new inevitably surfaces. The curious researcher who comes among them will be richly rewarded. This book came out of that kind of interaction with a specific group of Rossmoorians.

Each of the people about whom I have written added their energy and talent to making Rossmoor what it is. Magda organized the first big exercise class ever offered, and when it became unmanageable in size, Dita took over the overflow. Miriam, Tilda, Trudy, Brigitta and Suzanne all became ceramists for a time. Most of them played golf. Ilse came as a summer resident and soon was recruiting people from all over the Bay Area to come to live year-round as neighbors to her and "Wim." Magda found her way to Rossmoor without knowing Ilse first, but all but Brigitta and Miriam of those who followed came because they knew someone who knew Ilse. Ilse is still a central figure in the Jewish segment of Rossmoor's population.

They are among Rossmoor's rapidly disappearing fraternity of Jews who defied orders to be part of the Nazis' death marches. It is devoutly to be wished that such a fraternity will never be formed again, and fervently hoped that havens for such victims of biogtry will not be needed in the future. Still, in the climate of hate that prevails in the world today, the reader cannot assume that other huddlings of the hunted won't come into existence. Unless we gentiles who detest the profane hatred that has scapegoated Jews for all the ills of man for centuries, keep the stories of Nazi genocide alive and are constantly vigilant against those who would replay the macabre ghoulishness of 1933-1945, history could repeat itself.

PERSONAL DATA

Brigitta Konigstein Schneider - Born 1905, Budapest

Magda Zahler Markovits Oudegeest - Born 1904, Budapest

Frida Kwiatkowski Loeff - Born 1903, Vienna

Trudy Flamm - Born 1920. Vienna

Louise Hayman Hahn - Born 1899, Aachen

Miriam Lewinsohn Field - Born 1905, Suwalki

Ilse Schiff Gelnay - Born 1912, Berlin

Walter Gelnay - Born 1910, Vienna

"Dita" Gelnay Strass Dalton von Westerborg - Born 1907,
    New York City

Tilda Gelnay Eisner Scadron - Born 1903, New York City.

Suzanne Zahler Kenley - Born 1910, Budapest